Romantic Europe and the Ghost of Italy

JOSEPH LUZZI

Romantic Europe and the Ghost of Italy

Yale University Press
New Haven &
London

Published with assistance from the Louis Stern Memorial Fund.
Copyright © 2008 by Joseph Luzzi.
All rights reserved.
This book may not be reproduced, in whole or in part, including illustrations, in any form (beyond that copying permitted by Sections 107 and 108 of the U.S. Copyright Law and except by reviewers for the public press), without written permission from the publishers.

Set in Sabon by Keystone Typesetting, Inc., Orwigsburg, Pennsylvania.
Printed in the United States of America by Sheridan Books, Ann Arbor, Michigan.

Library of Congress Cataloging-in-Publication Data
Luzzi, Joseph.
Romantic Europe and the ghost of Italy / Joseph Luzzi.
p. cm.
Includes bibliographical references and index.
ISBN 978-0-300-12355-5 (cloth : alk. paper)
1. Italian literature—History and criticism. 2. Literature, Comparative—Italian and European. 3. Literature, Comparative—European and Italian. 4. European literature—18th century—Italian influences. 5. European literature—19th century—Italian influences. 6. Italy—Civilization. I. Title.
PQ4050.A2L89 2008
809'.894—dc22   2008016715

A catalogue record for this book is available from the British Library.

This paper meets the requirements of ANSI/NISO Z39.48-1992 (Permanence of Paper).
It contains 30 percent postconsumer waste (PCW) and is certified by the Forest Stewardship Council (FSC).

10 9 8 7 6 5 4 3 2 1

In loving memory of my wife
Katherine Lynne Mester
1970–2007
and for our daughter
Isabel Katherine Luzzi

All poetry essentially deals in anachronism.
— Goethe

Contents

Acknowledgments   ix

Introduction: Italy's Ambivalent Modernity   1

Part I: Genus Italicum

1   Did Italian Romanticism Exist?   25
2   Italy without Italians: Goethe, Staël, and Foscolo   53
3   The Death of Italy and Birth of European Romanticism   77

Part II: Heirs of a Dark Wood

Prologue   97

4   Dante and Autobiography in the Age of Voltaire   104
5   Alfieri's *Prince*, Dante, and the Romantic Self   124
6   Wordsworth, Dante, and British Romantic Identity   141

Part III: Corpus Italicum

7 Italy as Woman and Wound, Dante to Leopardi   163

8 The Body of Parini   195

   Epilogue: Italy's Broken Heart   213

   Notes   221

   Index   285

Acknowledgments

This book distills a literary education that began at the Yale graduate school over a decade ago. Giuseppe Mazzotta, my dissertation adviser, imparted my two most abiding lessons: that poetry is not just a form of art but a way of thinking, and that Italian literary history offers an indispensable challenge to the constellation of ideas associated with the elusive term *modernity*. He remains my ideal reader. Paolo Valesio taught me, among other things, the nature of rhetoric; if any of my critical writing bears a creative twist, it is largely to him that I owe the courage of the attempt. David Bromwich guided me toward a better understanding of the moral and philosophical questions that followed upon this book's initial interests in aesthetics and literary history. After Yale, Millicent Marcus led me to the ingredient that allowed my argument to realize its final form: a commitment to studying Italy's pressing historical and literary issues within their cultural contexts. Her spark of intellectual warmth helped animate the years of research that went into the preparation of this manuscript.

It is very much in this spirit of literary education that I acknowledge my debts to colleagues and students at Bard. The freedom to range across the centuries and disciplines in my teaching and the stimulating everyday conversations on campus encouraged me to complete this project in what I hope to be a critical idiom accessible to the nonspecialist. The college's administration and its Languages and Literature Division have been exceptionally supportive of my work; and I especially wish to thank my fellow teachers of foreign languages for their friendship and collegiality. This study has benefited from conversations with many friends and colleagues, including Marino Balducci, Florian Becker, Gabriela Carrión, Bob Connor, Kristin Phillips Court, Stuart Curran, Nicola Gentili, Geoffrey Harpham, Nancy Leonard, Geoffrey Sanborn, Benjamin Stevens, Karen Sullivan, Joseph Wittreich, Marina Van Zuylen, and especially Scott McGill. Above all, I thank my family, the Luzzis and the Mesters, for their remarkable and enduring support.

Earlier versions of chapters originally appeared in the following journals, whose editors I thank for their gracious permission to reprint: chapter 1 in *Comparative Literature* 56 (2004): 168–91; chapter 2 in *Modern Language Notes, Italian Issue* 117 (2002): 48–83 (Johns Hopkins University Press); chapter 4 in *Studies on Voltaire and the Eighteenth Century* (2002, no. 6): 349–70; and chapter 5 in *Italica* 80 (2003): 176–93. Two John F. Enders Travel Grants from Yale University (1998 and 1999), a Pforzheimer Grant from the Keats-Shelley Association of America (2002), and especially an NEH Fellowship from the National Humanities Center (2004–5) provided generous research funding. The librarians and copyeditor, Karen Carroll, at the National Humanities Center provided expert help as the manuscript neared completion. Finally, it is a pleasure to thank at Yale University Press Jonathan Brent for inviting me to submit my work; Annelise Finegan and Ann-Marie Imbornoni for their superb editorial assistance; and Andrew Frisardi for his exceptional copyediting of my manuscript. The three readers of my manuscript at the Press offered invaluable suggestions for improving the argument.

I first seriously read Romantic literature in a seminar offered by Geoffrey Hartman in 1996, and the poetry that opened my ears to Foscolo, Leopardi, Manzoni, and the Italian Ottocento as a whole was that of Wordsworth. My father, Pasquale Luzzi, had recently passed away, and for some reason the solitude of poems like "Tintern Abbey," "Michael," and "A slumber did my spirit seal" became a place I could spend time with him. This book was born from those silent conversations, where I dealt for the first time with loss and the bonds we create between the living and the dead. I have tried to translate these emotions into a study of the myth of Italy and reception of Italian Romanticism in nineteenth-century Europe and, in the process, do justice to my father's sacrifices and the Italy he gave me.

Though I had written this book in the happiest of circumstances, I have had to complete it in sorrow beyond words. My wife, Katherine, passed away just months before publication. She leaves behind a legacy of grace, kindness, wisdom, and above all the love that lives on in our daughter, Isabel. This book is for them.

Introduction: Italy's Ambivalent Modernity

I

A recent advertisement campaign by the Italian national airline, Alitalia, invites prospective leisure travelers to "fire [their] therapist" and fly to Italy. Another Alitalia advertisement depicts a couple kissing while flanked by majestic columns, with a slogan above them that challenges us to visit Italy and "do something monumental." A third image presents an attractive woman who is savoring cannoli, with the caption: "Let's give in to temptation." The rhetoric of this publicity draws on a myth, formed by writers in the early nineteenth century, of Italy as a premodern, sensual, and unreflective (hence, analyst-free) oasis in a dry and frenetic modern world. For the nineteenth-century author, as for today's tourist, the words *Italy* and *Romantic*—as well as *romantic* with the lowercase *r*—were synonymous.

This book examines the metaphors, facts, and fictions about Italy that were born in the Romantic age and that continue to haunt the Western literary imagination. My initial investigation of Italy in nineteenth-century Europe raised a host of questions that have sustained this study. Why does the protean term *modernity* obsess us? Why do we imagine that some cultures, like Italy's, resist the forms of alienation associated with the modern age?[1] Can one extrapolate from the Italian literary tradition Giambattista Vico's paradigmatic *sapientia italorum* (Italic wisdom)? Who were the Italian ghosts whose reception shaped the contours of European Romanticism? Why did the Enlightenment wall erected between church and state stand higher in some countries than in others — and why, in Italy, was this wall low enough to step over? How did definitions of literature change in the Romantic age, and how did these new notions of the literary draw on figurative representations of ancient and modern Italy? In addressing such questions, I aim to provide the first work in English that considers Italian Romanticism and, more broadly, the modern myth of Italy in a comparative European context.

In both popular imagination and historical fact, clichés about Italy continue simultaneously to attract us to the Peninsula and to thwart us from an informed understanding of it. This oscillation between seduction and misunderstanding defines the reception of Italy's contentious Romantic movement.[2] Paradoxically, foreigners ignored or critiqued Italian Romantic literature for the same reasons that they praised and imitated the remote Italian past. Italy's supposedly premodern status in European literature of the early nineteenth century resulted in, on the one hand, a loving mystification by foreigners of Italy's ancient and Renaissance heritage; on the other, foreign dismissal of more modern Italian forms of cultural expression because of their tradition-bound, classicizing elements. The very qualities that endeared the Italian Romantics to people at home often alienated them from foreigners. Of course, not all that foreign authors said about the Italian Romantics was inaccurate or ideologically suspect, for there were indeed fundamental differences that set apart nineteenth-century Italian literature from contemporary writing abroad. I limit myself here to four distinguishing features.

The burden of antiquity. It is not enough to claim that Italian Romantics felt ancient cultures in their blood, because one could also say this of other national traditions, perhaps most notably the philo-Hellenic Germany of August Wilhelm and Friedrich Schlegel and their Jena circle. To a degree unparalleled in Europe, however, many modern Italians imagined themselves to be the heirs of that same ancient Roman heritage whose mythological forms and aesthetic codes foreign, antineoclassical writers increasingly vilified. More often than not, Italian Romantics viewed mythology and classical literature as a unifying matrix that established a direct link between themselves and Greco-Roman antiquity, and not as mere emblems of cultural authority. In fact, two of Romantic Italy's principal authors, Ugo Foscolo and Giacomo Leopardi, believed that the future of Italian culture rested precisely in those self-consciously neoclassical and allegorical modes of representation attacked by contemporary theorists, most notably Germaine de Staël.

High culture and national identity. In contrast to the general European critique of neoclassical poetic diction, especially in England (for example, William Wordsworth's "Preface to *Lyrical Ballads*"), high cultural forms, including epic poetry, continued to serve as vital sources of political and social organization in nineteenth-century Italy. Lofty literary allegories, in authors ranging from Dante and Petrarch to Foscolo and Leopardi, played a crucial role in the Risorgimento, the "resurgence" or drive for a belated national unity finally achieved in 1861, when the Kingdom of Italy was proclaimed. Italy's historical disunity compelled many writers to place their most complex works in the service of their nonexistent nation; the Romantic critic Francesco De Sanctis even claimed that nationhood represented literature's fundamental transhistorical value, a view that would influence public intellectuals as diverse as the idealist philosopher Benedetto Croce and the Marxist theorist Antonio Gramsci. The relationship between high cultural expression and national identity reached its apotheosis in the monumental *I promessi sposi* (*The Betrothed;* 1827), by Alessandro Manzoni, who spent nearly fifteen years translating his novel into Tuscan in hopes of finally establishing this dialect as Italy's standard language.

The religious imagination. An abiding concern with Catholicism in Italian Romantic literature—as distinguished from the more secular literary movements abroad, with their burgeoning interests in folklore, anticlericalism, and rustic life—resulted in widespread use by Italian authors of a spiritual rhetoric, even when treating worldly and nonreligious themes. For example, in one of the more radical theoretical statements of the era, Manzoni claimed that he discerned a Christian component in Romantic theory. Similarly, Foscolo's influential poem "Dei sepolcri" ("On Sepulchers"; 1807) concludes by offering a prophecy for Italy's future that draws its terminology and moral energy from Dante's *Commedia* (specifically, Cacciaguida's prediction of Dante's exile in *Paradiso* 17), and then translates its Christian doctrine into a suitable nationalist idiom.

The resistance to modernity. Many Italian Romantics chafed at the imposition of social models and technological improvements predicated upon rationalist progress. They sought, rather, to reconcile tradition with innovation by planting the seeds of the future Italy in the soil of its past, thereby honoring the lost cultural forms and deceased exemplars of a putative Italian spirit that trumped centuries of political fragmentation.[3] Foscolo composed "Dei sepolcri" in response to Napoleon's Edict of St. Cloud (1804), a defensible modernizing project that outlawed the construction of graveyards within city limits in order to curtail the spread of infectious diseases from improperly interred corpses. But, in Foscolo's view, to separate the cities of the dead and the living was equivalent to tearing Italy's branches and trunk (its forms of modern cultural expression) from its roots and soil (its two thousand–plus years of accumulated traditions). "Dei sepolcri," therefore, proposes Florence's basilica Santa Croce—final resting place of Galileo, Machiavelli, and Michelangelo, among others—as a new Italian pantheon and symbolic antidote to a Napoleonic reform Foscolo deemed symptomatic of an abstract disregard for the obligations of Italians to their cultural patrimony.

Though these four elements do not fully account for the exceptional nature of Italian Romanticism, they do allow for a preliminary understanding of the movement's principal characteristics. A synthesis of all four of these traits appears in "Dei sepolcri" by Foscolo, the author who is arguably the protagonist of this study. One of the lovers he knew in his youth labeled him a novel-in-miniature, a tag his biography corroborates. He was born in Greece to an Italian father and a Greek mother; with the rest of his family, he expatriated to Italy while he was still a child, and the country became his cultural, linguistic, and political *patria*. A soldier in the Napoleonic campaigns, he was eventually imprisoned and exiled for his controversial beliefs and publications. In the midst of all these displacements and entanglements, he managed to conduct numerous affairs and even to hold briefly the prestigious chair in rhetoric at the University of Pavia before he turned thirty.[4] His final exile brought him in 1816 to England, where, after a foray into the gilded literary societies of London, he ended his days unnoticed by almost everyone except his creditors and an illegitimate daughter with whom he had recently reunited. After a life dedicated to developing alter egos and literary personae (Jacopo Ortis, Didimo Chierico, the *exul immeritus* [unmerited exile] Dante Alighieri), Foscolo died in hiding under a series of pseudonyms. His split career in Italy and England provided him an invaluable comparatist perspective on his own Italian culture, and his concern with the reception of his nation's traditions inspired him to write what is still the most substantial work on the question of Italy in nineteenth-century Europe. As with many Italian authors of the age, the profound neoclassical bent in Foscolo made him an ambiguous Romantic in the eyes of countryman and foreigner alike. Foscolo, in fact, chafed at many tenets of Romanticism and had some unpleasant things to say about this movement, which to his mind was overly metaphysical and "Teutonic." Yet, alongside Leopardi and Manzoni, he remains one of the three most significant Italian writers of the era; and no Italian was more influential than he in spreading the cause of Italian literature in Romantic Europe.

An obsession with the relationship between Italy's living and dead haunted Foscolo from the beginning of his career. His first novel, *Ultime lettere di Jacopo Ortis* (*Last Letters of Jacopo Ortis*; 1798), set in the Napoleonic era, is the story of a doomed love affair between a suicidal young Italian patriot and a married woman, and is a sepulchral text *per eccellenza*. The protagonist, patriot Jacopo Ortis (a thinly veiled portrait of Foscolo himself), and the betrothed, Teresa, discover their love by the tomb of Petrarch at Arquà; Ortis repeatedly pays homage to the tombs of the Florentine basilica Santa Croce; and, before committing suicide, he leaves orders to be buried under a cypress, the botanical symbol for death. To Ortis, the desire for fitting burial ground for all Italians is inseparable from the wish to forge the Italian nation. Foscolo writes of Ortis's visit to Petrarch's tomb:

> Io mi vi sono appressato come se andassi a prostrarmi su le sepolture de' miei padri, e come un di que' sacerdoti che taciti e riverenti s'aggiravano per li boschi abitati dagl'Iddii. La sacra casa di quel sommo italiano sta crollando per la irreligione di chi possiede un tanto tesoro. Il viaggiatore verrà invano di lontana terra a cercare con meraviglia divota la stanza armoniosa ancora dei canti celesti del Petrarca. Piangerà invece sopra un mucchio di ruine coperto di ortiche e di erbe selvatiche fra le quali la volpe solitaria avrà fatto il suo covile. Italia! placa l'ombre de' tuoi grandi. (November 20, 1797; 22)

> (I [Ortis] approached the house [of Petrarch] like one about to prostrate himself on the tombs of his ancestors, or like one of those priests who used to frequent, in silent reverence, the woods inhabited by the gods. Owing to the impiety of the owners of this treasure, the sacred home of that sublime Italian is falling down. In vain will travellers come from distant lands and look with pious wonder for the rooms still echoing with the heavenly poems of Petrarch. Instead they will weep over a heap of ruins covered with nettles and weeds, in which the solitary fox has perhaps made its lair. O Italy, appease the shades of your great men!) (18)[5]

Foscolo begins by paralleling the genetic connection joining Ortis to his ancestors and the cultural link between him and a literary father, Petrarch. He sanctifies this fusion of biological and aesthetic reflection with the religious image of holy men wandering, lost in contemplation, through divine woods. Employing what Benedict Anderson describes as "ghostly national imagining," Foscolo deepens the spiritual rhetoric by proposing that the neglect of Petrarch by Italians stems from "irreligione" (impiety) rather than inferior cultural literacy.[6] Italy must learn to placate the souls of its great by finding them suitable places of final rest, so that future generations of Italians can make pilgrimages to these graveyards and honor their towering exemplars. Give us Italians proper tombs, Foscolo suggests, or we will never achieve our nation.

Sepulcher and nation coincided in a work of Foscolo that followed *Ultime lettere di Jacopo Ortis,* "Dei sepolcri," an unusually challenging text whose nearly three hundred lines of rarefied diction, mythological allusion, and highly wrought syntax somehow convey the delicacy and intimacy of Keatsian lyric. "Dei sepolcri" attests to the belief, held by Foscolo and many Italians, that Virgil's celebrated ancient Troy from the *Aeneid* was not merely a literary-historical myth from the world of high culture; it could be the emblem of modern Italy's tragically unfulfilled destiny. Though once a great empire with roots in the magnificent city of Hector, Foscolo's Italy was, by the time of "Dei sepolcri," no more than a "geographical expression" (Prince von Metternich). Suffocated by foreign rule, Italy needed a unifying narrative to speed along the process of Risorgimento that had been making fitful, tentative progress since the French Revolution. Foscolo's solution to the *questione d'Italia* was as remarkable as it was unexpected: he sought his foundation myth among Italy's dead instead of its living.

Surprisingly enough, Foscolo never addresses the matter of spiritual life in this poem; a materialist pessimism, shaded by Lucretian natural philosophy, leads him away from the issue of the soul.[7] If we take Foscolo at his word, belief in immortality is one of those beautiful fictions that make existence bearable:

> Ma perchè pria del tempo a sé il mortale
> Invidierà l'illusïon che spento
> Pur lo sofferma al limitar di Dite?
> Non vive ei forse anche sotterra, quando
> Gli sarà muta l'armonia del giorno,
> Se può destarla con soavi cure
> Nella mente de' suoi? (23–29)

> (Then why should man,
> mortal as he is, reject the illusion
> that keeps him from the abyss when breath fails,
> when he can no longer hear the music of the day?
> If only he can wake a like illusion
> in the minds of those who tend his grave
> with loving care, he still lives on
> under ground.) (22–29)[8]

Illusïon here does not mean lie but rather artifice, in the Latin etymological sense of *artifex* (maker of art, from the compound of *ars* and *facere*). In *Ultime lettere di Jacopo Ortis,* the eponymous protagonist decides to commit suicide when he no longer has illusions to sustain him,[9] and in "Dei sepolcri" Foscolo translates his faith in illusion into a general act of love for humankind.

About halfway through, "Dei sepolcri" shifts from what Glauco Cambon calls an anthropology of mourning (*Foscolo* 162–63) to a funereal politics, by proposing that memory of the dead is a socially conditioned ethos designed to strengthen the ties that bind:

> A egregie cose il forte animo accendono
> L'urne de' forti . . . e bella
> E santa fanno al peregrin la terra
> Che le ricetta. (151–54)

> (The graves of the strong
> inflame a young mind to radiant
> deeds . . . and make the land
> that shelters them sacred, a beacon to travelers.) (151–54)

Then follows a series of dazzling periphrases, Dantesque in style and neoclassical in diction and tone, that establishes a parallel between the heroes of modern Italy and ancient Greece:

> E tu prima, Firenze, udiva il carme
> Che allegrò l'ira al Ghibellin fuggiasco,
> E tu i cari parenti e l'idïoma
> Desti a quel dolce di Calliope labbro
> Che Amore in Grecia nudo e nudo in Roma
> D'un velo candidissimo adornando,
> Rendea nel grembo a Venere Celeste;
> Ma piú beata chè in un tempio accolte
> Serbi l'Itale glorie, uniche forse
> Da che le mal vietate Alpi e l'alterna
> Onnipotenza delle umane sorti
> Armi e sostanze t'invadeano ed are
> E patria e, tranne la memoria, tutto.
> Che ove speme di gloria agli animosi
> Intelletti rifulga ed all'Italia,
> Quindi trarrem gli auspicj. E a questi marmi
> Venne spesso Vittorio ad ispirarsi.
> Irato a' patrii Numi, errava muto
> Ove Arno è piú deserto, i campi e il cielo
> Desïoso mirando; e poi che nullo
> Vivente aspetto gli molcea la cura,
> Qui posava l'austero; e avea sul volto
> Il pallor della morte e la speranza.
> Con questi grandi abita eterno: e l'ossa
> Fremono amor di patria. (173–97)

> (Florence, it was you who first
> heard the song that cheered the exiled
> Ghibelline [Dante], for all his anger. You

gave loving parents and your own language
to the Muse's darling [Petrarch], the laureate poet
who wrapped the boy-god of love, naked
in Greece, naked in Rome, in the whitest
veil and returned him to the lap of Venus
in heaven. But your greatest bliss is this:
to have united in one temple the glory
of Italy — all that is left of its glory
since the undefended Alps and power's changing
fortunes have plundered our arms, wealth,
altars, fatherland, everything save memory.
Bliss, for whenever the hope of glory
shines again in these minds that are brave,
and in Italy, *these* tombs will be our portent.
Here Vittorio [Alfieri] often came for inspiration.
Angry at Italy's patron gods,
he strode the most desolate reaches of the Arno
in silence, scanning field and sky,
filled with longing. Since no living creature
could soothe his cares he stood here,
his face stern, white as death,
shining with hope. Now he dwells
forever with these giants, and his bones shudder
with love of the fatherland.) (175–201)

Florence emerges here as a bona fide second Troy, source of a once-great Italian civilization that, though sunk in decline — and, what is worse, oblivion — stands to revive through the poet's song. The modern Florence of Santa Croce serves Foscolo as the privileged locus for cultural pilgrimage, because of both its Renaissance prestige and its lack of negative associations with the papacy and Napoleonic imperialism that made Italy's ancient *mater,* Rome, anathema to many Risorgimentalists.[10] "Dei sepolcri" establishes Florentine cultural supremacy through a biographical survey of Tuscan art (Michelangelo, 159–60), science (Galileo, 160–64), politics (Machiavelli, 155–58), and especially literary history (Dante, 173–74; Petrarch, 175–79; and Alfieri, 189–97). The overtures to Florence's luminaries address long-standing dilemmas plaguing the Italian quest for unification. For example, Foscolo identifies Petrarch as the poet laureate writing in Tuscan, the dialect of his predecessor Dante. The promotion of Tuscan suggests Foscolo's belief in the power of that *idioma* to end Italy's linguistic fragmentation, a position later taken famously and definitively by Manzoni. By grouping Italy's sages in ritual order, Foscolo counters the political disharmony of Italy with the architectonic and symbolic coherence of Santa Croce, the pantheon that "in un tempio accolte / Serb[a] l'Itale glorie" (united in one temple the glory / of Italy) ("Sepolcri" 180–81; "Sepulchers" 184–85).

In addition to conflating nationalist and religious rhetoric, the Foscolian myth of Santa Croce channels the prestigious voices of Italian literary history, especially Dante's. Foscolo begins the mighty last quarter of his poem with a traditional epic invocation:

> E me che i tempi ed il desio d'onore
> Fan per diversa gente ir fuggitivo,
> Me ad evocar gli eroi chiamin le Muse
> Del mortale pensiero animatrici. (226–29)

> (O Muses, you who alone give life
> to our human thoughts, summon me now—
> driven by these times and my love of honor,
> a wandering stranger—to call up heroes.) (228–31)

The lines recall the opening of *Purgatorio,* where the similarly wandering, persecuted Dante invokes the Muses so that "la morta poesì resurga" (dead poetry may rise again) (*Purg.* 1.7). "Dei sepolcri" collapses the temporal and spatial distance separating the civilizations of modern Florence (154–98) and ancient Greece (197–225) by sanctioning each with the same "god [who] / speaks from this solemn peace [of Santa Croce]" and "who kindled Greek courage / and wrath to rout the Persians at Marathon, / hallowed by the grave of Athens' fallen" ("Sepulchers" 201–2, 203–5):

> (Ah sí! da quella
> Religïosa pace un Nume parla:
> E nutría contro a' Persi in Maratona
> Ove Atene sacrò tombe a' suoi prodi,
> La virtú greca e l'ira.) ("Sepolcri" 197–201)

Then recourse to a crucial episode in Dante serves Foscolo in cementing the bonds between ancient Troy and modern Florence. In *Paradiso* 17, Cacciaguida tells Dante the protagonist what Dante the author, writing some years after the fictional date of the *Commedia* (1300), already knows: that in 1302 Dante will suffer bitter exile, wandering from court to court in central and northern Italy, and often be the victim of intrigue:

> La colpa seguirà la parte offensa
> in grido, come suol; ma la vendetta
> fia testimonio al ver che la dispensa.
> Tu lascerai ogne cosa diletta

> più caramente; e questo è quello strale
> che l'arco de lo essilio pria saetta.
>   Tu proverai sì come sa di sale
> lo pane altrui, e come è duro calle
> lo scendere e 'l salire per l'altrui scale.
>   E quel che più ti graverà la spalle,
> sarà la compagnia malvagia e scempia
> con la qual tu cadrai in queste valle;
>   che tutta ingrata, tutta matta ed empia
> si farà contr' a te; ma, poco appresso,
> ella, non tu, n'avrà rossa la tempia. (*Par.* 17.52–66)

(The blame, as always, will follow the injured party, in outcry; but vengeance shall bear witness to the truth which dispenses it. You [Dante] shall leave everything beloved most dearly; and this is the arrow which the bow of exile shoots first. You shall come to know how salt is the taste of another's bread, and how hard the path to descend and mount by another man's stairs. And that which shall most weigh your shoulders down will be the evil and senseless company with which you shall fall into this vale; which shall then become all ungrateful, all mad and malevolent against you, but, soon after, their brows, not yours, shall redden for it.)[11]

The above lines are reborn in "Dei sepolcri" with the prophecy of Cassandra:

>   Oh se mai d'Argo,
> Ove al Tidíde e di Laérte al figlio
> Pascerete i cavalli, a voi permetta
> Ritorno il cielo, invan la patria vostra
> Cercherete! (263–67)

>   (In Greece,
> you'll serve as Diomedes' stableboys, you'll pasture
> horses for Laertes' son, and if heaven
> should ever let you return, you'll look
> in vain for your fatherland.) (266–70)

Like Cacciaguida, she predicts setbacks and humiliations for her exiled people who, like Dante, will lose forever their homeland. But, Cassandra adds, Troy will never die, for beneath the rubble of its graves, the Penates "avranno stanza" (will yet have a home) ("Sepolcri" 269; "Sepulchers" 273). Cacciaguida offers his prophecy from a Christian perspective that preaches patience, forbearance, and spiritual indifference to secular travail. Though Foscolo, of course, could not have known that his own definitive exile would occur a decade or so after "Dei sepolcri," he echoes Dante by relaying the prophecy of Troy's destruction in the measured tones of one speaking *sub specie aeter-*

nitatis. By infusing Cassandra's prophecy with the moral and spiritual energies of Cacciaguida's vatic words, Foscolo imparts to his modern resurrection of Troy a Christian subtext that provides, if not the doctrine, at least the rhetoric of sacrifice and sanctification that will transform Trojan bodies into Italian blood. The recuperation of the Dantesque voice serves as more than the thematic key to Foscolo's modern political prophecy. By grafting an outline for Italy's future onto a paradigmatic medieval text, Foscolo lays bare the procedure and worldview of "Dei sepolcri," in which all constructs, from a single line of lyric to the forging of a collective identity, must chart the future with the maps of a transcendental cultural patrimony.

The lessons of Foscolo's "Dei sepolcri" surface throughout this book as emblematic both of Italy's vexed relationship with modernity and the signal differences that distinguish the Italian Romantic movement from its foreign counterparts. In the first place, and in a manner reminiscent of his Renaissance humanist predecessors, Foscolo perceived ancient culture not as an abstruse corpus of erudite texts but as an intimate fund of practical learning. Second, he transformed a potentially rarefied high cultural form, the fusion of lyric and epic that is "Dei sepolcri," into a politically engaged work meant to spur Italians toward a common cultural identification they desperately needed. Its complexities notwithstanding, "Dei sepolcri" was in fact an extremely influential presence in the literary milieu of its time, surpassing even the popular and melodramatic *Ultime lettere di Jacopo Ortis* in number of copies sold.[12] Next, his adaptation of Dantesque Christian elements, even while reflecting on pagan and nationalist themes, suggests the degree to which Catholic legacies and spiritual aims distanced Italian literary expression from the more secular European literary forms then in vogue. Last, and most important, Foscolo's consecration of the pantheon of Santa Croce reveals the tradition-conscious resistance to progressive reform held by an author who did not wish to see past and precedent leveled by a modernizing project.

In 1865, on the six hundredth anniversary of Dante's birth, Florence was named the Italian capital, thanks in part to Foscolo's efforts. The excavation of the actual Troy by Heinrich Schliemann began in 1870, the concluding year of Italian unification, when formerly papal Rome joined the Kingdom of Italy. The following year, as the dust emerged from the ruins of the city of Hector and Cassandra, Foscolo's bones were transferred to Santa Croce, where they now remain.

II

"Works of art are of an infinite solitude," Rainer Maria Rilke writes some hundred years after "Dei sepolcri," recommending solitude and discouraging his letter correspondent from criticism, a network of "partisan opinions, which have become petrified and meaningless, hardened and empty of life," or "clever word-games, in which one view wins today, and tomorrow the opposite view."[13] Though it does not take a Rilke to warn us of the perils of professional interpretation, one does well to note the geographical and temporal coordinates of this counsel. He was writing from Viareggio, near Pisa, in 1903. Like many before and after him, he had gone to Italy for warmer air, greater liberation from society, and a fuller understanding of the terms *poet* and *poetry*. Rilke, however, and most early twentieth-century Western authors, preferred Paris to Italy as the site of artistic exile. Foreigners, Rilke's contemporary Gertrude Stein once said, belonged to France. Only there, she claimed, was tradition so firm as to allow one an existence of unreality—the city of light was where the twentieth century was.[14] Closer to our own day, New York, mythologized in the poetry of Hart Crane and Walt Whitman en route to becoming a commercial and inspirational magnet for the international art scene, has assumed a comparable centrality in the Western imaginary. It remains to be seen whether the "scar of the spirit" left by 9/11 will challenge the city's artistic preeminence, as it remains to be seen which cities will succeed the Romes, Florences, Parises, and New Yorks as centers of the collective creative universe.[15] Perhaps our global village, with its fluid borders and economic and political structures, has rendered obsolete the notion of a single cultural capital. Johann Wolfgang von Goethe's maxim—"Wer den Dichter will verstehen muß in Dichters Lande gehen" (He who wishes to understand the poet must travel to the poet's land)—might strike today's writer as anachronistically Romantic.[16] To reach the land of poets, Goethe left his job as Weimar's secretary of state and traveled incognito to Rome, "die hohe Schule für alle Welt" (the world's university), where he remained for two years of intense private study. But in the transition from the Grand Tour to modern tourism, and in the age of the Internet, the drama of our cultural pilgrimages may have decreased in proportion to their ease of execution.

For Goethe, and for most of his contemporaries, the land of the poets was Italy. He writes, in a passage I will return to, "No one can take a serious look around [Rome], if he has eyes to see, without becoming solid, without forming a more vivid concept of solidity than he has ever had before." This observation defies the experience of most other Romantics, who ventured to Italy to become, in a manner of speaking, less solid, for they sought not Goethe's sturdy neoclassical forms but rather that ethereal and infinite loneliness mentioned by Rilke. Nathaniel Hawthorne writes in a work that supremely depersonalized Italy, *The Marble Faun*, that in Goethe's treasured Rome "the present moment is pressed down or crowded out, and our individual affairs and interests are but half as real. . . . Side by side with the massiveness of the Roman past, all matters, that we handle or dream of, now-a-days, look evanescent and visionary like."[17] Hawthorne's solution to the vertiginous layering of actual and literary history in the eternal city was to allegorize the elements of his narrative consistent with the inherited standards and motifs that had been employed by the predecessor travelers anthologized in his novel. He often compares his protagonist Miriam to Staël's Corinne, portrays the few Italians in his book in line with the primitive depictions in Goethe, and refers the reader to earlier descriptions of the Italian terrain. Aware of the clichés threatening an author writing about so familiar, well-traveled a site as the Colosseum, Hawthorne cuts short his desultory moonlight sketch of it to announce: "Byron's celebrated description is better than the reality" (153).[18]

"The Scipios' tomb contains no ashes now; / The very sepulchres lie tenantless / Of their heroic dwellers," Byron himself writes in a similar vein, invoking the rhetoric of belatedness, displacement, and loss that characterized his and most Romantic readings of Italian ruins.[19] Goethe, for his part, craved anonymity in Italy—hence his disguise and pseudonym, Johann Möller—but he balanced this social isolation with a quest for artistic, moral, and literary-historical communion with the ancients, who provided a classical *Bildung* that he then imported into Germany. Goethe's rebirth in Rome was personal as well as nationalist: he considered his entrance into the eternal city to be his second nativity. The Roman sojourn also exacted a necessary death. Upon Goethe's arrival in Italy, his Romantic alter ego, the young Werther—the literary ancestor of Foscolo's Ortis, among other terminal melancholics—was laid to final rest.[20]

In contrast to the vitalistic Goethe, François-René de Chateaubriand, Percy Bysshe Shelley, Staël, and others went to Italy to die a bit.[21] Most Romantics brought to Italy a horizon of concerns that only solitude could satisfy: to fathom the imagination; to escape native social strictures and structures; to develop a personal style unfettered by national tradition and outside of the firing range of the national critic. It may seem tragically fitting that a fair share of such writers perished at a young age during their Italian exile. After all, their initial decision to leave home for the Peninsula suggests their willingness to sacrifice personal concerns in the name of a literary calling. As with Dante's Ulysses of *Inferno* 26, no familial or patriotic bond could keep some Romantic artists from the aesthetic *esperienza* they believed only Italy could provide. A Ulysses-like intellectual shipwreck haunts Dante throughout the *Commedia*; the Romantics find a similar specter in Staël's legendary Corinne, who died young, brokenhearted, and almost midverse among her adoring Roman fans. In this grand if unwitting parallel, the artistic Italian shipwreck of Corinne denied her that same spouse, family, and country that, in the *Commedia,* the *libido sciendi* or longing to gain experience of the world steals from Ulysses. Staël's ill-fated heroine remains the consummate symbol of European Romanticism. Her life enacts the melodramatic themes of the poetry she performs; her willful cosmopolitanism belies a lurking sense of displacement; and her brilliant flame of a career flickers into night, just as quickly as it sparked into the Roman sun. No wonder, then, that the story of this female Romantic allegory was entitled *Corinne, ou l'Italie,* since Corinne both personifies Italy and enacts its tragic modern history.[22]

Few terms are as elusive and contentious as the Romanticism for which Corinne stands as emblem.[23] "In tutta la guerra del romanticismo," Manzoni writes in "Sul romanticismo" ("On Romanticism"; 1823), "non è dunque perita che la parola. Non è da desiderarsi che venga in mente ad alcuno, di risuscitarla: sarebbe un rinnovare la guerra, e forse un far danno all'idea che, senza nome, vive e cresce con bastante tranquillità" ("Sul romanticismo" 457). (In all the wars about Romanticism, the only thing that has perished is the word "Romanticism." Resurrection of the word is not desirable; this would only renew the wars and perhaps damage the idea, which, without a name, lives and grows tranquilly enough ["On Romanticism" 315].) The ongoing wars over this word, from the Romantic age to present-day academic criticism, confirm Manzoni's prophecy. Some argue that we are the heirs of Romanticism, the era of nature, nationalism, and the self. Others contend that Romantic reveries represent a false consciousness contaminated by political irresponsibility, sublimated desire, and biases of class, gender, and race. Textured interiority for one critic becomes toxic solipsism in the view of another; one reader describes a poet's gaze on his favorite hill as a loving contemplation, another interprets it as an aristocratic turning of a blind eye to the plight of the rural poor. Those of us with a personal or professional stake in Romanticism crowd round its dead body with competing agendas of comparable depth and conviction. But no matter how close the reading or sharp the polemic, the debates over Romanticism will yield no obvious victor or definitive judgment, whether we seek to bury the movement or to praise it.

Both defenders and detractors of Romanticism will agree that the age had its extravagances, especially in terms of the claims it made on behalf of the aesthetic. Perhaps more than any other period, the era witnessed startling pronouncements about the role and reach of poetry. Keats equated beauty with truth; Friedrich Schlegel declared all modern poetry to be Romantic; Shelley proclaimed poets the unacknowledged legislators of the world; and Manzoni suggested that one might discern the universal laws of literature, if not the word of God, in Romantic aesthetics. The proliferation of literary periodicals and institutions during this era tethers these airy statements to solid earth. The era was, as has been remarked, one of poetry.[24] Since the present age affords poetry no such privileges, we might regard these Romantic assertions with skepticism if not disbelief, and certainly with a tinge of irony. Yet it is doubtful that, say, a Wallace Stevens could have claimed that the theory of poetry was a theory of life without the preexistence of Romantic poetics. The lavish declarations on poetry's behalf by Shelley and others have not come without their price. We seem incapable of subtracting our experience of Romantic poems from our accompanying awareness of the daunting theoretical assertions made on their behalf. Thus, the Romantic text, perhaps more than any other, comes to us nailed against the cross of its own -*ism*.

However they judge Romanticism, most scholars would agree that a collective transition took place sometime after the French Revolution, and persisted for at least half a century, in Europe's general understanding of the term *literature*. In the early nineteenth century, the qualities of iconoclasm, originality, and specialization — as opposed to the Enlightenment norms of sociability and literary versatility — became accepted virtues of *homo poeticus*. In the current critical parlance, this shift from the cosmopolitan and clubbish belles lettres and encyclopedic reach of a Voltaire to the local, dialect-based, and self-reflective poetry of a Wordsworth signifies the birth or invention of a distinctly modern understanding of literature.[25] The idea of the writer as a producer of poetry or creative prose who must isolate himself from worldly affairs and social ties also sprang to prominence in the Romantic age. This is, of course, not to say that Enlightenment writers did not suffer for their work or sacrifice for their art in equal measure, since a great many of them (for example, Alfieri, Denis Diderot, Jean-Jacques Rousseau, and Voltaire) underwent exile to protect their authorial integrity. With the notable exception of Alfieri, however, these Enlightenment writers did not, like the Romantics, leave home as poets or creative writers but rather as authors of a more general stamp (*philosophes* or *gens de lettres*), and with a more direct sociopolitical rather than an aesthetic literary agenda. Again, it would be difficult to imagine perhaps the greatest twentieth-century paean to literary exile — James Joyce's pledge, in *Portrait of the Artist as a Young Man,* to leave Ireland so that he could forge abroad and in the smithy of his soul the uncreated conscience of his race — without its Romantic precedents. The quasi-religious asceticism of the Romantic view of literature as something worth giving up one's homeland for, equal to the sacrifice of loneliness and poverty, or as a conduit of otherworldly and even miraculous inspiration, tends now to elicit postmodern ridicule or ideological demystification. Without entering into the polemics about the status of the literary in its Romantic and post-Romantic forms, this study proposes that the early nineteenth-century understanding of literature needed more than a theoretical apparatus or manifesto: it required a physical home. That home, and the story of this book, is Romantic Italy.

Part 1, "*Genus Italicum*" (The Italian People), seeks to fill the yawning gap in Anglo-American scholarship by addressing the questions: Did Italian Romanticism exist (chapter 1)? How did issues of nationalism, religion, cultural mythmaking, and political ideology limit the international spread of the controversial Italian Romantic movement, whose intentions were considerably more cosmopolitan than its effects (chapter 1)? What myths did Romantic Italy represent to foreign writers, and how did Italians respond to these collective fictions? Why did foreigners' experience of Italy often ignore contemporary Italians themselves (chapter 2)? How did Italy become Europe's mausoleum for Shelley, mother for Byron, and museum for Goethe (chapter 2)? Why did Romantics outside of Italy speak of the birth of an anti-Enlightenment concept of literature, and a properly European Romanticism, in the same breath that they proclaimed the death of modern Italian culture (chapter 3)?

Part 2, "Heirs of a Dark Wood," proposes that the reception of Dante's *Commedia* united writers throughout Europe in their refashioning of the Enlightenment *mémoire* into a defining genre of the Romantic age, autobiography. I explain the reasons for the powerful Romantic "misreading" of Dante in an autobiographical key by discussing why Romantics were just as influenced by the set of biographical clichés surrounding Dante—his supposed heroism, political radicalism, and republican mentality—as by his actual work. Chapter 4 explores how the international turmoil surrounding Voltaire's infamous rejection of Dante in 1756 ("Nobody reads Dante anymore") inadvertently helped establish the philosophical terms of debate for the Romantic obsession with the life of Dante. The next two chapters chart the question of Dante in and around the autobiographical writings of Alfieri and Wordsworth. Overall, the section explores why so many in Dante's wake, Christian or not, Romantic or post-Romantic, have made the philologically questionable decision of exploring the contours of their own lives in Dante's hell instead of his heaven.

Part 3, "*Corpus Italicum*" (The Italian Body), examines the nexus between gender and geopolitics in the metaphorical representation of the Italian body politic. Chapter 7 traces the career of a major Romantic trope, Italy as a beautiful and wounded woman, from its origins in Dante to its culmination in Leopardi. The traditional Italian female national allegory contained a lovely though vulnerable female Italian exterior and a stalwart, masculine ancient Roman interior; rather than seek to resolve this temporal and gender dichotomy, Italian authors thematized the irreconcilable historical tensions within the figure. Chapter 8 explores Foscolo's obsession with the body of the Enlightenment poet Giuseppe Parini, whose battered and bruised form incarnated for Foscolo the historical iniquities faced by Italy in its drive for unification. The epilogue focuses on Corinne's "broken heart"—in Staël's use of her heroine's emotional breakdown as a representation of Italy—and also considers two other related constructions of Italianate female identity: Goethe's mistress from *Römische Elegien* (*Roman Elegies;* 1788–90) and Forster's Lucy Honeychurch from *Room with a View* (1908).

This study hopes to reinvigorate the unfortunately limited Anglo-American critical discussion of Foscolo, Leopardi, and Manzoni, the ambivalent *tre corone* (three crowns) of Italian Romanticism, who collectively vacillated between promoting, censuring, and ignoring the movement at different stages of their careers.[26] A lifelong dedication to the Italian *questione della lingua* (language question) as well as a unique brand of theological poetics, served to prevent Manzoni, whom Goethe labeled a Roman Catholic without bigotry, from acquiring the European reputation of a fellow historical novelist like Walter Scott. Foscolo, against the vogue of his age, promoted mythological allusion, allegory over symbol, recondite diction and syntax, and archaic metrical forms. Of the three, Leopardi, did find his share of readers abroad, in part because of his fluency in some of the major strands of Continental philosophy; but like Foscolo he continued to believe in the value of mythological and ancient forms of representation while his contemporaries were striving for a more colloquial and antineoclassical register of expression. A final aim of the book is to gauge the persistence of the myth of Italy in the wake of Romanticism. To that end, the book concludes with an epilogue, in which there is a reading of the figurative death of the prototypically Romantic Italy fashioned during the Grand Tour and the emergence of a new role for the Peninsula in the sentimental education of the modern tourist. Notwithstanding this dramatic rhetoric of decay and regeneration, I should add that humor and, above all, a light touch marked this transition. When Italy went from being the world's university of Goethe to the world's finishing school of E. M. Forster, readers witnessed the disappearance of chaste, neoclassical splendors in the name of a more sensual and practical set of living tools that only Italy could provide the foreigner. If Ralph Waldo Emerson and his Romantic predecessors went to Italy to seek truth, Forster's George Emerson traveled there to find beauty. Unbeknownst to each, and as Keats reminds us, the head of truth often finds itself chasing the tail of beauty. What unites truth and beauty in Forster's novel, and brings together these related Emersonian quests, is no less than love. George's yearning for Lucy's body becomes his need for her suppressed wisdom, just as today our enchantment by Italy's physical splendor is inseparable from our faith in its genius of place.

In methodological terms, I intend to translate, across the Atlantic and into a contemporary critical idiom, what has been until now a quintessentially native Italian reading of *il romanticismo italiano*. The history of Romantic criticism in Italy is illustrious, partly for the obvious reason that the nation's nineteenth-century literature infused tremendous energy into the process of unification. However, the visceral connection between Italian Romanticism and Italian national identity has led to the establishment of a predominantly political and historical mode of interpreting the literary Ottocento, an approach that is unlikely to pique the interest of the non-Italian reader. With the notable exceptions of more comparative and theoretical work on the period by scholars including Glauco Cambon, Mario Praz, and Ezio Raimondi, the many valuable studies of the Italian Romantics by major critics like Walter Binni, Giuseppe Antonio Borgese, Francesco Flora, Mario Fubini, Giuseppe Petronio, Mario Puppo, and Sebastiano Timpanaro are generally of a historicist, philological, or literary-historical stamp. A more recent group of distinguished scholars on Italian Romantic literature, both in Italy (including Pino Fasano, Sergio Givone, Salvatore Nigro) and abroad (Margaret Brose, Andrea Ciccarelli, Robert Dombroski), has certainly both adopted and in some cases helped develop the new approaches and methodologies associated with the theoretical turn that redefined literary studies. Yet the marginality of the Italian Romantics endures. The present study does not pretend to add substantively to our knowledge of, say, the textual sources or external events that informed the composition of masterpieces like *I promessi sposi* or "Dei sepolcri." This has been done admirably in any number of venues, since the acknowledged excellence of the Italian critical tradition has always been its historicism, philology, and textual criticism. I hope instead to enliven the existing discussion of these and other Italian Romantic works by interpreting them in light of developments in recent Continental and Anglo-American academic criticism, including deconstruction, gender, and cultural studies. What will hopefully emerge is the same productive "outsider" perspective on a question of Italian literary history that has yielded useful results in the Anglo-American interpretations of fields ranging from Dante and Renaissance studies to Italian cinema and travel literature.[27]

Though indebted to recent theory, I try throughout to capture what I consider to be the enduring literary qualities of the works in question and, in the process, introduce primary Italian Romantic texts into the broader comparative literary discussions from which they have too often been excluded. We do not yet know if world literature, the latest paradigm for describing the collective literary endeavors of the globe, will be kinder to modern Italy than was its predecessor discipline, comparative literature. My intuition is that it will be.

Comparative literature, at least in its anglophone golden age (c. 1950–80), in approaches ranging from Romance philology to deconstruction, was an eminently high-European affair, with a focus on the close linguistic analysis of major literary traditions (and political powers) like America, England, France, and Germany. World literature, with its dependence on translation and its eye to more hidden cultural vistas, appears to be a more suitable vantage point from which to observe the international spread of Italian Romanticism.[28] Few of the formidable comparatists of post–World War II criticism—including M. H. Abrams, Erich Auerbach, Harold Bloom, Paul de Man, and Geoffrey Hartman—consider the Italian Romantics; René Wellek does briefly, but his approach is derivative and his results perfunctory. Though they focus on a champion of Italian cultural prestige, Staël, two studies of European Romanticism by Lilian Furst (1979) and John Isbell (1994) ignore the question of Italian Romanticism.[29] Virgil Nemoianu (1984) discusses Italy in his comparative analysis of the second-generation Biedermeier phase of European Romanticism (1815–48), but he limits himself to Manzoni's contribution to the historical novel without considering the systemic value of other Italian authors and texts.[30] More recent comparatist works by Richard Eldridge (2001), Michael Löwy and Robert Sayre (2001), Ian Balfour (2002), and Paul Hamilton (2003) all deal with matters central to Italian Romanticism: respectively, the philosophical revision of Enlightenment thinking, resistance to the socioeconomic forms of the industrial age, nexus between poetry and religion, and self-conscious theorizing of Romanticism.[31] Yet none of these texts explores the Italian case; nor does the edited anthology *Romanticism in National Context* (1988).[32] There exist at least two major Italian inquiries into the question of Italy's relation to Romantic Europe: Mario Puppo (1985) and Ezio Raimondi (1997).[33] Though the philological nature of their studies reflects the best in traditional Italian scholarship, especially the sweeping intellectual synthesis of Raimondi, neither critic engages any of the major theoretical critical paradigms that have redefined French and Anglo-American interpretations of Romanticism.

In considering the possible contributions of this study, it becomes painfully clear how much more preliminary work will be required for Italian Romanticism to enter the critical mainstream. We lack English translations of most of the major literary works of the Ottocento, including many creative and expository masterpieces by Foscolo, Leopardi, and Manzoni as well as important work by their less famous contemporaries Giuseppe Gioachino Belli, Vincenzo Monti, Ippolito Pindemonte, Ermes Visconti, and a host of others. The Romantic debates that ensued in Italy after the publication of Staël's essay on translation in 1816 have also escaped, with few exceptions, the attention of translators and foreign critics.[34] A problem of more recent provenance but equal gravity is the paucity of work on the less canonical and more broadly cultural aspects of Italian Romanticism, especially with regard to the role of women.[35] On a more positive note, recent Anglo-American criticism has devoted increased attention to the question of how the history and politics of the Risorgimento relate to Romantic ideologies and cultural contexts.[36] New advances in scholarship also help us understand the intellectual currents that relegated Italy to its marginal status in the modern theoretical understanding of "Europe."[37] Whatever the critical future may hold for Italian Romanticism, it seems to me that the best response to a literary text has always been another literary text; hence the comparatist approach of the present study. Any reader who encounters the "ermo colle" (lonely hill) in Leopardi's "L'infinito" ("The Infinite") can never interpret the "sportive wood" of Wordsworth's "Tintern Abbey" the same way again; similarly, studying the dialectic between local and national history in Manzoni's *I promessi sposi* alters forever one's understanding of the revolutionary upheaval in Victor Hugo's *Quatrevingt-treize* (Ninety-three; 1874) or Scott's *Ivanhoe* (1819).

The Romantic Italy that emerges from these pages will hopefully seem eccentric by any standards. Charged with the burden of forging a nation and carrying an ancient civilization into an uncertain modern world, many nineteenth-century Italian writers, like their imaginary progenitor Aeneas, buckled under the weight of their own high ambitions. For most Italian Romantics, as for the Europeans, there could be (pace Foscolo) no second Troy. Yet, in Italy and abroad, the obsession with cultural origin persists. Michel Foucault, through the leveling motion of his critical archaeology and genealogy of Western intellectual discourse, has worked to demystify the metaphysical assumptions attendant upon such collective backward glances. These subsequent pages take a less rationalizing stand. Any surrender to memory, whether personal or public, involves a bend in the direction of the imagination; the words we use to describe this look backward, by virtue of their present removal from past experience, can signal our exile to the realm of anachronism, as potentially creative as it is inaccurate. Manzoni writes that, in the realm of art, the true cannot be established by the usual rational models, for all agree that there should be something invented in imaginary works, "che è quanto dire, del falso" (which is equal to saying there should be something false) ("Sul romanticismo" 452; "On Romanticism" 313). I take his distinction between the real and the true to heart. Following Manzoni's lead, we might discern that, even in a presumably rational venture like the pan-European reconstruction of the Italian past in the Romantic age, the more questionable truths of the poet should be weighed in equal measure with the more verifiable truths of the historian or cultural critic.

Romantic myths about Italy were at times neither honest nor empirically sound, and often permeated with unseemly political motives and obfuscating ideologies. Yet many of these myths attest to the spell that "Italy"—for two thousand years now, an imaginary construct as much as an actual place—casts outside its borders. These archetypal fictions nourish the abiding sense of connection to Italy felt by many foreigners, who, like Goethe, have walked and continue to wander around the Forum or inside Santa Croce as though the ruins or vaulted arches were an intimate cultural inheritance. The epigraph to this study by Goethe—written, not incidentally, in an essay on Manzoni—reminds us that the journey from experience to poetic form via memory marks a distance between us and that same experience, however beautiful or meaningful its subsequent rendering.[38] Similarly, the particular anachronism that Italy offered in the Romantic age suggests our abiding desire to return to cultural homelands that never existed.

PART I

Genus Italicum

I

Did Italian Romanticism Exist?

Friedrich Nietzsche's essay "On the Uses and Disadvantages of History for Life" has haunted literary historians across the critical spectrum.[1] He writes:

> Die historische Bildung unsrer Kritiker erlaubt gar nicht mehr, daß es zu einer Wirkung im eigentlichen Verstande, nämlich zu einer Wirkung auf Leben und Handeln komme: auf die schwärzeste Schrift drücken sie sogleich ihr Löschpapier, auf die anmutigste Zeichnung schmieren sie ihre dicken Pinselstriche, die als Korrekturen angesehn werden sollen: da war's wieder einmal vorbei. Nie aber hört ihre kritische Feder auf zu fließen, denn sie haben die Macht über sie verloren und werden mehr von ihr geführt, anstatt sie zu führen. Gerade in dieser Maßlosigkeit ihrer kritischen Ergüsse, in dem Mangel der Herrschaft über sich selbst, in dem, was die Römer impotentia nennen, verrät sich die Schwäche der modernen Persönlichkeit. (141–42)

> (The historical culture of our critics will no longer permit any effect at all in the proper sense, that is an effect on life and action: their blotting-paper at once goes down even on the blackest writing, and across the most graceful design they smear their thick brush-strokes which are supposed to be regarded as corrections: and once again that is the end of that. But their critical pens never cease to flow, for they have lost control of them and instead of directing them are directed by them. It is precisely in this immoderation of its critical outpourings, in its lack of self-control, in that which the Romans call *impotentia*, that the modern personality betrays its weakness.) (87)

Nietzsche believed that this thirst for historical knowledge engenders a confusing surplus of images and ideas that tempers the immediacy of experience and produces an ironic detachment from the present in the weakened or "impotent" modern personality. We can live as heroes, he argues, only by freeing ourselves from this "ungeheure Menge von unverdaulichen Wissenssteinen" (huge quantity of indigestible stones of knowledge), and embracing, like his beloved ancient Greeks, the "geschlossen und ganz" (rounded and closed) horizon of the present. In the current historicist critical climate — and in an information age marked by its capacity for retrieving, synthesizing, and storing historical information — it is difficult not to appreciate the prophetic qualities of his text. By reducing critical awareness to historical self-consciousness, however, Nietzsche perhaps overstates his case. As David Perkins writes, the aim of literary history is "not merely to reconstruct and understand the past" but "to explain how and why a work acquired its form and themes and, thus, to help readers orient themselves" (177). In his critique of Nietzsche, Perkins argues that literary history is also "literary criticism," and its "function lies partly in its impact on reading" (177–78). Less optimistic, René Wellek and Austin Warren encompass the concerns of Nietzsche and his commentators by asking: "Is it *possible* to write literary history, that is, to write that which will be both literary and a history?"[2]

Beyond this skeptical query lingers a more practical but no less troubling question: as difficult as literary history may be to write, can sound literary criticism exist without it? One need only think of I. A. Richards's experiment at Cambridge in the 1920s, when he challenged students to interpret poems without providing them with any literary-historical context. The responses ranged from the plausible to the absurd, and the task of extrapolating critical principles from the "astonishing variety of human responses" proved daunting.[3] The results of Richards's survey lent empirical legitimacy to what became a touchstone of reader-response theory: as a rhetorical structure and aesthetic construct, the literary text inevitably draws on the reader's historically conditioned *Erwartungshorizont* (horizon of expectations) with regard to such elements as genre, theme, and tone.[4] Questions about the vexed relationship between literary criticism and literary history persist. Can we speak intelligently of literature without the dreaded "blotting-paper" of Nietzsche's critic-historian? What occurs when we read a text or corpus of texts without also reading around or behind them — that is, without taking into account biographies, information on readership, political and historical data, a sense of the author's formal concerns, even literary anecdotes or gossip? Nietzsche labeled the historicizing critic a "neuter"; but without the requisite literary-historical groundwork, without this *neutrality,* can one ascend to higher aesthetic ground and approach Nietzsche's coveted "monumental" criticism? The strange career of Italian Romanticism would suggest this is not possible, for the expectations that have shaped foreign responses to Italian culture since the Romantic age continue to preempt most people outside of Italy from reading modern Italian literature objectively and productively.

Leading Romanticists have attested to the "carving up" of nineteenth-century English studies into discrete critical, historical, and ideological units that seldom dialogue with their counterparts.[5] The student of the Italian Ottocento cannot contemplate the energy involved in this professional partitioning without some jealousy. Although English and, to a lesser extent, French and German Romanticism are well enough established in the anglophone critical discourse to guarantee their survival in this carved-up terrain, Italian Romanticism has been a casualty of the new literary historiography. Today's comparative literary historians tend either to focus on canonical texts and traditions or try to recover voices from the literary past that ideology has stifled and that inherited aesthetic standards have rejected.[6] Consequently, many "middle-ground" works or literary cultures that are neither canonical nor marginal have escaped comparative study, and one of these betwixt and between literary cultures, Italian Romanticism, has well nigh disappeared from the foreign critical scene. Italian Romanticism was far more cosmopolitan in scope than its foreign critics have acknowledged; the relative lack of attention to it abroad has occurred because of issues of nationalism, religion, and cultural mythmaking.

I

In the provocatively entitled *Il romanticismo italiano non esiste* (Italian Romanticism does not exist; 1908), Gina Martegiani writes that so-called Italian Romanticism merely echoed the foreign, European strand of Romantic thought derived primarily from German theory and such Nordic movements as the Sturm und Drang. She argues that Italian authors between the French Revolution of 1789 and the European revolutions of 1848 were actually provincial "anti-romantici" (anti-Romantics) who countered the cosmopolitan cult of genius and individuality with a neoclassical group mentality.[7] Gods are gods because they lack goals and self-consciousness, Martegiani reports, quoting Friedrich Schlegel's *Lucinde* (1799) — but her Italian Romantics never sought this heaven on earth, as they aspired solely to patriotic acts (96–97). Even the influential principle of Romantic irony elaborated by Friedrich Schlegel in his *Athenäum* fragments did not affect Martegiani's ersatz Italian Romantics. In her critique of Manzoni's "anima semplice" (simple soul), she remarks that whereas the authentic Romantic could view his own life as a spectator and harness the creative energies of his divided self, Italians of the Ottocento countered this ironic state with some practical act (105–7). In short, Martegiani claims that the Italians failed to satisfy the sine qua non of any self-respecting Romantic: they did not take the absolute seriously enough.

Notwithstanding the extravagance of Martegiani's claims, they reflect the highly partisan and polemical nature of Italian Romanticism's reception, beginning with the politically charged debates that accompanied its inception. After Napoleon's defeat and the negotiations of the Congress of Vienna in 1814–15, the Austrians assumed control of the most developed part of the Peninsula, Lombardy, where the regime established the journal *Biblioteca italiana* (Italian library) to showcase its policies and rally the Italian intelligentsia to its cause.[8] Though Foscolo initially went on record against writers who aligned themselves with the ruling class, he eventually accepted—to the astonishment of his literary cohorts—the regime's mandate that he prepare the editorial plan for the new journal. By the time Staël's incendiary article on translation appeared in *Biblioteca italiana* in 1816, Foscolo had gone into exile to avoid assuming editorship of the journal and swearing allegiance to the Austrian government.[9] Most of the reactions to Staël's article were derivative, abusive, and of dubious worth—with the notable exception of work in the journal *Il conciliatore* (The reconciler; 1818–19) and, to a lesser extent, in the journal *Antologia* (Anthology; 1821–33). In the tradition of the great Milanese Enlightenment periodical *Il caffè* (Café; 1764–66), organized by Manzoni's grandfather Cesare Beccaria and the Verri brothers, the liberal *Il conciliatore* offered informed debate on the pressing issues of the day, including those of a scientific and technical nature. The journal also benefited from the contributions of authors, including Foscolo's protector Vincenzo Monti and Staël's translator Pietro Giordani, who had left the *Biblioteca italiana* in disgust once they recognized its propagandistic agenda. *Il conciliatore* provided the forum in which the principal voices in the *questione del romanticismo*—Giovanni Berchet, Pietro Borsieri, Ludovico di Breme, Silvio Pellico, and Ermes Visconti—explained and promoted the tenets of Romanticism; equally important (and in keeping with the nonpartisan approach suggested by its name), it also published the views of the movement's opponents. However moderate in intent, the journal came under constant censorship and was eventually forced to disband; some of its contributors, most famously Pellico, were jailed.[10] Less interested than *Il conciliatore* in the receding polemics between the *classici* and *romantici*, the Florentine *Antologia*, founded by Gino Capponi and Giovan Pietro Vieusseux, pursued a practical, cosmopolitan agenda aimed at fostering a sense of Italian cultural unity. Notwithstanding its measured editorial policy, it, too, eventually ran afoul of the authorities and was suppressed by the grand duchy of Tuscany.

At a crucial early juncture in the reception of Italian Romanticism, Francesco De Sanctis dedicated four courses to the subject at the University of Naples (1872–76), lectures that were subsequently edited and published by two distinguished disciples, Francesco Torraca and Benedetto Croce.[11] Essentially, De Sanctis argued that the history of the period centered on the struggles between the liberal schools of thought organized around the measured, reformist Manzoni and the more radical protocols associated with the democratic revolutionary firebrand Giuseppe Mazzini.[12] Following De Sanctis's critical watershed, the two most influential voices in the debates about Italian Romanticism belonged to the self-proclaimed *poeta vate* (poet-prophet) Giosuè Carducci and the philosopher-historian Croce. Carducci's distaste for the movement prejudiced generations of Italians against what he claimed was the egotistical, overwrought, nostalgic, sentimental, and—worst of all—international-minded writing that imitated the few legitimate masters of *il romanticismo italiano*.[13] Though decidedly less zealous, Croce voiced his skepticism about the movement in the form of a distinction between Romanticism's theoretical advances and, by contrast, its practical failures, especially the paralyzing sentimentality abhorred by Carducci.[14] Croce's negative assessment influenced another major voice in the debates, Giuseppe Borgese, whose *Storia della critica romantica* (History of Romantic criticism; 1905) argued that the supposed originality and innovativeness of the Italian Romantics represented no real departure from those same entrenched classical principles they believed they were overturning.

Perhaps more damning than the negative evaluations of Martegiani and others is the silence that has followed them outside of Italy. Great comparatist texts by de Man, Hartman, Wellek, and even the formidable Italianist Erich Auerbach devote little or no energy to linking the Italian Romantics to larger questions of European culture and literary history—a striking fact when one considers that the first three were leading scholars of European Romanticism.[15] The aforementioned *Romanticism in National Context* studies over a dozen national Romantic traditions (including relatively minor movements in Greece, Hungary, and Switzerland) but does not cover Italy.[16] Though the dramatic polemics over Italian Romanticism involved such prominent foreign authors as Goethe, Staël, and Stendhal, we lack translations of most Italian contributions to the debate and many related works by the canonical authors Foscolo, Leopardi, and Manzoni.[17]

However ignored Italian Romantics are abroad, within Italian literary circles—pace Martegiani—they remain the subject of an ongoing critical outpouring.[18] Each year brings scores of new articles, biographies, and critical editions explicating the metaphors and detailing the intimacies of the three crowns and lesser-known contemporaries.[19] Most Italian scholars view many of these Romantics not only as authors of the first rank but also as heroes who contributed their literary energies to the Risorgimento. Foscolo, for example, was considered by Mazzini, a so-called *padre d'Italia* (father of Italy), to be the model of Italian political virtue—a tag that both helped and hindered his literary reception. Another founder of modern Italy, General Giuseppe Garibaldi, was known to carry a copy of Foscolo's *Ultime lettere di Jacopo Ortis*. Manzoni, for his part, was named senator in 1860, the year Garibaldi invaded southern Italy and set in motion the process of unifying the Peninsula. Leopardi remains fixed in Italian lore partly because of his early patriotic poems "All'Italia" ("To Italy"; 1818); "Sopra il monumento di Dante" ("By Dante's Tomb"; 1818); and "Ad Angelo Mai" ("To Angelo Mai"; 1820), a text devoted to the Vatican archivist who discovered Cicero's antityrannical *De republica*.[20]

The connection between Romanticism and the Risorgimento in Italian minds is suggested by the following description of Vittorio Alfieri, arguably the nation's most important pre-Romantic author. The introduction to the definitive edition of Alfieri's works refers to him as a "prosatore civile e politico" (civic and political author), whom Europeans and Americans alike remember as much for his devotion to liberty as for his writings—a view that echoes De Sanctis's paradigmatic reading of Alfieri in *Storia della letteratura italiana* (*History of Italian Literature*; 1871).[21] Unlike the French or even the American Revolution, however, the Italian Risorgimento did not have enough of an international effect to guarantee that one of its poet-patriots—an ambivalent one, for that matter, who celebrated his aristocratic lineage and came to abhor the French revolutionary uprising—would enter public memory abroad. Indeed, English readers today must still rely on an edition from 1876 for the complete translation of Alfieri's tragedies.[22]

Traditionally, scholars have assigned three primary explanations for the exceptional nature of Italian Romanticism—that is, the movement's ubiquity in Italian scholarship yet its invisibility in foreign criticism. First, Italian authors of the early nineteenth century continued to emulate that same Greco-Roman classical culture that the rest of Romantic Europe had begun to regard with suspicion.[23] Second, Italian Romanticism promoted a pious Catholicism that was out of step with the more rational Protestant cultures of northern Europe.[24] Third, Italian Romantic authors failed to transcend the chaos and contingencies of Italian history and politics to address international currents of thought.[25]

A comparative reading of a standard Romantic trope, the crossing of the

Alps, shows how these factors worked in unison to distinguish Italian authors from their foreign contemporaries and isolate the Italian Romantic movement from its European counterparts. For many Romantic poets and their predecessors, the summits of the Alps embodied the natural sublime, both as a literary topos and as a physical locus whose genius loci could provide inspiration lacking in the world below.[26] Wordsworth's apostrophe to "Imagination" in book 6 of the *Prelude,* one of the more celebrated Alps crossings in Romantic literature, represents a rare instance in which the work of this elusive and contentious poet fits into a broader European framework.[27] He begins by acknowledging the failure of verbal representation in the face of certain registers of experience ("Imagination—here the Power so called / Through sad incompetence of human speech"). The very inscrutability and "awful" qualities of this same inchoate internal domain, however, prove inseparable from the corresponding "glory" that ensues "when the light of sense / Goes out." The mineral world that Wordsworth encounters after crossing the Simplon Pass falls short of the images of the Alps his mind had prepared for him. But, in this disappointment and reckoning that the material of life inevitably pales in comparison with the spectral energies of the "invisible world" of feeling and thought, the poet discerns the contours of a soul. The apostrophe contains the following typically "Romantic" markers: a confrontation between the forces of the imagination and the machinations of nature ("That awful Power [imagination] rose from the mind's abyss / Like an unfathered vapour that enwraps, / At once, some lonely traveller"); praise of the infinite over the finite ("Our destiny, our being's heart and home, / Is with infinitude, and only there"); an awareness of the dangers and seductions of the natural sublime ("I was lost; / Halted without an effort to break through"); and a tendency to translate personal aesthetic experience into universal moral precept ("But to my conscious soul I now can say— / 'I recognise thy glory'").

In contrast to their northern counterparts, Italian Romantics depicted the Alps in a less ethereal manner. Two of the more celebrated examples of the topos come from Foscolo's *Ultime lettere di Jacopo Ortis* and Manzoni's *Adelchi.* Foscolo's passage describes the flight of his protagonist, Ortis, from both the proscription list of Napoleon and an unhappy love affair with the betrothed Teresa:

> Ho vagato per queste montagne. Non v'è albero, non tugurio, non erba. Tutto è bronchi; aspri e lividi macigni; e qua e là molte croci che segnano il sito de' viandanti assassinati. Là giú è il Roga, un torrente che quando si disfanno i ghiacci precipita dalle viscere delle alpi, e per gran tratto ha spaccato in due queste immense montagne. ... La natura siede qui solitaria e minacciosa, e caccia da questo suo regno tutti i viventi. I tuoi confini, o Italia, son questi! ma

sono tutto dí sormontati d'ogni parte dalla pertinace avarizia delle nazioni. (February 19 and 20, 1799; 111)

(I have wandered among these mountains. There is not a tree, not a hut, not a blade of grass. It is all bare, with gnarled branches, rough, grey boulders, and many crosses scattered about which mark the spots where travellers have been assassinated. Over there is the Roia, a torrent which when the ice melts rushes from the entrails of the Alps, and for a long stretch splits this immense mountain in two.... Nature takes her seat here, solitary and threatening, and drives all living things from this realm of hers. These, O Italy, are your borders! But every day they are crossed at every point by the obstinate greed of other nations.) (110)[28]

As opposed to the hermetically sealed interiority of Wordsworth's crossing, Foscolo's Alps encompass discussions of geography, habitation, and homicide. More important, Ortis's preoccupation with the current strife afflicting Italy tethers to the earth and its nations his reflections on the natural power of the mountains. Even when he appears on the verge of immersing himself in lyrical reflection about the force of these environs ("Nature takes her seat here, solitary and threatening"), the shadows of history cool the heat of Ortis's introspection and remind him of his political coordinates ("These, O Italy, are your borders!"). If Wordsworth discovers his home in the "invisible world" of the imagination, Ortis's sense of political engagement grounds his poetic sensibilities in a more visceral geography. All is scattered, harsh, sickly, and rocky on the rooftop of Europe, and the images in Ortis's mind, as throughout the novel, center on the idea of death, with none of the regenerative yearning in Wordsworth ("Our being's heart and home, / Is with infinitude, and only there").

Manzoni's text comes from the verse tragedy *Adelchi* (*Adelchis*; 1822), which narrates the political intrigue and spiritual crises in Charlemagne's eighth-century war with his rival the Longobard King Desiderio:

Dio gli accecò, Dio mi guidò. Dal campo
inosservato uscii; ...
. . . .
   ... e abbandonando
i battuti sentieri, in un'angusta
oscura valle m'internai: ma quanto
più il passo procedea, tanto allo sguardo
più spaziosa ella si fea. Qui scorsi
gregge erranti e tuguri: era codesta
l'ultima stanza de' mortali. Entrai
presso un pastor, chiesi l'ospizio, e sovra
lanose pelli riposai la notte.

Sorto all'aurora, al buon pastor la via
addimandai di Francia. — Oltre quei monti
sono altri monti, ei disse, ed altri ancora:
e lontano lontan Francia; ma via
non avvi; e mille son que' monti, e tutti
erti, nudi, tremendi, inabitati,
se non da spirti, ed uom mortal giammai
non li varcò. — Le vie di Dio son molte,
più assai di quelle del mortal, risposi;
e Dio mi manda. — E Dio ti scorga, ei disse:
indi, tra i pani che teneva in serbo,
tanti pigliò di quanti un pellegrino
puote andar carco; e, in rude sacco avvolti,
ne gravò le mie spalle: il guiderdone
io gli pregai dal cielo, e in via mi posi. (2.167–93)

(God blinded them, God guided me. I left
The camp unobserved, . . .

. . . .

    . . . and I abandoned all
Well-trodden paths.
I entered into a dark,
Narrow valley, but as I walked along
It became spacious, more and more airy.
There I saw roaming flocks and wretched sheds,
Resembling mankind's ultimate abodes
In a wasteland. A shepherd hosted me
For the night, and I slept on woolen hides.
When I awoke at dawn I asked the way
To France of the good shepherd, and he said:
"Beyond those mountains are other mountains
And others still, and then, but very far,
There is France. But there is no way to go.
There are thousands of mountains, steep and bare,
And dreadful. No one lives there but spirits;
No mortal man did ever pass them." "God's
Ways are many," I replied, "many more
Than a mortal man has, and God sends me."
"Then may God guide you," he said; and out of
The loaves he kept in store he gave me many,
As many as a pilgrim can carry;
In a bag of coarse cloth he put them and
I shouldered it, as I prayed our God
To reward him. And then I set out.) (239–40)[29]

Perhaps Manzoni's most successful theatrical work, *Adelchi* realizes his lifelong goal of combining accurate historical writing with an exaltation of the Catholic faith. From a comparative European perspective, however, this Alps crossing is sui generis. The above journey of Charlemagne's Deacon Martino inspires him to trumpet the inner workings of nature, the contingencies of human history, and the providential relationship between the ways of God and man. But beyond the content of Martino's words, the syntactic and rhetorical structure of his speech reveals the distance separating Manzoni from his fellow European authors. Biblical parataxis, embodied in the staccato repetition of uncoordinated clauses ("Dio gli accecò, Dio mi guidò"; later, "Dio mi manda," followed by "Dio ti scorga"), combines with explicitly Christian imagery and phrasing (the mutual blessings; sharing of bread; Dantesque "oscura valle" [dark valley]; repeated allusions to God; and lexical choices "pastor" and "pellegrino" [shepherd and pilgrim]) to create an otherworldly atmosphere in which the nature of the Alps becomes subsumed by a religious vision. Whereas Wordsworth's Alps are a place where an imaginative soul transcends rational and sensorial experience, and Foscolo's Alps are a site where political consciousness asserts the primacy of the empirical over the imagined, Manzoni's Alps are an embodiment of the liminal space where religion and history meet. Martino will eventually cross the alpine border that separates the worlds of man and God and, in so doing, will set apart Manzoni's representative strand of Italian Romantic thought from that of most European contemporaries.

Foscolo's and Manzoni's eccentric treatment of the natural sublime suggests the difficulty of integrating Italian Romanticism into a comparative discussion. An avowedly neoclassical author for most of his life, Foscolo's stalwart interest in mythology and his defense of allegorical representation epitomized the type of thinking that often came under attack in the polemics over Italian Romanticism stimulated by Staël. The case of Manzoni is even more ambiguous. After producing his pioneering historical novel, *I promessi sposi*, he disavowed the legitimacy of this very genre.[30] In *Del romanzo storico* (*On the Historical Novel*; c. 1851) he writes that the so-called historical novel is a hybrid monster, neither pure fiction nor pure history, and hence a contaminated construct that he will henceforth discard in the name of historical writing proper.[31] However, beyond Manzoni's stated reason for reporting historical events, there may lurk a more unsettling motive: perhaps he believed that the Italian drive for unification, tenuous as it was at that time, could not afford the luxury of historical fantasy.

With the benefit of two hundred years of hindsight, however, it becomes clear that the traditional explanations for the exceptional nature of Italian Romanticism—that is, its classicism, Catholicism, and nationalist-historical dimensions—do not tell the whole story. Although the predominantly historicist and neoclassical approach to mythology by Italians in this period differed in kind from the more metaphysical understanding of ancient cultural forms elsewhere, especially in Romantic England and Germany, one does well to note the fluency in the language and symbolism of mythology displayed by many northern European contemporaries of the Italian Romantics. For example, Marilyn Butler has demonstrated that the cultlike devotion to ancient Greek concepts of love inspired some of the best poetry written by Shelley and his circle late in the second decade of the nineteenth century.[32] Keats laced his finest poetry with mythological allusions, as did the accomplished German classicist and translator of Sophocles Friedrich Hölderlin. One can barely speak of German Romanticism without addressing the profound philo-Hellenism of Johann Joachim Winckelmann, Goethe, the Schlegels, and the post-Romantic Nietzsche, to name only the more prominent exponents. Scholars who emphasize the exceptionality of Italian classicism also fail to account for a simple fact of Italian cultural history. Most Italians of the Ottocento did not view mythology and classical literature as mere emblems of artistic and cultural authority. Rather, they considered the classical heritage a legitimate birthright that enjoined them to ancient Rome, and hence to Troy and ancient Greece.[33] Foscolo, we will see, felt as at home in the temples of Ilium as Wordsworth did in the hills of the Lake District.

The claim that the Catholicism of the Italian Romantics hindered their reception abroad is also problematic. We study many other Romantics precisely because of their religious extremism and idiosyncrasies. Søren Kierkegaard and Novalis come readily to mind, as well as Samuel Taylor Coleridge and Friedrich Schlegel, both of whom experienced religious conversions. Wordsworth's spirituality comprised everything from pantheism to conservative Anglicanism, yet these doctrinal issues have never prevented scholars from studying his poetry. Nor has the Catholic strand in such French Romantic authors as Chateaubriand and Alphonse de Lamartine blocked our interest to the extent that Manzoni's Catholicism supposedly has.

The weakest explanation for the dismissal of Italian Romanticism is the claim that Italian Romantics were too bound up in the history of their unification and political dispersion to have mattered to the rest of Europe. This argument fails to account for the fact that it was often Italy's historical crises and political fragmentation that brought so many foreigners to its shores and made its culture of interest to the international community. Since the Romantic period is celebrated for genres like the historical novel, it seems unlikely that the historicist focus of many Italian writers should have kept their texts out of foreign hands. Moreover, the demands of Italian culture and history resulted in those works that we now believe contain the most enduring and general appeal, especially *I promessi sposi* and, to a lesser extent, *Ultime lettere di Jacopo Ortis*.

Given the limitations of these traditional explanations for the isolation of Italian Romanticism in Europe during the Romantic age and its subsequent marginality in comparative literary studies, I wish to propose three new and interrelated reasons: first, the emergence of a prescriptive nationalist hermeneutics in nineteenth-century Italian criticism; second, the antimodern flavor of Manzoni's views on the providential link between religion, aesthetics, and history; and third, the diffusion of Italy as a premodern culture in the Romantic foreign imaginary. My analysis of these three factors will return us to Foscolo and Manzoni as well as introduce an unexpected voice: that of the neorealist film director Roberto Rossellini.

II

When an author writes a text, he often imagines a special group of ideal readers. Although that privileged group may never appear or be peripheral to the actual reception of the text and the meanings it produces, when these imagined or ideal readers do arrive they can perpetually haunt the text's afterlife. The responses of this ideal group may come to be accepted as definitive by a majority of readers, and the text may then be promoted to the status of cultural monument. We sometimes call the author who achieves this readership a prophet or sage. Yet, as the case of Foscolo suggests, the making of the prophet can also be the unmaking of the writer.

In an essay written to commemorate the transfer of Foscolo's bones to the cathedral of Santa Croce in 1871, the patriot Mazzini railed against Italy's mania for constructing lavish tombs to honor its dead. Italians, Mazzini claimed, should instead study Foscolo's literary works, which in Mazzini's eyes were fictions that masked profound nationalist truths. The particular poem that Mazzini had in mind was "Dei sepolcri," which introduced Italians to the revolutionary concept that the tombs of Santa Croce were sites of national value that demanded physical communion and spiritual homage. Like most Italian readers, Mazzini emphasized the patriotic components of "Dei sepolcri" without delving into its universal elements, which include meditations on the rituals of mourning and the relationship between the living and the dead.[34] Although one might expect a reading of this nature from a politician-critic like Mazzini, his interpretation of the poem remains representative. His practice of equating nation with text reflects what one might term the "nationalist hermeneutics" that permeated nineteenth-century Italian critical discourse, especially in De Sanctis, whose work became a point of reference for many critics in the newly unified nation.[35] De Sanctis read Foscolo's *Ultime lettere di Jacopo Ortis* as the turning point in which a tired and defeated national consciousness receives a necessary jolt from an upstart author; and "Dei sepolcri" stands as the mature poet's creation of a new idiom that reflects a remade Italian spirit.[36]

Even Borgese, a scholar largely unsympathetic to De Sanctis's claims on behalf of the life-bestowing originality of Romantic literature, admitted that De Sanctis's preeminence among Italian critics past and present validated his observations on the link between nationalism and literary form. De Sanctis, he writes, was Manzoni's disciple in that he believed literature's essential task was "to fill with probable imagination the gaps left by documentary historiography in the tale of human destiny as well as in the moral advice emerging therefrom" ("Romantic Period" 67). Perhaps the same sense of political engagement that drove Manzoni away from the aesthetic hybrid of the historical novel and back to history writing proper compelled De Sanctis to emphasize the organic unity of Italian literary history, which emerges from his pages as a high cultural corrective to centuries of national fragmentation. Just as Foscolo's "Dei sepolcri" provided Italians with an artistic testament to the unifying achievements of exemplary Italians, so did De Sanctis's *Storia della letteratura italiana* serve as a scholarly and didactic justification of this cultural common ground by charting the steady progress in which the genius of Italian letters defined and advanced the stubbornly fragmented national consciousness. Croce refuted De Sanctis's idea that literature's effect could be felt in other areas of Italian life, arguing that only a work's formally successful *poesia* or failed *non-poesia* (poetry or non-poetry) mattered to the critic. But he helped establish his mentor's canonicity by promoting De Sanctis's Hegelian principle of literature as a pure form capable of progressing through concrete historical time.[37]

In addition to the nationalist hermeneutics that reached their apotheosis in De Sanctis, modern theories of the nation help explain the interpretive closure that has enveloped Foscolo's "Dei sepolcri." In his pioneering study of nationalism, Anderson asks the reader to imagine the scandal that would ensue if a "busybody" attempted either to discover the name of the Unknown Soldier or fill his tomb with actual bones.[38] He writes that citizens would always rebuff such efforts in order to preserve the mysterious nature of these ceremonial graves. For the modern citizen, inside the tomb lies no single soldier but an entire nation, and to name or individuate the deceased would reduce the national ghost to an ordinary self. Tombs of the Unknown Soldier thus translate the private suffering of war into transcendental sources of collective identity. Students of nationalism will by now recognize the religious rhetoric that most theorists of nationalism cite as central to the formation of national identity. Scholars generally agree that the nineteenth-century cult of the nation grew in part because the discourse of national identity during this era was able to promise citizens abstract immortality in the wake of Enlightenment skepticism about religious belief and doctrinal transcendence. The life that one sacrificed to God or king in the medieval and early modern periods became, with the advent of modernity, a life offered in the name of one's country. Few understood this better than Foscolo.

From his earliest work, Foscolo dedicated his career to establishing a cult of literary history that made Italy's great writers into priests of their broken polity. Whereas Goethe's *Die Leiden des jungen Werthers* (The sorrows of young Werther; 1774) keeps us in suspense as to whether the protagonist will take his own life over his amorous despair, Foscolo's *Ultime lettere di Jacopo Ortis* compels us to wonder just when that inevitable suicide will occur.[39] The novel begins, "Il sacrificio della patria nostra è consumato" (The sacrifice of our homeland is complete), a language of consecration and national reflection that extends to Ortis's sense of his own mortality (October 10, 1797; *Ultime lettere* 11; *Last Letters* 7). By the novel's end, Ortis will voluntarily follow the abstraction "Italy" to the grave, offering himself as a political martyr for future generations of Italians. Years after this novel appeared, Foscolo stated that, unlike Werther's suicide, which he claimed was a result of a melancholic and morbid personality, Ortis's self-slaughter reflected his "sentimenti repubblicani" (republican feelings) and "tempra fiera e virile" (proud and manly spirit).[40] Using similar rhetoric, Ortis writes to his beloved Teresa on the morning of his suicide:

> Che se il Padre degli uomini mi chiamasse a rendimento di conti, io gli mostrerò le mie mani pure di sangue, e puro di delitti il mio cuore. Io dirò: ... Ho spartito il mio pane con l'indigente; ho confuse le mie lagrime alle lagrime dell'afflitto; ho pianto sempre su le miserie dell'umanità. Se tu [Padre] mi concedevi una patria io avrei speso il mio ingegno e il mio sangue tutto per lei. (March 25, 1799; 134–35)

> (If the Father of men were to call me to account, I would show him my hands unstained by blood, and my heart unstained by crime. I would say, ... "I have shared my bread with the poor; I have mingled my tears with the tears of the afflicted. I have always wept over the misery of mankind. If you had granted me a homeland, I would have spent all my intellect and my blood on its behalf.") (135)[41]

In the manner of Lucan's representation of Cato in the *Pharsalia,* Foscolo presents Ortis's suicide as a form of political protest.[42] What Ortis kills is not merely the self but a degenerate and corrupt state; in taking his own life, he takes on the sins of his nation.

Similar political and nationalist impulses also fueled Foscolo in composing "Dei sepolcri," which has become a symbol of national identity that, for all it has gained in cultural prestige and influence, has lost much in terms of the variety of interpretations it elicits. The fault lies partially with Foscolo himself. In contrast to the long tradition of sepulchral poetry that preceded it, the poem thematizes that eminently modern concept, the nation. In response to criticism of "Dei sepolcri," Foscolo writes in "Lettera a Monsieur Guill[on]" that, unlike the graveyard poetry of his British pre-Romantic predecessors, his intent in "Dei sepolcri" was chiefly political:[43]

> Per censurare i mezzi d'un libro bisogna saperne lo scopo. Young ed Hervey meditarono sui sepolcri da cristiani: i loro libri hanno per iscopo la rassegnazione alla morte e il conforto d'un'altra vita; ed a' predicatori protestanti bastavano le tombe de' protestanti. Gray scrisse da filosofo; la sua elegia ha per iscopo di persuadere l'oscurità della vita e la tranquillità della morte; quindi gli basta un cimitero campestre. L'autore considera i sepolcri politicamente; ed ha per iscopo di animare l'emulazione politica degli italiani con gli esempi delle nazioni che onorano la memoria e i sepolcri degli uomini grandi: però dovea *viaggiare piú di Young, e d'Hervey e di Gray*, e predicare non la risurrezione de' corpi, ma delle virtú. (44n; Foscolo's emphasis)[44]

> (To criticize the methods of a book, one should know its intentions. Young and Hervey meditated on sepulchers as Christians. The aim of their work is to show resignation in the face of death and the comfort of another life. And for Protestant preachers, Protestant tombs will do. Gray writes as a philosopher: his *Elegy* wishes to persuade us of the obscurity of life and tranquility of death, and so a countryside cemetery is suitable for him. The author [Foscolo] considers sepulchers politically, and he seeks to inspire Italians politically by showing them examples of nations that honored the memory and sepulchers of their heroes. But he had *to travel farther than Young, Hervey, and Gray* and preach the resurrection not of bodies but of virtues.)

The last third of "Dei sepolcri" is a paean to the future Italian nation. The following lines have come to embody what many Italians consider to be the Foscolian moment *per eccellenza* of the Risorgimento:

> Un dí vedrete
> Mendico un cieco errar sotto le vostre
> Antichissime ombre, e brancolando
> Penetrar negli avelli, e abbracciar l'urne,
> E interrogarle. Gemeranno gli antri
> Secreti, e tutta narrerà la tomba
> Ilio raso due volte e due risorto
> Splendidamente su le mute vie
> Per fare piú bello l'ultimo trofeo

> Ai fatati Pelidi. Il sacro vate,
> Placando quelle afflitte alme col canto,
> I Prenci Argivi eternerà per quante
> Abbraccia terre il gran padre Oceáno.
> E tu onore di pianti, Ettore, avrai
> Ove fia santo e lagrimato il sangue
> Per la patria versato, e finchè il Sole
> Risplenderà su le sciagure umane. (279–95)

(One day you shall see a blind beggar groping under your ancient shadows, and, muttering, penetrate the burial vaults, and embrace the urns, and question them. The secret recesses shall groan, and the tombs tell all, Ilium razed twice and twice rerisen magnificently above its silent roads to make finer the final trophy of the fatal sons of Peleus. The holy bard, calming those tormented souls with his song, shall make immortal the Argive princes through all lands embraced by the great father Oceanus. And you, Hector, shall be honored by tears wherever men lament and hold sacred blood poured out for a fatherland, and as long as the sun shall shine on the calamities of man.) (Kroeber, 183)

The lines that precede the above passage tell of Cassandra's prediction that, though Troy would fall, the household gods would remain protected in tombs of the fallen Trojans. One day the blind seer Homer would come to question the spirits and speak of their trials to the world. It does not take a classical scholar to see the chain of succession that Foscolo establishes: from Troy and Hector sprang the Rome of Aeneas, whose story Virgil would sing; this in turn would lead to contemporary Italy and the luminaries of Santa Croce, whose burial vaults Foscolo himself figuratively embraces and questions, so that, like Hector's, the blood these visionaries spilled for their nation can be sanctified. By anchoring the Italian nation in a cultural tradition that stretches back to ancient Troy, Foscolo establishes the mythical dimensions of the Italian people and conflates the diachronic parameters of Italian history with its roots in the synchronic, infinite temporality of myth. He does this by borrowing from Christian rhetoric: the secret recesses of the tomb "gemeranno" (shall groan) just as hell groaned during Christ's harrowing; the city of Ilium, again like Christ, will have its resurrection; and the blood shed for the fatherland, Italy, will become sacred, just as the Trojan princes have become immortal in first the ancient Roman and then the modern Italian imaginary. The song of the poet himself will reanimate the memory of Troy and rescue it from the dark tombs. In the final act of perhaps the most powerful meditation on sepulchers in early nineteenth-century Europe, Foscolo fuses pagan, Christian, nationalist, and literary-historical rhetoric in one sacred bond consecrated to the nonexistent Italian state and embodied in the form of a silent tomb. Here, in marvelous fashion, Foscolo claims for himself the title of Italy's Orpheus: animator of the dead and bard of the nation. For better and for worse, many Italian readers like Mazzini took Foscolo at his word and made him into a cultural icon whose work is celebrated more as a perfect treasure of national patrimony than as an imperfect but astonishingly open literary text.

III

It is a truism that the separation between church and state was a fundamental development of the so-called Enlightenment project and, more broadly, of modernity itself. Whereas some of the philosophical highlights associated with the high Enlightenment — for example, John Locke's tabula rasa, Kant's categorical imperative, and Rousseau's noble savage — may have faded from public memory, few educated people in the West would now fail to acknowledge the church-state division, whether or not they accept it. The ubiquity of the concept makes the following remark by Manzoni all the more startling: "In questo sistema mi pare di vedere una tendenza cristiana" ("Sul romanticismo" 453). (In Romantic theory I seem to discern a Christian inclination ["On Romanticism" 313].) The comment strains credulity not because Romantic literature lacked its strong theological traditions, often excesses; but, even for an age alternately celebrated and criticized for its tendency toward spiritualism and sublimation, Manzoni's statement stands out as a defiant advocate for the link between the new Romantic aesthetic and an existing religious doctrine. This single sentence helps explain why Italy's most important nineteenth-century author — whose *Promessi sposi* was hailed by a major contributor to the *questione del romanticismo* as Italy's first "leggibile" (readable) novel — never attained the broad international audience one would have expected for him.[45] It has, in fact, become a critical topos in both Italian and foreign criticism to speculate why Manzoni, a writer of such national renown that his death was commemorated by a worshipful Giuseppe Verdi's *Requiem* in 1874, is little known outside of Italian borders.

Though Manzoni's identification of a Christian tendency in Romantic thinking may seem out of step with modern thought, it is in keeping with how Italians throughout their cultural history have attested to the force of the Catholic Church in the nation's creative and intellectual life. What I will term the "providential imagination" has defined Italy's rationalist protocols and aesthetic endeavors stretching back to Dante through Vico, and forward through to Rossellini, whose works show that ultimately, and often in the face of apparent evil, a sovereign God prevails in the lives of humankind and permeates the universe with his active presence.[46] In contrast with the more passive and distant godhead favored by many of the Deist *philosophes,* the providential imagination in the Italian tradition underscores two defining characteristics of the nation's cultural energies in the post-Enlightenment era: the acknowledgment of the limits of rationality and the comparative lack of a great metaphysical tradition on a par with such nations as Germany (pace Croce).

Nowhere in Italian letters is the exquisitely mutable term *providence* more present than in Manzoni's *I promessi sposi,* whose reception has been conditioned by the nature and degree of its religiousness.[47] One of novel's more adept readers, Rocco Montano, notes that Manzoni's Catholicism tends to obstruct discussions of his work, and that to get around the issue more secular-minded critics have interpreted Manzoni as either a democrat, Jansenist, liberal, or even, as De Sanctis read him, a reformist "child of 1789."[48] The influential scholar Attilio Momigliano went so far as to call *I promessi sposi* an "epopea della Provvidenza" (epic of providence), and took great care to distinguish Manzoni's spirituality from the vogue of Romantic thinking.[49] Less flattering, others, often of the Marxist school and in line with Gramsci's slight that the poor in Manzoni lack an inner life, have read the religious element in Manzoni as an unwelcome sign of his paternalism and reactionary thought. What has blocked many, Montano notes, has been an ignorance of Manzoni's nuanced, complex, and sometimes antithetical notion of providence.[50] Precisely what Manzoni avoids, he notes, is the so-called *lieto fine* (happy ending) version of providence, in which all is worked out for the Christian believer, with the good and bad rewarded or punished according to their just merits — an interpretation that limns the history of his great novel's reception.[51] Yes, the separated protagonists Renzo and Lucia do marry at book's end, Montano concedes, but only after a tale of surpassing woe and ill fortune that narrates famine, injustice, pestilence, revolt, and war. Indeed, as has been noted, over eight thousand people die from the plague, including nine-tenths of the clergy and one of the peasants' most cherished protectors, the saintly Father Cristoforo.[52] For all the back-and-forth between Manzoni's critics over the question of providence in his novel, two things are certain: the centrality of the concept for Manzoni has, first, divided his Italian critics into antagonistic camps whose polemics often divert them from considering the novel's other aesthetic, cultural, and historical elements; and, second, it has contributed to Manzoni's isolation from the international mainstream of literary reception, especially in the domain of the historical novel, the genre he was institutional in creating.

In his study of Manzoni's limited European reception, Mario Puppo notes that it was not just the fact of Manzoni's religious faith but also its highly rationalist nature that made his work a poor fit for the more mystical, authoritarian Catholic traditions in neighboring Spain. Puppo also comments that the liberal, antiauthoritarian Manzoni was likely too moderate for the revolutionary zeal of French Romanticism; too measured for the fantastic, irrational imagination of Romantic Germany; and (falsely) considered to be too much of Walter Scott's epigone to make an impact in England (*Poesia e verità* 121–22).[53] In line with Puppo, a common denominator in much of the criticism on Manzoni, both in Italy and abroad, has been its concern over how to incorporate his work into the creative, cultural, and intellectual life of a nation trying to distance itself from institutions and legacies central to *I promessi sposi*, especially the political sway of the Catholic Church and the quasi-feudalistic reforms beholden to *noblesse oblige*.

The conceptual underpinnings that rendered Manzoni's brand of Romanticism so difficult to export are spelled out in his letter "Sul romanticismo," which does not, as is commonly supposed, explicitly connect Romantic theory to Christian doctrine; rather, the letter suggests that the principles and practices of Romanticism mesh with those of Christianity.[54] Like Christianity, Manzoni writes, Romanticism freed literature from paganism, promoted the true and the good, and critiqued a moral and mortal voluptuousness.[55] The impenetrability and untranslatability of Manzoni's religious reading of Romanticism, however, lies not in his defense of the movement's Christological associations — since, of course, many and powerful were the Christian avatars of the Romantic age.[56] Rather, at stake in Manzonian Romanticism was an obsession with an ideal that was sanctioned by his providential understanding of history and literary history. Manzoni steadfastly believed that literature's primary function was to arrive at a divinely underwritten idea of truth. It was this quality that compelled Goethe to criticize Manzoni for dividing his characters into the true and the ideal, motivated Foscolo to write that Manzoni was too concerned with historical accuracy to be a good poet, and drove Manzoni himself away from the historical novel soon after the appearance of his masterpiece.[57] Manzoni writes:

> Dove poi l'opinioni de' Romantici erano unanimi, m'è parso, e mi pare, che fosse in questo: che la poesia deva proporsi per oggetto il vero, come l'unica sorgente d'un diletto nobile e durevole; giacché il falso può bensì trastullar la mente, ma non arricchirla, né elevarla; e questo trastullo medesimo è, di sua natura, instabile e temperario, potendo essere, come è desiderabile che sia, distrutto, anzi cambiato in fastidio, o da una cognizione sopravvegnente del vero, o da un amore cresciuto del vero medesimo. ("Sul romanticismo" 451)

(The area, then, in which the opinions of the Romantics were unanimous, it seemed and seems to me, was this: that poetry should make truth its objective, as the unique source of a noble and enduring delight. Although the false can fascinate the mind, it can neither enrich nor elevate it. This pseudofascination is, by its nature, unstable and temporary, since it is capable, as should be the case, of being destroyed or even changed into something tedious. Such a change may be brought about by a transcendent sense of truth or by an ever-increasing love of truth.) ("On Romanticism" 312)

Manzoni was too subtle and erudite a thinker not to realize how slippery and protean—and loaded—the term *truth* is, so he quickly qualified his use of it:[58]

> Non desidero d'ingannarmi, quanto indeterminato, incerto, e vacillante nell'applicazione sia il senso della parola "vero" riguardo ai lavori dell'immaginazione. Il senso ovvio e generico non può essere applicato a questi, ne' quali ognuno è d'accordo che ci deva essere dell'inventato, che è quanto dire, del falso. Il vero, che deve trovarsi in tutte le loro specie, *et même dans la fable,* è dunque qualche cosa di diverso di ciò, che si vuole esprimere ordinariamente con quella parola. (452)

> (I do not wish to deceive myself about how indeterminate, uncertain, and vacillating in application the term "true" is with regard to works of the imagination. The obvious and generic sense of the word cannot be applied to works of the imagination, for we all agree that there should be something of the invented in imaginary works, which is equal to saying there should be something false. Truth, which should find expression in all forms, [and even in fiction,] is therefore something different from the normal meaning of the word.) (313)

Although Romanticism is just as uncertain as to what constitutes the magical signifier *truth* as are other systems of thought, Manzoni continues, it is actually less vulnerable in its attempts to get closer to the word because "la parte negativa, specificando il falso, l'inutile, e il dannoso, che vuole escludere, indica, e circoscrive nelle idee contrarie qualcosa di più preciso, un senso più lucido di quello, che abbiamo avuto finora" (in its negative form [Romantic theory] specifies the false, useless, and damaging aspects that it seeks to exclude. It indicates—and circumscribes with opposing ideas—something more precise, a sense more lucid, than anything we have had until now) ("Sul romanticismo" 452; "On Romanticism" 313). This is a surprising claim, when one considers that the two leading Italian poets of the age—Foscolo and Leopardi—emphasized literature's links to fantasy and illusion, and that most of Europe's major theoretical statements on Romantic poetry also sought to underscore the power of the imagination in its metaphoric and nonrational compass.

Manzoni then intensifies the bond between poetry and truth by bringing in the element that sanctioned the connection in the first place, the transcendental basis of his aesthetics:

> Era questa tendenza nelle intenzioni di quelli, che l'hanno proposto, e di quelli, che l'hanno approvato? Sarebbe leggerezza l'affermarlo di tutti, poiché in molti scritti di teorie romantiche, anzi nella maggior parte, le idee letterarie non sono espressamente subordinate al cristianesimo; sarebbe temerità il negarlo, anche d'uno solo, perché in nessuno di quegli scritti, almeno dei letti da me, il cristianesimo è escluso. Non abbiamo, né i dati, né il diritto, né il bisogno di fare un tale giudizio: quella intenzione, certo desiderabile, certo non indifferente, non è però necessaria per farci dare la preferenza a quel sistema. Basta che quella tendenza ci sia. (452–53)

> (Did those who first proposed and approved Romantic theory ever intend this Christian inclination? It would be frivolous to assert that this was everyone's intention, since in many Romantic theoretical writings, indeed in the greater part of them, literary ideas are not subordinated expressly to Christianity. It would be cowardly, however, to deny this Christian component, even in a single writer, for in none of these Romantic writings, at least in those I have read, is Christianity excluded. We have neither the facts, the right, nor the need to make such a judgment. Such a possible Christian intent, while certainly desirable and no small matter to us, is not, however, necessary to make us voice our preference for Romantic theory. It is enough for us that this Christian tendency is present in Romantic thought.) (313)

Manzoni's justification for the above is that the tenets of Romanticism — by dissociating literature from paganism and the amoral immanence of neoclassical letters and by promoting literary elements aligned with transcendental truth — converge with the goals of Christianity. He adds that other systems and disciplines besides Romanticism, though they profess their difference from Christianity, may eventually bend in its direction. For example, he claims that though the political economy of the eighteenth century adopted strictures that seemed antithetical to the Gospel, eventually its critics, in line with biblical teachings, realized the immorality of liberal principles predicated upon the acquisition of wealth derived from the ruin of others. "E quanto più considero," he concludes the section, "tanto più mi pare, che il sistema romantico tenda a produrre, e abbia cominciato a produrre nelle idee letterarie un cambiamento dello stesso genere" ("Sul romanticismo" 454). (The more I consider the matter, the more it seems to me that Romantic theory tends to produce — and has already begun to produce — a similar change in literary thinking ["On Romanticism" 314].)

In *I promessi sposi*, the singularity of Manzoni's theoretical insights finds expression in the passages devoted to the archbishop of Milan, Cardinal Federigo Borromeo, who enters the narrative after the sequence of chapters (19–21) dedicated to the conversion of l'Innominato (the Unnamed), the legendary blackguard hired by Don Rodrigo to sequester Lucia after her betrayal at the hands of the dubious Monaca (Nun) of Monza. After the Unnamed undergoes an excruciating process of self-examination stimulated in part by his awareness of Lucia's supreme goodness, he ventures out to see the visiting Cardinal, for whom Manzoni interrupts the narrative proper to give an extended biographical sketch. Born in 1564, Borromeo was "degli uomini rari in qualunque tempo, che abbiano impiegato un ingegno egregio, tutti i mezzi d'una grand'opulenza, tutti i vantaggi d'una condizione privilegiata, un intento continuo, nella ricerca e nell'esercizio del meglio" (one of those few men—rare in any age—who devote the resources of an exceptional intellect, of vast wealth and of a privileged position in society in an unbroken effort to seek out and practice the means of making the world a better place) (*Promessi sposi* 409; *Betrothed* 401).[59] While it is tempting to read into this account an autobiographical connection between the lives of the noble Manzoni and the public-minded and patrician Cardinal, the focus of the sequence on Borromeo lies in his handling—administrative as much as spiritual—of the Unnamed's conversion. In Borromeo's actions, Manzoni finds justification for the institutional value of the Catholic Church within the political and social structure of a fragmented Italy desperate for unification.[60] A common thread in the description of the Cardinal points to his practical acumen: he gave a high percentage of his income to the poor; strategically invested his money to heal social rifts; and, most memorably, established the celebrated Ambrosiana Library in Milan. The manner in which he adjudicates and administers his gifts was as consequential as the charity itself:

> Diceva, come tutti dicono, che le rendite ecclesiastiche sono patrimonio de' poveri: come poi intendesse infatti una tal massima, si veda da questo. Volle che si stimasse a quanto poteva ascendere il suo mantenimento e quello della sua servitù; . . . diede ordine che tanti se ne contasse ogni anno dalla sua cassa particolare a quella della mensa; non credendo che a lui ricchissimo fosse lecito vivere in quel patrimonio. (412–13)

> (He would often say—as all priests say—that the income of the Church is the patrimony of the poor. The practical meaning which he attached to these words can be seen from the following example. He ordered an estimate to be prepared of the total cost of his own personal expenditure and that of his servants. . . . He then ordered that the full corresponding sum should be transferred every year from his private account to that of his household. For he did not think it right that he, with his great wealth, should live on the patrimony of the poor.) (404)

Much of the rhetoric used to describe Borromeo in chapter 22 centers on his administrative capacities (for example, "applicandosi assiduamente alle occupazioni che trovò prescritte" [he applied himself assiduously to the tasks prescribed to him]; "nelle regole che stabilì per l'uso e per il governo della biblioteca" [in the rules he set up for the use and administration of the library]) (*Promessi sposi* 410, 414; *Betrothed* 402, 405). His fusion of charity and managerial skill is manifest in his interview with the Unnamed, who at one point begs the Cardinal to leave him and go administer to the throng of decent believers waiting outside his office. But the Cardinal replies: "Lasciamo le novantanove pecorelle. . . . Sono in sicuro sul monte: io voglio ora stare con quella ch'era smarrita" (*Promessi sposi* 430). (Never mind the nine and ninety sheep. . . . They are safe on the mountainside; and I mean to stay here with the one that was lost [*Betrothed* 417].) In addition to invoking the Dantesque signifier from the opening of the *Commedia* (where the fallen Pilgrim's way in life is "smarrita" [lost] [*Inf*. 1.3]), the passage cites the biblical parables of the good shepherd leading his flock in Matthew 18:12–14, and, more emphatically, its conversionary inflection in Luke 15:4–7.[61] The blessed stirrings that rent asunder the Unnamed's life of evil coalesce into feelings of joy after he receives Borromeo's embrace; it is the text's first mention of pleasure with regard to this hitherto tormented character.

News of his conversion spreads like wildfire: "Il giorno seguente, nel paesetto di Lucia e in tutto il territorio di Lecco, non si parlava che di lei, dell'innominato, dell'arcivescovo" (*Promessi sposi* 481). (In the village where she lived and throughout the territory of Lecco, people were talking on the following day of little else but Lucia, the Unnamed, and the Archbishop [*Betrothed* 460].) Thus, the private pain and transport of the Unnamed becomes, through the charity and ministry of Borromeo, and in the tradition of Augustinian and Dantesque conversionary narratives, an *exemplum* for future penitents. The tale, furthermore, serves as a testament to Manzoni's idea of providential design:

> Ma ora, chi si sarebbe tenuto d'informarsi, e di ragionare d'un fatto così strepitoso, in cui s'era vista la mano del cielo, e dove facevan buona figura due personaggi tali? Uno, in cui un amore della giustizia tanto animoso andava unito a tanta autorità; l'altro, con cui pareva che la prepotenza in persona si fosse umiliata, che la braverìa fosse venuta, per dir così, a render l'armi, e a chiedere il riposo. (*Promessi sposi* 481–82)

(But now no one was likely to feel shy about asking questions or stating opinions regarding a widely known story, in which the hand of Providence could be clearly seen—a story with two such remarkable heroes, one of whom [Borromeo] united so vigorous a love of justice with so lofty an authority, while the other was a man [the Unnamed] in whom tyranny itself seemed to be humbled, and gangsterism itself to have laid down its arms and sued for peace.) (*Betrothed* 460)

By emphasizing the institutional reach of Borromeo's Christian doctrine, Manzoni's portrait of the Cardinal provides the biographical corollary to the principles of morality, truth, and utility elucidated in his defense of the putatively Christian Romantic aesthetic.

One can imagine how this idealized portrait of the altruistic, efficient Cardinal came to be identified with a Manzonian religiosity that met considerable resistance in the more rationally inclined Europe and West of the author's day and afterward. Instead of pushing the poor to revolt or revolution, Manzoni's novel asks of them to believe in a better world to come—either on earth or in heaven—and instead of asking of governmental institutions to do the work of reform, Manzoni inscribes this progressive motion in well-intentioned paternalistic institutions like the Church and the noble class that Borromeo supremely embodies. In terms of the literary elements of Borromeo's representation, one thinks of Goethe's critique of Manzoni, that he unnecessarily divides his characters into the historical and the ideal, and his related claim that, for the poet, nobody is historical. In contrast to both Goethe and Foscolo, Manzoni looks to the events of the past as the backbone for his aesthetic work, for it is in the acts of men and women—especially the humble and disenfranchised often ignored by the historians—that he sought evidence of the providential design that made his work anomalous.[62] Since much of Manzoni's portrait of Borromeo is open to autobiographical speculation, it is fitting that he ended his biographical description of the Cardinal—also an author of many literary works and a leading intellectual light of his age—by asking the very words that one day others would ask about Manzoni himself: "Come mai, tutte insieme, non sono bastate a procurare, almeno col numero, al suo nome una fama letteraria presso noi posteri?" (*Promessi sposi* 420–21). (How is it that those works of [Borromeo's], by their sheer number if nothing else, have not won him literary fame among the members of the present generation? [*Betrothed* 410].)

IV

In addition to domestic cultural issues, the persistence of a certain foreign notion of Italy—one that has little to do with Italian Romanticism itself—has hindered the movement from reaching an international audience. Countless late eighteenth- and early nineteenth-century authors, ranging from the neoclassical Goethe to the Romantic Staël, favored Italy as a site for aesthetic exile, self-induced or otherwise. But with few notable exceptions—Stendhal generally, Shelley in more cosmopolitan moments—most of these foreigners believed that Italy's magnificent cultural residue from antiquity and the Renaissance overwhelmed any signs of cultural activity in modern Italy. For all its historical preeminence, the Italy of Goethe and others lacked a viable contemporary history; it was a land of ruins, actual and figurative—an enduring stereotype that has done much to limit the international spread of the Italian Romantic movement. Following in the footsteps of Foscolo and other Italians who sought to redress the obvious inequities of this foreign myth, the director Roberto Rossellini offered a critique of the Grand Tourist's Italy in his controversial film *Voyage to Italy* (1954).

In a typically elaborate metaphor, André Bazin compares the bricks of a house and the rocks of a ford to distinguish the neorealist cinema of Rossellini from traditional nineteenth-century European realism. According to Bazin, realism in the manner of, say, Émile Zola represents individual units of reality as though they were the bricks of a house. In themselves, the representative units have no individual value or nature; we do not trouble to inquire as to their beauty or composition. What matters is that these individual units have enough form and resistance to cohere into an organic whole. Only in contributing to this overall design do the individual units of realist representation achieve meaning. The realist house, Bazin contends, is already there in the individual brick. Not so with the neorealist Rossellini. Bazin writes that, rather than the bricks of a house, Rossellini's representative units resemble the rocks in a ford. Just as one might cross a ford by jumping from rock to rock, one might glean meaning from Rossellini's completed narrative by stopping along the route of the story. And as the rocks of a ford are in themselves integral units that do not depend on the structural totality of the ford for their identity (unlike the format and functional bricks, each rock is unique), so do the elements of Rossellini's narrative retain individual significations and functions independent from any teleology or post hoc analysis. Bazin writes that, in contrast to the synthetic and analytical modes of traditional realism, Rossellinian neorealism resists both a *prise-de-position* and the imposition of authorial worldview: "Le film néo-réaliste a un sens, mais à posteriori, dans la mesure où il permet à notre conscience de passer d'un fait à l'autre, d'un fragment de réalité au suivant, tandis que le sens est donné à priori dans la composition artistique classique: la maison déjà est dans la brique." (Neorealist film has a meaning, but it is a posteriori, to the extent that it permits our awareness to move from one fact to another, from one fragment of reality to the next, whereas in the classical artistic composition the meaning is established a priori: the house is already there in the brick.)[63]

Bazin's emphasis on the identity between the object and its photographic image in Rossellini provides us with the means to explore how he uses this "cinema of facts" and "pure acts" to critique the foreign gaze upon Italy that has limited the reach of Italian Romanticism. In *Voyage to Italy,* Rossellini exploits the tension between impersonal and subjective perspectives to deconstruct the visual images of Romantic Italy in the Western foreign imaginary. The film starts as a marvelous subversion of the Grand Tour. A well-heeled couple from London, Katherine and Alexander Joyce (Ingrid Bergman and George Sanders) travel by car to Naples to claim the inheritance of their deceased Uncle Homer, an eccentric expatriate who lived in Italy during World War II. The ancient Homeric and modern Joycean echoes of these protagonists' names only serve to remind the audience that this bourgeois journey to settle a will and sever a marital tie is deeply anti-epic. With free indirect point-of-view shots (reminiscent of Pier Paolo Pasolini's "cinema of poetry"), Rossellini uses the perspective of Katherine—the audience perceives Naples through her eyes and consciousness—to describe the stereotypical Romantic aspects of Italy, equating them with fanatical mysticism, earthy and unbridled fertility, and the primitive roots of Italian culture.[64] Most important, Rossellini utilizes Katherine's reactions to Italian art to critique the way foreigners have translated Italy into a pseudo-Romantic romance with death.

The Joyces' view of the Italians returns us to some of the Romantic stereotypes about national character circulated by Staël and her contemporaries. Like Staël's Grand Tourist Oswald in *Corinne* (1807), perhaps the most influential foreign statement on Italy of its time, Alex Joyce is stolidly British in his sensibilities and aspirations, unable to tolerate "lazy" Italy because it distracts him from his "work" and "duty" back home. Katherine, meanwhile, like Staël's heroine Corinne, opens herself to Italy's charms, particularly its art and poetic inspirations. She recites the verses of a former but now deceased admirer, Charles Lewington, to Alex, who in turn mocks this "strange" and "romantic" poetaster. The clichéd English Romantic visitor to Italy, Lewington is "thin, tall, fair, spiritual, [and] ill," and he composes the following Romantic-sounding lines after visiting the National Archaeological Museum of Naples: "Temple of the spirit, no longer bodies, but pure ascetic images, compared to which mere thought seems flesh, heavy, dim." Katherine admires these effusions, yet her husband derides her aesthetic sensibilities, symptomatic to him of what he later terms her "ridiculous romanticism."

Following her husband's arrogant disavowal of her yearnings, Katherine decides to visit the museum herself—which, however, has quite a different

Figure 1. Katherine Joyce (Ingrid Bergman) in *Voyage to Italy*, directed by Roberto Rossellini (1954; Sveva/Junior/Italia Films [Italy] and SGC/Ariane/Francinex [France]).

effect on her than it did on Lewington. Katherine drives to the museum lost in reflection and oblivious to the white noise of Neapolitan streets that teem with nuns, pregnant women, communist banners, chaotic traffic, and, as throughout the film, the echoes of folk music and passionate, disjointed conversations. Unlike her museum guide, for whom the classical statues initiate a series of personal and anecdotal reflections, for Katherine the statues are, she later tells Alex, not the ascetic figures invoked by Lewington. Rather, they exhibit a "complete lack of modesty." The Neapolitan tour guide lives organically inside the cultural history that the works embody; at one point, he even remarks that one of the statues resembles his daughter Maria. Katherine, however, feels alienated from this cultural history and the pagan and naturalistic impulses it only faintly masks. The inert yet threatening forms occasion no sense of aesthetic pleasure or spiritual reflection in Katherine. She comes to the statues seeking spirit and communion but finds instead embarrassment, solitude, and — Rossellini suggests by layering the scene with an ominous musical score — fear. In a magnificent reversal, Rossellini uses Katherine's visible sense of alienation to transform the romance of Italy and the pageantry of its history into a kind of anti-Romantic gesture (fig. 1). For Katherine Joyce, the putative sepulcher celebrated by Foscolo contains no eternal Italian spirit nor national genius; rather, it is like the "mere thought" of Lewington's verse:

"flesh, heavy, dim." Like the rocks in Bazin's metaphor of the ford, the statues are "facts" and "things" in and of themselves; they resist being subsumed or sublimated into a grand narrative or myth about Italian cultural history. Seeking Romantic transport, or at the very least the liberating symbolism of the cultural sublime, Katherine only finds a bare and confined Naples, the perfect analogue for her own spiritual poverty.[65]

Katherine's thwarted quest for Romantic Italy offers a clue as to why we are deaf outside of the Peninsula to the achievements of the Italian Romantics. Philosophy, Novalis claimed, was nothing but homesickness; for many European writers of the early nineteenth century, and later for Katherine Joyce, Italy became this imaginary homeland. "Or dov'è il suono / di que' popoli antichi?" (Now / where are all the ancient voices?), Leopardi asks in "La sera del dì di festa" ("Sunday Evening" 33–34; 1820), and his foreign contemporaries responded that this originary cultural music emanated from Italy itself.[66] The Romantic Italy created by nineteenth-century writers continues to inform our understanding of modern Italian culture and helps answer the question posed in the title of this chapter. Yes, Italian Romanticism did and does exist in Italy, as evidenced by the indisputable cultural, literary, even political achievements (and their continued influence) of the alternately self-proclaimed and ambivalent Italian Romantic authors of the early nineteenth century. But no, Italian literature between the French and European revolutions (1789–1848) was not "Romantic" in the way that most major European writers of the period understood the term then, and in the way that most comparative literary historians understand it today. The modern habit of thinking about Italy as an eminently premodern corpus of cultural traditions, a habit that emerged in the Romantic literary movements of Europe in the early nineteenth century, has made it difficult for foreigners to import the innovations and eccentricities of the Italian Romantics. The peculiar cultural and historical status of early nineteenth-century Italy — its heavily nationalistic critical discourse, traditions of providential aesthetic thought, and its mythologized role in the foreign literary imaginary — created a distinctly "Italian" brand of Romantic thinking that has had little purchase abroad.

Since Italy has always existed as much in the imagination as it has in fact, it seems appropriate to conclude on a note of psychological speculation. Perhaps Italy's ancient traditions, premodern antidotes for anxiety and alienation, supposedly fluid relations between the living and dead, and unthreatening political and historical marginality compel foreigners to preserve Italy as the haunted Lewington's "temple of the spirit." In this way, those outside of Italy can have a land in which traditions are safely and magnificently housed in a kind of cultural sepulcher, free from modernity and its uncertainties — in the spirit of Foscolo's "Dei sepolcri," our own private second Troy.

2

Italy without Italians: Goethe, Staël, and Foscolo

E non si tosto [noi italiani] viaggiamo, i forestieri che ci conoscono per popolo unicamente musico ci pregano di cantare; nè pensano com'ei ci fan piangere sempre!

(And as soon as we Italians travel, the foreigners who recognize us as a uniquely musical people ask us to sing—but they do not realize how they always make us weep!)
— Ugo Foscolo

Stimulated by the pioneering work of Edward Said and other theorists of literary geopolitics, recent criticism has explored the ideological bias behind the regional and national stereotypes ascribed to Italians at home and abroad.[1] Scholars have been especially active in examining the marginal position of the Italian south—the so-called *mezzogiorno,* land of the midday sun—vis-à-vis the north, a situation that has been described as "orientalism in one country."[2] Just as Said demonstrates that Westerners constructed a primitive and archaic Muslim Middle East in contrast to the supposedly more modern and ordered Occident, students of the *mezzogiorno* show that northern Italians promoted their own industriousness and European character by distinguishing themselves from a backward and provincial south.[3] In addition to these analyses of regional power politics, scholars have also examined the degree to which nationalist sentiments both in Italy and throughout Europe stimulated writers and citizens to define themselves collectively and often negatively against neighboring cultures.[4]

What has escaped attention in much of the literature on Italy's place in the foreign imaginary, however, is how a sense of cultural identity that was Continental in scale motivated its adherents to assign Italy certain characteristics, functions, and qualities. A critical mass of major nineteenth-century foreign writers, in constructing their common European heritage and sense of national identity, created a Romantic myth of Italy that persists to the present. These predominantly northern European authors established a dichotomy between their own supposedly rational, progressive cultures and the correspondingly irrational, backward society of their southern neighbor Italy.[5] Many foreign writers believed, moreover, that Italy's monumental past (especially that of Rome) represented the privileged historical source of their own individual nations and cultures.[6] In linking themselves to this storied Italian past, authors tended either to ignore or dramatize the shortcomings of contemporary Italy, which emerged paradoxically in the Romantic age as the culturally impoverished antithesis of its own illustrious heritage. The marginal status of contemporary Italian culture in Romantic Europe, however, was not wholly negative, for foreign authors sometimes used the example of a premodern and primitive Italy to critique the ambiguities and forms of alienation that accompanied modernity.

A process occurred between roughly 1775 and 1825 in the imagination of Romantic Europe that can be described as Italy's transition from Europe's museum to its mausoleum. This chapter approaches the issue of an *Italia senza italiani* (Italy without Italians) by surveying how some major foreign authors of the age constructed the following categories for describing Italy and the Italians.[7] First, Italy's magnificent cultural residue from antiquity and the Renaissance overwhelmed any signs of cultural activity in modern Italy, which assumed the didactic function of the "world's university" (Goethe quoting Winckelmann). In this geographically remote classroom—especially in Goethe's *Italienische Reise* (*Italian Journey*; published 1816–29)—European exiles and Grand Tourists could educate themselves and experiment with their identities for a fixed amount of time before returning to their homelands and their attendant responsibilities. Second, Italy and its people were effeminate, a gender characteristic that helped explain their prowess in the imaginative arts and their role in providing cultural access and opportunities to otherwise hearth-bound northern European women. Third, Italians were raw and violent, often to the point of being murderous; yet this same volatility also contributed to their remarkable creative accomplishments. Last and most important, Italian society and public order basically did not exist. Thus, any sense of law and morality in the country had to be created internally by individual Italians, who had no recourse to the written laws and public institutions enjoyed by northern Europeans. Although indicative of a chaotic Italian social structure, these private codes of honor and morality in Italy could also represent a positive antidote to the passive reliance by northern Europeans on official legal discourse. The concluding discussion explores the manner in which Foscolo's *Lettere scritte dall'Inghilterra* (Letters from England; 1817) critiqued this line of national stereotyping—especially as expressed in Staël's *Corinne, ou Italie*—by promoting a protocol for comparing nations that draws on his understanding of Vichian cultural and linguistic anthropology.

In order to distinguish vital ancient Italy from moribund contemporary Italy, foreign writers developed an impromptu cultural lexicon that employed such binary oppositions as male-female, living-dead, freedom-oppression, and Protestant-Catholic. During his Italian exile, Shelley wrote to fellow author Thomas Love Peacock on December 22, 1818, that the *città eterna*, for all its cultural splendor, seemed remarkably devoid of life: "The impression of it [Rome] exceeds anything I have ever experienced in my travels. . . . Rome is a city, as it were, of the dead, or rather of those who cannot die, and who survive the puny generations which inhabit and pass over the spot which they have made sacred to eternity. In Rome, at least in the first enthusiasm of your recognition of ancient time, you see nothing of the Italians."[8]

Poets, of course, should never be confused with demographers, yet the remark is both curious and typical. According to census data, the actual population of Rome at the time of Shelley's observation was well over a hundred thousand, which made it the third most populous city in Italy and one of the more populated urban areas in all of Europe.[9] More important, in terms of the literary culture that might have appealed to an Italianist as brilliant as Shelley, the year 1818 was one of the more explosive in modern Italian history.[10] The contentious *questione del romanticismo italiano* stimulated debate in such journals as Visconti's *Il conciliatore*, which distilled major currents of international thought for Italian readers and numbered among its contributors foreign authors on the level of Stendhal. The years of Shelley's exile (1818–22) also witnessed the publication of signal literary works by Italian authors as diverse as Berchet, Leopardi, Manzoni, Monti, and Pindemonte, to name a few.[11] Shelley's interests, however, did not primarily lay with Italy's living. In his eyes—or at least in the "first enthusiasm" of his encounter with Rome's "ancient time"—the cultural moment of the Italian past obscured "the puny generations" in its wake.

The above letter continues: "The English burying-place is a green slope near the walls, under the pyramidal tomb of Cestius, and is, I think, the most beautiful and solemn cemetery I ever beheld." In contrast with lifeless contemporary Rome, the natural aspects of the English burial ground burst with growth: the sun shines on its "bright grass," which is "fresh" and "green." Even the dead themselves appear animated, for their somatic state seduces the poet into wishing a similar level of consciousness for himself ("one might, if one were to die, desire the sleep [the deceased] seem to sleep"). For Shelley, the physical aura of the tombstone and its surrounding nature inspire thoughts that triumph over the corporeal state of death that the sepulcher normally signifies. The Italian landscape functions in a similar manner for him: its ruins and monuments, temporal markers usually associated with decay and death, fire his mind to "people . . . with its wishes vacancy and oblivion." Like many of his contemporaries, Shelley chooses to counter physical death with symbolic life while meditating beside an Italian cemetery that is Protestant and English. Shelley would even choose this "beautiful and solemn" spot as his place of final rest.[12]

A text by Shelley's friend and fellow Italophile, Byron, reveals the degree to which Italy became a collective sepulcher in the minds of many Europeans. In the best seller *Childe Harold's Pilgrimage,* Byron contrasts Italy's glorious past with the cultural and political decadence afflicting it at present. Italy, Byron writes, is "Mother of Arts" and "Parent of Our Religion" (4.417, 419).[13] Europe, he continues, "shall yet redeem [Italy]" and conquer the "barbarian tide" that threatens it (422–23). After establishing Italy as Europe's sacred female archetype and source of culture and faith, Byron elegizes Santa Croce:

> In Santa Croce's holy precincts lie
> Ashes which make it holier, dust which is
> Even in itself an immortality,
> Though there were nothing save the past, and this,
> The particle of those sublimities
> Which have relaps'd to chaos: — here repose
> Angelo's, Alfieri's bones, and his,
> The starry Galileo, with his woes;
> Here Machiavelli's earth return'd to whence it rose. (478–86)

Byron's encomium of Santa Croce and its fallen heroes dramatizes the notable absence of those cultural avatars who lie outside of the cathedral's walls: the *tre corone* (three crowns) Dante, Petrarch, and Boccaccio. Byron asks:

> Where did they lay
> Their bones, distinguish'd from our common clay
> In death as life? Are they resolv'd to dust,
> And have their country's marbles nought to say? (499–502)

Italy without Italians 57

Figure 2. Johann Zoffany, *The Tribuna of the Uffizi*. Reprinted by permission of The Royal Collection © 2002, Her Majesty Queen Elizabeth II.

To Byron, the scattering of Italy's dead reflected its current political fragmentation. In order for the nation to be forged, Italians needed to gather these illustrious sepulchers into a single spot, where they could host pilgrimages to the heroic dead that could serve as a nationalist ritual for the then nonexistent Italy. The half-full and half-empty tombs of Santa Croce thus embody the country's genius and unrealized destiny.[14]

Artists of the period employed similar images and themes. Johann Zoffany's *The Tribuna of the Uffizi* (1772–78/79; fig. 2) typifies the social practices and patterns of cultural consumption of the Enlightenment traveler. In a room filled with the greatest hits of the Italian Renaissance, patrician gentlemen mingle among works whose cultural prestige and proven excellence refine the sensibilities and confirm the clout of Grand Tourists.[15] Commissioned by Queen Charlotte, the painting adheres to the protocols of the Grand Tour group portrait genre; yet the vision of the artist is in full effect in what Olivar Millar describes as Zoffany's "hypothetical 'hang'" of the Tribuna.[16] Though the format of the painting's genre did not allow for the inclusion of contemporary Italians, the intensity of dialogue and exchange among the British Grand

Figure 3. Jacques Sablet, *Roman Elegy*. Musée des Beaux Arts, Brest. Photo Credit: Réunion des Musées Nationaux / Art Resource, NY.

Tourists and the works of art suggests that the value of the Tour derived from forms of interaction independent of actual Italian society.[17] The implied distance between foreigner and Italian increases when one considers that, for many in Zoffany's age, Italy lacked a basic sense of "society" altogether, because of its permissiveness and its decline from former glories.[18]

The formal and thematic distance between Zoffany's *Tribuna* and Jacques Sablet's *Élégie romaine* (*Roman Elegy*; 1791; fig. 3) encompasses, of course, the shift toward the more introspective and symbolic modes of representation that pervaded most European art forms in the latter part of the eighteenth century. Notwithstanding its obvious differences from its predecessor, Sablet's painting also provides visual analogues to the characteristics imputed to modern Italian society during the epoch of the Grand Tour. Sablet and his contemporaries rarely introduced living Italians into their depictions of the social encounters of Europeans abroad in Italy, and his image of two anonymous gentlemen brooding in a cemetery contains many elements that permeated the visual representations of the Peninsula in the early 1800s: an Italy without

Italians, the fascination with Italy's graves and its ruins, and the use of Italy as a backdrop to solitary meditation. The setting for Sablet's painting is a locus classicus in the foreign gaze at Italy: that same Protestant Cemetery in Rome described by Shelley. As in Shelley's letter to Peacock, in Sablet's work the only surge of life in the landscape appears in the idyllic pastoral at the base of Cestius's tomb (Piramide di Caio Cestio). In an otherwise barren landscape, this spot teems with animal and human presence and contrasts the shadow of death with verdant images bathed in light. Just as Shelley describes Cestius's tomb as a natural refuge of life and hope in an otherwise "dead" city of Rome, Sablet presents the Protestant burial ground as a living antidote to the spectral images and energies that haunt his canvas.

I

Goethe in der Campagna (*Goethe in the Roman Campagna*; 1786–87; fig. 4), by Johann Heinrich Wilhelm Tischbein, captures the recurring emphasis on clarity and serenity that marks Goethe's writings on Italy. Stretched out in repose and cloaked in a white mantle that lends to his figure a "timelessly sculptural quality," Goethe contemplates a ghostly Roman landscape of ruins, bas-reliefs, and other icons of antiquity (Bignamini and Wilton, 74). Absent from Tischbein's *Goethe* are the social interactions and public scenes of instruction that informed Zoffany's *Tribuna;* absent also is the melancholic brooding of Sablet's *Elégie romaine,* which was inspired by Goethe's eponymous collection of poetry. The prevailing atmosphere in Tischbein's portrait is one of "solid" (a favorite word of Goethe in *Italienische Reise*) composure and confidence. The aesthetic, cultural, and social observations of the *Italienische Reise* suggest that the solidity of Goethe's Italian gaze, in sympathy with the gazes of Zoffany and Sablet, demanded that the scenes before him be devoid of Italians.

Italienische Reise offers a privileged perspective on the status of Italy in the foreign imaginary for a host of reasons.[19] First, though Goethe reworked and at times substantively altered the notes, letters, and diary entries from 1786 to 1788 that serve as the basis for the published versions of the *Italienische Reise* (vol. 1, 1816; vol. 2, 1817; and vol. 3, 1829), the text is based on an actual journey. Moreover, the celebrated section on Goethe's first Roman sojourn (November 1786–February 1787) undergoes relatively minor changes in the transition from private journey to public statement. Thus, unlike Staël's *Corinne* or Byron's *Childe Harold's Pilgrimage,* the accounts of Rome in the *Italienische Reise* do not take second place to the formal and thematic concerns of a fictional narrative. Second, for all the controversy that attends the

Figure 4. Johann Heinrich Wilhelm Tischbein, *Goethe in the Roman Campagna*. Städelsches Kunstinstitut, Frankfurt am Main. Photo Credit: Kavaler / Art Resource, NY.

half-fact, half-fiction status of the *Italienische Reise*, scholars agree that the text charts the evolution of the mature aesthetic vision that transformed Goethe into a principal voice not only in German culture but in general European culture. Analysis of the *Italienische Reise* provides, therefore, insight into the role that the reception of Italian culture played in a *Bildung* whose influence and scope was and remains Western if not global in scale. Third, Goethe's vision of Italy was more neoclassical than Romantic; thus, his influential writings on Italy reveal that the late eighteenth- and early nineteenth-century myth of Italy reached across a wide spectrum of aesthetic and cultural orientations. Finally, as part of the vast network of foreign travel accounts of Italy circulating in Europe in the early 1800s, the *Italienische Reise* follows a traditional itinerary that allows for fruitful comparative analysis alongside the constructions of Italy by many contemporaries.[20] For example, Goethe describes that same Cestius's tomb represented by Sablet and Shelley:

> Heute war ich bei der Pyramide des Cestius und abends auf dem Palatin, oben auf den Ruinen der Kaiserpaläste, die wie Felsenwände dastehn. Hievon läßt sich nun freilich nichts überliefern! Wahrlich, es gibt hier nichts Kleines, wenn auch wohl hier und da etwas Scheltenswertes und Abgeschmacktes; doch

auch ein solches hat teil an der allgemeinen Großheit genommen. (November 10, 1786; *Italienische Reise* 134)

(Today I was at the pyramid of Cestius, and on the Palatine in the evening, up there on the ruins of the imperial palaces, which stand like rocky cliffs. I confess that I cannot describe any of this to you! Truly, there is nothing small here, although a few things may be objectionable and tasteless; but even they reflect the general grandeur.) (*Italian Journey* 111)[21]

In Goethe's imagination, the cultural splendors of Italy have no man-made equal; only in nature itself can one find a comparable grandeur. In contrast to the prevailing Romantic aesthetic, however, the Italian traveler Goethe shuns the lures of the natural sublime in favor of a more earthly ("solid") aesthetic protocol: "Kehr' ich nun in mich selbst zurück, wie man doch so gern tut bei jeder Gelegenheit, so entdecke ich ein Gefühl, das mich unendlich freut, ja, das ich sogar auszusprechen wage. Wer sich mit Ernst hier umsieht und Augen hat zu sehen, muß *solid* werden, er muß einen Begriff von *Solidität* fassen, der ihm nie so lebendig ward" (November 10, 1786; *Italienische Reise* 135; my italics). (Returning now to myself, as one so gladly does at every opportunity, I discover a feeling that infinitely delights me, and that I shall even venture to put into words. No one can take a serious look around this city, if he has eyes to see, without becoming solid, without forming a more vivid concept of solidity than he has ever had before [*Italian Journey* 111].) Instead of the limitless yearning and introspection that typified his age's encounters between the subject and the landscape, Goethe's panoramic sweep of Rome focuses on the formal mastery of the ancient Romans and the lines, shapes, and volumes they produced.[22] Observation mingles with introspection, and concern for the self becomes inseparable from a quest to fathom the impersonal mysteries and structures of the physical world. Goethe's immersion in the forms of antiquity compelled him to remark that, after his initial wonder in seeing Italy, he experienced a sense of solidarity with the world of objects and a deeper sense of its intrinsic worth.[23] In short, Italy in Goethe's eyes was what it had been for his *maître à penser* Winckelmann and many others: "die hohe Schule für alle Welt" (the world's university) (December 13, 1786; *Italienische Reise* 149; *Italian Journey* 122). Like the university, Italy represented a locus of education and self-exploration, at a physical remove from the confines of one's normal life (for Goethe, Weimar), and of limited temporal duration (for European aristocrats, the length of the Grand Tour, which ranged considerably from several months to several years). Yet, as we will see with Staël's Oswald, not all Grand Tourists were as keen as Goethe to perpetuate the lessons learned in their Italian *hohe Schule* once they returned home.

If Italy was a privileged didactic forum for Goethe, what of the Italians themselves? Scholars remain divided on that contentious issue.²⁴ At first glance, the *Italienische Reise* would seem to suggest that, in Goethe's eyes, the Italians of modern Rome were as ephemeral as the forms of classical Rome were abiding. Goethe's reading of Italian society, however, reflects his quest for that same "objective" understanding that motivates his aesthetic activities in Italy.²⁵ Goethe intentionally distanced himself from the Italians in order to fathom more clearly the principles—or, to apply a more modern term, the social poetics—by which Italian society functioned. Anthropological inquiry never escapes the shadow of aesthetic vision in his portrait of Italy.

Goethe writes on December 29, 1786, that he has observed enough of Italian society to know how things operate in Rome. What he has witnessed does not impress him: "Denn die vielen kleinen Zirkel zu den Füßen der Herrscherin der Welt deuten hie und da auf etwas Kleinstädtisches" (*Italienische Reise* 153). (For the many little social circles at the feet of the mistress of the world now and then betray a certain provincialism [*Italian Journey* 125].) Chafing at the pettiness in the *hic et nunc* of the eternal city, Goethe protests, "Ich will Rom sehen, das bestehende, nicht das mit jedem Jahrzehnt vorübergehende" (*Italienische Reise* 153). (I want to see the enduring Rome, not the one that passes away every ten years [*Italian Journey* 125].) Italy provides him with a privileged historical perspective that, notwithstanding the clarity that it lends to his view of the long *durée* of European civilization, occludes from sight the Italian present.²⁶ Rome becomes the vantage point that permits him a bird's eye view of world history: "Besonders liest sich Geschichte von hier aus ganz anders als an jedem Orte der Welt. Anderwärts liest man von außen hinein, hier glaubt man, von innen hinaus zu lesen, es lagert sich alles um uns her und geht wieder aus von uns. Und das gilt nicht allein von der römischen Geschichte, sondern von der ganzen Weltgeschichte" (*Italienische Reise* 153–54). (From this vantage point [of Rome], history especially is read differently from anywhere else in the world. In other places one reads from the outside in, here we imagine we are reading from the inside out, everything lies spread out around us and also extends out from us. And that holds true not only of Roman history, but also of all world history [*Italian Journey* 126].)²⁷

However detached from modern Italy Goethe's world-historical consciousness may appear to be, the entries from the first Roman sojourn contain acute observations on Italian mores and society. He writes of the clashes between the primitive and modern cultures of Rome:

> Von der Nation wußte ich nichts weiter zu sagen, als daß es Naturmenschen sind, die unter Pracht und Würde der Religion und der Künste nicht ein Haar

anders sind, als sie in Höhlen und Wäldern auch sein würden. Was allen Fremden auffällt, und was heute wieder die ganze Stadt reden, aber auch nur reden macht, sind die Totschläge, die gewöhnlich vorkommen. Viere sind schon in unserm Bezirk in diesen drei Wochen ermordet worden. (November 24, 1786; *Italienische Reise* 143)

(The only thing I can say about this [Italian] nation is that it is made up of primitive people who, under all their splendid trappings of religion and the arts, are not a whit different from what they would be if they lived in caves or forests. What particularly strikes foreigners, and today again is the talk of the entire city — but only talk — is the homicides that take place so routinely. Just in the last three weeks four persons have been murdered in our district.) (*Italian Journey* 117)

Goethe's depiction of the violent Italian national character reflects personal, philosophical, and religious concerns. In personal terms, the mention of homicide in Rome could not fail to evoke in Goethe's mind the infamous murder of Winckelmann in 1768. Immediately after introducing the murderous qualities of the Romans, Goethe remarks: "Heute ward ein braver Künstler [Schwendimann] . . . überfallen, völlig wie Winckelmann" (*Italienische Reise* 143). (Today a fine artist named Schwendimann . . . was attacked, exactly like Winckelmann [*Italian Journey* 117].) Winckelmann, who was assassinated in Trieste while returning to Germany from an extended sojourn in Rome, introduced Goethe to the city's Greco-Roman treasures with his *Geschichte der Kunst des Altertums* (History of ancient art; 1764).[28] Goethe implies that the Italians — because of their propensity for violence and Catholicism — prevented Winckelmann from achieving his intellectual fulfillment.[29] In subsequent descriptions of the Italian *Volk*, he repeatedly returns to the tropes of aggression and transgression inherent in his allusion to the murder of Winckelmann.

From a philosophical perspective, Goethe's view that the Italians were a naturally primitive people (*Naturmenschen*), whose "splendid trappings of religion and the arts" could not obscure the fact that they lived as if they were still "in caves or forests," reflects a commonly held supposition in the intellectual circles of his age.[30] In a work by Goethe's friend, Friedrich Schiller's *Über naïve und sentimentalische Dichtung* (*On Naive and Sentimental Poetry*; 1800), the belated or modern artist lacks the effortless reciprocity between self and community that served the primitive, ancient writer in making his work mirror an external reality that was, according to this Hellenistic myth, intrinsically beautiful and meaningful. Schiller, who believed that Goethe was the contemporary German embodiment of this naive artist, urged modern writers to return self-consciously to the raw genius and force of their remote predecessors: "Sie *sind*, was wir *waren*; sie sind, was wir wieder *werden sollen*"

(*They* [the naive poets] *are what we* [moderns] *were; they are what we should once again become*) (Schiller's and translator's italics).[31] By describing Italians as primitive and violent, Goethe suggests that they, like Schiller's naive artists, remain capable of the powerful aesthetic visions of their remote ancestors. Like most of his contemporaries, including his friend and mentor Johann Gottfried Herder, Goethe subscribed to a fairly traditional, Rousseauistic primitivism that celebrated the early ages of man for their nobility and liberty. Though capable of great violence, these supposedly heroic forebears of humanity—like Goethe's modern Italians—also lived free from the excesses of skepticism and reflection that plagued modern man.[32]

In terms of religion, Goethe's invocation of Winckelmann's murder forms part of his extended critique of Roman Catholicism on behalf of his own Protestantism. He claims that one reason why Winckelmann never reached his full greatness was because he was forced to submit to the will of his ignorant Catholic patron, Cardinal Albani. The mention of Albani recalls an earlier entry from this same date (January 13, 1787), in which Goethe openly slights the cardinal in one of his many attacks on the Catholic faith.[33] The insult appears at the end of a passage in which he derides the Italian religious festival of Epiphany, during which worshippers recited poems in "barbarische Rhythmen und Töne" (barbarous rhythms and sounds) (*Italienische Reise* 159; *Italian Journey* 130). Goethe went so far as to remark that when an Italian commits a crime, even one as egregious as homicide, he inevitably flees to a church whose amnesty places him above the law: "Der Mörder erreicht eine Kirche, und so ist's gut" (November 24, 1786; *Italienische Reise* 144). (The murderer manages to reach a church, and that ends the matter [*Italian Journey* 118].) In this scene, as throughout the *Italienische Reise*, his Protestantism fuels his critical view of Roman Catholicism's attachment to spectacle and ritual, its promotion of feeling over reason, and its tendency to mire Italians in rebarbative mores and social protocols.[34]

Goethe's unkind treatment of superstitious Catholic Rome recalls Shelley's description of Rome as a dead city, in which the cultural legacies of the ancients cannot die and will "survive the puny generations" that now inhabit the eternal city. In order to find the abiding and enduring Rome, Goethe, like Shelley after him, focused more on the objects the Italians had left behind than on the Italians themselves. In training his sight on these classical forms, Goethe went perhaps further than any of his contemporaries in establishing the ancient Greco-Roman cultural heritage as the common artistic and scientific ground of the modern European.[35] A later and—not incidentally—female writer, Staël, examined more closely these Italians that Goethe overlooked. In so doing, she fulfilled the unrealized dream of Goethe himself: that of expanding the marvelous observations of his *Italienische Reise* into a systematic study of the beliefs, culture, and mores of the alternately uncivilized, splendid, and murderous Italians.[36]

II

Alongside Byron, Goethe, and Scott, Staël was one of the most widely read authors of her age; her massively influential *Corinne* reads like a guide to the standard Romantic devices of its day.[37] It displays a preoccupation with national character, champions the emotions over the intellect, celebrates the natural over the man-made, and renders homage to the power of art to shape morality and society.[38] The novel, fittingly, also explores another Romantic obsession, the sepulcher. Like Goethe and Sablet before her, and Shelley after her, Staël describes the Protestant Cemetery by Cestius's tomb. On a typical Romantic outing early in the novel, Corinne and Oswald decide to spend the day at the tombs outside of Rome. Their visit, predictably, provides fodder for a series of reflections on the indebtedness of future societies to those that have preceded them. In the midst of these meditations on mortality, the site of a certain tomb piques their interest. Corinne asks Oswald to accompany her to Cestius's remains, for, she says: "Les protestans qui meurent ici sont tous ensevelis autour de cette pyramide, et c'est un doux asile, tolérant et libéral" (5.2; *Œuvres* 693). (Protestants who die here are all buried round this pyramid and it is a gentle haven, tolerant and liberal) [*Corinne, Italy* 80].)[39] Oswald enthusiastically seconds Corinne's political rhetoric: "C'est là que plusieurs de mes compatriotes ont trouvé leur dernier séjour. Allons-y" (5.1; *Œuvres* 693). (It is there that several of my compatriots found their last resting place. Let us go there [*Corinne, Italy* 80–81].)

As in Shelley's encomium of Cestius's tomb, in Staël the landscape surrounding the grave and its monuments prove more vital than the Italians themselves. She writes that there is something remarkable about the *campagna di Roma*. On the one hand, it is a wasteland ("un désert") that lacks both trees and dwellings; on the other hand, the landscape teems with life: "Mais la terre est couvertes de plantes naturelles, que l'énergie de la végétation renouvelle sans cesse" (5.1; *Œuvres* 692). (But the ground is covered with natural plants, which are continually renewed by their vigorous growth [*Corinne, Italy* 78].) After establishing this contrast between the countryside's lack of Italians and its excess of robust natural vegetation, Staël writes that these "plantes parasites se glissent dans les tombeaux, décorent les ruines, et semblent là seulement pour honorer les morts" (parasitical plants insinuate themselves into the tombs, decorate the ruins, and seem to be there only to honor the dead) (5.1;

Œuvres 692; *Corinne, Italy* 78). The natural growth outside of Rome seems to shun any contact with living Italians, instead expending its energies on the remote ancient Rome that casts an overwhelming shadow over the present.[40] Staël writes that the uncultivated stretches of land in the outskirts of Rome are the bane of administrators, agriculturists, and those who wish to exploit the land for instrumental value. But for the foreign traveler who comes to Italy to dream, paint, and write, these alternately barren and fecund patches of the Italian landscape embody the soul of creative vision: "Mais les âmes rêveuses, que la mort occupe autant que la vie, se plaisent à contempler cette campagne de Rome, où le temps présent n'a imprimé aucune trace" (5.1; *Œuvres* 692). (But imaginative souls, concerned as much with death as with life, enjoy contemplating this Roman countryside where the present day has left no mark [*Corinne, Italy* 78].)

Nowhere is the eclipse of contemporary Italy more dramatic than in the crucial episode in which Oswald, after embarking upon a simultaneously tempestuous (emotionally) and innocent (physically) relationship with Corinne, decides to abandon his lover and return home. As his boat approaches England, Oswald equates his native land with public order and political freedom. By contrast, memories of Italy leave only the faintest emotional film on the surface of his civic musings:

> En approchant de l'Angleterre, tous les souvenirs de sa patrie rentrèrent dans l'âme de Oswald; l'année qu'il venait de passer en Italie n'était en relation avec aucune autre époque de sa vie. C'était comme une apparition brillante qui avait frappé son imagination, mais n'avait pu changer entièrement les opinions, ni les goûts dont son existence s'était composée jusqu'alors. Il se retrouvait lui-même; et, bien que le regret d'être séparé de Corinne l'empêchât d'éprouver aucune impression de bonheur, il reprenait pourtant une sorte de fixité dans les idées, que le vague enivrant des beaux-arts et de l'Italie avait fait disparaître. (16.4; 811)

> (As he drew near to England, all the memories of his native land came back to Oswald. The year he had just spent in Italy had no connection with any other period of his life. It was like a brilliant apparition which had completely struck his imagination but had not been able to alter completely the opinions or tastes which had constituted his life till then. He found his former self again, and although the feeling of being separated from Corinne prevented him from having any feeling of happiness, he nevertheless returned to a certain rigidity in his ideas that the intoxicating wave of the arts and Italy had washed away.) (304)

Like Goethe's *hohe Schule für alle Welt,* Oswald's Italy represents a place at a physical remove from his true home and being—in England, Oswald "finds his former self again." Italy, thus, provides him with a discrete period in which to explore the creative and fanciful aspects of his personality. Unlike Goethe's experience, however, Oswald's time in Italy produces little lasting effect. As "brilliant" as the time abroad is, ultimately the Italian experience proves as weightless as that seductive "apparition," Italy itself. Staël contrasts the Italian and English cultures with a set of oppositions: whereas Italy is "intoxicating," England is "rigid"; Italy "strikes the imagination," while England "enters into the soul"; and Italy represents the "arts," but England embodies "opinions and tastes." The question of which nation would hold ultimate sway over Oswald was a foregone conclusion: solid England would easily crush ethereal Italy, in affairs of the heart as well as in foreign affairs.[41]

The industry, order, prosperity, and wealth of his native land astonish Oswald upon his return. He even begins to pity Italy ("Oswald pensait à l'Italie pour se plaindre" [Oswald thought of Italy to pity it]) (16.4; *Œuvres* 811; *Corinne, Italy* 304). To his mind, Italy's institutions and society reflected confusion and weakness, especially when compared to England, where "la raison humaine était partout noblement empreinte" (human reason had left its noble imprint everywhere) (16.4; *Œuvres* 811; *Corinne, Italy* 304). Oswald marvels, moreover, at the dignity and modesty of the English women and their capacity to translate domestic tranquility into a public virtue. This backhanded critique of the fiercely independent and iconoclastic Corinne (heartless and husbandless) sets the stage for a series of reflections on the gender of Italy:

> Les tableaux séduisans, les impressions poétiques faisaient place dans son cœur au profond sentiment de la liberté et de la morale. . . . Il échangeait le désir indéfini d'un bonheur romanesque contre l'orgeuil des vrais biens de la vie, l'indépendance et la sécurité. Il rentrait dans l'existence qui convient aux hommes, l'action avec un but. La rêverie est plutôt le partage des femmes, de ces êtres faibles et résignés dès leur naissance. (16.4; 811)

> (The entrancing pictures, the poetic impressions [of Italy], gave way in [Oswald's] heart to the deep feeling of liberty and morality. . . . He was exchanging the vague desire of romantic happiness for pride in the true goods of life, independence and security; he was returning to the life suited to men, action with a goal. Reverie is more for women, beings who are weak and resigned from birth.) (304)

In Oswald's eyes, Italy, like a woman, seduces and entrances, plies with art; England, a more masculine land, provides the "true goods" of life: independence, liberty, and security. Italy, in short, becomes in Staël's novel the woman of the world.[42] In addition to being a woman, Italy is also mistress of the arts; in *Corinne,* the fields of creative endeavor are associated with the feminine categories of caprice, reverie, and weakness.[43]

In contrast to the social bonds that regulate the English society of Oswald,

Staël writes that Corinne's Italy lacks even the most basic form of social order: "C'est un peuple qui ne s'occupe pas d'autres" (10.2; *Œuvres* 742). (They [the Romans] are people who do not bother about others [*Corinne, Italy* 172].) The lack of society in Italy, Staël writes, suggests the lack of a regulatory Italian public sphere capable of sound moral judgment: "Comme la société ne s'y constitue juge de rien, elle admet tout" (6.2; *Œuvres* 700). (Since society does not set itself up as judge of anything, it allows everything [*Corinne, Italy* 93].) Yet *Corinne* ultimately celebrates the society-less Italian culture for three qualities that Staël found lacking in modern Europe: the emancipation of women; the flourishing of the arts; and the triumph of personal, emotional justice over public, rational law. She brings all three of these elements to bear in one masterful series of episodes that culminates in the death of Corinne. During this extended sequence, Staël offers a critique of European modernity predicated upon her construction of a premodern *eccezione italiana*.

The events leading to Corinne's death begin with Oswald's flight from Italy and from Corinne. During a visit to Corinne's father, Oswald encounters Lucile Edgermond, who is the antithesis of her older half sister, Corinne. Whereas Corinne is intellectual and creative, Lucile is simple and unimaginative; while Corinne is independent and iconoclastic, Lucile is submissive and traditional; and where Corinne speaks her mind, Lucile holds her tongue.[44] In contrast to domestic Lucile, Corinne declaims lofty poetry to the Roman public while strumming on a guitar; she is the Romantic artist incarnate.[45] Before meeting Lucile, Oswald asks Corinne how she can desire the applause of an Italian people who lack free institutions, once again setting his pride in the British social order against his disdain for Italian anarchy. Corinne responds that art is the last refuge of a nation despoiled by foreigners of its arms and government. In celebrating the artistic heritage of Italy, Corinne also endorses the distinctly European nature of this legacy, which the modern world repaid by subjugating the Italians: "L'Europe a reçu des Italiens les arts et les sciences, et maintenant qu'elle a tourné contre eux leurs propres présents, elle leur conteste souvent encore la dernière gloire qui soit permise aux nations sans force militaire et sans liberté politique, la gloire des sciences et des arts" (6.3; *Œuvres* 703). (Europe has received the arts and the sciences from Italy, and now that it has turned their own gifts against them it still often disputes the last glory that is allowed to nations without military power or political liberty, the glory of the sciences and the arts [*Corinne, Italy* 99].)[46]

If art is the last recourse of a nation stripped bare by its oppressors, Staël implies, then it is also the last refuge of a woman. Corinne herself could not pursue her artistic interests in England, where social protocols and domestic responsibilities prevented her from finding an avenue for her creative aspirations. In fleeing England and becoming a celebrated artist and the toast of Italian society, however, she acquired the very qualities that made her unmarriageable in Oswald's eyes.[47] In sum, Corinne Italy's is a place where an independent woman can make her way in the world: "Dès le premier jour de ma jeunesse, je promis d'honorer ce nom de Romaine, qui fait encore tressaillir le cœur. Vous m'avez permis la gloire, ô vous, nation libérale, qui ne bannissez point les femmes de son temple" (20.5; *Œuvres* 861). (From my earliest youth, I promised to bring honour to the name of Roman which still thrills my heart. You have allowed me glory, oh, liberal nation, you who do not banish women from your temple [*Corinne, Italy* 401].)[48]

Oswald vacillates at first between Corinne the Italian artist and Lucile the English maiden. He eventually admits to himself that, "bien que Corinne enchantât l'imagination de milles manières" (although Corinne charmed the imagination in a thousand ways), Lucile represents an unassailable "genre d'idées" (class of ideas) with which Oswald finds himself in complete harmony (16.5; *Œuvres* 814; *Corinne, Italy* 312).[49] The ideas Lucile epitomizes are those that led Oswald to pity Italy and praise England. He believes he will find an enduring domestic bliss in England with Lucile that trumps the ephemeral, romantic, and illusory happiness he experienced in Italy with Corinne. In the end, in the name of country, duty, and family, Oswald rejects Corinne and the Italy she embodies.[50]

Utilizing Corinne's insider-outsider's perspective, Staël censures those same English political and social forces that conspire to conquer Oswald's love for Corinne and Italy.[51] After he marries Lucile, Oswald and his wife travel to Rome, ostensibly so that he can cure his poor health in the Italian sun. The actual reason, however, is that he wishes to assuage his guilt in having abandoned Corinne for her half sister. When he arrives in Italy, Oswald learns from Prince Castel-Forte, an Italian nobleman who is Corinne's closest friend — and who embodies Italian qualities that Oswald scorns — that Corinne is gravely ill to the point of death. Corinne denies Oswald's request to see her, relaying to him via Castel-Forte that, though Oswald has had all the advantages of society, he can lay claim to no single sacrifice or act of generosity in the name of love. Oswald asks Castel-Forte if he shares Corinne's indictment, to which the prince gives the memorable reply:

> "Je pense que vous l'êtes. . . . Les torts, qu'on peut avoir avec une femme ne nuisent point dans l'opinion du monde; ces fragiles idoles, adorées aujord'hui, peuvent être brisées demain, sans que personne prenne leur défense, et c'est pour cela même que je les respecte davantage; car la morale, à leur égard, n'est défendue que par notre propre cœur. Aucun inconvénient ne résulte pour nous de leur faire du mal, et cependant ce mal est affreux. Un coup de poi-

gnard est puni par les lois, et le déchirement d'un cœur sensibles n'est l'objet que d'une plaisanterie; il vaudrait donc mieux se permettre le coup de poignard." (20.2; 855)

("May I say that I think you are [guilty]. . . . The wrong you may do a woman may not hurt you in the eyes of the world. The fragile idols adored today may be smashed tomorrow without being defended by anyone, and it is for that very reason that, as far as they are concerned, I respect them more. Morality is upheld only in our hearts. We suffer no inconvenience when we cause them pain, and yet the pain is terrible. A dagger blow is punished by the law but the rending of a sensitive heart is only the subject of a joke. So it would be better to allow yourself to strike with a dagger.") (389)

By pronouncing Oswald's moral culpability through the mouthpiece of the Italian Castel-Forte, Staël indicts Oswald's passive reliance on a set of British legal codes and societal restraints that are public and official in nature. She suggests that, however undeveloped the Italian public sense of morals compared to democratically progressive Britain, in Italy an internal sense of right and wrong ("Morality is upheld only in our hearts") may prevail in a manner that Oswald cannot fathom. A crime of the heart against love or a woman, Castel-Forte reminds Oswald, is one that no constitutional code can punish; only one's conscience can prevail upon one's self in this regard. Oswald, who endlessly praises the laws and customs of Britain and derides the supposed lack of social mores in Italy, is rebuked by Castel-Forte for having failed to develop an individual code of honor. The prince himself, as a representative member of the Italian aristocracy, emerges as the emblem of a particularly Italian way of considering law and morality. He respects the fragile and the weak, beings who, like Italy, have suffered at the hand of others. Oswald, the prince claims, has rent asunder the sensitive heart of Corinne. Although society will never punish him for this act, he may have just as well struck her with a dagger and, in so doing, at least be held accountable for his transgression.

After Corinne dies, Oswald sinks into a depression that nearly causes him to lose his wits and his life. But familial, patriotic, and social duty, the very things that took him from Corinne, bring him back to Lucile, England, and domestic order ("Lord Nelvil donna l'exemple de la vie domestique la plus régulière et la plus pure" [Lord Nelvil was a model of the purest and most orderly domestic life] [20.5; Œuvres 863; Corinne, Italy 404]). Italy and Corinne—and the accompanying fantasies of art, female imagination, and private morality that they embody—are absorbed into the smothering folds of a simple English country life. Staël neither condemns nor exculpates Oswald; like Castel-Forte, she leaves him to confront his conscience: "Je . . . ne veux . . . ni le blâmer, ni l'absoudre" (20.5; Œuvres 863). (I want neither to blame nor to absolve him

[*Corinne, Italy* 404].) *Corinne*'s readers themselves must, therefore, judge Oswald's transgression, which begins in the privacy of Oswald's heart but eventually encompasses issues of gender, morality, and nationalism.[52] Was Oswald compelled to betray Corinne by the masculine, public ideals of his British upbringing that left no room for the decidedly "feminine" charms of Italian art and culture? Or did Oswald's betrayal result from his inability to translate English public morality into a private sense of justice—a virtue that his Italian contemporaries were forced to develop in their own anarchic society? In deciding Oswald's fate, the reader passes judgment on a protagonist whose observations of and opinions on Italy did perhaps more than any other figure in literary history to forge an exportable notion of *l'Italia moderna*.

III

The Italian exile in England, Foscolo, was perfectly poised to participate in the international debates about Italy that *Corinne* stimulated. Foscolo, in fact, was one of the very few Italian authors to enter the international arena and address foreign stereotypes about his homeland, for he spent the last decade or so of his life (1816–27) living in England and writing for the British about Italian culture, history, and politics.[53] The stalwart patriot Foscolo discovered in England that some of the generalizations about Italy that marked Staël's *Corinne* (and later Goethe's *Italienische Reise*) were among the greatest impediments to his nation's cause. Staël, in particular, came to epitomize for Foscolo the foreigner's misapprehension of Italy, and his first composition as an exile and last work of noncritical prose, *Lettere scritte dall'Inghilterra* (Letters written from England; 1817–18), challenged the line of thinking about Italy promoted by Staël.

A comparative look at the cultures, fashions, and mores of England and Italy, the uneven *Lettere scritte dall'Inghilterra* evokes two alternate philosophical approaches to human nature early in the text.[54] The first belongs to the *maestro ginevrino* (Genevan Master), Rousseau, who believed that man was "d'innocenza angelica" (of angelic innocence), but that eventually "la società lo ha corrotto" (society corrupted him) through the social contract (450). A second thinker, Thomas Hobbes, posited that humankind's natural belligerence rendered society a perpetual state of war. Foscolo quickly rejects both Rousseau's and Hobbes's views on the grounds that they are fit only for "poeti tragici" (tragic poets) (450). As opposed to the abstract and ahistorical musings of Rousseau and Hobbes (compared to "ciffre d'algebra" [algebraic numbers]), Foscolo promises a more modestly empirical study of man in his most familiar and quotidian cultural contexts: "Per te, o lettore, sarà piú grato spettacolo a guardare quell'uomo della natura che troverai nella tua famiglia e nella tua città" (451). (For you, O reader, it would be a more pleasing spectacle to see humankind in the natural state in your own family and community.) More important, he proposes to buck the fashionable trend of emphasizing the differences between English and Italian cultures, and suggests instead that, for all their surface discrepancies, each shares a common author in nature itself: "Italiani ed Inglesi avendo per autore e rammentatore la sola Natura ripetono con idiomi e vestiarj moderni caratteri al tutto diversi" (451). (The Italian and English, created and given their speech by a common nature, repeat their lines and wear their modern costumes in completely different ways.) In order to grasp the essential kinship between England and Italy, a certain amount of cultural distance from each is needed. Exile affords Foscolo this detached perspective: "E se tu pure non hai piú nè patria nè casa—guardalo ne' tuoi pellegrinaggi" (451). (And if you [reader] also lack a country and a home—then look at [humankind] in your wanderings.)

Foscolo's allusion to the patterns of historical *corsi* and *ricorsi* that simultaneously create and regulate cultural differences draws heavily on his reading of Vico, who enjoyed a renaissance throughout Europe in Foscolo's era.[55] The reappraisal of Vichian thought in early nineteenth-century Europe contributed to the development of the following Romantic practices: the celebration of the poetic force of supposedly barbarous and primitive times; the use of interpretive philology as a way to fathom the complexities of a temporally remote culture; and the privileging of poetic language over what Foscolo describes as the abstractions and doctrines comprising the "corrottissima decrepitezza della civiltà" (most corrupt decadence of civilization).[56] In Vichian philosophical philology, the linguistic sign embodies the mysteries and prodigies of a given culture, because it reveals the essence of the way a people lived and viewed itself.[57] Following Vico, Foscolo writes in *Lettere scritte dall'Inghilterra* that the histories, rhythms, and sounds of words shape the meanings they intend to signify: "La lingua (Italiana) ch'io scrivo, o lettore, oltre le facoltà perfezionatele o procacciatele dall'età, . . . n'ha una nata seco e di cui trecento anni d'inerzia, d'usi forestieri e di servitú l'avrebbero del tutto spogliata, se non fosse facoltà ingenita ed è: un'ardente diritta evidente velocità" (*Lettere dall'Inghilterra* 453). (The [Italian] language I write, reader, besides the powers perfected or fostered by age, . . . possesses a native one which three hundred years of inertia, foreign habits, and servitude would have utterly removed, were it not congenital; and it is a glowing, straightforward, manifest speed [Cambon, *Foscolo* 312–13].)

For Foscolo, the sullying of *la lingua italiana* by foreigners was comparable to the manner in which these same foreigners compromised Italian political freedom. He writes in *Lettere scritte dall'Inghilterra* that he lost all hope in the future of Italian freedom when he learned of the three thousand Italian soldiers who lost their lives on the plains of Russia during Napoleon's campaign of 1813. Yet, he continues, the inherent genius and qualities of the Italian language guarantee that a certain ferociousness and freedom will always reign in Italian hearts:

> I suoi primi scrittori ricavavano le idee dai sentimenti del loro cuore e dall'esperienza della lor vita; se ne accertavano nella loro mente con sincera meditazione; però poteano significarle senza vocaboli astratti: e per farle sentire e vedere anche agli altri, illuminavano le loro frasi di metafore d'oggetti agevoli a sensi; e costringendo la loro sentenza in un conflato di affetti e d'immagini, la vibravano quasi saetta che senza fragore nè fiamma lasciava visibile tutto il suo corso in un solco di calore e di luce e arrivava infallibile al segno. (453)

> (Its [Italy's] first writers drew their ideas from their heart's feelings and from their experience of life; they ascertained those ideas through sincere meditation; therefore they could signify them without recourse to abstract words: and to make others feel and see them as well, these early writers lit their clauses with metaphors involving objects accessible to their senses; and thereby compressing their sentences into a conflation of emotions and images, they would fling it like an arrow which, noiseless and flameless, still left a whole visible track of heat and light and unfailingly hit the mark.) (Cambon, *Foscolo* 313)

The rhetorical energy for the above derives almost verbatim from Vico, who writes in his *Scienza nuova* (New science; 1725) that the earliest poets in primitive or unreflective cultures—such as Homer's Greece and Dante's Tuscany—naturally spoke in an image-laden idiom resembling song.[58] The poets of these cultures, Vico argues, do not create or construct the life around them but merely record it, a view that Vico expresses in "Discoverta del vero Dante" (Discovery of the true Dante): "La *Commedia* di Dante Alighieri ella è da leggersi per tre riguardi: e d'istoria de' tempi barbari d'Italia, e di fonte di bellissimi parlari toscani, e di esemplo di sublime poesia."[59] (*The Divine Comedy* of Dante should be read in three ways: as a story of Italy's barbaric times, the source of extremely beautiful Tuscan expressions, and an example of sublime poetry.) Similarly, Foscolo believed that the mysteries of a culture were accessible not through any abstract meditation on human nature à la Rousseau and Hobbes and their *ciffre d'algebra* but rather through a Vichian anthropology that aspires toward a historical understanding of the raw materials of this culture, especially its language.

It is upon this Vichian foundation that Foscolo set his critique of foreign views of Italy in *Lettere scritte dall'Inghilterra*. The majority of foreigners could never understand Italy, he suggests, because they seek to do so abstractly, without studying its language and carefully observing its customs. Of all foreign views, he finds Staël's most guilty in this regard. In opposition to her portrait of Italians as effeminate, false, and servile, Foscolo writes that the early Italians were "anime maschie, alti intelletti, uomini liberi, amatori del vero" (masculine souls, high intellects, free men, and lovers of truth) (453). Soon, however, "la mollezza intiepidí le passioni" (soft living cooled the passions), and Italy was overrun by foreign invaders, who corrupted culture, education, and religion: "l'educazione commessa a' frati sfibrò gl'ingegni; i letterati erano arredi di corti spesso straniere, le accademie pasciute dai Re, e la Inquisizione le udiva" (education given over to the priests weakened the mind, writers were ornaments in courts that were often foreign, and the academies were sponsored by kings and monitored by the Inquisition) (453). The result of this bastardization of Italian culture by foreigners was that the Italian language became "musica senza pensiero; finchè la filosofia del secolo scorso, e poi la vittoria trapiantarono in Italia lo stile francese che ne sviò da' Latini e da Greci" (music without thought, until last century's philosophy and then political events transplanted a French style in Italy that distracted us from the ancient Latins and Greeks) (453).

Foscolo's contempt for the "snaturato" (unnatural) *stile francese* fuels his censure of Staël's portrait of Italy — a work he is generally believed to have known only superficially.[60] Ironically enough, his critique follows the eminently Staël-like protocol of ascribing individual tendencies to national character. After criticizing "la Metafisica" (metaphysics) and its adverse effects on contemporary art and literature, he writes that Staël's moving description of Santa Croce in *Corinne* would seem to be based not on reviled French abstraction but rather on genuine feeling and pathos. Unfortunately, he continues, Staël states that Giovanni Boccaccio was buried in Santa Croce, when in fact his tomb rests "parecchie miglia fuor di Firenze" (many miles outside of Florence) (460). This is just one of the many factual errors by Staël that Foscolo brings to light. For example, she confuses the tombs of Leonardo Bruni and Pietro Aretino based on the incidental fact that both hailed from Arezzo.[61] He argues that her typically French adherence to metaphysics led her into confusion not only about the identity of Bruni and Aretino but about Italy as a whole: "[La Metafisica] illuse una donna di bellissimo ingegno a fondare avvenimenti storici sopra la favola, e a descrivere l'Italia con mille invenzioni" (461). ([Metaphysics] tricked a woman of great intelligence into establishing historical events upon fables and describing Italy with a thousand fanciful things.) Foscolo writes that Staël's view of Italian culture was the cursory glance of a woman peering from a speeding carriage: "La Metafisica sedusse la stessa donna a galoppare seco in carrozza, e penetrare in un voltar d'occhi negli usi, nelle opinioni, nella letteratura, e nelle viscere delle nazioni" (461). (Metaphysics seduced this same woman into bringing it along with her in her carriage while she penetrated, in the blink of an eye, the customs, opinions, literature, and lifeblood of national life.)

Foscolo contends that Staël circulates "teorie incomprensibili" (incomprehensible theories) with both "neologismo tedesco" (German neologism) and "entusiasmo ginevrino" (Genevan, or Rousseau-like, enthusiasm) (461). These allusions to Rousseauistic and Nordic, Germanic Romantic thought in Staël suggest the degree to which Foscolo believed that her reading of Italy epitomized the major branches of contemporary intellectual debate. He felt that the tendency of Staël and others toward circumstantial historical and sweeping cultural generalizations was part of a larger European trend:[62] "Oggi ogni scrittore va spaziando per la storia e la letteratura di tutti i secoli scorsi, e di tutte le lingue contemporanee; la vanità mista alla impossibilità ne induce a mostrare quello che non sappiamo; e gli autori studiano con noi . . . le vite degli uomini grandi ne' *Dizionari;* le scienze, nelle *Enciclopedie;* e la letteratura, ne' *Giornali* e nelle *Gazzette*—e la è moda europea" (494). (Today, each writer goes wandering through the history and literature of all the past centuries and all the contemporary languages. Vanity, mixed with the impossibility of the endeavor, inspires him to show us what we do not know. And writers study with us . . . the lives of great men in the dictionaries, the sciences in encyclopedias, and literature in journals and gazettes—and this is the European fashion.) Foscolo notes with chagrin that such fashionable theoretical readings of history criticize Italians for their excessive reliance on Greek and Latin literature and refusal to read more modern literature. In contrast, his defense of Italian culture's propensity for Greco-Roman literature formed an integral component of his position in the debates about Italian Romanticism. The document most responsible for introducing the Romantic polemics into Italy, Staël's essay "De l'esprit des traductions" ("The Spirit of Translation"), exhorted Italian writers to reject their neoclassical patrimony and translate the supposedly more progressive literary works from northern Europe. Foscolo, however, writes in *Lettere scritte dall'Inghilterra* that "ogni sentenza ne' libri antichi ravvolge affetti e pensieri profondi, invisibili a chi non ha occhio esercitato da rimirarli" (each judgment in the classics reveals profound emotions and thoughts that are invisible to the untrained eye) (494). The study of antiquity was not, in Foscolo's eyes, the intellectual cult of Goethe's *hohe Schule für alle Welt,* nor was it the inert bastion of neoclassical erudition as portrayed in Staël's "De l'esprit des traductions." Rather, ancient Greek and Roman literature represented to him a network of cultural codes that could continue to shape both individual and collective life.⁶³ By promoting the classical cultures as his preferred model of Italian identity, Foscolo sought to disengage Italy from what he believed were the northern European aesthetic protocols that had come to dominate the high cultural practices of Europe.⁶⁴

Stimulated by his moral and intellectual commitment to classical literature, and disciplined by his understanding of Vichian cultural and linguistic anthropology, Foscolo's *Lettere scritte dall'Inghilterra* rejects any presentist reading of Italy based on literary fashion, political ideology, and received ideas. He censures the methodology that led Staël to describe Italy as a place in which justice and law have disappeared and in which a cultural window dressing of arts and monuments masks a chaotic social structure. By focusing on the Italian past not as a residue of a once glorious culture, whose present-day function was to provide aesthetic and moral instruction to an international European elite, Foscolo also implicitly critiques the view of Italy that emerges from Goethe's *Italienische Reise*. *Lettere scritte dall'Inghilterra* seeks to reorient the foreigners' gaze upon Italy so that it can survey those aspects of Italian culture that have been obscured from view, namely, the Italian language, social customs of the Italians themselves, and a long chain of historical events that brought the Italian nation to its present woes. In illuminating these overlooked characteristics, he initiates his principal concern while in exile in England: to provide Europe with an insider's view of Italian culture resistant to the clichés that had come to dominate the foreign imaginary. In this sense, Foscolo's perspective makes him a kind of obverse Corinne — a male poet who leaves Italy for England and who, like Corinne, attains a privileged perspective for comparative cultural analysis because of his status as an exile who has intimate knowledge of both English and Italian life.

Foscolo's attempt to debunk the Romantic myth of Italy had mixed results. The *Lettere scritte dall'Inghilterra* remains untranslated into English, and the Romantic generalizations persist about Italy as a feminine, premodern, and sepulchral space whose present cannot escape the burden of her past. Illustrious exiles in the wake of Staël and her contemporaries — including Elizabeth Barrett and Robert Browning, D. H. Lawrence, Henry James, James Joyce, and Ezra Pound, to name a few — traveled to the Peninsula in search of that same Italy that provided late eighteenth- and early nineteenth-century authors the freedom to develop as artists and the detached perspective to contemplate their societies back home. The Western romance with Italy, tinged both with ideological overtones and genuine affection, remains as complex today as that earlier *amour manqué* in Romantic Europe: the courtship of Oswald and Corinne, which embodied the uses and abuses that northern Europe made of its beloved if barbarous neighbor to the south.

3

The Death of Italy and Birth of European Romanticism

    Throughout Romantic Europe, definitions of literature connected certain crises of modernity with Italian art and history, especially those related to issues of exile, nostalgia, and cultural belatedness. More specifically, anti-Enlightenment notions of the "literary" drew on poetic representations of modern Italy as a dying culture. Some of the views that helped artists break with long-standing French neoclassical principles were admittedly extravagant. In fact, a number of empirically false observations on Italy served Romantics in reconceptualizing a construct as vast as literary history, which Romantics infused with original considerations on the nexus between geography and culture. A pioneering study by Franco Moretti describes the ascription of aesthetic qualities to physical environs as an "artistic atlas," and argues that this intellectual mapmaking shaped the narrative structure of the modern European novel.[1] In anticipation of such theories, Goethe's notion of *Weltliteratur,* the evolutionary process whereby the various national literatures gradually unite and achieve a splendor that rivals ancient letters, draws on the classically inflected aesthetic mapmaking of his Italian travels. Many theoretical statements on literature by the Romantics mesh with contemporary descriptions of Italy's artistic terrain, which became emblematic to some of a divided modern consciousness in search of cultural origins. Shelley wrote to Leigh Hunt, on the same day he described Rome as a "city of the dead" to

Peacock: "There are *two* Italies—one composed of the green earth and transparent sea, and the mighty ruins of ancient time, and aërial mountains, and the warm and radiant atmosphere which is interfused through all things. The other consists of the Italians of the present day, their works and ways. The one is the most sublime and lovely contemplation that can be conceived by the imagination of man; the other is the most degraded, disgusting, and odious" (December 22, 1818).[2] The observations square with the Romantic tendency to spatialize literary history, a defining discipline of the age that connected literary activity to macrocosmic trends including nationalism and the rediscovery of oral, folkloric traditions.

Building on advances in Enlightenment literary historiography, writers in the nineteenth century began to ask with increasing frequency such questions as: What is the relationship between literature and the nation?[3] Is literature a shaping agent as well as a product of political and social developments? Does the history of literature contain a geographic and demographic dimension? Perhaps their Enlightenment predecessors did not ask these questions as often because they were less bothered by the crises that fueled the dialectic between historical self-consciousness and literary theory in pre-Romantic Europe. Schiller's *Über naive und sentimentalische Dichtung* distills this collective unease into a theory of literary history, which acts as the matrix in which a belated poet, conscious of his distance from both his own childhood and the early stages of humanity, reconnects through art and the imagination to a lost anterior plenitude. With Schiller, the creation of modern art, no matter how magnificent, entails a self-consciousness whose pathos and sentimentality were alien to earlier, less reflective, and more socially integrated poets. He uses *naive* as a neutral marker of the earlier poet's place in history and not his self-originating psychological attitude. It was precisely a lack of self-awareness that made the ancient Greek poet naive; implicitly, this is why it is so difficult to speak of the self or individuality in Schiller's ancient Greece. Subjectivity, for Schiller, exists as a form of compensation. We became selves, he suggests, when we became conscious of the loss of that organic connection between humankind and the world that rendered subjectivity a moot point in the supposedly reciprocal relations between internal and external life of antiquity. Thus, in Schiller, a theory of literary history becomes no less than a theory of human nature.

Schiller's psychology of the literary moment and its implicit geopolitical assumptions were incarnated in the arch-Italianate Goethe. For many Germans, and for Schiller in particular, Goethe represented a literary history-in-miniature; he was the author who took it upon himself to give his inchoate nation a cultural tradition worthy of the ancients. An accident of clime and time, Schiller writes, prevented Goethe from his true birthright of the Greco-Roman Mediterranean. But, he continues, in this cultural, spatial, and temporal exile, Goethe's inherent "naive" characteristics productively combined with the fluke of his "sentimental" surroundings. The ensuing aesthetic dialogue represented the painful, glorious birth pangs of German literary history:

> Wären Sie als ein Grieche, ja nur als ein Italiener geboren worden, und hätte schon von der Wiege an eine auserlesene Natur und eine idealisierende Kunst Sie umgeben, so wäre Ihr Weg unendlich verkürzt, vielleicht ganz überflüssig gemacht worden. . . . Mit Ihren ersten Erfahrungen hätte sich der große Stil in Ihnen entwickelt. Nun, da Sie ein Deutscher geboren sind, da Ihr griechischer Geist in diese nordische Schöpfung geworfen wurde, so blieb Ihnen keine andere Wahl, als entweder selbst zum nordischen Künstler zu werden, oder Ihrer Imagination das, was ihr die Wirklichkeit vorenthielt, durch Nachhülfe der Denkkraft zu ersetzen, und so gleichsam von innen heraus und auf einem rationalen Wege ein Griechenland zu gebären.
>
> (Had you been born a Greek or even an Italian, surrounded by the beauties of an exquisite nature and an idealized art, the path you have chosen would have been made infinitely shorter, perhaps even obviated. . . . Out of your very first experiences would have come the grand style! But here and now, born a German, your Greek mind transplanted into this northern world, you are faced with the choice of becoming a Nordic artist or of recreating in your imagination the art which reality withholds from it. With the help of rational thinking you substituted, in your imagination, the ancient ideal of art for the poor reality around you.)[4]

Unlike his English and French contemporaries, says Geoffrey H. Hartman, Goethe lacked a strong native literary tradition: there was no German nation as there was no German Renaissance.[5] Hartman also notes that a Wordsworth could afford to downplay the importance of book learning and emphasize the influence of nature because of his desire to transcend the neoclassical refinement and alleged pedantry of predecessors like Thomas Gray and Alexander Pope. Goethe enjoyed no such literary-historical "traction" (164); he would have to refashion nonnative traditions, ancient and modern, to achieve the appropriately Germanic literary form. The site of this transformation and the pedagogic forum for his cultural apprenticeship was Italy.

Goethe's rhetoric of regeneration in the *Italienische Reise* suggests a transformation that is at once cultural and personal. "Alle Träume meiner Jugend seh' ich nun lebendig" (Now I see all my childhood dreams come to life), he writes upon entering the *città eterna* (November 1, 1786; *Italienische Reise* 126; *Italian Journey* 104).[6] Later, he reports that this arrival was the start of a new life ("einen zweiten Geburtstag" [my second natal day]; "eine wahre

Wiedergeburt" [a true rebirth]) (December 3, 1786; *Italiensiche Reise* 126; *Italian Journey* 121). The fusion of nationalist and affective concerns surfaces early in the first Roman sojourn. Goethe writes that only after seeing the eternal city was he able to appreciate fully his friends and fatherland, and that his eventual importation of Rome's cultural treasures would provide both him and others a lifetime's worth of instruction and edification.[7] But, echoing Shelley and his "two Italies" alluded to above, before locating his trove, Goethe must first separate the Italic cultural wheat from the chaff: "Gestehen wir jedoch, es ist ein saures und trauriges Geschäft, das alte Rom aus dem neuen herauszuklauben, aber man muß es denn doch tun und zuletzt eine unschätzbare Befriedigung hoffen. Man trifft Spuren einer Herrlichkeit und einer Zerstörung, die beide über unsere Begriffe gehen. Was die Barbaren stehenließen, haben die Baumeister des neuen Roms verwüstet" (November 7, 1786; *Italienische Reise* 130). (Let us admit, nevertheless, that it is hard, sad work to sort out the old Rome from the new, but one has to do it and hope for inestimable satisfaction at the end. We encounter traces of a magnificence and a destruction that are both beyond our comprehension. What the barbarians left standing, the builders of new Rome have ravaged [*Italian Journey* 107].) For Goethe, as for many fellow Romantic travelers, the time within the Italian classroom is limited, and the cultural lessons learned only attain their true value at home, far removed from the originals—copies of which, thanks to his friend Tischbein, Goethe can bring back to Germany (December 29, 1786; *Italienische Reise* 152; *Italian Journey* 124). The *translatio studii* of ancient Roman forms into modern Germany would, in Goethe's mind, provide a unifying set of cultural practices upon which to set the foundation of the German *Kulturnation* (cultural nation). He sought, therefore, not merely to trace the roots of German culture back to antiquity via a virtuoso display of erudition. Rather, through a radical cultural hermeneutics, he hoped to make ancient Roman culture his and his people's organic own. By the end of his first stay in Rome, he had internalized the lessons of the ancient city and was subsequently able to translate what he termed his "private museum" into a German idiom.[8]

Ideological appropriations of Italian culture in the manner of Goethe had been at least a hundred years or so in the making. Though travel to Italy (especially from northern Europe) had existed for centuries before the eighteenth century, it was in this period that the Grand Tour emerged as the sine qua non for the education and edification of the European elite.[9] But it was later, around the age of Goethe, that travelers' direct contact with Italy's artifacts and traditions began to shape the construction of personal and national identity on a collective, systematic scale. For example, both Joseph

Addison and Edward Gibbon found the beauty of the Venus de Medici in Florence's Uffizi to be surpassing. However, the associations that their aesthetic bliss occasioned markedly differed. For the neoclassical Addison, the perfect proportions of the statue set off a sequence of cultural meditations: they remind him first of a Greek epigram then of the other statues of Venus in Italy.[10] Writing from his tour in 1764, Gibbon unsettles the kinds of divisions between art and experience painstakingly erected by Addison. Although he, too, meticulously describes the formal qualities of the Venus, he also notes that the sight of the statue is "la sensation la plus voluptueuse que mon œil ait jamais eprouv[é]" (the most voluptuous sensation my eyes have ever experienced), as though to imply that a purely technical analysis of the work would cheat its riveting effect on the viewer's imagination, even desire.[11]

Still later, for Shelley the amount of objective information gleaned from select pieces of Italian art was incidental. The basis of his aesthetic encounters was the reciprocity between the self and the object that the work inspired, either in the form of personal epiphany, existential insight, or material for his own poetry: "I have seen a quantity of things here [in Italy]—churches, palaces, statues, fountains, and pictures; and my brain is at this moment like a portfolio of an architect, or a print-shop, or a common-place book."[12] His subsequent disquisition on Raphael's painting of St. Cecilia favors speculation over formal analysis: "You forget that it is a picture as you look at it; and yet it is most unlike any of those things which we call reality.... The central figure, St. Cecilia, seems rapt in such inspiration as produced her image in the painter's mind" (64–65). In the transition from Addison's cool formalism and visual philology to Shelley's heated hermeneutics, the measure of sensitivity to the aesthetic object's intrinsic qualities diminishes in proportion to its capacity to shape the viewer's inner world. The experience of art becomes more freighted with autobiographical meaning if also perhaps less enjoyable, therapeutic, or didactic. By extension, in the late eighteenth and early nineteenth centuries, the actual details of the Peninsula's culture, for all their impact on the lives of visitors, often receded into the background in relation to the attention paid to their affective claims on their viewers and readers. The shift is from a tourism of appreciation to one of appropriation.

A poet with a less ideological agenda than Goethe's, Keats, also writes of Italy in a manner that evokes a dialogue between autobiographical and sociopolitical reflection. "On First Looking into Chapman's Homer" begins with the admission that, notwithstanding the poet's travels to the bard's homeland, he had never "breathed its [antiquity's] pure serene" until he read Chapman's translation of the *Iliad* (7).[13] Keats's contemporaries Goethe and Staël shared this notion that physical and verbal translation, rather than the original source, best relays the force of a text. For Goethe, personal contact with ancient Roman cultural forms attained full value when these same forms were transformed into a native, national idiom.[14] Staël similarly claimed that, however much we enjoy an original, the translation brings a finer and more lasting "naturalized" pleasure.[15] Much less programmatic, Keats nonetheless suggests that a mediated verbal trace in English means more to him than visits to "many western islands . . . / Which bards in fealty to Apollo hold," and to the "demesne" in which "deep-browed Homer ruled" (3–4, 6). Only through Chapman's English version of the ancient Greek can the *Iliad* and *Odyssey* enter his "ken" (10).

In Keats's poem "Happy is England!" however tightly the poet clings to a sense of national identity, his repetition of "yet" and overtures to the nuances and historical inflections of antiquity bespeak his "languishment / For skies Italian" (5–6). England provides Keats "tall woods and high romances"; this genre-sensitive invocation of medieval and Renaissance epic à la Mallory and Spencer reflects the poet's belief that his powerful nation stands at the pinnacle of secular power and progress. Yet often this English "worldliness" weighs upon him, and the poet would "half forget" England and its "artless daughters," in order to exchange them for "beauties of deeper glance" (8–9, 13). The land of artful oblivion, for Keats and countless others, lay under "skies Italian" (6). The civic-minded Goethe translated his devotion to ancient Italy into the source for modern Germanic culture; for the more delicate Keats, the *translatio* was of an emotional, existential register. It would be left to Staël, a self-proclaimed European Romantic and an author who combined Goethe's ideological edge with Keats's melancholic reverie, to reconcile the public Italy of the German polymath with the private one of the English poet.

I

Can one speak of a "European" Romanticism? The long-standing debate, which received its most dramatic academic installment in the comparatist Wellek (1949) contra the nominalist A. O. Lovejoy (1929), remains open.[16] At present, the discussion tends to veer into one of two directions. In the tradition of Wellek and his contemporaries Abrams, Bloom, de Man, and Hartman, many literary comparatists and theoreticians situate the Romantic text within an international network of aesthetic, creative, and intellectual currents that reveal the conceptual and formal similarities of the various literary movements of nineteenth-century Europe.[17] Arguing on behalf of a consistently "Romantic" tendency in the canonical literature of the early nineteenth century, this group adduces, in varying degrees and measures, a common concern with poetic imagination, psychological interiority, symbolic representation, historical self-consciousness, the mystification of nature, and the critique of neoclassical and Enlightenment modes of expression.[18]

The synthetic and unifying tendencies of this critical camp flourished in the comparatist heyday of the 1950s to 1980s, particularly in methodologies like formalism and deconstruction, in which transnational linguistic and literary issues took precedence over individual and contingent cultural context. Times have changed, for the current trend is to regard with historically or politically oriented suspicion those conceptual comparative paradigms that led to the promotion, in postwar Anglo-American criticism, of the idea of a European Romanticism. Whereas Lovejoy used intellectual history to sunder the monolithic tag "European Romanticism" into its constituent national parts, critics of the present are likely to underscore the unique local historical conditions and ideological frameworks that make it difficult to speak of a pan-Continental movement. For example, Marilyn Butler, arguing against Wellek and his fellow comparatists, indicates that most British authors between 1760 and 1830 had no sense that they were creating anything "Romantic," but were reacting to specific historical phenomena and cultural matrices that had little to do with Continental literary matters.[19] A similar sentiment of historicist caution appears in Stuart Curran, who cites the wide divergences in dates, political context, religious climate, and above all cultural environment among the various national Romantic movements.[20] Perhaps most influential of all in challenging the former hegemony of Wellek and others has been Jerome McGann, who critiques the ideologies of Romantics and their later interpreters for seeking to elevate certain aesthetic qualities to the status of the universal, without considering the political factors and economic superstructures informing such claims.[21]

In reviewing the oscillation over either a variegated or a unified European Romanticism, however, I believe that both views are defensible, and that ultimately one's stance depends on a choice of mutually tenable perspectives. Indeed, Hartman once wrote provocatively—and to my mind correctly—that, had Lovejoy written Wellek's article, Wellek would have countered with Lovejoy's.[22] My compromise view is not wholly original, for even most skeptics of a European component would concede that Romanticism was less a school of thought than a general mood and atmosphere that "spread rapidly throughout the European continent, leaving deep traces in the formation of some of the major national cultures of the nineteenth century" (Ciccarelli, *People's Voice* 3). No less an authority than Manzoni argued that the actual, polemically charged word *Romanticism,* because it meant so many different things in so many different contexts, should never be mentioned. He asked instead that we consider the legacy of Romanticism as an "idea without a name" — that is, an aesthetic and moral attitude and mode that permeated early nineteenth-century European literary culture. To Manzoni's mind, "Questo, non che esser caduto, vive, prospera, si diffonde di giorno in giorno, invade a poco a poco tutte le teorie dell'estetica; i suoi risultati sono più frequentemente riprodotti, applicati, posti per fondamento dei diversi giudizi in fatto di poesia" ("Sul romanticismo" 456). (This [Romanticism] is far from decaying but lives, prospers, and diffuses itself day by day and invades little by little all aesthetic theory, with results that are increasingly reproduced, applied, and considered the basis of good judgment in poetic matters ["On Romanticism" 315].)[23] Rather than seek to resolve the Romantic debate in a binary either/or fashion, one might take Manzoni's cue and construe the concept of European Romanticism, like Romanticism itself, as a fluid signifier. This protean category "European Romanticism" denotes a series of discrete episodes, ever-changing concepts, and diverse ideas that can be distinct in different countries yet also coherent from a Continental perspective. Only by examining aspects of the Romantic controversy on an individual and ad hoc basis can one accurately judge whether an international European Romanticism or an isolated, local Romantic effect is at work. Moreover, in certain cases *both* a distinctly national and a broadly European component obtain, as we see in the transition in definition of writer from Voltaire's *gens de lettres* (person of letters) to Alfieri's *libero scrittore* (free author).

A master of many rhetorical forms and registers, Voltaire considered himself France's official historian, though he also composed works of poetry (including epic), science, and, of course, philosophy. Not surprisingly, his definition of *gens de letters* emphasizes versatility, both of character and intellect, and the ability to work with various disciplines, forms, genres, and themes:

> L'esprit du siecle les a rendus [les *gens de lettres*] pour la plûpart aussi propres pour le monde que pour le cabinet; & c'est en quoi ils sont fort supérieures à ceux des siecles précédens. Ils furent écartés de la société jusqu'au tems de Balzac & de Voiture; ils en ont fait depuis une partie devenue nécessaire. Cette raison approfondie & épurée que plusieurs ont répandue dans leurs écrits & dans leurs conversations, a contribué beaucoup à instruire & à polir la nation: leur critique ne c'est plus consumée sur des mots grecs & latins; mais appuyée d'une saine philosophie, elle a détruit tous les préjugés dont la société étoit infectée; prédictions des astrologues, divinations des magiciens, sortiléges de toute espece, faux prodiges, faux merveilleux, usages superstitieux; elle a relegué dans les écoles mille disputes puériles qui étoient autrefois dangereuses & qu'ils ont rendues méprisables: par-là ils ont en effet servi l'état. On est quelquefois étonné que ce qui bouleversoit autrefois le monde, ne le trouble plus aujourd'hui; c'est au véritables *gens de lettres* qu'on en est redevable. (7:599–600)

(The spirit of the century has made most [men of letters] as much at ease in society as in their study. This is the great advantage they hold over men of letters of preceding centuries. Up to the time of Balzac and Voiture [prominent authors in the first half of the seventeenth century] they were not admitted to society; since that time they have become a necessary part of it. The profound and clear reasoning which many have infused into their books and their conversation has done much to instruct and polish the nation. Their criticism is no longer spent on Greek and Latin works but, with the aid of a sound philosophy, it has destroyed all the prejudices with which society was afflicted: astrologers' predictions, the divinings of magicians, all types of witchcraft, false prodigies, false marvels, and superstitious customs. This philosophy has relegated to the schools thousands of childish disputations that had formerly been dangerous and have now become objects of scorn. In this way men of letters have in fact served the state. We are sometimes amazed that matters which formerly disturbed the world no longer trouble it today. We owe this to true men of letters.) (248–49)[24]

The principal concern of Voltaire's writer is the applicability of literary skill to problems in and of the world, and the means to achieve this praxis are rigorously formal. Rather than inspiration or native talent, more mundane qualities like taste and verbal flair sanction his versatility; hence Voltaire's promotion of sociability and utility. His writer, one might say, is not born; he or she is made. The talent that permits the writer his breadth derives from the attainment of *la clarté, l'élégance,* and *le dessein* (clarity, elegance, and intention), virtues that Voltaire and his Enlightenment peers associated with good writing and fine living. The famous dictum of his contemporary Buffon, *le style est l'homme même* (the style is the man), suggests that the formal qualities of one's prose manner laid bare the elements of one's personality: one was how and what one wrote. Style, thus conceived, absorbs the need for any introspective inquiry into the self, for the agreed-upon conventions of literary excellence translate into viable models of social conduct and moral behavior. Recent work has exposed the ideological assumptions underlying the presumed stylistic universality that sanctioned these high-Enlightenment protocols.[25] The cultural hegemony enjoyed by the *philosophes,* though it permitted the international promotion and diffusion of French standards, did not come without cost for other less "universal" literary cultures. For example, some Italians, whose own Enlightenment was a tenuous affair, limited mostly to Milan and the group associated with the journal *Il caffè,* viewed the supposedly abstract, transhistorical, and universal Enlightenment program as a predominantly French phenomenon. One of these uneasy children of the Italian Enlightenment, Alfieri, devoted his career to reorienting the definition of literature away from its roots in French universalist rhetoric and toward a specifically Italian, and incidentally pre-Romantic, path.

Alfieri's discovery of a new idea of literature entailed his rewriting of Italian cultural history by means of a critique of the aesthetic principles that sustained his early intellectual development. His earliest autobiographical texts, the *Giornali* (Journals; 1774–77), demonstrate his debt to the intellectual and cultural milieu that inspired Voltaire's definition of *gens de letters:*

> Se rendre conte à soi même des actions de chaque jour, n'est le plus souvent qu'un tems perdu, parce qu'on répète facilement le lendemain les mêmes deffauts, dont on a rougi le soir d'avance. Plusieurs philosophes ont cependant regardé cette méthode comme très bonne, en ce que tôt ou tard un homme de sens doit se corriger, de ce qui doit nécessairement lui déplaire, en se regardant aussi souvent dans ce fidèle miroir, car personne ne nous connoît mieux que nous mêmes. (November 23, 1774; 407)[26]

> (To attempt to understand our own daily behavior is, generally speaking, a waste of time, for tomorrow we easily repeat the same mistakes that made us blush last night. Many *philosophes*, however, have considered this method quite useful. By continually looking at himself in a truthful mirror, sooner or later a man of sense ought to correct what truly displeases him, for no one knows us better than we know ourselves.)

Alfieri follows the *philosophes* here in viewing the self as an essentially neutral core capable of progress ("tôt ou tard un homme de sens doit se corriger"). Because he equates self-examination with diary writing, literary pursuits will presumably sustain his desire for self-improvement. The desire for self-correction that a later entry describes, and the language of eighteenth-century moral philosophy inherent in its use of terms like *amour propre*, reveal the extent to which the young Alfieri elaborated his inner conflicts in the idiom that Voltaire elevated to the status of literary model.[27] Alfieri was a native of the traditionally Francophile Piedmont — French was the first language he mastered — and these journal entries date from his first extended sojourn in Paris. All of these factors suggest that his early notions of literature and authorship derived primarily from his exposure to the vogue of French literary thought. Indeed, in considering his early writing, Alfieri accused himself of having been "un asino scimiotto di Voltaire" (a fool aping Voltaire).[28]

The transition from the French-inspired, universal-minded Alfieri to his Italian nationalist edition transpired after his dramatic decision, at the age of twenty-seven, to dedicate himself to the task of becoming Italy's premier tragedian. His autobiographical *Vita scritta da esso* (*Memoirs;* 1804) rests upon this Archimedean point in his life in which he decides to become a writer. Though the conversion topos is one of the most hallowed in Italian literary history, Alfieri appears to be the first Italian author to conceive of this traditionally Roman Catholic, Pauline, and Augustinian phenomenon in aesthetic and cultural terms.[29] In the first, nonliterary half of his life, he describes events in terms of his lack of recourse to the aesthetic means of translating experience into literary form. He writes of the Swedish landscape, one of the many stops in the incessant wandering of his life: "Compariva la fresca verdura: spettacolo veramente bizzarro, e che mi sarebbe riuscito poetico se avessi saputo far versi" (3.8; *Vita* 96). ([The] most beautiful verdure [produced] a surprising and truly romantic effect. Had I known how to write verses I should have turned it all into poetry [*Memoirs* 100].)[30] The longed-for literary conversion finally takes place when Alfieri reaches maturity, toward the beginning of the fourth book of the *Vita*, when he announces his intention of introducing himself to the public as Italy's next great playwright.[31] The path to literature for Alfieri involved, to use his own terms, a process of Italianization (*italianizzarsi*) and de-Frenchification (*disfrancesarsi*): "Primo passo adunque verso la purità toscana essere doveva, e lo fu, di dare interissimo bando ad ogni qualunque lettera francese. Da quel Luglio in poi non volli più mai profferire parola di codesta lingua, e mi diedi a sfuggire espressamente ogni persona e compagnia da cui si parlasse. Con tutti questi mezzi non veniva perciò a capo d'italianizzarmi" (4.1; *Vita* 169). (The first step towards the attainment of pure Tuscan had to be, and was, the total abandonment of all French reading. From that July [1775], in order to avoid conversing in the French language, I religiously shunned every society in which it was spoken, yet I did not succeed in *Italianizing* myself [*Memoirs* 156].)

This process of Italianization via mastery of the prestigious Tuscan dialect of Dante, Petrarch, and Boccaccio entailed the rejection of those rhetorical principles that allowed the Enlightenment writer to move effortlessly between genres. In contrast to the Enlightenment promotion of versatility of genre and idiom, Alfieri writes that French does not translate into Italian any more fluidly than comedy into tragedy or poetry into prose:

> E questa impossibilità di spiegarmi, e tradurre me stesso, non che in versi ma anche in prosa italiana, era tale, che quando io rileggeva un atto, una scena, di quelle ch'eran piaciute ai miei ascoltatori, nessuno d'essi le riconosceva più per le stesse, e mi domandavano sul serio, perché l'avessi mutate: tanta era l'influenza dei cangiati abiti e panneggiamenti alla stessa figura, ch'ella non era più né conoscibile, né sopportabile. Io mi arrabbiava, e piangeva: ma invano. Era forza pigliar pazienza, e rifare: ed intanto ingoiarmi le più insulse e antitragiche letture dei nostri testi di lingua per invasarmi di modi toscani; e direi, (se non temessi la sguaiataggine dell'espressione) in due parole direi che mi conveniva tutto il giorno *spensare* per poi *ripensare*. (4.1; 168–69)

(The difficulty of explaining or translating my sentiments either into Italian verse or even prose was such that when I re-read in this language an act or scene which had appeared to delight my auditors in French, they no longer knew it to be the same and inquired the reason for the change. Such was the influence of a new dress that the same personage became insupportable and incapable of being recognized. I raged, I wept, but it was necessary to assume patience and begin my task anew. I was obliged to ransack classical Italian texts, however insipid and anti-tragical, in order to become master of the native Tuscan. In short, if the expression may be forgiven, I had daily to "unthink" first and "rethink" after.) (155)

Alfieri's description of the swerve from a French to an Italian model of composition in terms of "unthinking" reveals the antirationalist disposition of his *libero scrittore*. The Italian models he initially consults, however, repel him because of their ostentation and empty formalism.[32] His answer to this quandary, as it was for many of his Italian Romantic successors, was a return to ancient sources. He writes that, after devoting himself to the study of Italian literature for those first six anti-French months, he began to experience "una onesta e cocente vergogna di non più intendere quasi affatto il latino" (a genuine shame that I had entirely forgotten Latin) (4.2; *Vita* 178; *Memoirs* 163). From that moment on, his immersion in Greek and Latin tragedies replaces his earlier dependence on the prestigious French theatrical models of Pierre Corneille, Molière, and Jean Racine as well as the once-fashionable Italian playwrights Giovanni Della Casa and Pietro Metastasio.

But the exorcism of French rhetoric is not yet complete. Alfieri admits that the "lungaggine e fiacchezza" (long-windedness and feebleness) of his style persists, "finché andava traducendo me stesso dal francese" (while I continued to translate my own works from the French) (4.2; *Vita* 179; *Memoirs* 163). So, in April 1776, he sets about the process of *disfrancesarsi* and chooses Florence as this site of linguistic conversion, the same city in which Manzoni famously went *sciacquare i panni nell'Arno* (literally, to rinse his clothes in the Arno; figuratively, perfect his Italian).[33] During his Florentine sojourn, he listens to each sound of Tuscan with "umiltà e pazienza" (deference and patience) (4.2; *Vita* 184; *Memoirs* 169). By September of 1776, the vehicle of his thoughts is this "doviziosissima ed elegante lingua" ([most] copious and elegant language) (4.2; *Vita* 185; *Memoirs* 170); by October of the same year, his writing is "intoscanito" (Tuscanized) (4.3; *Vita* 186; *Memoirs* 171). Having mastered a new rhetorical system and freed himself from the hegemony of French language and culture, Alfieri chances upon a tragedy of Voltaire's, whose subject matter resembles one of his own plays. He decides not to read Voltaire's text, for in literary composition, he argues, it is better to be original rather than perfect ("se non buono, almeno ben mio") (4.5; *Vita* 197; *Memoirs* 183). His paradigmatic shift, and accompanying redefinition of Voltaire's *gens de lettres*, is thus complete.

Through his sustained critique of French neoclassical aesthetic principles and their universalist rhetoric, Alfieri promoted a definition of writer at once firmly grounded in the specific demands of Italian history yet also indicative of the unifying effects that Italy's cultural traditions later exerted throughout nineteenth-century Europe. Only an Italian author such as he would opt for a local Tuscan dialect—which was, after all, a foreign language even to him, a native of Piedmont—rather than the accepted international prestige of French. Yet his insistence on combining the high-literary and everyday colloquialisms of this regional vernacular anticipated the rediscovery of local dialects (for example, Wordsworth's "language of real men" from *Lyrical Ballads*) that would become central to the Romantic eschewal of neoclassical diction and the corresponding rediscovery of oral and folkloric traditions. Moreover, Alfieri's patriotic promotion of *italianità* (Italian identity) at all costs also anticipates the dramatic degree to which nationalist authors throughout Europe championed the literary traditions of their own native soil against the abstract, cosmopolitan literary practices of the French Enlightenment. Indeed, Alfieri's tendency to define his Italian identity against the negative example of France recalls the powerful anti-French nationalist impulses that dominated nineteenth-century political life in other European countries, especially England.[34] It is fair to say that Alfieri, by devoting himself with religious fervor to promoting his land's canonical works as its best hope for cultural renewal, idealized Italian literary history. But through his mythmaking—a Romanticizing of Italy similar to that which took place abroad—he paved the way both for a literary rebirth in his native land and for foreigners to view Italian cultural history as a viable alternative to increasingly obsolete high-Enlightenment (especially French) literary ideals. Many in Alfieri's wake also sought to *italianizzarsi* and *disfrancesarsi*.

II

Staël was the rare foreign author cognizant of Alfieri's effect on Italian literary history. In a passage in *Corinne* reminiscent of Schiller's portrait of another ancient transplant, Goethe ("But here and now, born a German, your [Goethe's] Greek mind transplanted into this northern world"), she writes of Alfieri: "Alfieri, par un hasard singulier, était, pour ainsi dire, transplanté de l'antiquité dans les temps modernes; il était né pour agir, et il n'a pu qu'écrire: son style et ses tragédies se ressentent de cette contrainte. Il a voulu marcher par la littérature à un but politique" (7.2; *Œuvres* 713). (By a strange chance,

Alfieri was, as it were, transplanted from antiquity to modern times. He was born to act, but he could only write. His style and his tragedies are affected by this constraint. He wanted to achieve a political objective by means of literature [*Corinne, Italy* 118].)[35] Her astute exposé of Alfieri seizes on his feeling of historical unease and desire to create a readership in whom the faults and frailties of his own Italy would cede to the "actions et . . . sentiments des anciens Romains" (deeds and feelings of the ancient Romans) (7.2; *Œuvres* 714; *Corinne, Italy* 119). She claims, however, that his quixotic desire to be a literary history-of-one was doomed to fail; he was no Goethe.[36] The weight of Alfieri's own character overburdened his creative expression: "Mais on y voit toujours l'empreinte d'Alfieri, et non celle des nations et des temps qu'il met en scène" (7.2; *Œuvres* 714). (One always sees on [his tragedies] the stamp of Alfieri's nature and personality and not of the nations and periods he presents on stage [*Corinne, Italy* 119].) With a deft stroke, Staël dashes Alfieri's lifelong hopes of separating himself from the accursed French "monkeys" (Alfieri's own term in the *Vita*), for she saddles both Alfieri and the French with a common aesthetic will-to-power: "Bien que l'esprit français et celui d'Alfieri n'aient pas la moindre analogie, ils se ressemblent en ceci, que tous les deux font porter leurs propres couleurs à tous les sujets qu'ils traitent" (7.2; *Œuvres* 714). (Although the French mind and Alfieri's bear no resemblance to each other, they are alike in this, that both give their own characteristics to all the subjects they treat [*Corinne, Italy* 119].)[37]

Building on Staël's critique of Alfieri, this concluding section shows how her representation of the death of the heroine Corinne signals an unwitting challenge to the kind of nationalist and "Italianized" aesthetics of Alfieri. In the masterful sequence culminating in Corinne's last song, Staël structures the protracted demise of her heroine according to pan-European Romantic poetic principles that transcend the local concerns and contingencies motivating Alfieri's anti-French campaigns. Though Staël aims in *Corinne* to replace the aesthetic tenets of Enlightenment literary theory with more properly Romantic models, she also strives to maintain the overriding spirit of cosmopolitanism and universality that marked most Enlightenment literary paradigms. The death of her Corinne thus occurs in the shadows of both the literary ancien régime of Voltaire and the brave new nationalist world of Alfieri. In fitting Romantic fashion, Staël achieves this theoretical synthesis by way of a broken heart.

The sequence that leads to the death of Corinne begins with a reflection on national identity. Corinne and her half sister, Lucile, separated during early childhood, only meet as adults late in Staël's novel, when Corinne lies dying. When Corinne and Lucile finally do meet, Corinne learns that Lucile is the wife of that same man responsible for her breakdown and impending death, Oswald. Lucile has come to visit Corinne to apologize to her about her marriage, gain her forgiveness, and establish a relationship with the English-Italian half sister from whom she was separated in childhood. Because Lucile married Oswald unaware of the fact that he had been involved with Corinne, Corinne assures Lucile that she does not begrudge her actions. Instead, she offers Lucile advice: "Il faut que vouz soyez vous et moi tout à la fois" (You must be both you and me at the same time), both the demure English maiden celebrated by Keats in "Happy England" and the fantastic creature of Italian national allegory that Corinne herself represents (20.4; *Œuvres* 860; *Corinne, Italy* 398). Corinne is not wholly selfless in offering this advice. She wishes, in prosopopoeia-like fashion, that her former paramour Oswald "retrouve dans vous et dans sa fille quelques traces de mon influence, et que jamais du moins il ne puisse avoir une jouissance de sentiment sans se rappeler Corinne" (should find again in you [Lucile] and in his daughter some traces of my influence, and that at least he may never enjoy a feeling without recalling Corinne) (20.4; *Œuvres* 860; *Corinne, Italy* 398). To push the trope of prosopopoeia further, Staël invokes the silent figure of Dido, who in *Aeneid* 6 refuses to acknowledge Aeneas when he visits the underworld after having abandoned her and caused her suicide. When Oswald visits the dying Corinne as she prepares to perform her last song, a musical poetic improvisation before the Roman public, she first reaches out to Oswald, "mais retomba l'instant d'après, en détournant son visage, comme Didon lorsqu'elle rencontre Énée dans un monde où les passions humains ne doivent plus pénétrer" (however, she [Corinne] fell back, turning away her face like Dido when she met Aeneas in another world, impervious to human passions) (20.5; *Œuvres* 861; *Corinne, Italy* 400). Like Dido, in death Corinne rejects an Aeneas that in life she could not live without.

 Corinne's approach to death is softened by her sense that she is dying in the name of a larger cultural construct that will lend her a tinge of immortality; this construct, I will argue, was European Romanticism. Her death song, appropriately, begins with an apostrophe to Rome that is funereal both in theme and tone: "Recevez mon salut solennel, ô mes concitoyens! Déjà là nuit s'avance à mes regards, mais le ciel n'est-il pas plus beau pendant la nuit? Des milliers d'étoiles le décorent; il n'est de jour qu'un désert. Ainsi les ombres éternelles révèlent d'innombrables pensées que l'éclat de la prospérité faisait oublier. Mais la voix qui pourrait en instruire s'affaiblit par degrés" (20.5; *Œuvres* 861). (Fellow citizens, listen to my solemn greeting. Darkness already draws near to my vision, but is not the sky more beautiful at night? Thousands of stars adorn it. By day, it is but a desert. The eternal shadows reveal countless thoughts which gleaming posterity made us forget. But the voice which could tell of them gradually grows faint [*Corinne, Italy* 400–401].) Corinne's beloved Rome "fait encore tressaillir le cœur" (still thrills her heart) and "ne sacrifi[e] point des talents immortels aux jalousies passagères" (do[es] not sacrifice immortal talents to passing jealousies) (20.5; *Œuvres* 861; *Corinne, Italy* 401). Her fellow Romans, moreover, always applaud "l'essor du génie" (the flight of genius), in that victor who draws on "l'éternité pour enrichir le temps" (eternity to enrich the scope of time) (20.5; *Œuvres* 861; *Corinne, Italy* 401). Though Corinne stands at the brink of a bodily death because of her star-crossed romance with Oswald, the Rome she invokes is exempt from mortality because of its associations with all that is enduring, permanent, and infinite. The rhetoric that surrounds her Rome, moreover, recalls those literary qualities that Staël was busy promoting in such works as *De l'Allemagne* (On Germany; 1810) and "De l'esprit des traductions." As the apostrophe to Rome suggests, these specifically Romantic qualities centered on the powers of the imagination, the sublime, and the mystical, all of which Staël located in a northern European, Germanic literary imagination that she urged other cultures (especially Italy) to imitate and translate.

Staël identifies Corinne's dying body with that most mortal of countries, modern Italy: "Belle Italie" (Beautiful Italy) promises Corinne its charms but "en vain" (in vain), for Italy can do nothing for a "cœur délaissé" (deserted heart) (20.5; *Œuvres* 862; *Corinne, Italy* 402). Just as Oswald leaves Corinne naught but the charms of her own art, so has Europe stripped modern Italy of its ancient glory and left distinctions of a strictly cultural variety—its language, literature, and the fine arts.[38] After suggesting Italy's impotence, Corinne accepts her death: "C'est avec douceur que je m'y soumets" (I submit to it serenely) (20.5; *Œuvres* 862; *Corinne, Italy* 402). At this point, the elegiac tone of her last song intensifies. The deadly muses, love and unhappiness, inspire her, and the angel of death, white wings and shroud of darkness withal, awaits her. Corinne then turns once more to her adopted city: "Et vous, Rome, où mes cendres seront transportées, pardonnez, vous qui avez tant vu mourir, si je rejoins d'un pas tremblant vos ombres illustres; pardonnez-moi de me plaindre. Des sentiments, des pensées, peut-être nobles, peut-être fécondes, s'éteignent avec moi, et, de toutes les facultés de l'âme que je tiens de la nature, celle de souffrir est la seule que j'aie exercée tout entière" (20.5; *Œuvres* 862). (And you, Rome, where my ashes will be conveyed, you who have seen so many die, if, with trembling step, I join your illustrious dead, forgive me for complaining. Perhaps noble, fruitful feelings and thoughts die with me, and of all the faculties of the heart I receive from nature, that of suffering is the only one I have fully put into practice [*Corinne, Italy* 402].)

Dead Rome stimulates the haunted imagination of the foreign Romantic writer Staël, just as funereal Florence incited the progressive political meditation by the Foscolo of "Dei sepolcri." In Staël's elegy, the definition of writer established by Voltaire, which we saw *italianizzato* by Alfieri, now resurfaces in the Roman necropolis of Corinne. In choosing Rome as her place of final rest, Staël expresses her faith in the capacity of the eternal city to sanctify her passing by including her in its illustrious cultural pantheon. Her heart now irrevocably broken — "Mon cœur n'a plus d'asile" (My heart no longer has a refuge) — the heroine aches for the peace of Rome's "tombeaux silencieux" (silent tombs) (20.5; *Œuvres* 862; *Corinne, Italy* 402). Whereas in "Dei sepolcri," the tombs "gemeranno" (will moan) in witness to acts on behalf of the nation ("Sepolcri" 283; "Sepulchers" 286), here Staël has her protagonist's "Last Song" bear silent and lyrical witness to the coming of night.[39] In so doing, she engulfs her national allegory of Italy, Corinne, in the funereal lyricism of a broadly European Romantic aesthetic rooted in the soil of ancient Italian culture.

In an Enlightenment writer like Voltaire, the writer or *gens de lettres* enjoyed a feeling of literary solidarity and community based largely on accepted principles of composition, that is, the rhetorical models of *la clarté, l'élégance,* and *le dessein* that reflected a French universalist cultural program. In a subsequent critique of this Enlightenment model in Alfieri's program of *italianizzarsi* and *disfrancesarsi*, the result was an aggressively nationalist poetics tinged with nostalgia and disgust at the modern Italian culture that inspired Alfieri's return to Italian antiquity. Staël strikes a balance between the communal notion of Voltaire's *république de lettres* and Alfieri's social iconoclasm and fierce nationalism. In joining her international and progressive Corinne with Rome's illustrious dead, Staël uses her construction of the ancient Roman past to promote a pan-European aesthetic that combines the emphasis on the imagination, sublimity, and poetic vision in Alfieri with the cosmopolitanism and rhetorical virtuosity typical of Voltaire. In so doing, she lends the Roman necropolis a genius loci of a distinctly European Romantic dimension that remains beholden to long-standing Enlightenment principles. Rome accepts Corinne after native England has spurned her; and the liberal Roman nation allows Corinne her glories, while refusing to discriminate against her gender or national identity. But one does well to remember that the cultural sanctification Corinne enjoys in Italy — however European in its embrace of progressive international currents — isolated her in social terms. Too independent and having too much of a past to become Oswald's wife, she suffers in solitude much like Alfieri's *libero scrittore*. Corinne's reputation, however, will outlive the society in which she dies, and her character traits persist in the form of her sister, Lucile, who promises to teach Corinne's ways to her and Oswald's child. Corinne's legacy, especially as outlined in the last song, represents a poetics of exile and a "religion of the imagination" that would shape European Romantic practices for the next few decades.[40] In Corinne's end we thus discover a European Romantic beginning of Italian inflection—for, in her own words, the sky can often be more beautiful at night, as the day's death encroaches.

PART II

Heirs of a Dark Wood

Prologue

Since the rediscovery of the art and literature of the Middle Ages was a defining characteristic of Romanticism, it is no surprise that one of the most prominent medieval authors in European history, Dante, would figure centrally in the formation of the principles and practices of the new cultural moment. More mysterious, however, remain the reasons that a certain idea or representation of Dante came to dominate the literary reception of the poet, both in the high literature of the age and in the public imaginary. The nature of this paradigmatic notion of Dante becomes all the more striking, when one considers that it does not often square with the messages and motifs of the masterpiece that established his Romantic preeminence, *La divina commedia*.

The question of Dante occupies a central role in the relationship between Italian cultural traditions and the formation of Europe's Romantic movements because, more than any other single text or concern, it illuminates the deeper cultural and theoretical motivations that fueled the foreign obsession with Italy's past. "Dante Alighieri" became a convenient shorthand and code of access enjoining the two vast epochs of principal interest to the foreign traveler, Roman antiquity and the northern Italian Renaissance. As obscure as Foscolo, Manzoni, and their contemporaries were, Dante was proportionately famous; yet it was not always so. The story of his rise from Enlightenment obscurity to Romantic ubiquity stands as an analogy for Italy's collective ascent from Grand Tourist cultural destination to nineteenth-century "paradise of exiles" (Shelley). Dante's reception replays in miniature the drama of the nationalist hermeneutics that alternately expanded and restricted Foscolo's reputation; the transcendental imagination that both secured Manzoni's place in the pantheon of Italian letters and limited his foreign readership; and the tension between antiquity and modernity that simultaneously drew literary tourists like Goethe and Staël to the Peninsula yet distracted them from a fuller understanding of the nation's contemporary realities. The presence of Dante's *Commedia* in nineteenth-century reading lists also provides insight into the methodological principles that led to the distinctive nature of Romantic criticism and its refashioning of major genres and frameworks for literary analysis.

This Romantic rehabilitation finds its purest distillation in the endless pages devoted to understanding the personality and worldview of Dante himself. The Romantics were intensely interested in his biography, especially the poetic and legendary form established by Boccaccio in *Trattatello in laude di Dante* (Little treatise in praise of Dante; c. 1351–65) and perpetuated by the humanist Cristoforo Landino in his landmark edition of the *Commedia* in 1481.[1] The work most responsible for Dante's English rebirth, Henry Francis Cary's translation of the *Commedia* (entitled *The Vision*; 1814), claims that Dante associated only with men of "grave and tragic deportment," an allusion to the poet's shared characteristics with John Milton.[2] Most Romantics viewed Dante as a heroic sojourner rather than a religious pilgrim. In the *Commedia*, however, heroism serves only to aid the Pilgrim in his spiritual ascent. In the lower reaches of hell, Virgil even warns the Pilgrim away from acts of self-glorification. Dante later admits to Virgil that, were he to die at the time of his journey through the afterworld, he would be placed in the terraces of *Purgatorio* among the proud. One could even argue that the central theme of *Paradiso*, the canticle in which Dante encounters God, is the overcoming of the self. Yet it was the fierce Dantesque self that piqued Romantic interest.

In the critical apotheosis of the Romantic Dante, Thomas Carlyle blatantly misinterprets an encounter in *Inferno* 15 as an instance of Dante's robust heroism: "It must have been a great solacement to Dante, and was, as we can see, a proud thought fr[om] him at times. That he, here in exile, could do this work [the *Commedia*], that no Florence, nor no man or men, could hinder him from doing it, or even much help him in doing it. He knew too, partly, that it was great; the greatest a man could do. 'If thou follow thy star,' *Se tu segui la tua stella* — so could the Hero, in his forsakeness, in his extreme need, still say to himself: 'Follow thou thy star, thou shalt not fail of a glorious haven!' "[3] In the scene in question, Dante actually debunks the pretentious glory mongering of his former teacher, Brunetto Latini. An eminent statesman and educator in thirteenth-century Tuscany, Latini, like Dante, suffered exile. Unlike Dante, however, Latini failed to acknowledge his own sins and shortcomings. Even in the *Inferno,* he pontificates to the penitent Pilgrim, as though Dante were still his adoring pupil. Dante lampoons his former teacher by exposing the ostentation and empty erudition of his Latinisms, rhetorical inversions, and false allegiance to the realm of medieval astrology. Latini's allusion to Dante's *stella* (lucky star) and later to his *glorïoso porto* (glorious haven) in lines 56 and 57 of the canto reveals his belief in a most un-Christian, astrologically ascertainable fate. We learn how contemptible Dante finds such a notion in lines 93–96:

> ch'a la Fortuna, come vuol, son presto.
>   Non è nuova a li orecchi miei tal arra:
> però giri Fortuna la sua rota
> come le piace, e 'l villan la sua marra.
>
> (I am prepared for Fortune as she wills. Such earnest [talk by Latini] is not strange to my ears, therefore let Fortune whirl her wheel as pleases her, and the yokel his mattock.)[4]

Dante's aggressive rebuttal provides Latini with a lesson in something that he could never fathom: humility. In failing to note how Dante's Christian faith undercuts Latini's inflated rhetoric, Carlyle becomes yet another victim of Dante's ferocious irony.

Giuseppe Mazzotta describes our abiding autobiographical reflection on the *Commedia* à la Carlyle in terms of a hermeneutic tendency to reduce the manifold complexities of the text into a "domesticated commonplace of our own selves."[5] An emphatically self-referential author, who addresses the reader no less than twenty times and obsessively casts and recasts his own previous writing, the palinodic or self-revising Dante certainly invites interpretations of a personal kind.[6] Yet the dangers of emphasizing the individuality in Dante have long kept scholars on edge. In Italy, the heroic Dante developed with the Romantic tradition, especially in De Sanctis, to read Dante as a political martyr and patriotic symbol of Italy's fraught Risorgimento. Dante's acts on behalf of his fragmented nation were rightly legendary. He composed the first defense of the Italian language in *De vulgari eloquentia* (On eloquence in the vernacular; c. 1304–5) and theorized the return of Roman imperial glory in *Monarchia* (Monarchy; c. 1317). Most important, he laced his *Commedia* with diatribes on how the corruption of Italy's politicians and city-states were depriving their nation of its unity and compromising its capacity for self-governance. Partly in reaction to De Sanctis's historicist cult, Croce wrote that only Dante's poetic achievements (*poesia*) and formal limitations (*non-poesia*) deserve critical scrutiny. In a move similar to Croce's, T. S. Eliot promoted an impersonal Dante, who, he claimed, managed better than any other poet to synthesize the forms and norms of literary history ("tradition") into an "individual talent."[7]

Later Dante specialists took issue with the Romantic Dante as forcefully as Croce and Eliot. Arguing against Jacob Burckhardt, Etienne Gilson claimed in 1937 that, well before the supposed autobiographical watershed of Dante, complex literary models of the personal identity existed in the writings of Augustine, Boethius, Abelard, and Héloïse. Since Gilson's statements, the collective inquiry into the Dantesque *io* (I) suggests that Dante was not the first recognizably modern individual or self, for scholars have generally acceded to Gilson's view that many influential literary meditations on personal identity—laced, implicitly and explicitly, with what became the preoccupations of modern individuality—preceded Dante's.[8]

Yet, though Dante's self-representation in the *Commedia* may not have been as original as Burckhardt and the Romantics proposed, the question of the Dantesque self remains a fundamental interpretive issue for any serious reader of the poem. John Freccero's reading warrants attention in this regard. Though he has argued persuasively and perennially for the autobiographical Dante, Freccero's sense of this last word is by no means Romantic. In fact, by establishing the parallels between Dante's *Commedia* and Augustine's *Confessions*—that is, by showing how Dante follows Augustine in retrospectively reviewing and rewriting his earlier life from the perspective of a Christian conversion—Freccero proposes what one may term an "anti-Romantic" reading of the Dantesque self. Instead of the strengthening of self that most Romantics gleaned from Dante's text, the Christian allegorical structure that subtends Freccero's Augustinian reading has this same Dantesque self transcend individual desire and ego to fuse with a divine collectivity. The Romantics, on the other hand, believed that Dante's modernity resulted partly from his ability to fashion images that escaped the restrictive allegorical codes that accompanied certain stock medieval tropes (for example, the *selva oscura* [dark wood] of earthly life; more generally, the body as material prison of the soul). De Sanctis went so far as to claim that, because Dante was above all *poeta,* therefore "si ribella all'allegoria" (he rebelled against allegory) (*Letteratura italiana* 211; *Italian Literature* 1:176).[9] So the biblical *allegoresis* sanctioning Freccero's reading of the Dantesque self suggests the distance we have traveled from the more symbolic Dante of the Romantics, who valued the *Commedia* for its ability to conflate the individual nature of the poetic image with its possible, indeterminate, and potentially non-Christian associations and meanings.

The heroic, individualistic, and predominantly secular Dantesque self of the

Romantics reflects the quest of many European writers of that age for cultural origin and genealogy. Authors like A. W. Schlegel and Friedrich Schelling promoted Dante as a landmark in modern individuality in order to situate the birth of their artistic and intellectual concerns in a historical source whose visionary character imbued their endeavors with a transcendental basis and bias. The Romantics' identification with Dante, however, as with most ventures in genealogy, also marked the distance they believed that they had traveled from this alternately familiar and strange Dantesque point of origin. A. W. Schlegel encapsulated the dialogue between familiarity and alterity that lay at the core of his contemporaries' thinking on Dante:

> Wir haben an dem Gegensatz unseres Zeitalters, dann auch an der nachherigen Entwicklung der romantische Poesie, für welche Dantes Werk vorbildlich und prophetisch war, einen Reflexionspunkt, und können die ganz einzige Synthesis der heterogensten Elemente, welche es darbietet, deutlicher mit den Gedanken fassen, weil wir zugleich mit dem Dichter eins und von ihm durch die neuere Bildung getrennt sind.
>
> (It is thanks to the differences between our respective ages and the subsequent development of Romantic poetry, that we today have reached a moment of reflection which allows us to appreciate Dante's work as both prophetic and exemplary. We are today in a better position to recognize its unique synthesis of the most heterogeneous elements; for we are both at one with the poet and at the same time divorced from him through our modern education.)[10]

The desire to reconcile the credible and the incredible, to be both at one with a prophetic poet like Dante yet divided from him through modern understanding, obsessed artists throughout the period in their quest for what Wordsworth termed "knowledge not purchased by the loss of power" (*Prel.* 5.125).[11] Schlegel's quotation also shows that, for all the attraction of the Romantics to Dante, light years separated them from him. His brother Friedrich Schlegel defined the Romantic artist as always becoming but never being, hence a creature defined by desire. Dante, by contrast, is all about closure. By poem's end he could write: "già volgeva il mio disio e 'l *velle*, / sì come rota ch'igualmente è mossa, / l'amor che move il sole e l'altre stelle" (my desire and will were [already] revolved, like a wheel that is evenly moved, by the Love which moves the sun and the other stars) (*Par.* 33.143–45). His architectonic mind, moreover, privileged what the Romantics avoided: he is allegory to their symbol, epic to their lyric, and one hundred cantos in symmetrical triune division to their scattered and broken fragments. The *Commedia* became an unattainable holy grail that inspired Romantics to imitate the questing spirit of Dante's poem in full knowledge that they would never realize the teleological arc of its theological patterns. It is no surprise, therefore, that the Romantics "misread" Dante by focusing on the very thing he overcame, the self, and by arresting their imitative journeys of the poem at its lowest stage: the *Inferno*. Few Romantic readers ventured into *Purgatorio* or *Paradiso*; as Victor Hugo writes, the human eye, at least in Romantic Europe, was not made to look upon such light, and when the *Commedia* becomes happy, it was thought to be boring.[12]

Since the Romantic Dante, we have seen a dizzying array of Dantesque selves: Gabriele Rossetti's mystical and antipapal Dante (1843), Eugène Aroux's socialist and revolutionary Dante (1854), T. S. Eliot's impersonal Dante (1920), Auerbach's secular Dante (1929), the Dante-as-proper-name of the deconstructionists in the 1970s and 1980s, and more recently a gender-inflected Dante.[13] The protean categories of analysis have felt in some way the remarkable amount of critical energy expended by the Romantics in their autobiographical rehabilitation of Dante's sagging Enlightenment reputation. In literary-historical terms, the rebirth of Dante was indeed sudden and dramatic. Less than one hundred years after Voltaire's remark from 1756 that "nobody reads Dante anymore," the *questione di Dante* was a closed one, with the verdict decidedly swung against Voltaire and his treasured neoclassical culture. By the early nineteenth century, the canonical status of the *Commedia* was so well established as to prompt Peacock (and later Wordsworth) to deride the resurgence of Dante as a cult. Between 1800 and 1850, no fewer than 181 editions of the *Commedia* were published in Europe, from Scotland to present-day Slovakia, edited by writers as accomplished as Rossetti, Foscolo, and Mazzini.[14] Dantesque themes of exile, religious pilgrimage, and the political struggles of the artist — what Byron called Dante's poetry of "liberty" ("Persecution, exile, the dread of a foreign grave, could not shake his principles")[15] — saturate the writings of, among others, Byron, Chateaubriand, Foscolo, Hugo, Mazzini, Shelley, and Ludwig Tieck.[16] A high number of the period's major authors either made some significant critical statement on Dante or incorporated elements of his work into their own compositions. From ephemera to acknowledged masterpieces, Dante's presence asserted itself at various levels of European, and not just Italian, cultural life. The identification with Dante was so pervasive that by 1823 Stendhal could claim: "Le poète romantique par excellence, c'est le Dante." (Dante is the Romantic poet par excellence.)[17]

This transition in the *fortuna di Dante* fueled another, much more dramatic change in Europe whose full effects have not yet been revealed. Between roughly 1750 and 1825, European writers revised the way they wrote about, interpreted, and imagined their own lives. As distinguished from Romanticism and its autobiographies, the Enlightenment is more properly understood as the age of the memoir, which generally denotes writings on the self that are concerned with the external events surrounding an author's profession, reputation, or public image and not his interiority or quest for personal identity. On the other hand, the Romantic age is considered the period of self-conscious inquiry into an interior drama that is then cloaked with literary form. Between the French and European revolutions of 1789 and 1848, there was an explosion in retrospective narratives that, in the manner of Rousseau's *Confessions* (1782), thematized the development of interior identity. From the self-representations of the pre-Romantics Rousseau and Alfieri to Wordsworth's *Prelude* and Friedrich Schlegel's *Lucinde,* these texts varied greatly in content and formal structure. They shared, however, a concern with the question of individual personality, the development of artistic sensibility or creative vocation, and the desire to unravel the threads of emotional history and private thoughts. If so-called Romantic autobiography might be reduced to any single trait, it could be this sense of the sometimes daunting, often inscrutable strangeness that writers imagined they carried inside themselves. If that sense of inner strangeness now seems either well-rehearsed or self-indulgent, we need only recall how astonishing (and perverse) it would have appeared to the generations of authors — the Johnsons, Lessings, Montesquieus, Parinis, and so on — who never heard its voices. The reticence toward the burgeoning Romantic idiom of the self and its Dantesque inflection finds its most forceful expression in the writer whose name stands synonymous with his Enlightenment age: Voltaire.

4

Dante and Autobiography in the Age of Voltaire

On ne lit plus le Dante dans l'Europe.

(Nobody reads Dante anymore in Europe.)
— *Voltaire*

This remark from Voltaire's *Lettres philosophiques* in 1756 has produced endless wordplay on the fact that, for Dante, the age of light was truly obscure. A glance at the publication history of the period would seem to confirm Voltaire's observation: in his lifetime, 1697–1778, only sixteen editions of the *Commedia* appeared, a figure nearly surpassed in the first decade of the nineteenth century alone. A closer look at the literature of eighteenth-century Europe shows, however, that the *Commedia* did find its readers. Many major writers remarked about the work, and some devoted themselves either to attacking or defending it.[1] The eighteenth century produced thirty-two editions of the *Commedia* in four European countries; in the seventeenth century, only three were published, all in Italy. After 1629, Europe saw no new publication of the text until 1702. In contrast to the paucity of writing on Dante during the 1600s, the range of Dante criticism during the eighteenth century was indeed broad. But the force of Voltaire's declaration endures, and it unfortunately has compelled many scholars to dismiss the *Commedia* from their studies of Enlightenment literature.[2]

The international debates over the *Commedia* that Voltaire helped instigate provide insight into how writers of the period viewed the blooming genre of autobiography, and Voltaire's influential attacks on Dante reveal the hostility of many *philosophes* and neoclassical critics toward personal and transcendental narratives like the *Commedia*. He dismissed Dante's poem for the same reasons that he spurned those forms of autobiographical representation — including Rousseau's *Confessions* — that focused on individuality instead of universal human nature. Through his critique of the *Commedia* on autobiographical grounds, however, Voltaire unwittingly helped establish an interpretive framework for the "individual Dante" that soared to prominence in the Romantic age. The great effect of Voltaire's views on Dante is paradoxical, for he was a casual reader of the *Commedia* at best and an erratic one at worst.[3] However, because of the respect and notoriety that he enjoyed in his lifetime, his words on Dante became slogans and rallying cries. A full understanding of what Voltaire said about the *Commedia* — and of how these words influenced contemporary literary culture — must encompass his beliefs on what constituted good writing. Voltaire considered literature to be part of an autonomous and artificial realm of aesthetics and culture.[4] In his eyes, belles lettres were the province of individuals of rarefied taste who would meet to cultivate their literary appreciation in a *locus amoenus* like the *temple de goût* (temple of taste) or his own estates of Cirey, Les Délices, and Sans Souci. His famous remark at the conclusion of *Candide* — "Il faut cultiver notre jardin" (We must cultivate our garden) — captures the essence of a literary philosophy that saw the pursuit of letters as a means of attaining freedom from one's ignorance. Voltaire reserved, however, this process of self-emancipation for a select few who could immerse themselves in the study of books only by casting aside worldly concerns.[5] Herein lies the impasse in his understanding of literature that repeatedly surfaces in his reading of Dante: his exaltation of literary activity failed to incorporate literary pursuits in the motion of progressive philosophical reform that sustained his otherwise liberal attitudes toward society. For Voltaire, reading belonged in a place apart, and few ideas could inspire his contempt as could the illusion that poetry and politics might share each other's responsibilities.[6]

Voltaire's literary pastoral, however, differed from other Arcadian literary worlds of his age. The Voltairean garden was never merely a place where one donned a mask and played at letters for a while, only to shed the disguise once the demands of the city encroached upon the stillness of the literary grove. As we read in the final chapter of *Candide*, in which the protagonists' suffering momentarily subsides and they find hope in cultivating a garden on the border of the city, Voltaire saw the garden of letters as a liminal and not a marginal space. From this Archimedean point outside of historical events, he critiqued society through satire, literary evaluation, and philosophical speculation. The garden was ultimately the only place where the iconoclast Voltaire felt at home; exile and displacement were, therefore, preconditions for the independence that he only experienced in small, episodic doses.[7]

For all the harmony that suffused these spots of temporary repose, Voltaire was merciless in defending them from enemies, one of whom he perceived early in Dante. Voltaire's polemic against the *Commedia* centered on an aspect of Enlightenment literary theory that has become associated with his name: taste. Long before he remarked in 1756 that nobody read Dante, Voltaire's preoccupation with standards of taste had led him in his *Essai sur la poésie épique* (Essay on epic poetry; English ed., 1727; French ed., 1733) to ignore Dante and focus instead on now-forgotten writers like Alonso de Ercilla y Zuniga and Giangiorgio Trissino.[8] Thus, his anti-Dante polemic began in the very un-Voltairean realm of silence; this silence, however, was pregnant with the accumulated indifference to Dante that characterized the so-called *grand siècle* of French classicism during the reign of Louis XIV. In this era, the typical attitude toward the *Commedia* was disdainful: Corneille, Racine, and Blaise Pascal ignored Dante. In *L'art poétique* (1674), Nicolas Boileau-Despréaux, the leading critic of his age, does not mention the *Commedia* in his attacks on such Christian epics as Torquato Tasso's *Gerusalemme liberata* (Jerusalem delivered; 1581). A work cherished by Voltaire, Pierre Bayle's *Dictionnaire historique et critique* (Historical and critical dictionary; 1697), discusses Dante only because of his slur in *Purgatorio* 20 against Hugh Capet, France's first Capetian king.[9] The second edition of the *Dictionnaire* (1702) devotes some pages to Dante, but the tone is neutral, the content anecdotal and biographical, and thematic criticism of the poem itself is conspicuously absent (5:370–82).

After the *Essai sur la poésie épique*, Voltaire did not discuss Dante until 1738, when he and Émilie du Châtelet began to translate and study the *Commedia* at Cirey. This period witnessed Voltaire's introduction to the Italian language and the birth of a passion for Italian culture and history that sustained him throughout his life.[10] In the midst of his Italophilia, Voltaire produced his most flattering remarks on Dante in the May 9, 1746, address that marked his acceptance into the Académie française. After exhorting French poets to evoke not only their inner landscapes but also "les objets sensibles de toute la nature" (the sensory objects in all nature), he writes, "Il n'est rien que le Dante n'exprimât, à l'exemple des anciens: il accoutuma les Italiens à tout dire" (M 23:208). (Like the ancients, there was nothing that Dante did not express. He encouraged the Italians to say all.) His work on the subject next appears in 1753 in a letter addressed to "Monsieur de ***, professeur en histoire," which contains a translation from the *Commedia,* and in the *Annales de l'empire* drafted that same year. Voltaire added the infamous quotation that serves as this chapter's epigraph to an edition from 1756 of the *Lettres philosophiques* (Philosophical letters; 1734), in which he mentions in passing: "On ne lit plus le Dante dans l'Europe, parce que tout y est allusion à des faits ignorés" (M 22:174). (Nobody reads Dante anymore in Europe, because his work is nothing but allusions to now-ignored facts.) As harsh as these words may sound, Voltaire wrote them with a neutrality that disappeared in the later criticism.

During this period, the *Essai sur les mœurs* (Essay on morals; 1756) contains Voltaire's most complex thoughts on the *Commedia*. In chapter 82, Voltaire describes the *Commedia* as a "poème bizarre, mais brillant de beautés naturelles" (a strange poem, though it is glimmering with natural beauties) (M 12:58). Then, in what became a continuous thread of his reading, he writes that Dante managed to raise himself "au-dessus du mauvais goût de son siècle et de son sujet" (above the bad taste of his epoch and subject matter) (M 12:58). In the *Essai* and the texts preceding it, Voltaire stresses the eccentricity of the *Commedia* without condemning it, praises Dante the poet for transcending the aesthetic limitations of his age, and displays a residual sympathy for a work that, for all its obscurity, manifests flashes of brilliance.

Even before the accumulation of Voltaire's statements fed the polemical fires in Italy's arcadian societies, he had compelled writers to publicize and politicize their readings of Dante. Giuseppe Baretti, an exile from Turin living in London, responded in 1753 with *A Dissertation upon the Italian Poetry in Which Are Interspersed Some Remarks on Mr. Voltaire's Essay on the Epic Poets*. He writes: "When I read Monsieur de Voltaire's *Essay on the [E]pic [P]oetry of all the European [N]ations from Homer down to Milton* and found it filled with so many contemptuous reflections on the language and works of the Italians, I thought the author should rather have written it in his own language, than have dishonoured that of England by making it the conveyance of his impertinence."[11] Baretti's words testify to the international and temporal sweep of the *question du Dante*. As we will see, however, his defense only pushed Dante further into the exile that Voltaire had decreed for him.

The *Dissertation* begins by placing Voltaire's hatred of Dante in the context of French neoclassicism. According to Baretti, after a golden age in the baroque France of Louis XIII, the return to cultural sobriety under the aegis of critics like Bayle and Boileau led the French to reject the Italian literary tradition. By acknowledging Boileau as the judge and jury of French letters, Baretti foreshadows Voltaire's own usurpation of this role. He describes the French as a docile and passive nation: "If a man of great dignity introduces a mode, all the nation conforms itself to his taste immediately" (93). Baretti fails, however, to develop the notion of taste implicit in these observations. Critics of his age struggled with the question of whether it was possible to establish a model of literary taste that transcended cultural differences. Marc Akenside's "Ballance of the Poets" (attrib. 1746) — with its evaluation of poetic skill according to such categories as critical ordinance, versification, and moral — is a naive example of the depths to which rationalistic impulses drove less astute critics.[12] Neither Voltaire nor the other major theorists who argued over the possibility of universal taste were so literal-minded. According to Voltaire, taste in literature was universal insofar as it was beholden to such abstract qualities as clarity, design, and measure. But Voltaire's thoughts on art — though they did not address the relationship between aesthetic and sociopolitical factors as explicitly as his contemporary Winckelmann — never strayed far from his ideas on society.[13] He understood that the literary virtues he promoted reflected the tastes and lifestyle of a cosmopolitan Parisian and not of a foreigner or French peasant. His aesthetic theories embodied the qualities of his own social milieu, which in turn rewarded him for upholding its values by sanctioning his views on art.[14]

To Voltaire, refinement in letters was akin to the aristocratic notion, which later resurfaced with an angry, antidemocratic tinge in thinkers like Nietzsche, that a chosen few, given to leisure, could translate their aesthetic understanding into the fine art of living. Voltaire considered literature — like clothing, cuisine, gardening, and even animal husbandry — an art of civilization and thus the antithesis of the natural and primitive. In *Le temple du goût* (The temple of taste; 1731), he describes French literary neoclassicism as a "sanctuaire" (sanctuary) that, through the cultural politics of the Sun King, Richelieu, and Colbert, summoned to its cause a "troupe immortelle" of fine arts: "L'Europe jalouse admira / Ce temple en sa beauté nouvelle" (Jealous Europe admires the fresh beauty of this temple) (M 8:561). These allegorical lines invoke a monumental, polished cultural enclave into which the *gens de lettres* enter through a door hidden from the world. Such highly aestheticized realms embodied the types of spaces from which writers in support of Voltaire attacked Dante. Anti-Dante polemicists understood that the cultural concerns of their arcadian worlds conflicted with the themes of the *selva oscura,* the representative image of Dante's hell described in the opening lines of *Inferno*. Arcadian writers were, for the most part, uncomfortable with the carnality and excesses of *Inferno*, the canticle in which Dante unmasks any pretense of literature to self-sufficiency.[15]

Although Baretti fails to discredit Voltaire's aesthetics on theoretical grounds, the point in his *Dissertation* about the influence of personality and cultural politics on literary taste reflects the contemporary resistance to neoclassical tenets in movements including the English cult of sensibility and German Sturm und Drang. In antineoclassical fashion, Baretti historicizes Dante's achievement by introducing him as the father of Italian language and literature. However, his reading of Dante's place in linguistic and literary history never celebrates the poet's medieval world in the manner of an important predecessor like Vico; Baretti even rejects the "vain ostentation of erudition" of certain Italian authors (like Vico) who sought to parallel Homer and Dante (100). Ever the Enlightenment gentleman, Baretti rivals Voltaire in his wish to produce a version of Dante suitable for the drawing room. In line with many of his contemporaries, he used translation to tame the supposedly primitive elements in Dante. He renders, for example, the dark pathos of the words of Ugolino's starving children in *Inf.* 33.61–63 ("Padre, assai ci fia men doglia / se tu mangi di noi: tu ne vestisti / queste misere carni, e tu le spoglia") with the comparatively stiff, stentorian: "Dear father! Our torments would be less, if you would allay the rage of your hunger upon us.[16] It is you who have clothed us in this miserable flesh; now then divest us of it!" (103). Baretti aimed to rid Dante of the undesirable characteristics that Voltaire's reading imputed to him; but he ultimately defended Dante along the same lines on which Voltaire attacked him and produced a diluted, arcadian interpretation of the text.[17]

The debates over Dante became even more international after the publication of Baretti's *Dissertation,* and, as one would expect, the Dante question drew more intense energy in Italy than anywhere else in Europe.[18] After languishing in the 1600s, Dante criticism experienced a revival in Italy in the first half of the eighteenth century.[19] Likewise, a line of poets inspired by Dante's verse began to challenge the centuries-long dominance of the followers of Petrarch, Ariosto, and Tasso. This situation inspired Voltaire's friend Saverio Bettinelli to seek to expel Dante from the literary garden. A worldly Jesuit who traveled to the courts of Russia and Poland, the academies of Italy, and the salons of Paris, Bettinelli was also acquainted with some of the *philosophes* who composed the *Encyclopédie.* Hoping both to dissuade young Italian writers from imitating Dante and to defend an increasingly besieged cosmopolitan ideal of neoclassicism, Bettinelli issued what is likely the most debilitating of all eighteenth-century attacks on Dante: *Lettere virgilianae* (Virgilian letters).[20] He first wrote the letters in 1755 and then included them as a preface to a collection of poetry he edited in 1758 entitled *Versi sciolti di tre eccellenti moderni autori* (Blank verse from three excellent modern authors). The anthology featured Bettinelli, Carlo Frugoni, and Francesco Algarotti (another friend of Voltaire's). The letters propose to meditate on Italian literary history, but they barely masque their promotional intent. They seek to provide a suitably elegant cultural context and atmosphere for the arcadian and refined *Versi sciolti,* which Bettinelli hoped would challenge the renewed — and, to his mind, dangerous — interest in Dante. Bettinelli's attack comes in the second Virgilian letter, whose setting is as suggestive as the author's words.

The second letter describes a make-believe land whose arcadian inhabitants masquerade as Greek and Latin poets. Dante's guide in the *Commedia* becomes his adversary in Bettinelli's text, for in the second of the *Lettere virgilianae,* the narrator Virgil recounts the arrival into the arcadian literary circle of a frightening soul who can do nothing but praise Dante.[21] Virgil describes this soldier-poet as a writer of Dantesque poetry who has devoted himself so subserviently to the cult of his master that he appropriates the qualities of haughtiness and disdain that biographers, beginning with Boccaccio, associated with Dante. Bettinelli's poetaster is one of the few eighteenth-century literary characters for whom the *Commedia* serves as a model of personal identity, and Bettinelli makes him pay dearly for it. He juxtaposes the immaturity and uncouthness of the Dantesque intruder with the serene detachment of the arcadian poets: "Ma noi, che per indole siamo più pazienti, e per professione più mansueti, l'invitammo a sedere con noi sull'erba" (637). (But we, who by nature are more patient and because of our work more accommodating, invited him to sit with us on the grass.) The poets in Bettinelli's pastoral shower Dante's representative with a mixture of grace and condescension they deem appropriate to their office.

Virgil then announces that Dante's language is unintelligible to the arcadians, because he speaks an Italian that the Latin poets cannot understand. This pronouncement by the Roman poet rewrites one of the more powerful scenes in the *Commedia, Inferno* 26. In this canto, Virgil intervenes during Dante's interview with the burning spirit of Ulysses and tells him that he will communicate with the flames and thereby save Dante from any potential disdain that the Homeric Ulysses and his companion Diomedes may have for his "detto" (speech) (*Inf.* 26.75). In *Inferno* 26, Virgil represents a cultural ally who helps the Pilgrim communicate with an ancient Greek. In Bettinelli's text, however, Virgil underscores the differences in language — and, by implication, in genre — between classical Latin epic and Dante's medieval Italian work. Virgil next takes the *Commedia* and joins the Greek and Roman poets who have secluded themselves from the others: "Io presi il grosso volume, e in un cerchio di greci e di latini sedetti in disparte con esso alla mano" (637). (I took in hand the heavy volume and sat with it in a circle of Latins and Greeks.) By setting this act of reading in a pastoral space within yet another pastoral space, Bettinelli implicitly reverses Dante's negative treatment of such acts of reading in the Limbo canto; for in *Inferno* 4 Dante ironizes the literary *locus amoenus* by placing it inside a structure of spiritual reference that exposes the limitations of the ancient worldview. The Greek and Latin poets of Limbo, no matter how learned or brilliant, are condemned to live in desire "sanza speme" (without hope) (*Inf.* 4.42). By situating the literary pastoral of Limbo in the early part of hell, Dante shows that even the greatest achievements of literature must answer to a transcendental Christian order. Bettinelli's scene produces therefore a Chinese-box effect, in which Dante's own ironies are turned against him, and in which the poets of Limbo once again enjoy a spot of aesthetic tranquility apart from the quotidian and Christian world.

Bettinelli's letter then derides Dante's lack of adherence to the rules of neoclassical poetry by describing how the *Commedia* is not an epic in the technical sense that the *Iliad* and Virgil's own *Aeneid* are; the *Commedia* is thus unclassifiable, the work of an unsophisticated poet. Dante also fails, according to Bettinelli, because he attributes to Virgil anachronistic knowledge of medieval matters. Here, as elsewhere, the aim of the *Lettere virgilianae* is to distance Bettinelli's treasured ancient Roman culture from the Middle Ages, with the implication that literary community results not from any bloodline or national tie but from a disembodied kinship of elite spirits. Overall, Bettinelli's approach to the *Commedia* reduces the terms of interpretive debate to contemporary notions of taste that frustrate any attempt to understand Dante in his medieval context. The same figures that Dante reverentially places in Limbo come back to haunt him in Bettinelli's letter. When the *Commedia* is mentioned, Ovid laughs, Lucretius yawns, and Horace describes it as an eccentric poem that is neither *utile* (useful) nor *dulce* (pleasing).

Like Voltaire, however, Bettinelli finds a way to enjoy and praise the *Commedia*—by sifting it for gems.[22] His choices are standard, for all the assembled classical poets enjoy the passages featuring Ugolino and Francesca da Rimini. The reactions of these arcadian litterateurs are eminently classicizing: some wish to turn the *Commedia*'s best parts into odes, others to translate them into Latin and Greek, and some to convert them into elegies. But the rest of the poem fits no categories and only incites derision. The arcadians also express their displeasure with the character of Dante's Pilgrim, who becomes frightened at the slightest peril, falls asleep when he should not, awakes with difficulty, and asks too many questions for Virgil's liking. The Pilgrim exhibits none of the impersonal heroism that Bettinelli associated with the protagonists of the epic genre, of which he imagined the *Commedia* to be a failed example. He negatively contrasts Dante with the traditional epic hero who is passively linked to a larger sociopolitical and cultural network that gives meaning to his actions from without and endows him with a sense of personal identity.[23] The letter concludes by praising Dante the man but disdaining Dante's work. Dante,

Bettinelli writes, is the first to conceive of an epic in a barbarous age from which the present is rapidly and fortunately departing: he is great despite his time. His ultimate value, Bettinelli claims, is that he was a pioneer who allowed his literary successors their achievements. For Bettinelli, however, Dante's contribution to literary history and his "alcune centinaia di bei versi" (few hundred beautiful verses) do not make him a classic author (641).

In 1760, just a few years after the publication of *Lettere virgiliane*, Bettinelli visited Voltaire at his Genevan house Les Délices, where the two discussed Dante and the Italian literary tradition. As is clear from the following letter to Bettinelli from December 18, 1759, Voltaire's position on the *Commedia* continued to alternate between mockery and grudging respect during the period before Bettinelli's visit: "Je fais grand cas du courage avec lequel vous avez osé dire que Dante était un fou, et son ouvrage un monstre: j'aime encore mieux pourtant ce monstre que tous les vermisseaux appellés Sonetti qui naissent et qui meurent par milliers dans l'Italie, de Milan jusqu'à Ottrente" (D8663). (I admire the courage with which you ventured to claim that Dante was mad and that his work was a monster. I still prefer this monster to all those miserable worms called sonnets that come and go by the thousands in Italy, from Milan to Trent.)[24] In 1765, the accumulation of statements of this nature formed the basis for a special article in Voltaire's *Dictionnaire philosophique* (Philosophical dictionary):

> Vous voulez connaître le Dante. Les Italiens l'appellent *divin;* mais c'est une divinité cachée: peu de gens entendent ses oracles; il a des commentateurs, c'est peut-être encore une raison de plus pour n'être pas compris. Sa réputation s'affermira toujours, parce qu'on ne le lit guère. Il y a de lui une vingtaine de traits qu'on sait par cœur: cela suffit pour s'épargner la peine d'examiner le reste. (M 18:312)

> (You wish to know Dante. The Italians call him divine, but it is a hidden divinity. Few people understand his oracles. He has his commentators, which is perhaps yet another reason for not being understood. His reputation will always endure, since scarcely anyone reads him. There are in his work twenty or so passages that we know by heart, and there is thus no need to bother with examining the rest of him.)

Like many others of the day, Voltaire's reading expresses intolerance for the poem's mystical, spiritual elements; impatience with its symbolism and hermeticism; an inclination to dissect the text into its greatest hits; and indifference to the work as a whole. Above all, his criticism lacks a historically minded approach that is sensitive to the *Commedia*'s contexts and intended horizon of concerns. This is not to say that Voltaire is ahistorical in the traditional sense of the word. In fact, the paragraphs following the above citation explore the relationship between the biography of Dante and the content of the *Commedia*.[25] This historicism, however, is typical of the rigid, developmental attitude inherent in Voltaire's philosophy of history. His interests were less the peculiarities and details of a given period and more its overall spirit, and the way this spirit informed his theories of historical progress. Whereas other historians situated Dante in a primeval forest of crude yet powerful barbarism, Voltaire disdainfully set him on a shelf in the antiquarian shop.

The primary intent of Voltaire's remarks about Dante in the *Dictionnaire philosophique* may have been literary, but, as in all his Dante criticism, the antidoctrinal and nonsectarian bias of his religious thought is manifest.[26] He ridicules Dante's theological allusions, and remarks that the only parts of the *Commedia* worth conserving are those that have managed to stand outside of time: "Mais il y a des vers si heureux et si naïfs qu'ils n'ont point vieilli depuis quatre cent ans, et qu'ils ne vieilliront jamais" (M 18:313). (But there are some verses so felicitous and natural that they have not aged in four hundred years and never will age.)[27] His mention of the powerful naivety of Dante's poetry anticipates Schiller's theories in *Über naïve und sentimentalische Dichtung*, though with a proviso. For Voltaire, the anteriority of the primitive poet, however pure and raw, represents not a stage of plenitude from which the later writer has fallen but a state of ignorance out of which he has progressed. Like most *philosophes*, Voltaire found Dante's Middle Ages to be a period of backwardness and superstition—a dark age in comparison with Voltaire's own century of light.[28]

Voltaire's writings on Dante from this period turn on three interrelated Enlightenment notions, each of which helps explain why many thinkers of the time rejected the *Commedia*: taste, human nature, and self-representation. To begin with literary taste, it follows that critical principles like Voltaire's would leave little room for a text that he thought to be unclear, unmeasured, and extravagant—in the words of his own *Dictionnaire philosophique*, a "salmigondis" (hodgepodge) (M 18:313). His exclusion of Dante on formal grounds, however, reflects philosophical suppositions that transcend the realm of mere literary appreciation. Voltaire's attacks on the *Commedia* draw on one of the most crucial and controversial notions in the Enlightenment: that people are born the same, regardless of where and when they are born, and that human nature is universal and general.

Even if thinkers like Voltaire understood the great extent to which individual experience shaped aesthetic judgments, most defended the belief that a general human nature supersedes the impulse to relativism and subjectivity.[29] The stakes, both intellectually and politically, were too high for them not to do so. The faith of most *philosophes* in human perfectibility, the eradication of prejudice, and the study of humankind in the Enlightenment understanding of anthropology depended on the premise that human nature is the same for all.[30] The *philosophes* sought to look past subjective differences in order to discover how individuals could divest themselves of prejudices, habits, and flukes of circumstance that impeded them from attaining those universal and progressive qualities that only rational thought could ascertain.[31] The world of individuals may be one of inexorable variety, the typical *philosophes*' argument went, but if one were to abstract this diversity into metaphysical categories, one could discern common denominators that subsumed these differences. Crucial to this argument was the idea of common sense.[32] Many *philosophes* grounded aesthetic judgments in common sense because they believed that individuals living together in society shared modes of thought that transcended their subjective differences and peculiarities. With these universal points of contact in the human psyche, Voltaire and his associates imagined that it was possible to extrapolate guiding principles — not rules — for evaluating art. From this perspective, it is logical that Voltaire would set his critique of Dante on the same philosophical foundation that supported the aesthetic notions of his fellow *philosophes*. But his reading of the *Commedia,* for all its bile, does reveal an abiding interest in Dante that distinguishes him from the other Encyclopedists, none of whom left any lasting contribution to Dante studies. The Encyclopedists' preoccupation with *l'humanité* as a universal category that one could analyze in a speculative manner left little place for the kind of historicist, autobiographical interest in the *Commedia* that pre-Romantic writers soon showed.

The manner in which Voltaire approached the historical world of the *Commedia* was consistent with how he interpreted his own past. Like the majority of the *philosophes,* he composed few works that addressed the content of his own life. This fact is indeed strange when one considers that by 1766 Rousseau already had begun to write his *Confessions,* and that other memoirs and related genres flourished in the age. Voltaire and other *philosophes* did pose the sort of questions about personal identity that later compelled Romantic writers to turn to the *Commedia.* The forms, however, in which many *philosophes* chose to couch their inquiry into the self — whether the memoir, philosophical tract, or historical overview of literary production — tended not to focus on their individual feelings and thoughts about their own lives. Rather, *philosophes* generally sought to understand how their personal lives fit into a larger conception of humanity and human nature. An awareness of this premise helps one understand how Voltaire's indifference to self-representation and autobiography informed his attacks on the *Commedia.*

Voltaire left only three texts that are autobiographical in nature. The first, the "Article de Voltaire sur Voltaire" (Article by Voltaire on Voltaire; 1755), is a small notice that he sent to the publishers of the *Dictionnaire des théâtres de Paris* at their request (M 1:1–2). Fewer than a thousand words in length, the text proceeds in a businesslike fashion to list Voltaire's works along with their publication history. Only a modicum of self-representation appears in the text, including the author's characteristic defensiveness with regard to his much maligned epic, the *Henriade*. His second autobiographical text, *Mémoires pour servir à la vie de M. de Voltaire écrits par lui-même* (Memoirs on the life of Voltaire, written by himself; 1759), is far more evocative of Voltaire's attitudes toward Dante and their relation to the question of identity.[33] The text begins in the gardens of Cirey, to which Voltaire has just returned from the "vie oisive et turbulente de Paris" (idle and turbulent life of Paris), where he had tired of the "bassesses et . . . brigandage des misérables qui déshonoraient la littérature" (baseness and . . . thievery of the miserable sorts who were dishonoring literature) (M 1:7). Horticultural imagery marks each stage of this bittersweet return: Voltaire's companion Émilie du Châtelet decorates the refuge with "jardins assez agréables" (most agreeable gardens); and the two of them together "cultiv[aient] à Cirey tous les arts" (cultivated all the arts at Cirey) (M 1:8). The motivation for the text's emphasis on movement, growth, and activity rather than on introspection and self-analysis soon becomes clear. After describing how he introduced Isaac Newton into France in 1738 with his *Eléments de la philosophie de Newton*, Voltaire pronounces John Locke "le seul métaphysicien raisonnable" (the only reasonable metaphysician) (M 1:21). Although Voltaire's espousal of these two English philosophers as part of his ongoing critique of Cartesianism is well known, scholars seem not to have remarked upon the implications of Voltaire's affinity for Locke in autobiographical matters and, by implication, his dismissal of an author like Dante.[34]

After mentioning Newton and Locke, Voltaire stymies with one breath any hope for understanding the history of his own self: "Le fait est que nous ne savons rien de nous-mêmes, que nous avons le mouvement, la vie, le sentiment et la pensée, sans savoir comment; que les éléments de la matière nous sont aussi inconnus que le reste; que nous sommes des aveugles qui marchons et raisonnons à tâtons; et que Locke a été très-sage en avouant que ce n'est pas à nous à décider de ce que le Tout-Puissant ne peut pas faire" (The fact is, we know nothing about ourselves. We have movement, life, feelings, and thoughts without knowing how. The world of nature is as unknown to us as everything else. We are like blind people who march and reason in the dark. Locke was very wise in asserting that it is not for us to decide what the Almighty cannot do) (M 1:21). The digression levels the epistemological support for the autobiographical introspection and subjective emphasis that later fueled the Romantic interest in the poet and protagonist of the *Commedia*. The Romantics, in fact, employed their readings of the *Commedia* to address and then reject the five postulates suggested by Voltaire: we know nothing of ourselves; we have life without knowing how; the external world that we inhabit is unknowable and alien; we move through life in blinders if not blindness; and the workings of providence are no concern of ours. René Descartes' positing of innate notions concerning the existence of God are part of what Voltaire calls philosophy's tendency to write a "roman de l'âme" (novel of the soul), which, according to Voltaire, the empirically minded Locke was able to replace with his more sober history of the soul.[35]

The impact of Locke's thought on Voltaire's autobiographical writings recalls the influence of his landmark *Essay Concerning Human Understanding* (1690) on a major Enlightenment experiment in personal identity by the Abbé de Condillac. In the opening chapter of *Traité des sensations* (Treatise on sensations; 1754), Condillac asks the reader to imagine "une statue organisée intérieurement comme nous, et animée d'un esprit privé de toute espèce d'idées" (a statue organized internally like us and animated by an intelligence devoid of any semblance of ideas).[36] The author activates the statue's senses one by one and, in the process, establishes a continuum in which the marble object acquires an emotional and intellectual life. All that separates the originally inert slab of marble from its eventual attainment of a spiritual life — what may even be termed a soul — is thus an amalgam of sense perceptions experienced over time. Condillac goes beyond merely arguing against God's existence: he reduces it to a calculus.

In the consciousness of this *machine à sentir,* no qualitative difference exists between the most complex form of aesthetic evaluation and a pang of hunger, since both develop from the gradual transformation and elaboration of that first sense perception: "Le jugement, la réflexion, les desirs, les passions, etc., ne sont que la sensation même qui se transforme différement" (11). (Judgment, reflection, desire, the passions, etc., are nothing but that sensation itself that transforms in different ways.) Presumably, only those literary works that share the regulated and quantifiable nature of the statue's own mode of experience will be best suited for the enjoyment and edification of the animated marble. The economies of taste established within Condillac's closed, self-referential system of feeling and evaluation would probably have rejected "bizarre" (Voltaire's word of choice for Dante) and unclassifiable works (Bettinelli's description of Dante's untraditional epic). In Condillac's model, one expects a certain predictability and repeatability from the work of art — an internal logic akin to the way the statue bases its experiences on the infinite and inexhaustible elaboration of an initial sense perception. As Ernst Cassirer puts it, for Condillac, the mind neither creates nor invents; it repeats and constructs.[37]

Like Condillac's experiment in identity, Voltaire's self-representation attests to the influence of certain currents of philosophical speculation.[38] In his *Mémoires* from 1759, the most evocative portrait is not of himself but of Frederick II of Prussia. In describing the king's typical day, he imbues the text with a Rabelaisian irony that deepens his emphasis on the precariousness endemic to any attempt at representing a human life. Frederick awakes at the hour of five in summer or six in winter, and he dresses in a stark room that embodies stoic virtue. If he was stoic at dawn, however, by breakfast the king is epicurean: "Il faisait venir deux ou trois favoris. . . . On prenait le café. Celui à qui on jetait le mouchoir restait un demi-quart d'heure tête à tête" (M 1:26–27). (He had two or three of his favorites join him. . . . They would have coffee. The one to whom he would throw his handkerchief would stay a while for a tête-à-tête.) This first unexpected shift in the king's behavior anticipates a dizzying variety of activities. From eight to eleven, Frederick handles affairs of state; from eleven to lunch, he reviews his troops; after lunch, he finds a couple of hours to compose poetry, enjoy a reading, and play the flute. Finally, at the end of the day, the philosopher-king dines and engages in spirited philosophical discussion in a room decorated with scenes of debauchery. Like Rabelais' comically hyperactive Gargantua, the Prussian king "ne perdait heure du jour" (did not waste a single hour of the day).[39]

Frederick emerges from Voltaire's description not as a well-rounded man but as a skilled actor who dons mask upon mask. Voltaire even uses a term of disparagement from his Dante criticism (*bizarre*) to describe Frederick's world. The absence in the *Mémoires* of any sustained and coherent individual identity is not limited to Frederick: it includes Voltaire himself. Following the death of Émilie du Châtelet, Voltaire returns to Frederick's court and, like a figure from a romance epic, sets an allegory of desire in motion: "Astolphe ne fut pas mieux reçu dans le palais d'Alcine" (M 1:36). (Astolfo received no better a reception at the palace of Alcina.)[40] The time at court proves rejuvenating for Voltaire, who is now free to pursue his literary interests: "Je m'étais fait une vie libre, et je ne concevais rien de plus agréable que cet état" (M 1:36). (I created for myself a free life, and I could conceive of nothing more agreeable than this state.) The magic spell of the enchantress-king Frederick, however, proves irresistible. While Voltaire settles into life in Berlin, his host sends him a fateful letter:

Une maîtresse ne s'explique pas plus tendrement. . . . Ce fut le dernier verre que m'enivra. Les protestations de bouche furent encore plus fortes que celles par écrit. Il était accoutumé à des démonstrations de tendresse singulières avec des favoris plus jeunes que moi; et oubliant un moment que je n'étais pas de leur âge, et que je n'avais pas la main belle, il me la prit pour la baiser. Je lui baisai la sienne, et je me fis son esclave. Il fallait une permission du roi de France pour appartenir à deux maîtres. Le roi de Prusse se chargea de tout. (M 1:36–37)

(A mistress would not have explained herself more tenderly. . . . It was the final intoxicating sip. The protests from [Frederick's] mouth were even stronger than the ones from his pen. He was used to demonstrations of exceptional tenderness from favorites younger than I. Forgetting for a moment that I was not the same age as these younger favorites, and that I did not have a shapely hand, he took my hand to kiss it. I kissed his, and I made myself his slave. I needed permission from the King of France to be able to serve two masters. The King of Prussia took care of everything.)

Voltaire's loss of liberty extends to the personal (Frederick mocks his vanity and screens his mail), political (he falls out of favor in France because of his split allegiances), and literary-philosophical (he is compelled to spend his days editing the king's works). At the crucial moment where his freedom and happiness depend on a self-knowledge and sense of identity that he denies himself a priori, Voltaire's sense of self seems to escape him.[41]

Neither Voltaire's memoir nor his Dante criticism allows any external presence — whether God, nature, or destiny — to unsettle the closed economies of his textual worlds. According to Voltaire, Frederick's actions are best understood in relation to one another, independent of their reference to any behavioral or moral code. Likewise, in Voltaire's opinion, one should read the best passages of the *Commedia* without considering the world of references that lies outside of them. The prophecies, allusions, and allegories of Dante may point somewhere, but Voltaire expresses no interest in ascertaining where that may be. In a similar fashion, he exhibits no desire to extrapolate from the incidents and experiences of his life a retrospective notion of personal identity.

After the remarks from the 1750s and 1760s examined above, Voltaire remained quiet about Dante for some time. Then, two years before his death, he delivered his final and perhaps most vicious attack on Dante, in the *Lettres chinoises, indiennes et tartares* (Chinese, Indian, and Tartar letters; 1776). Voltaire's discussion of Dante in this text is consistent with the main points of stage two of his Dante criticism (1756–65). In letter 12, Voltaire once again labels the *Commedia* "bizarre," and he ridicules its mix of ancient and modern elements (M 29:495–98). Following Bettinelli, Voltaire also claims that one of the *Commedia*'s principal faults is that Dante himself is an uninteresting hero. The heroes he finds more engaging are located in Ariosto and Tasso, whose epic protagonists define themselves through their exploits and not through any self-generated notion of identity. Voltaire's remarks on Dante's failure as a protagonist corroborate the observations he made in his last autobiographical text, the *Commentaire historique sur les œuvres de l'auteur de la "Henriade"* (Historical commentary on the author of the *Henriad;* 1776; M 1:67–123). As the title suggests, this third-person memoir describes at length how the *Henriade* was composed. Voltaire first alludes to a Virgilian legend and says that he, like the Roman poet, had his epic saved from the flames. He then writes that his well-publicized problems in composing the *Henriade* arose from the fact that he was not yet familiar with the rules of the epic genre. By shrewdly invoking these rules, Voltaire expresses his desire to protect at all costs neoclassical tenets that were being threatened by the new literary movements he abhorred — movements that were embracing such texts as the *Commedia*.

In the *Commentaire*, Voltaire avoids interiority and self-representation even more deftly than he did in the earlier *Mémoires*. The transition from the *Mémoires* to the *Commentaire* of the above scene with Frederick II epitomizes this anti-autobiographical impulse. Just as he did in the *Mémoires*, Voltaire recounts in the *Commentaire* his visit to Frederick's court after the death of Emilie du Châtelet. In the *Commentaire*, however, he retells this dramatic episode in a bloodless tone:

> [Voltaire] ne put résister à cette lettre que ce prince lui écrivit de son appartement à la chambre de son nouvel hôte dans le palais de Berlin, le 23 août; lettre qui a tant couru depuis, et qui a été souvent imprimée.... [Voltaire] était attaché au roi de Prusse par la plus respectueuse tendresse et par la conformité des goûts. Il a dit cent fois que ce monarque était aussi aimable dans la société que redoutable à la tête d'une armée; qu'il n'avait jamais fait de soupers plus agréables à Paris que ceux auxquels ce prince voulait bien l'admettre tous les jours. Son enthousiasme pour le roi de Prusse allait jusqu'à la passion.... Le roi composait en haut des ouvrages de philosophie, d'histoire, et de poésie; et son favori cultivait en bas les mêmes arts et les mêmes talents. Ils s'envoyaient l'un à l'autre leurs ouvrages. (M 1:92–93)

> ([Voltaire] could not resist this letter that the prince [Frederick] had written him on August 23, from his apartment to the room of his new guest in the Berlin palace. This letter has since traveled widely and has been printed often. ... [Voltaire] was attached to the King of Prussia by the most respectable affections and by a similarity in tastes. He said countless times that this king was just as loveable in society as he was redoubtable at the head of an army. He also said that he had never had such wonderful dinners in Paris as those to

which the Prussian king wished to invite him every day. Voltaire's enthusiasm for the king was a passionate one. . . . The king composed philosophical, historical, and poetic works from above; meanwhile, his favorite cultivated these same arts and talents from below. They would send their works to each other.)

Voltaire's sentiments in response to Frederick's cajoling and flattery, so vivid in the *Mémoires,* now resurface as a string of platitudes and protests exaggerated enough to betray a lurking sense of anxiety. In the *Commentaire,* Frederick, the one-time Ariostean magician, becomes no more than a collection of accolades to whom Voltaire does not even refer by name. Even the delicate and ambiguous nature of their mutual affection now assumes the form of an anodyne "passion" between two friends immersed in bookish pursuits. The partial eclipse of the self, prophesied in the *Mémoires* with its Lockean disclaimers about self-representation, is, by the time of the *Commentaire,* total.

This practice by literary men of offering the story of their lives as a public record was common in Voltaire's age. One of Voltaire's fellow *philosophes,* Hume, left a literary self-portrait that is no less striking than Voltaire's in its indifference to self-representation. Written in 1776 four months before his death, the Scottish *philosophe*'s autobiography is in many respects the testimonial that Condillac's *machine à sentir* would have written.[42] Hume begins the text with a polite nod to the manners of his day: "It is difficult for a man to speak long of himself without vanity; therefore, I shall be short" (v). Lest his readers accuse Hume of presuming any undue interest in his personal life, he adds that "this narrative shall contain little more than the history of my writings" (v). As in Voltaire's *Commentaire,* in Hume's *My Own Life* the literary works in themselves constitute the author's identity. The movement in Hume's memoir is everywhere from the general to the particular: a sanguine temper leads to the blithe, well-adjusted nature that allows Hume to handle the setbacks of public indifference to both his *Treatise of Human Nature* (1737) and *Enquiry into Human Understanding* (1748). He narrates his intellectual development in a way that negates any contingency, accident, or historical fluke that might have obstructed his literary pursuits. All events in the narrative appear to proceed according to the "plan of life which [Hume] steadily and successfully pursued" (vi), and even so personal and distressing a matter as a terminal medical condition only strengthens Hume's resolve and deepens his fatalism: "I possess the same ardor as ever in study, and the same gayety in company. I consider, besides, that a man of sixty-five, by dying, cuts off only a few years of his infirmities; and though I see many symptoms of my literary reputation's breaking out at last with additional lustre, I know that I could have but few years to enjoy it. It is difficult to be more detached from life than I am at present" (xv). However unsettling this last sentence, it is consistent with the author's beliefs on selfhood.[43] For all Hume's emphasis on the differences separating the sense perception of one individual from another, he was a man of his age in his belief in a common human nature that can temper subjectivity and prevent it from dissolving into unbounded relativism. His *My Own Life* discloses the steady process by which a neutral core with certain characteristics and attributes, Hume himself, manages to become progressive, and to a certain degree universal, through an intellectual growth that remains indifferent to the peculiarities of individuality.

Along with Voltaire's *Commentaires,* Hume's *My Own Life* is part of the branch of anti-autobiographical, philosophical self-portraits that appeared at the same time as the more properly pre-Romantic autobiographies of Rousseau and the Sturm und Drang Goethe. As an astonishing letter from Voltaire to Hume on October 24, 1766, reveals, a *philosophe* like Voltaire could not accept the growing preoccupation in literary circles with the elaboration of the self that Rousseau was representing. Voltaire writes: "Vous dites qu'il fait l'histoire de sa vie. Elle a été trop utile au monde, & remplie de trop grands événements, pour qu'il ne rende pas à la posterité le service de la publier. Son goût pour la vérité ne lui permettra pas de déguiser la moindre de ces anecdotes, pour servir à l'éducation des princes qui voudront être menuisiers comme Emile" (D13623). (You say that [Rousseau] is writing the history of his life [the *Confessions*]. This life has been too useful to the world and too filled with great events for its author not to serve posterity by publishing its story. Rousseau's taste for truth will not permit him to disguise the least of his anecdotes — in order to serve the education of princes who will want to become carpenters like Émile.) From the perspective of Voltaire's abstract concerns about humanity and human nature, the "petites misères" (little miseries) of Rousseau's personal life "ne méritent pas qu'on s'en occupe deux minutes; tout cela tombe bientôt dans un éternel oubli" (do not warrant the slightest attention, for they will all soon fall into eternal oblivion) (D13623).

This letter to Hume concludes with a fatalistic overture to the insignificance of personal matters: "Il y a des sottises & des querelles dans toutes les conditions de la vie. . . . Tout passe rapidement comme les figures grotesques de la lanterne magique. . . . Les détails des guerres les plus sanglantes périssent avec les soldats qui en ont été les victimes. . . . Dans ce torment immense qui nous emporte & qui nous engloutit tous, qu'y a-t-il à faire?" (D13623). (There are idiocies and quarrels in all conditions of life. . . . All passes rapidly, just like those grotesque figures of the magic lantern. . . . The details of the bloodiest wars perish along with those soldiers who were their victims. . . . In all this immense torment that carries us away and envelops us, what are we to do?)

The resignation that pervades this letter resurfaced with comparable poignancy in the final pages of Voltaire's *Commentaire,* whose words on approaching death recall those of Hume in *My Own Life.* "Dans ce dernier temps [Voltaire] avait une profonde indifférence pour ses propres ouvrages, dont il fit toujours peu de cas, et dont il ne parlait jamais" (M 1:123). (In this last period, [Voltaire] was profoundly indifferent to his own works. He invariably paid little attention to them and never spoke about them.) Even Voltaire's usually irrepressible sense of irony does not mitigate the ambivalent pathos of the following words: "N'imprimez pas tant de volumes de moi; on ne va point à la postérité avec un si gros bagage" (M 1:123). (Do not publish so many volumes by me. One can hardly travel to posterity with such heavy baggage.) So great is Voltaire's indifference to attempts by others to monumentalize him while he is alive that, when a Genevan edition of his completed works appears with texts in it that he never wrote, he does not bother to correct it. With both bemusement and bewilderment, he says of the scramble to publish, praise, attack, and even erect a statue of him: "Je me regarde comme un homme mort dont on vend les meubles" (M 1:123). (I think of myself as a dead man whose furniture is being sold away.)

Voltaire's self-portrait in the *Commentaire* in 1776 reflects his thinking on Dante that same year in the *Lettres chinoises.* In the *Lettres chinoises,* he rejects the protagonist Dante for the same reasons that he attacks the autobiographical project of Rousseau in his letter to Hume discussed above. In a literary career spanning the middle fifty years of the eighteenth century, Voltaire did not believe the literary text to be a suitable place for self-exploration. By eschewing the hero of the *Commedia* in favor of the epic protagonists of Ariosto and Tasso, Voltaire voiced his critique of the model of the self in the *Commedia*—that is, Dante's historically naive and primitive origins, his doctrinal Christian faith, and his eccentric originality. Voltaire celebrated the heroes of traditional epic not because of what they say about individual experience, but because they embody public ideals and codes of behavior that he believed to be the hallmarks of the truly great literary figure. To posit, however, that he did not think that literature was capable of exploring the human condition is to miss entirely his intent. He believed that the question of the self was best approached through philosophical works that deal with human nature, history, and mores—and not through what he considered to be the failed attempt at epic of Dante. Like many of his contemporaries, Voltaire refused to take the *Commedia* seriously as a model of autobiography, in part because he did not place much value in the developing genre itself.

In Voltaire's lifetime of ironies, the following becomes one of the most telling: his announcement in 1756 that no one reads the *Commedia* helped to incite critical discussions that resuscitated the poem once and for all. Voltaire's throwaway line represents, therefore, a turning point in modern Dante scholarship. Like many other *philosophes,* Voltaire died a decade or so before the French Revolution; had he lived to see its events, I suspect that his reading of Dante would have become more sustained. At the very least, the aftermath of 1789 made it increasingly difficult to argue for the autonomy and self-enclosure of the literary world. The classicizing cultural politics of the ancien régime gave way to a new generation of writers who read Dante partly because they identified with his text and partly because their former masters did not. Always a creature of his time, Voltaire would probably not have been able to resist expanding his own views of the ever more popular medieval poet. Once the revolution had blurred the boundaries between the gardens of literary retreats and the streets of Paris, the issues the *Commedia* raised acquired a gravity and immediacy that they did not have in the spaces of aesthetic self-enclosure Voltaire associated with belles lettres. During the long period of upheaval that followed the events of 1789, the age's literature revealed how writers increasingly found the abstract speculations of the *philosophes* on human nature to be insufficient guides to representing individual human life. Ironically, those same aspects of the *Commedia* that Voltaire scorned — Dante's individuality, mystical yearning, and unrefined nature — would inspire his pre-Romantic successors in their autobiographical quests.

5

Alfieri's Prince, *Dante, and the Romantic Self*

Leggere, come io l'intendo, vuol dire profondamente pensare; pensare, vuol dire starsi; e starsi, vuol dir sopportare.

(To read, as I understand it, means to think deeply; to think deeply means to stand firm; and to stand firm means to endure.)
— *Vittorio Alfieri*

Alfieri wrote these words circa 1778, the year in which his former *maître à penser* Voltaire died a celebrity in Paris.[1] Although Voltaire does not appear in the epigraph, he haunts it. As opposed to the pleasure and cultivation inherent in Voltaire's notion of reading, Alfieri's statement introduces a concern with ethics and character that ignores the question of aesthetic appreciation and literary value. This journey from reading to endurance suggests Alfieri's tendency to translate literary pursuits into a quest for freedom and self-esteem if not survival. "Si esamini la storia," he continues, "e si vedrà, che i popoli tutti ritornati di servitù in libertà, non lo furono già per via di lumi e verità penetrate in ciascuno individuo; ma per un qualche entusiasmo saputo loro inspirare da alcuna mente illuminata, astuta, e focosa" (1.8; *Del principe* 127). (Examine history, and you will see that all peoples who turned from servitude to liberty did so not because each individual was enlightened by truth but because of a certain enthusiasm that a few enlightened, shrewd, and fiery minds were able to inspire in them [*Prince and Letters* 22].) For Voltaire, the term *lumière* (enlightenment) entailed committing intellectual labor to cultural and political reform out of a nearly impersonal sense of moral obligation and social responsibility. In the above citation, however, Alfieri equates the Italian version of the word (*illuminato*) with a cult of personality that only genius can inspire. His rhetoric of fire, lightning, and laceration challenges the most self-consciously august and abiding metaphor of the *siècle des lumières*, the light of truth, with a Machiavellian overture to mob psychology and republican cynicism. Fittingly, these words appear in *Del principe e delle lettere* (*The Prince and Letters*; 1786), which claims that only individual talent, brute strength, or force of will — not ideas — can effect social change. Alfieri arrived at this conclusion partly through a powerful though questionable reading of the author whom Voltaire sought to exclude from literary debate: Dante. In promoting Dante as his privileged model of self, Alfieri, to a greater degree than any of his pre-Romantic contemporaries, established a paradigmatically autobiographical reading of Dante that shaped critical interpretation of the *Commedia* in the early nineteenth century.

In contrast with the early eighteenth century, the *Commedia* flourished in the period between the deaths of Voltaire and Alfieri (1778–1803). During this time, sixteen new editions of the text appeared in Europe, almost a third of which were published outside of Italy.[2] Landmark translations and critical studies of the *Commedia* in the 1780s and 1790s stimulated interest in the poem that remained constant throughout the age of Romanticism.[3] The concern with Dante contributed to and drew on the emergence of another eminently Romantic phenomenon: modern autobiography. Although the period's most sophisticated theoretical approaches to Dante's influence on questions of subjectivity appeared in Germany, the *Commedia* had the greatest impact on literary self-representation in Italy.[4] Several important new editions of Dante's text appeared in the Peninsula in the late eighteenth century, and the many biographical sketches or *vite* of Dante in these same works reflected the growing preoccupation with the poet's life.[5] Beyond mere antiquarian or philological curiosity, the biographical reconstruction of Dante's life became part of a dialogue between the study of the *Commedia* and contemporary attitudes toward the self.

Nowhere is the presence of the *Commedia* in autobiographical discourse more prominent than in Alfieri, who came to identify with Dante after rejecting the Enlightenment notion of the *homme de lettres* and several major assumptions associated with this term. In polemical response to Voltaire and the *philosophes*, Alfieri's turn to Dante led him to center his autobiography on the theme of the writer's rejection of all cultural, political, and social ties in the name of the abstraction "literature." Alfieri's impossibly high demands on poets stemmed from his belief in literature's historical vocation of remaking the world—a conviction, however quixotic, that had great impact on the manner in which many of his Romantic successors understood the psychology and responsibilities of the creative writer. Alfieri's desire for personal and public reform through literature led him to redefine certain key concepts of the Enlightenment—including genius, humanity, and literary taste—in terms that reveal Dante's influence.

Along with Rousseau and the early Goethe, Alfieri has assumed the status of a transitional and epochal pre-Romantic figure.[6] Born during the height of Enlightenment thought in 1749, Alfieri's early intellectual formation occurred during the pro- and anti-*philosophe* debates of the 1760s and 1770s. Because of his self-imposed Parisian exile (1786–92), he was also firsthand witness, early friend, and eventual enemy of the French Revolution. Finally, he lived long enough to be a contemporary of those young writers whom we now consider first-generation Romantics.[7] Given the many allusions Alfieri makes to Dante and their similarities in style and personality, the limited scope of the criticism on their relationship is surprising.[8] Alfieri's relationship with Dante encompassed three distinct phases: reading (1771–78), incorporation (1778–90), and identification (1790–1803).[9] The principal event of Alfieri's reading stage was in 1776, when he composed an *Estratto di Dante* (Extract from Dante), in which he transcribed and annotated his favorite verses of the first twenty-two cantos of *Inferno*. During the period of incorporation, Alfieri composed *Del principe e delle lettere,* which contains numerous references to Dante. The culmination of this second phase was in 1790 when Alfieri adapted the Ugolino episode of *Inferno* 32–33 into his own hybrid theatrical genre, the *tramelogedia* (musical tragedy); during this time, he also relied heavily on the writings of Dante in his satires and in the anti-French tract he began to write, *Il misogallo* (Against Gaul; 1814).[10] The third and most crucial stage of Alfieri's involvement with Dante began in 1790 with the initial draft of his *Vita,* the work that made his identification with the medieval poet complete if rather tragic.

The young Alfieri described himself as an *homme de lettres* in the idiom of the French Enlightenment. He first read Voltaire in 1765, well before he began to engage the great authors of the Italian tradition. In fact, by Alfieri's own admission, between 1765 and 1775 he read almost exclusively French authors, and his first major work, *Esquisse du jugement universel* (Sketch of the universal judgment; 1772) carries throughout French Enlightenment influences. Although the text may appear Dantesque in structure and intent—as the title indicates, it narrates an apocalyptic Last Judgment, with an attendant parade of self-advocating sinners — it could not be further removed from the Christian gravitas of the *Commedia*. God appears in the guise of an eighteenth-century gentleman who has just had his morning chocolate; heaven takes the form of a royal court where angels serve as chamberlains and address God as "Votre Majesté"; and Jesus jokes about the temptations of dishonest women. A pastiche of sources ranging from Lucian to Helvétius, the text's most dramatic encounter between Alfieri's emerging literary sensibility and the thought of the *philosophes* occurs in the following passage that scholars have acknowledged to be autobiographical:

> J'ai été toujours, un tissu d'inconséquences, et j'ai réuni dans mon caractère tous les contrastes possibles. J'ai fait des longs voyages, dans les-quels j'échangeois mes propres ridicules, avec des ridicules étrangers, je renonçois à quelques préjugez, pour en investir d'autres. J'eus le deffaut d'aprouver rarement, ce qui se passoit autour de moi, et un penchant beaucoup plus fort, pour blâmer, que pour applaudir. Je ne m'employois à rien, un amour propre démésuré me fit croire au dessus de tous les emplois, si j'avois pourtant pensé juste, j'avois vu, qu'en tout pays, et en tout tems, il est libre à chacun d'en exercer le plus noble, qui est d'être utile à l'humanité. J'ai beaucoup parlé sur ce même grand ton, dont j'ai l'honneur de parler a Votre Majesté, mais le fait est, que, je n'ai jamais été utile à personne.[11]

> (I have always been a meaningless thing and have managed to contain every possible contradiction within my character. I took long voyages, during which I exchanged my native idiocies for foreign ones. I renounced some of my prejudices only to replace them with others. I had the defect of rarely approving of what went on around me, and a much stronger tendency to blame than to praise. I did not put myself to any use and an unbounded *amour propre* made me think I was above all tasks. If I had, however, seen things clearly, I would have realized that, in all places and times, each is free to do the most noble thing: that is, be useful to humanity. I have often spoken in this same grand tone in which I have the honor of addressing Your Majesty, but, the fact is, I have never been of any use to anyone.)

The moody self-analysis in the passage, as opposed to the satirical and comic tone of the other sinners, provides a hint of the author's problematic relationship with the forms of self-representation favored by the *philosophes*, the majority of whom constructed the self in order to uphold their metaphysical speculations on the essential neutrality of human nature and its perfectibility. The form of self-representation they favored was the *mémoire*, which typically fell into the following five categories: first, souvenirs or official *mémoires* that recount the major events that formed an author's profession, reputation, or public image; second, descriptions of a writer's *Bildung*, intellectual trajectory, or *cursus studiorum;* third, fictionalized stories of an aspect or period of an author's life, written in a transparent form; fourth, chronological versions by writers of their daily activities in the form of a diary or *journal intime;* last, life histories structured according to the methodological practices and principles of the historian.[12] In the versions of memoir adduced above, speculative concern for personal identity and abstract issues of selfhood is implicit and incidental. Alfieri, and his more famous precursor Rousseau, rejected this detached attitude toward subjectivity and transformed the question of the self into the thematic core of their autobiographies. Generally speaking, scholars believe that this self-conscious pursuit of an elusive inner identity in the manner of Rousseau's *Confessions* — in contrast to the more externally oriented process of self-representation that marks the *mémoire* — signals the transition from Enlightenment to Romantic, or modern, autobiography.[13] Viewed from this perspective, Alfieri's self-critique in the above quotation from *Esquisse du jugement universel* functions as a metacritique of the language of the self then current. Though Alfieri goes through the verbal motion of self-examination in the manner of the *philosophes*, he questions the very principles that sustained this process, especially utility ("je n'ai jamais été utile à personne") and the eradication of prejudice ("je renonçois à quelques préjugez, pour en investir d'autres").

Shortly after the *Esquisse*, Alfieri experienced the aesthetic conversion that led to his devotion to the solitary and exclusive pursuit of literature; this new conception of literary activity involved a shift from a Voltairean to a Dantesque model of the writer. The text that narrates this transition, *Del principe e delle lettere*, anticipates the psychology and mythology that Alfieri later adopted in his *Vita scritta da esso*. A precursor to such comparative critical works as Staël's *De la littérature considérée dans ses rapports avec les institutions sociales* (Literature considered in its relationship with social institutions; 1800), *Del principe e delle lettere* promotes sociological and political analysis over traditional literary-historical methods of aesthetic evaluation, rhetorical classification, and chronological ordering. Alfieri began the text in 1778 when his clandestine relationship with Louisa of Stolberg, then wife of the pretender to the English throne, Charles Edward Stuart, made him a political liability to his king, Vittorio Amadeo III.[14] When Alfieri requested permission to travel to Tuscany, the king agreed only after reminding him that he had given similar dispensation just months earlier. Alfieri viewed the need to receive travel permission as symbolic of how politics and literature were two masters he could not serve simultaneously. Of all the European countries, only England, Holland, and Switzerland in Alfieri's age had anything resembling a modern form of freedom of the press; overt censorship prevailed in France, Germany, and Italy.[15] Although laws varied greatly in Italy, Piedmont had notoriously harsh restrictions against freedom of expression.[16] Baretti, for example, anticipated Alfieri's fate by leaving the Piedmontese capitol of Turin in 1751 for the literary freedom of London. When Baretti returned to the Italian Peninsula in 1760, he decided to settle in Lombard Milan and not Turin, where his inflammatory satires were likely to invite censure. Eventually, the Piedmontese royal constitution of 1770–71 passed a law forbidding the king's subjects to publish any work outside of his kingdom without approval of the censors. The combination of these hostile laws and Alfieri's precarious situation with Louisa incited him to produce a trilogy of political treatises on freedom between 1778 and 1786: *Del principe e delle lettere, Della tirannide* (On tyranny), and *Etruria vendicata* (Etruria vindicated). Moreover, as if to foreshadow Alfieri's own possible fortune, in 1777 Carlo Denina, Alfieri's first Latin teacher as well as an autobiographer and Dantist of note, was arrested outside of Turin, and his politically charged books were seized and burned. Alfieri began shortly thereafter the negotiations with King Amadeus that resulted in his voluntary exile and the relinquishing of all his property in exchange for a yearly stipend. The following August, in 1778, he began to draft *Del principe e delle lettere*.

The events that led to the composition of this text embody the principle of zero-sum relations between writer and ruler that informs each of its pages. *Del principe e delle lettere* begins with the following premises: force not knowledge rules the world; any ruler may be and generally is ignorant; and the prince is the congenital enemy of mankind. Drawing on Voltaire's *Dictionnaire philosophique*, Alfieri then describes literature somewhat feebly as the Horatian *utile* and *dulce*. Because of this capacity for docile pleasure in literature, the prince will always favor elegant writers over sublime ones; the only writers that the prince should fear, Alfieri claims, are those who place literature at the service of humankind. The primary targets of his critique are neoclassicism and its touchstones, taste and utility. Within the stark economy of Alfieri's notion of literature, taste is portrayed as a reactionary desire to limit the scope of the literary with the socially conservative qualities of wit, elegance, and sophistication. Utility, at least in the Enlightenment sense of the term, was no less conservative in Alfieri's eyes, for to serve the existing system, he argues, is to abet a conspiracy of corruptions. Genuine utility comes only through the iconoclasm of sublime writers ("veritieri" and "feroci" [sincere and ferocious]) whose work every prince seeks to suppress (1.3; *Del principe* 121; *Prince and Letters* 14).

In addition to criticizing the state of European literature, Alfieri frees the writer from any traditional social tie or obligation. Because all governments are inherently corrupt, he writes, all writers should challenge them, and all literature worthy of the name must offend. He then adds that, as opposed to writers like Voltaire who signed his name "Gentleman-in-Waiting to the King," the author who struggles against authority is a champion of liberty. The second book begins with a dedication "ai pochi letterati, che non si lasciano proteggere" (to those few men of letters who accept no protection), writers including Hume, Milton, Homer, and Dante. The latter emerges as Alfieri's model of the poet-hero:

> Dante non fu protetto: che poteva egli dar di più? Mi si dirà forse: "Più eleganza": ma egli ebbe tutta quella che comportavano i tempi suoi; e l'ebbe di gran lunga superiore a tutti i suoi predecessori, che scritto aveano nella stessa sua lingua. Ma Orazio e Virgilio furono protetti: e diedero perciò quel tanto di meno, che la dipendenza e il timore andavano ogni giorno togliendo alla energia già non moltissima degli animi loro. Mi si opporrà, che Dante in una corte ripulita e delicata come quella d'Augusto non avrebbe adoprato tante rozze e sconce espressioni. Rispondo, che questo può essere: ma soggiungo, che Virgilio ed Orazio fuor di tal corte, non si sarebbero contaminati di tante vili adulazioni e falsità. Qual è peggio? (2.3; 148)
>
> (Dante was not protected; what more could he have achieved? You will perhaps say to me: "More elegance." But he had that degree of elegance which suited his times, and to a much greater extent than all his predecessors who had written in the same language. "But Horace and Virgil were protected." That is exactly why they were less admirable, because dependence and fear deprived them a little less every day of that energy which already was by no means superabundant in their hearts. The objection will be raised that Dante would not have used so many coarse improper expressions in a refined fastidious court like that of Augustus. I admit that this may be true: but I will add that except for that court, Virgil and Horace would not have defiled themselves with so much base adulation and falsehood. Which fault is worse?) (46–47)

This last query ("Qual è peggio?") suggests the transition taking place around this time in the types of questions that writers throughout Europe were asking of literary works. In reality, these requests had already been intuited by some of those same Enlightenment thinkers whom authors like Alfieri were attacking.[17] However, for Alfieri to balance the moral and ethical content of a work against its formal properties, and then to judge these former two qualities more important, reflects the tendency in his age to theorize about literature in terms that were increasingly hostile to neoclassical strictures.

The "Dante" that Alfieri created in *Del principe e delle lettere* was in part fictitious, and the manner in which he handled the dialectic in the *Commedia* between self-representation and self-transcendence was curious but consistent. Although Dante promoted a centralized and authoritarian Holy Roman Empire, Alfieri transformed the medieval poet into an iconoclastic political radical, and he viewed Dante more as a heroic poet rather than a religious pilgrim. Dante's writings do contain numerous examples in which the poet calls on his courage and inner reserve to deal with a pressing matter, yet these instances of heroism are crucial only insofar as they aid the Pilgrim in a spiritual ascent that eventually requires him to transcend the *principium individuationis*. But Dante's overcoming of the self did not concern Alfieri, for his Dante became a symbol of the literary life centered on values of protest, endurance, and moral imperturbability. The dialogue Alfieri establishes between a writer's moral and ethical makeup and the content of his work makes autobiographical reflection natural if not inevitable. He even stressed the relevance of biographical criticism in his critique of Enlightenment literary thought. Modern literature, he writes, is the result of a "semi-filosofia" (pseudophilosophy) widely disseminated in the eighteenth century "da alcuni scrittori leggiadri, o anche eccellenti, quanto allo stile; ma superficiali, o non veri, quanto alle cose" (by certain charming writers whose style is excellent but whose subject matter is superficial or untrue) (3.5; *Del principe* 221; *Prince and Letters* 124–25). He then blames these "scrittori leggiadri" for their indifference to heroism, failure to attend to human spiritual needs, and incomplete development of the notion of man. He writes: "E tutto ciò, perchè si rimirano i nostri con occhi offuscati da un pregiudizio contrario ai passati; e perchè si giudicano dagli effetti che hanno prodotto, non dall'impulso che li movea, e dalla inaudita sublime tempera d'animo, di cui doveano essere dotati, abbenchè con minor utile politico per l'universale degli uomini l'adoprassero" (3.5; 222). (All this is so because we behold our own heroes with eyes dimmed by different standards from those of the past; and because we judge them by the results they have produced, not by the impulse which moved them and the unique sublime frenzies of spirit with which they must have been endowed, though they used it with less political benefit to the majority of men [125].)

The above defense of heroism is crucial, for many Enlightenment writers, including Voltaire, had written against it in the name of social equality and cohesion.[18] Alfieri's repudiation of Enlightenment antiheroism drew on his dissatisfaction with any criticism that evaluated a work solely according to the standards of the present and without reconstructing its context and motives. He qualifies his exhortation to the literary hero in an idiom and lexicon consistent with his description of Dante, the *libero scrittore*: "*È questo impulso, un bollore di cuore e di mente, per cui non si trova mai pace, nè loco; una sete insaziabile di ben fare e di gloria; un reputar sempre nulla il già fatto, e tutto il da farsi, senza però mai dal proposto rimuoversi; una infiammata e risoluta voglia e necessità, o di esser primo far gli ottimi, o di non esser nulla."* (3.6; *Del principe* 225; Alfieri's italics). (*This impulse is a fervour of heart and mind from which there is no peace or respite; it is an unquenchable thirst for noble action and glory; it invariably considers past achievements nothing, the future everything; it never deviates from its goal; it is a passionate relentless desire and necessity to be foremost among the great or nothing at all* [*Prince and Letters* 128].) This description of the burning and resolute desire that compels the *libero scrittore* to bypass present concerns in the name of a reformed future recalls the text's portrait of Dante in 2.3. Alfieri's putative free authors will produce true literature, constitute a small but noble republic of letters, and enter into voluntary exile in order to regain "l'intero esercizio del loro intelletto e della lor penna" (complete use of intellect and pen) (3.8; *Del principe* 233; *Prince and Letters* 138). These are writers of genius not talent, who must move away from their public in order to communicate better with it. Moreover, they are not *gens de lettres*, in the sense of literary persons of broad learning and versatility, but primarily creative writers, whom Alfieri and many others after the French Revolution identified as the type of author most capable of producing high literature.

Alfieri claims in book 3 that writers in the manner of Dante, who are guided by natural and not artificial impulses, will work free from envy and government restraint, and will speak "per loro e per tutti" (for themselves and humanity) (3.8; *Del principe* 235; *Prince and Letters* 140). This tendency to link discussions of a writer's identity with general observations on the human condition corresponds to his rejection of key Enlightenment ideas on human nature. To a *philosophe* like Voltaire, a certain notion of humanity made a sustained interest in the question of the self a moot point. This was due in part to the assumption that an author wrote not as an individual, separate from society and beholden primarily to his own feelings and thoughts for a sense of identity, but rather as a representative of a larger social group that conferred identity upon him from without. One should learn who one was, Voltaire believed, primarily through one's relations with others and not through introspection. The breed of individual best capable of defining himself as the differentiated part of a greater external whole was the *philosophe* or *homme de lettres*, who felt at home in this constructed notion of totality and gave the feeling associated with it a name: *l'humanité*. The *philosophes* did not, in the manner of Descartes, arrive at an understanding of the link between the self and society through abstract, a priori principles. Rather, they promoted the radical concept that the literary practitioner should walk among men and women and observe them from eye level:

Notre *philosophe* ne se croit pas en exil dans ce monde; il ne croit point être en pays ennemi; il veut jouir en sage économe des biens que la nature lui offre; il veut trouver du plaisir avec les autres: & pour en trouver, il en faut faire: ainsi il cherche à convenir à ceux avec qui le hasard ou son choix le font vivre.... Les *philosophes* ordinaires qui méditent trop, ou plûtôt qui méditent mal, le sont envers tous le monde; ils fuient les hommes, & les hommes les évitent. Mais notre *philosophe* qui sait se partager entre la retraite & le commerce des hommes, est plein d'humanité.... [Il] sent qu'il est homme, & que la seule humanité intéresse à la mauvaise ou à la bonne fortune de son voisin.... De cette idée il est aisé de conclure combien le sage des stoïciens est éloigné de la perfection de notre *philosophe:* un tel *philosophe* est homme, & leur sage n'étoit qu'un phantôme. Ils rougissoient de l'humanité, & il en fait gloire. (*Encyclopédie* 12:510)

(Our philosopher does not think that he lives in exile in this world; he does not believe himself to be in enemy territory; he wishes to enjoy as a frugal steward the goods that nature offers him; he wishes to find pleasure in the company of others, and to find pleasure, he has to give pleasure, so that he seeks to adapt himself to those with whom he lives by chance or by choice.... The common run of philosophers who reflect too much, or rather reflect badly, behave in the same manner toward everyone: they flee men, and men avoid them. But our philosopher, who knows how to divide his time between solitude and social intercourse, is full of humanity.... [He] feels that he is human and that humanity itself impels him to take an interest in the good or bad fortune of his neighbor.... From this it is easy to conceive how far removed the impassive sage of the Stoics is from our philosopher: this philosopher is a man while their sage was only a phantom. They were ashamed of their humanity, he takes pride in his.) (*Encyclopedia* 286–89)[19]

The above quotation renders explicit the link between writer and society that authors like Voltaire and Hume elaborated in their memoirs, and also demonstrates how a writer's sense of belonging stems less from any rational process or creative discovery than from a social instinct inherent in human nature.[20] The "plaisir" that this feeling of humanity elicits is one that the *philosophe* experiences through a process of communal integration and identification ("[the *philosophe*] seeks to adapt himself to those with whom he lives by chance or by choice"). The emphasis on sociability and public-mindedness in the *Encyclopédie*'s definition of *l'humanité* is striking:

HUMANITÉ ... c'est un sentiment de bienveillance pour tous les hommes, qui ne s'enflamme guere que dans une ame grande & sensible. Ce noble & sublime enthousiasme se tourmente des peines des autres & du besoin de les soulager; il voudroit parcourir l'univers pour abolir l'esclavage, la superstition, le vice & le malheur. Il nous cache les fautes de nos semblables, ou nous empêche de les sentir. . . . Il ne nous porte pas à nous dégager des chaînes particulieres, il nous rend au contraire meilleurs amis, meilleurs citoyens, meilleurs époux; il se plaît à s'épancher par la bienfaisance sur les êtres que la nature a placés près de nous. (*Encyclopédie* 8:348)

(*Humanity* . . . is a feeling of good will toward all men. Ordinarily only great and sensitive souls are consumed by it. This noble and sublime enthusiasm is tortured by the sufferings of others and tormented by the need to relieve such suffering; it fills men with the desire to traverse the world in order to do away with slavery, superstition, vice, and misfortune. Humanity hides the faults of our fellow men from our eyes or prevents us from sensing them. . . . It does not impel us to break the bonds that tie us to other individuals, but on the contrary turns us into better friends, better citizens, and better spouses; it delights in doing good deeds and thus pours out its benefits over those whom nature has placed next to us.) (*Encyclopedia* 390)

Here, the feeling of humanity does not lead to a process of self-examination or desire for independence but instead to a strengthening of the ties that bind. In theory, this sentiment of humanity gave the *philosophes* that rare historical phenomenon: a mutually beneficial relationship between intellectual activity and community life. Alfieri used his reading of Dante to challenge this high-Enlightenment notion of human nature and the barriers it erected between a writer and the possibilities that literature held for the exploration of the self.

A philanthropic instinct of humanity cannot endure in the mind of Alfieri's *libero scrittore*, for he proposes that society threatens creativity and expression. Implicit, however, in the antagonistic relationship Alfieri sets up between the writer and society is the idea that a new version of human nature must issue from the free writer's pen. He reformulates the traditional Enlightenment ideal of humanity along the following lines. First, he challenges the belief that men and women are perfectible and capable of progress. Second, he argues that human nature is a historical process and not a metaphysical category. Third, he counters the cosmopolitanism of the *philosophes* with an ethics of exile. Last, he contends that times of supposed darkness and backwardness, such as the Middle Ages of Dante, actually represent enviable periods of faith and power. The following sonnet, one of two addressed by Alfieri to Dante in 1783, epitomizes his anti-Enlightenment bias:

> O grande padre Alighier, se dal ciel miri
> Me tuo discepol non indegno starmi,
> Dal cor traendo profondi sospiri,
> Prostrato innanzi a' tuoi funerei marmi;
> Piacciati, deh! propizio ai be' desiri,
> D'un raggio di tua luce illuminarmi.

> Uom, che a primiera eterna gloria aspiri,
> Contro invidia e viltà de' stringer le armi?
>   — Figlio, i' le strinsi, e assai men duol; ch'io diedi
> Nome in tal guisa a gente tanto bassa,
> Da non pur calpestarsi co' miei piedi.
>   Se in me fidi, il tuo sguardo a che si abbassa?
> Va, tuona, vinci: e, se fra' piè ti vedi
> Costor, senza mirar, sovr'essi passa.[21]

(O great father Alighieri, if you look down from the heavens, do not disdain me, your disciple, who draws deep sighs from his heart as he lies by your marble tombstone. If it pleases you to satisfy my great desire, illuminate me with a ray of your light. Does the man who would aspire to eternal glory need to battle jealousy and cowardice? "Son," [Dante answered], "I waged that kind of war, and greatly did I suffer for it. For I gave a name to people so low that they were not even worthy of trodding beneath my feet. If you trust in me, then at what are you lowering your gaze? Go, roar, and conquer; and, should you stumble upon such people, walk over them without a glance.")

Alfieri composed this poem after a visit to Dante's tomb that he later described in terms of a religious experience.[22] But any reflective pause he may have experienced at the grave becomes in sonnet 53 the righteous anger he claims is required of the *libero scrittore*. The poem's paternal images reveal his genetic identification with Dante ("O grande padre Alighier" in line 1 and "figlio" in line 9); and the word *discepol* in the second verse suggests Alfieri's devotion if not worship of the medieval poet. The opening lines also show Alfieri's habit of substituting the Enlightenment image of the light of truth with a flash of inspiration or genius ("d'un raggio di tua luce illuminarmi") (6). In a carefully staged dialogue between a belated pilgrim-poet (Alfieri) and the prototypical one (Dante), the funereal meeting ponders what the poet is to do in a world that has no use for him nor he for it. The sense of solitude in the sonnet is complete: rays of light from an illustrious predecessor poet may penetrate Alfieri's mind but no human presence will. The free writer Alfieri has become — in 1783 we are five years into his voluntary exile — has deepened his conviction that the path to glory must pass through a misanthropy that he unfairly attributes to Dante. By 1783, Alfieri has also decided that any feeling of humanity should express an intractable disgust with a world that only literature can redeem. Writing, subsequently, became for him an act of protest that sought more the respect of the dead than the approval of the living.[23]

Alfieri's proclivity to attribute misanthropy to Dante resulted from his exaggerated emphasis on the traits of pride and disdain that biographers and commentators typically have ascribed to the poet.[24] The *vite* of Dante followed two main lines of exposition: one poetic or legendary, in the manner of Boccaccio's *vita* of Dante; the other historical, in the style of Bruni's biography of the poet (1436). Alfieri owned commentaries on the *Commedia* that included both a poetic (Landino; 1481) and a historical (Vellutello; 1544) life of Dante. Each of these commentaries does allude to the prideful and disdainful aspects of Dante's character; nowhere, however, either in Dante's own writings or in the biographical works on him, is there the rage toward humanity that surfaces in Alfieri's representation of the medieval poet.

Alfieri's choice of Dante as the writer most capable of redefining the shape of humanity led to the period of his most intense identification with Dante. During this time, Alfieri produced his *Vita*, one of the earliest autobiographies in European literature to narrate the process by which an individual divests himself of all worldly ties in the name of his literary vocation. Although Alfieri did not begin to write his life story until 1790, this text splits his career into two halves: one in which he produced literary art (1772–90); and another in which he anthologized, edited, translated, and published it (1790–1803). If social decorum prevented a writer like Hume from introspective autobiography—and an Olympian sense of irony produced a similar restraint in Voltaire—Alfieri's introduction to the *Vita* conveys his desire to immerse himself in the literary self-representation that intermittently occupied the last fourteen years of his life and that led to observations like the following: "Il parlare, e molto più lo scrivere di sé stesso, nasce senza alcun dubbio dal molto amar di sé stesso.... Ed è questo dono una preziosissima cosa; poiché da esso ogni alto operare dell'uomo proviene, allor quando all'amor di sé stesso congiunge una ragionata cognizione dei propri suoi mezzi, ed un illuminato trasporto pel vero ed il bello, che non son se non uno" (introduction; *Vita* 3). (Self-love is unquestionably the chief motive which leads anyone to speak, and more especially to write respecting himself.... This precious gift is the principal motive of all the great actions of man, when he unites to a knowledge of his own powers an enlightened enthusiasm for the sublime and beautiful, which are in fact only one and the same thing [*Memoirs* 1].) It is useful to situate Alfieri's positive appraisal of unbounded, demiurgic enthusiasm (which he discerned in writers like Dante) within the larger context of the transition from Enlightenment to Romantic conceptions of poetic inspiration. Drawing on authors including Voltaire and Diderot, the anti-Dantist Bettinelli provided Italians with a monograph on the subject with *L'entusiasmo delle belle arti* (Enthusiasm in the fine arts; 1769), which critiqued the rationalist *style géométrique* associated with Descartes and promoted the importance of energy and personal experience in the creation of enduring artistic works. Bettinelli, however, never dissociated the effects of enthusiasm and poetic inspiration from good taste. He believed that imagination and taste enforced each another and worked in unison to create his treasured arcadian poetry. Later, in his attacks on Alfieri's tragedies, Bettinelli shrewdly indicated that the *entusiasmo* that pervades Alfieri's works had little to do with Bettinelli's own belletristic version.[25] Alfieri removed altogether the creative aspects of poetic enthusiasm from the compass of taste. He argued that writers on the order of Dante transcended existing norms of aesthetic evaluation and appreciation through the culturally disruptive yet morally productive agency of the creative act, which Alfieri understood to be the originary and violent space wherein the self was forged.

In the *Vita,* Alfieri drew on his reading of Dante to transplant the *libero scrittore* from *Del principe e delle lettere* onto his own life. He began the *Vita* in Paris in 1790, where he was witnessing the aftermath of a revolution he increasingly reviled.[26] In 1786, Alfieri chose to move to Paris to follow Louisa of Stolberg, who had been living in the French capital after finally succeeding in her attempt to divorce Stuart. For all its promise of personal and political freedom, France represented the antithesis of Alfieri's core beliefs. The same French artifice, sophistication, and elegance that Voltaire hoped would permeate all aspects of European creative and social life appalled Alfieri. Moreover, his avowedly aristocratic sympathies and cult of tradition reminiscent of his contemporary Edmund Burke made the postrevolutionary chaos synonymous in his mind with a world gone mad. If Voltaire conceived of his literary pursuits through metaphors of gardening ("il faut cultiver notre jardin"), Alfieri chose for his *Vita* images of turbulent seas, wild forests, and icy northern plains. Above all, the figures of speech he preferred were those related to horses and riding. Since real life provided infrequent opportunities to display his bravery, his autobiography often unwittingly assumes the form of a mock epic, with Vittorio racing to and from lovers' homes on a charging horse like a warrior or sentry who has gone ahead to warn troops of approaching danger.[27]

In the *Vita,* Alfieri's perennial obsession with originality fueled his critique of the Enlightenment model of the self and its belief in a general, abstract human nature.[28] Like so much else in the *Vita,* Alfieri's sentiments lie more with Vico's notion of the deterministic nature of historical and sociocultural context than with the metaphysical notion of tabula rasa that Voltaire popularized in his writings on Locke.[29] Alfieri's childhood is, by and large, one of ignorance and stagnation. He describes himself as "selvatichetto" (a little savage) and claims that, while young, he was a stranger to all forms of learning. Early chapters bear the titles "Continuazione di quei non-studi" (Continuation of those nonstudies) and "Primi studi, pedanteschi, e mal fatti" (First studies, pedantic and poorly done) and depict scenes in terms of the author's inability to compose poetry or respond with sensitivity to art. The early cultural and intellectual poverty forms a vivid contrast to the radical change that occurs when Alfieri actually does dedicate himself to writing, which occurs in 1772 after years of anomic wandering. Henceforth, the mock heroism of his travels cedes to the militant engagement of the man of letters, a fragile pursuit of glory that he embarks upon after careful consideration of the relationship between French and Italian literary history. As we have seen, before beginning *Del principe e delle lettere* in 1778, Alfieri banned himself from speaking French and set about the arduous task of learning Dante's Tuscan. His study of the Italian language involved immersing himself in its most illustrious practitioners: Dante, Petrarch, Ariosto, and Tasso. Beginning in the fourth book, his allusions to these writers increase. He decides to become a tragedian after he reviews the Italian literary tradition and realizes that it lacks a great playwright: "Questi quattro nostri poeti, erano allora, e sono, e sempre saranno i miei primi, e direi anche soli, di questa bellissima lingua italiana: e sempre mi è sembrato che in essi quattro vi sia tutto quello che umanamente può dare la poesia; meno però il meccanismo del verso sciolto di dialogo, il quale si dee però trarre della pasta di questi quattro, fattone un tutto, e maneggiatolo in nuova maniera" (4.10; 228). (These four poets [Dante, Petrarch, Ariosto, and Tasso] have always been, and will continue to be, prized by me above all others in our divine language. It appears to me that they afford a model of every species of poetry except blank-verse dialogue which itself must be produced from the basic material of all four of them, blended and modified [217].) Alfieri himself, presumably, would be the one to gather Dante, Petrarch, Ariosto, and Tasso into a single form and then add drama and the art of dialogue to this synthesis. By his own account, the process of incorporating the four *maestri* into his work — and learning from their failures as well as their successes — was a rare thread of continuity in a life of great personal and artistic vicissitudes.[30]

Of these four models, Alfieri first eschews Ariosto and Tasso as courtly writers that were too beholden to the whims of their patrons to be free and fierce (*Del principe* 3.2). Petrarch was also protected by a prince; his greatness, subsequently, was limited (*Del principe* 3.2). The only writer who entirely satisfies Alfieri's demands is the one to whom he refers as *Poeta,* Dante.[31] In this same section of *Del principe e delle lettere,* Alfieri asks if it is possible for a nation to produce two Dantes. Such a phenomenon, he argues, would result in all the greatness a literary culture needed. The *Vita,* in essence, answers this question by proposing Alfieri himself as a kind of second Dante, a sentiment, as we see below, anticipated in the earlier *Del principe e delle lettere:*

> E di Dante mi sono prevaluto per prova, perchè io molto lo leggo, e mi pare di sentirlo, e d'intenderlo: di Omero, di Sofocle, o di altri simili massimi e indipendenti scrittori mi sarei pure prevaluto per prova, se nella loro divina lingua mi fosse dato di leggerli. Ma in Dante solo mi pare d'aver io bastantemente ritrovata la irrefutabile dimostrazione del mio assioma; poichè Dante senza protezione veruna ha scritto, ed è sommo, e sussiste, e sempre sussisterà: ma nessuna protezione ha mai fatto, nè vorrebbe, nè potrebbe far nascere un Dante. Potrebbe la protezion principesca bensì, dove un tanto uomo nascesse, impedirlo; pur troppo! (3.2; 207)

> (And I have used Dante as an example because I read him often and I think I have a feeling for him and understand him. I should have availed myself of Homer, Sophocles, and other similar great independent authors as examples if it were within my power to read them in their own divine language. But in Dante alone I seem to have found sufficiently irrefutable proof of my axiom: because Dante wrote with no patronage and is unsurpassable, survives, and will always survive: but no protection ever has produced or could or would produce a Dante. If such a great man chanced to be born, princely patronage could indeed, alas, stifle him.) (109)

The definitive sign of Dante's presence in Alfieri's notion of the self lies in his evocation of how a feeling and understanding for an author ("mi pare di sentirlo, e d'intenderlo") can nourish a sense of personal identity. Here, in the incessant battle that Alfieri understood writing to be, he momentarily surrenders the anger in his pen for a tranquil moment of identification with an illustrious predecessor.

The same year in which he commenced the *Vita*, Alfieri also began a work, the *tramelogedia* entitled *Ugolino*, in which Dante's influence would have been at its most explicit; but, not incidentally, this theatrical adaptation of *Inferno* 32–33 never made it past the outline stage. By his own account, the *Vita* was intended as a postmortem to his career as writer. It is no surprise, therefore, that Alfieri decided to abort the *Ugolino*, the last text in which he composed an original tragic verse. Though never realized, the Ugolino-adaptation manqué suggests much about the question of literary self-representation in Alfieri's age and Dante's place in it. In 1790, to thematize and re-create in prose one's own life in the manner of Alfieri was neither accepted nor common; hence the myriad of qualifications and self-accusations that fill the *Vita*. It was also unusual to base, as Alfieri partly did, one's identity on Dante. This fact helps to explain why Dante's presence in the *Vita* is at once so diffuse and so hidden — and why Alfieri abandoned his *Ugolino* at the very point where he began a life story in which Dante figured so prominently. In all likelihood, a completed

Ugolino would have rendered official Alfieri's choice of Dante as model of the self in the *Vita,* a result that an autobiographer as concerned with originality as Alfieri could never have desired. In this last period of his life, he no longer wrote tragedies but devoted his energies to constructing an elaborate portrait of himself as Italy's premier tragedian and its self-proclaimed heir to the tradition of modern Italian letters beginning with Dante. The literary lion had reached his autobiographical winter.

Alfieri's Romantic successors, especially his poetic disciple the young Foscolo, continued to ask both of books and themselves questions similar to the ones Alfieri posed. Unlike Alfieri, however, these authors were not so confrontational in their fusion of Dante and autobiography, for the steady institutionalization of the relationship between Dante criticism and literary self-representation made such polemics unnecessary. Indeed, Dante's presence in the burgeoning autobiographical genre of the Romantic age became something of a rite of passage. Viewed from this perspective, Alfieri's elusive heroism derives in part from the following fact: he was among the first to allot to Dante a significant place in his autobiography at a time when many authors regarded with suspicion both Dante and introspective autobiographical writing. By translating Dante into an iconoclastic poet-hero, Alfieri neglected the medieval Christian poet's spiritual concerns and devotion to political empire. But it was Alfieri's talent to live and write so emphatically that the sheer force of his convictions, whether accurate or not, could sweep both himself and his readers toward some erstwhile *glorïoso porto,* where the self never escapes the shadows cast by literary history.

6

Wordsworth, Dante, and British Romantic Identity

Among the stacks of documents in the Wordsworth archive there lies a diary belonging to the poet's son-in-law, Edward Quillinan, who writes soon after his wife's death: "My Beloved Dora breathed her last at one o'clock a.m. — less five minutes by the stairclock at Rydal Mount. — *Io dico che l'anima sua nobi[l]issima si partì nella prima ora del nono giorno del mese. Dante. Vita Nuova. Beatrice.*"[1] Though unlikely to be published, these words attest to one of the more dramatic phenomena in modern literary history. Less than one hundred years after Voltaire had proclaimed Dante's obituary, his work had spread widely enough to articulate the thoughts of a grieving husband only indirectly connected to the literary scene. More than in other European countries, in England, where the medieval poet's influence rivaled his impact in Italy, the *Commedia* especially flourished.[2] In the quest of autobiographers to become, in G. W. F. Hegel's words, "true artists of themselves," the turn to Dante became an English literary rite of passage.[3] In 1818, Peacock's fictional Mr. Listless satirized the mix of study and posturing that constituted this cult: "I don't know how it is, but Dante never came in my way till lately. I never had him in my collection, and, if I had had him I should not have read him. But I find he is growing fashionable, and I am afraid I must read him some wet morning."[4]

Just one year after Stendhal proclaimed Dante the "poète romantique par excellence," however, Wordsworth issued his own untimely opinion on the *Commedia,* which has become symbolic of his characteristic antipathy for any literary trend: "It has become lately—owing a good deal, I believe, to the example of [A. W.] Schlegel—the fashion to extol him [Dante] beyond measure. I have not read him for many years; his style I used to think admirable for conciseness and vigour, without abruptness; but I own that his fictions often struck me as offensively grotesque and fantastic, and I felt the Poem [the *Commedia*] tedious from various causes."[5] In reality, when Wordsworth lashed out against Dante, he was responding not to the *Commedia* but to a politically charged, autobiographical version of Dante circulating in early nineteenth-century England.[6] Most writers of this era, especially the so-called second-generation Romantics (including Byron, Shelley, Keats, and lesser-known contemporaries like Leigh Hunt) viewed Dante as the literary-historical embodiment of the radical and extroverted poet-hero. Those who favored such a reading, particularly Shelley, often combined their praise for the heroic, republican image of Dante with attacks on what they took to be the introspective, divided, and conservative Wordsworthian self. Though not so overtly political in their readings of Dante, other writers, including Coleridge and William Hazlitt, also used their Dante criticism to censure what they found disagreeable in Wordsworth's subjectivity. In reaction to these direct and indirect polemics, Wordsworth pronounced harshly on the *Commedia* because of the text's associations with radical politics, German metaphysics, and the literary extravaganzas of his younger contemporaries. Beneath the surface of Wordsworth's professed anti-Dantism lie profound formal and thematic sympathies that link his *Prelude* to the *Commedia*—sympathies that make the persona of Wordsworth himself one of the closest, of all the major Romantic literary self-representations, to the spirit and scope of Dante.

Wordsworth probably first encountered Dante while he was an undergraduate at Cambridge in 1787–91. Though much has been made of the poet's uneven academic career, he did distinguish himself in one subject: "My Italian master was named Isola, and had been well acquainted with Gray the poet. As I took to these studies with much interest, he was proud of the progress I made. Under his correction I translated [Addison's] the *Vision of Mirza,* and two or three other papers of the *Spectator,* into Italian."[7] It may seem bizarre that the cash-starved young Wordsworth ("I was disturbed at times by prudent thoughts, / . . . About my future worldly maintenance") would pursue a subject that provided little promise for future employment and served mainly to prepare young aristocrats for the Grand Tour (*Prel.* 3.77, 79).[8] Wordsworth, however, was no typical student, and Cambridge had no usual program.[9] The university employed one of the most eminent Italianists in England, the aforementioned Agostino Isola, an associate of Samuel Johnson's and Oliver Goldsmith's and the rare teacher at Cambridge who managed to stimulate Wordsworth.[10] Isola edited Tasso's *Gerusalemme liberata* (Jerusalem delivered) in 1786 and Ariosto's *Orlando furioso* (Orlando enraged) in 1789, and was appointed to his post by his friend Thomas Gray, whose "Elegy" he translated into Italian. Gray was Wordsworth's favorite eighteenth-century poet, and it cannot have escaped the student-poet that, along with Milton, he was also an accomplished Italianist.[11] Though Gray's Italian studies are not well known, his predecessor Milton's represent an acknowledged component of his literary formation. For a young writer as conscious of his relation to literary history as Wordsworth, it was logical enough to study the language and literary traditions that had appealed to these two important models.

Though Wordsworth makes no specific mention of Dante at Cambridge, his immersion in the Italian canon would have made such an encounter likely. Any reticence of his toward Dante had much to do with the age's prevailing arcadian and Augustan academic tastes, which were generally critical of the *Commedia*.[12] Wordsworth actively defended Dante after Cambridge: "There is a mistake in the world concerning the Italian language; the Poetry of Dante and Michael Angelo proves, that if there be little majesty and strength in Italian verse, the fault is in the Authors and not in the tongue."[13] In *The Convention of Cintra* (1809), he quoted Dante's inscription over the gates of hell in a manner that suggests familiarity with the *Commedia*.[14] Thus, beginning most likely in 1787 and continuing to about 1809, Wordsworth read and commented on Dante with regularity; however, contrary to what some scholarship has argued, during these years he never directly alluded to Dante in his poetry.[15]

The young Wordsworth shared with the young Dante the desire to find a literary language capable of reaching the general public as well as the learned. Dante's vernacular defense in *De vulgari eloquentia*, his decision to write the *Commedia* in Tuscan instead of Latin, and Wordsworth's plea, in "Preface to *Lyrical Ballads*," for a post-Augustan "language really used by men," are defining moments in the perennial struggle to render poetic diction attuned to everyday experience. One of the few critics who intuited the affinities between the two poets, Robert Morehead, remarks in an unusual essay from 1818 in the *Edinburgh Review*:

> The modern school, with Mr Wordsworth at its head, has a contempt for the established language of poetry; and he, it is well known, even goes so far as to propose the adoption of a low and familiar diction, approaching to the language of a vulgar prose. Now Dante seems to have apprehended all that was

> just and sound in this idea, and to have, moreover, perceived what Mr Wordsworth has not, the precise bounds and limits to which it ought to be carried. No diction can be more familiar, more the language of conversation, more taken out of the unnatural forms of a false poetic elevation, than his, yet none can be less vulgar, less childish, more constantly bearing the impression, and reflecting the images of a powerful, unwavering, and highly cultivated mind.[16]

However negative the comparative assessment of Wordsworth, Morehead's words capture the common desire in both poets to challenge existing paradigms of diction in the name of a more culturally engaged poetic idiom. In their drive toward this experiential vernacular, two major early works of both poets — Dante's *Vita nuova* and Wordsworth's "Tintern Abbey" — inscribed the act of poetic composition within a reflective poetics predicated upon the retrospective translation of memory into linguistically accessible poetic images.[17]

The thematic horizon of "Tintern Abbey" provides clues as to why, despite Wordsworth's initial sympathy for Dante's work, most English writers resembled Morehead in attacking the Wordsworthian self in the same motion that they praised the poet and protagonist of the *Commedia*. To study "Tintern Abbey" in depth is to confront an unsettling fact: the more one reads, the less one knows about the protagonist who inhabits the text. Wordsworth deftly articulates the challenges presented by this type of poem in the notes to his "Intimations Ode": "Archimedes said that he could move the world if he had a point whereon to rest his machine. Who has not felt the same aspirations as regards the world of his own mind?" (*Prose* 3:195). The quest for an Archimedean point inspired him in "Tintern Abbey" to conceive a frustrating solution: one can construct a notion of the self even though it contains contradictory and mutually irreconcilable registers of experience. The opening lines of the poem give the impression not so much of introspection but of a kind of sinking or implosion. The repetitions (five years, five summers, five long winters, beheld before and again) blur the contours of the present tense in which the poet speaks. Similarly, the layering of past physical spaces upon present and future ones confuses the specificity of the spot by the Wye River where the narrator stands. Rather than any genius loci, we confront a genius of displacement. The narrative voice comes across as sluggish and opaque, submerged in its own "thoughts of a more deep seclusion" (7).[18] One cannot be sure from what or whom the narrator retreats: nature, himself, industrial encroachment, perhaps memories of France and its revolution.[19] The verses that follow contain a series of references to registers of personal experience to which only the poet has access; thoughts of nature pass into his "purer mind," leading to feelings of "little, nameless, unremembered acts / Of kindness and of love" (30, 35–36). "Tintern Abbey" certainly is a poem about someone, but it does not appear that the author intends for the reader to know just whom.

This opacity has confounded and even infuriated its audiences for some time now, but I believe it would be wrong to think of the narrative voice as somehow cagey or deceptive. This would imply that Wordsworth cared enough about the responses of his readers to wish to confuse or mislead them. To say this would be to ignore the plodding, almost tranquil feeling of self-enclosure of the poem, especially its early verses. In some sense, the poet's indifference to the reader *is* the poem, and the inaccessibility of the narrative presence should be read less as an obstacle and more as the poem's mode. In an earlier visit to the setting of "Tintern Abbey," the narrator would run more like a man fleeing what he dreads than heading toward the thing he loved. Within the poem's economy of information and images, one can only guess at what this means. It is clear, however, that this earlier period of the poet's life needed no poetry, no "remoter charm" to capture its essence; it resisted representation ("I cannot paint / What then I was") (76–77). In remembering this former self, writing poetry for Wordsworth becomes its own reward or wage, almost an emotional surplus value ("abundant recompence") (89). For what, we cannot be sure. It is difficult to accept Wordsworth's own version of the story, that it has to do with a temporal dialectic between youth and maturity. In other words, the mature Wordsworth narrating "Tintern Abbey" may have lost an earlier, unconscious connection to nature, but in its place he can now see how those effortless feelings that once bound him to the landscape have come to represent a deeper set of emotions, intuitions, and sentiments that connect him to all people and places. Such a reading makes Wordsworth into something he only officially became toward the end of his life, when it may have cost him his talent: a moralist and teacher. It appears that the recompense results from something far more ambiguous and idiosyncratic. The pleasure Wordsworth derived from writing about his own life is a good place to begin to approach this willful ambiguity.[20]

Wordsworth uses the word *pleasure* in the "Preface to the *Lyrical Ballads*" to distinguish the poet from the common run of people. He is a man among men, but he gets a more profound joy from his perceptions than others because of the nature and degree in which he experiences things. This makes the poet an eternal outsider, for he receives pleasure not just from partaking of the joyous but also at times in witnessing the painful. This pleasure is also why "Tintern Abbey," which begins in so ponderous and disjunctive a manner, appears to become conscious of its own "glad animal movements" as a poem and hit its perfect stride in the following passage:

> And I have felt
> A presence that disturbs me with the joy
> Of elevated thoughts; a sense sublime

> Of something far more deeply interfused,
> Whose dwelling is the light of setting suns,
> And the round ocean, and the living air,
> And the blue sky, and in the mind of man,
> A motion and a spirit, that impels
> All thinking things, all objects of all thought,
> And rolls through all things. (94–103)

Moral or epistemological points are made throughout the poem (for example, "These forms of beauty have not been to me / As is a landscape to a blind man's eye"; and "For I have learned / To look on nature, not as in the hour / Of thoughtless youth") (24–25; 89–91). But the energy of the poem, its "dizzy rapture," so to speak, suffuses the lateral shuffling from one state of consciousness or group of memories to the next. One gets the feeling that any recompense of an artistic, moral, or philosophical type that Wordsworth's memories may bring are beside the point. The real story lies in the process of evocation itself, and the palpable atmosphere of expressive joy it creates.[21] The poet's various remembered states in themselves are disconnected and inscrutable; within the poem, however, they are almost unbearably deep with resonance, at one point so intoxicating as nearly to paralyze the poet's consciousness, lay it to sleep.

This version of the Wordsworthian self was bound to offend people then, and it still does now. Perhaps most famously, Keats claimed that Wordsworth represented the egotistical sublime, and many later critics have taken these buzzwords as keys of interpretive entry. According to Hazlitt, Wordsworth saw only himself and the universe; Shelley wrote that Wordsworth had forsaken the voice of truth and liberty for the impoverished world of the self; and Byron unceasingly lampooned Wordsworth's nature-centric interiority. The above writers wanted a model of the self that was coherent, engaged with the world, and that sought its "abundant recompense" in the cultural, political, and social arenas. For paradoxical reasons, the anti-Wordsworthians chose Dante as their privileged model of the self.

A typical reading of Dante that reveals two characteristics of the debates over the *Commedia* in Romantic England — its anti-Wordsworthian scope and use of the German Romantic lexicon — is Hazlitt's "Lectures on the English Poets" (1818).[22] The profound disappointment Hazlitt felt after the early promise of Wordsworth's poetry is well known. "He who was more than man, with [Wordsworth] was none" (CW 5:163), Hazlitt writes, and in his ensuing description it becomes clear that, in Hazlitt's eyes, Wordsworth himself was a victim of his own "leveling muse." The image of Wordsworth he evokes is of a man trapped and confounded by his own intentions, too distracted by the sublimity of a daisy and pathos of a withered thorn to notice the world around him.[23]

Much of the anti-Wordsworthian strain in Hazlitt's reading of Dante drew life and direction from the "dreary" (the term is Wordsworth's) thought of the Schlegels. As early as his review in 1815 of Jean Charles Léonard de Sismondi's influential *Littérature du midi de l'Europe* (Literature of the south of Europe; 1813), Hazlitt followed the Jena school in classifying Dante as "the first lasting monument of modern genius" and "the origin of modern literature" (*CW* 16:40). Hazlitt had, in fact, reviewed A. W. Schlegel's seminal *Lectures on Dramatic Literature* in its English translation (1815); along with Coleridge, he was one of the few people living in England who immediately grasped their significance. Like most English writers, Hazlitt accepted Schlegel's depiction of Dante as the artist who linked the ancient and modern worlds; he even praised Dante's "modern genius" for those same traits that Wordsworth later implicitly condemned:

> His [Dante's] genius is not a sparkling flame, but the sullen heat of a furnace. He is power, passion, self-will personified. In all that relates to the descriptive or fanciful part of poetry, he bears no comparison to many who had gone before, or who have come after him; but there is a gloomy abstraction in his conceptions, which lies like a dead weight upon the mind; a benumbing stupor, a breathless awe, from the intensity of the impression; a terrible obscurity, like that which oppresses us in dreams; an identity of interest, which moulds every object to its own purposes, and clothes all things with the persons and imaginations of the human soul,—that makes amends for all other deficiencies. (*CW* 5:17)

The correlation that Hazlitt establishes between the figure of Dante and his poem—the "identity of interest" of authorial consciousness that "moulds every object to its own purposes"—draws on what was by the time of his lecture a critical commonplace beholden primarily to the Schlegels and Schiller. According to Schiller, the belated or modern artist lacks the effortless reciprocity between self and community that made the ancient writer's work capable of mirroring an external reality that was, according to this Hellenistic myth, intrinsically beautiful and meaningful. The modern artist, therefore, loses the world but gains himself in the purchase. In the ensuing self-consciousness, the identity is no longer between artist and world but between artist and art—a view echoed in Hazlitt's portrait of Dante: "The immediate objects he [Dante] presents to the mind are not much in themselves, they want grandeur, beauty, and order; but they become every thing by the force of the character he impresses upon them" (*CW* 5:17). In Hazlitt's reading, "modern" artists—who also went by the aliases "sentimental" or "Romantic"—necessarily invested and invented themselves in their work, to compensate privately for what they lost on a public scale. Dante, the "father of modern poetry," could no longer write as Homer did in his world of inherent "grandeur, beauty, and order" (*CW* 5:17). For Hazlitt, as for the Germans before him, Dante represented the privileged genealogical point at which moderns stopped mirroring the world and began to mirror themselves.

This version of the Dantesque self and its roots in German Romantic thinking received their most striking endorsement in Coleridge's lectures on the *Commedia* in 1818. Coleridge was probably the person most responsible for spreading Dante's fame in England, because he publicly praised Cary's translation of the *Commedia* and thereby stimulated the widespread demand for this Miltonic blank-verse rendering of Dante. Unlike most of his contemporaries, Coleridge's reading was shaded by conservative preconceptions. He believed that Dante's "intense democratical partizanship" contributed to his "comparative failure" in the combination of poetry and doctrine.[24] Whereas his political insights are personal, the critical ones are German, for the following observation derives almost verbatim from Schelling: "For Dante was the living link between religion and philosophy; he philosophized the religion and christianized the philosophy of Italy; and in this poetic union of religion and philosophy, he became the ground of transition into the mixed Platonism and Aristotelianism of the Schools" (441).[25] Taking Schelling's cue, Coleridge makes a strong claim for the primacy of the aesthetic over the philosophical and theological modes. The "poetic union" of philosophy and religion — not their specific rational or spiritual aspects — allowed Dante's dialectic between the real (Aristotelian) and ideal (Platonic) worlds to reform religious and intellectual life in the Middle Ages. This was possible because of the agency and personality of Dante himself, who Coleridge claims became a "living link" between secular and divine concerns.[26]

Schelling and German idealism are most present in the following remarks, which recall the poetry of Wordsworth as only Coleridge could: "Hence resulted two great effects; a combination of poetry with doctrine, and, *by turning the mind inward on its own essence* instead of letting it act only on its outward circumstances and communities, a combination of poetry with sentiment. And it is this inwardness or subjectivity, which principally and most fundamentally distinguishes all the classic from all the modern poetry" (442; my emphasis). In *Prelude* 3, Wordsworth describes his desire to separate himself from his peers and the often "injurious sway of place / Or circumstance" of his difficult time at Cambridge (102–3). The solace he finds in such "universal things" as "the common countenance of earth and sky" leads him to an act "of turning the mind in upon herself" (109–10, 116). The image is unforgettable and signatory, and it is possible that Coleridge, one of the few to have read the text before its posthumous publication in 1850, recalled it when he described modern poetry in terms of the mind's tendency to turn inward upon its own essence.

Another writer whose reading of Dante affected his understanding of Wordsworth was Shelley, arguably the finest Dantist of the age.[27] Though it may seem unusual to discuss Shelley's reading of Dante in light of his views on Wordsworth, doing so gives an idea of the deeply dialogic nature of English literary culture during the war of ideas that ensued after the defeat of Napoleon at Waterloo.[28] Shelley's lament "To Wordsworth" (1815) became one of the most celebrated documents in the ongoing indictment of the so-called later Wordsworth. Once the voice of "truth and liberty," Shelley writes, Wordsworth has left his former admirers, who now mourn the loss of their hero's integrity.[29] Shelley's activities in radical London in the period before his departure to Italy in 1818 made this opinion of Wordsworth's conservatism a matter of course. Less likely, however, is the fact that years later Shelley used another text, his acclaimed *A Defence of Poetry* (1821), to continue some of the lines of argument that "To Wordsworth" had opened.

In the *Defence*, Shelley begins his discussion of Dante with the following declaration: "The abolition of personal slavery is the basis of the highest political hope that it can enter into the mind of man to conceive."[30] When a group of those subjugated, women, became free, the poetry of sexual love ensued, a turn of events that transformed love into a religion, the high priests of which were poets. Simultaneously priests and preceptors in Shelley's imaginary polity, poets create this communal rapture by raising people from the "dull vapours of self" through their art. Dante, for Shelley, was one of these unacknowledged legislators of the world: "Dante understood the secret things of love even more than Petrarch. His *Vita Nuova* is an inexhaustible fountain of purity of sentiment and language: it is the idealized history of that period, and those intervals of his life which were dedicated to love" (*Defence* 497). It is plausible that, writing about Dante in 1821, Shelley also had Wordsworth in mind when he described this impoverished world of the self in terms of "dull vapours." Wordsworth was by nature incapable of acceding to Shelley's extroverted lyricism, and could never sympathize with a model of self whose character was demiurgic and whose interests were predominantly public. Shelley's notion of the activist and public-minded poet found perfect expression in his reading of Dante, whose poetry becomes a "bridge thrown over the stream of time, which unites the modern and an[c]ient world" (498).[31] Further stressing Dante's historical importance, Shelley describes him as a proto-Miltonic "Lucifer of [the] starry flock," who brought light to "benighted" thirteenth-century republican Italy (499–500).

Taken as a whole, the writings on Dante that began in Jena and made their way into English literary circles between 1810 and 1830 amounted to a cult that Shelley's interlocutor in the *Defence*, Peacock, gleefully satirized.[32] Wordsworth's reaction to this turn of events was perhaps predictable, but the form it took was unusual: he chose to ignore Dante at the pinnacle of the medieval poet's popularity, a pointed act of indifference that says as much about the literary and political culture he inhabited as his actual thoughts on Dante. His statements regarding the Italian literary tradition dropped off dramatically after 1810: he published no translations of Italian writers during this time and did not make a single extant allusion to the writings of Dante between 1810 and 1830. This is striking, given his engagement with Dante and Italian letters in the preceding decades. Part of Wordsworth's silence had to do with his reaction to political events in England during the early 1800s. A revival of the Italian cause led to renewed interest in Dante in the radical circles that pervaded English intellectual life during the years of domestic crisis after the Napoleonic Wars ended in 1815.[33] Works like Sismondi's multivolume *Histoire des républiques italiennes du moyen âge* (History of the Italian republics in the Middle Ages; 1807–18), reviewed by Hazlitt for the *Edinburgh Review* in 1815, made it clear in many English minds that the Italian cause was also a British one. Like Risorgimentalist Italy, England increasingly struggled to define its sense of national identity against that of France.[34] As part of their conflict with France, many English intellectuals promoted Italian traditions as preferable alternatives to French high culture and its neoclassical hegemony dating back to the Enlightenment and, before that, the *grand siècle* of Corneille, Molière, Racine, and others. Many young radical writers identified medieval and Renaissance Italian arts and letters as the preferred historical model for English culture and, simultaneously, argued that French paradigms were anathema to the spirit of English thought.[35]

Beginning with Napoleon's ceding of northern Italian territories to Austria with the Treaty of Campoformio in 1797, Italy's regions were perennial pawns in the chessboard of post–French Revolution European politics.[36] Wordsworth, on the whole, was sensitive to the Italian struggle and believed that England had a moral obligation to protect its weaker ally. However, he did not follow others in naming Dante as the foremost Italian patriot.[37] Rather, by way of exhortation at the conclusion of *The Convention of Cintra*, he quoted Petrarch to inspire Britain to recover the sense of moral leadership it had compromised by treating Spain unjustly. Wordsworth celebrated Wellington's victory at Waterloo as eminently "English" and expected that it would finally bring the domestic stability to England that first the French and then the Napoleonic revolutions had upset. A good gauge of just how disappointed Wordsworth's political expectations were after Wellington's victory—and how abhorrent he found the radical branches of postrevolutionary democracy — was his disapproval of the proletarian uprisings in Manchester that led to the massacre of Peterloo in 1819.[38]

Once one has read a poem such as "Michael" (*LB* 252–68), it becomes clear why Wordsworth chose neither to support movements like the one that resulted in Peterloo nor to sympathize with the image of Dante as a radical reformer. A feudal element obtains in his understanding of the unspoken, affective, and habitual bonds and codes that make it possible for manual laborers and working-class people to subsist and even prosper within a polity that does not legally set forth their rights. His genuine if naive belief that the only way to make any social covenant binding was through mutual trust, based on gestures of good faith, rendered formal declarations and contracts unnecessary if not pernicious. In "Michael," the land itself represents this covenant, in part because it embodies the past that two people, a shepherd and his son, have shared. A contractual agreement, abstract by nature and necessity, disembodies that same past and neutralizes the passions inherent in it. When the shepherd Michael and his son, Luke, exchange vows of loyalty before the latter leaves the family for the city, they stand by the future sheepfold. This site is the only possible place where this declaration can take place, for it is as inseparable a part of their identities and memories as their flesh and family. Remember your father and their fathers, the shepherd tells his son, and in so doing you will grasp the affective and human history that suffuses this natural spot ("corner stone"), which represents our common past, present, and future. Michael's subsequent words became a philosophy for Wordsworth:

> When thou return'st thou in this place wilt see
> A work which is not here, a covenant
> 'Twill be between us — but whatever fate
> Befall thee, I shall love thee to the last,
> And bear thy memory to the grave. (423–27)

The conditions of this covenant have been set by an accumulation of actors, objects, and circumstances (Michael and Luke's ancestors, the fields themselves, the building of the sheepfold) extrinsic to both father and son. Michael knows what these terms are because he has internalized that historical body of knowledge and feeling that makes this anticontractual agreement binding. His act of internalization involves respect for tradition, a sense of belonging equally to a family of living and dead blood relations, and knowledge of the historical responsibilities of one's vocation. But Michael makes the mistake — as Wordsworth did later in life — of believing that his own intuitive understanding of what constituted a binding covenant will just as naturally be felt in the blood by others (especially his son Luke). Wordsworth inserts a crucial conjunction ("but") that captures the absolute faith that Michael feels toward the covenant: the son need not even follow or honor it ("but whatever fate / Befall thee, I shall love thee to the last"). In Michael's own mind, the oath and its bonds are by nature inexorable, independent of whether the human actors who share it defer to its legitimacy. That "but," we learn by poem's end, is well-nigh tragic: the son leaves the father and sheepfold for a prodigal life in the city, forcing Michael to sell all he owns and end his days in poverty. This type of social and political thinking helps explain why Wordsworth turned a cold shoulder to the widely circulating Romantic image of Dante as a radical poet-crusader. For most of Wordsworth's contemporaries, Dante represented an explicitly engaged republican reformer who was willing to sacrifice all (family, country, title) in the name of his beliefs. Wordsworth, meanwhile, promoted a distinctly more conservative form of communitarian thought that found its expression, not in the impassioned political diatribes of a Dante, but in the homely atmosphere and homespun ideologies of works like "Michael."

But for all the circumstantial evidence condemning Dante that the letter to Landor in 1824 contains ("[Dante's] fictions often struck me as offensively grotesque and fantastic, and I felt the Poem [the *Commedia*] tedious from various causes"), critics have failed to address certain mitigating factors. To begin with, Wordsworth's invocation of a previous perspective ("[Dante's] style I used to think admirable for conciseness and vigour, without abruptness") suggests a break with what had been an earlier, more favorable opinion. The letter, in fact, demonstrates that Wordsworth had long been a serious reader of Dante, as is implicit from the good-humored allusion to the space the *Commedia* occupied in Wordsworth's library: "You promise me a beautiful Copy of Dante, but I ought to mention that I possess the Parma Folio of 1795,—much the *grandest* book on my shelves." Moreover, Wordsworth's request that Landor relay him his opinion of Dante's work implies an abiding concern that a merely "tedious" poet would not elicit. That Wordsworth chose the word *grotesque* to express his disapproval of Dante may also be significant, for both Coleridge and Cary had used this adjective to describe Dante, which could suggest Wordsworth's familiarity with the terminology and texts of the Dante criticism in circulation.[39] It is also worth noting that Hazlitt, in his alternately laudatory and condemnatory essay on Wordsworth in the "The Spirit of the Age" (1825), defended him from the label of "puerile" by remarking upon "his strong predilection for geniuses such as Dante and Michael Angelo" (*CW* 11:92).

Another mitigating factor in the rejection is the identity of the addressee himself, Landor. An ardent anti-Dantist, Landor held resolutely arcadian and neoclassical tastes. He wrote in a rarefied Latin whose elitism Wordsworth could never appreciate; but he did flatter Wordsworth in print, which by the 1820s went a long way with the increasingly self-monumentalizing poet.[40] Landor remained a devoted follower of Wordsworth until 1836, when he accused Wordsworth of plagiarizing his work and brought their friendship to an abrupt and dramatic halt. After breaking with Landor, Wordsworth returned once again to an actively pro-Dante stance. That the letter from 1824 was addressed to Landor therefore raises the possibility that Wordsworth said the unkind things he did in part to express solidarity with a friend whom he knew disliked the *Commedia*.

One could even claim a distinctly Dantesque element in Wordsworth's letter to Landor with regard to its treatment of the link between religion and the imagination: "This leads to a remark in your last [letter], 'that you are disgusted with all books that treat of religion.' I am afraid it is a bad sign with me, that I have little relish for any other—even in poetry it is the imaginative only, viz., that which is conversant [with], or turns upon infinity, that powerfully affects me,—perhaps I ought to explain: I mean to say that, unless in those passages where things are lost in each other, and limits vanish, and aspirations are raised, I read with something too much like indifference—but all great poets are in this view powerful Religionists" (D123). Whomever Wordsworth meant by the authors of a "religionist" verse capable of losing things in one another, abolishing limits, and raising aspirations, he could not in fairness have excluded Dante, whose penchant for combining metaphysical and spiritual discourse in verse rivaled Wordsworth's own.[41] These affinities show that, in actual poetic terms, Wordsworth still held many of the same beliefs and attitudes that had compelled him in the first forty years of his life to read Dante with frequency and pleasure. What had changed, and what did incite him to label the poet "tedious" and "grotesque," was less something between him and Dante and more between him and writers like Coleridge, Hazlitt, Shelley, and the radical political element that adopted Dante as model.[42]

In addition to these English contemporaries, the brunt of Wordsworth's attack on Dante included the vogue of German philosophy in Romantic England: "It has become lately—owing a good deal, I believe, to the example of [A. W.] Schlegel—the fashion to extol [Dante] beyond measure." Wordsworth's proverbial antipathy to the German metaphysical tradition associated with the Schlegels led to such statements as the following: "They [German authors] often sacrifice Truth to Originality, and, in their hurry to produce new and startling ideas, do not wait to weigh their worth. When they have exhausted themselves and are obliged to sit down and think, they just go back to the former thinkers, and thus there is a constant revolution without their being quite conscious of it. Kant, Schelling, Fichte; Fichte, Schelling, Kant: all this is dreary work and does not denote progress."[43] Throughout his life, Wordsworth criticized Hazlitt and Coleridge when he thought they were spending too much of their energies engaged in the abstract philosophy he associated with German metaphysics — which, deep down, he blamed for killing the poet in Coleridge. He could never, therefore, approve of a literary cult that he rightly imagined as having originated in Jena school theory. As a whole, the above factors suggest that Wordsworth's negative assessment of Dante was motivated by strategic concerns and was therefore anything but a straightforward dismissal. Above all, the attack on Dante in the letter to Landor illustrates how defensive Wordsworth had become with regard to his place in the literary hierarchy.

Wordsworth's vitriol toward Dante dissolved by 1837. From then on, with Landor no longer his friend and many of his radical antagonists from the Waterloo era no longer alive, he underwent a major and unnoticed change in his attitudes toward the medieval poet. Beginning in the late 1820s, allusions to Dante both in conversation and in his poetry reappear with frequency (all of the allusions to Dante in his verse are after the letter to Landor).[44] Perhaps the most conclusive evidence of this reorientation of opinion lies in Wordsworth's attitude toward Cary and his translation of Dante, *The Vision*. Though Coleridge's endorsement of Cary's translation is well known, Wordsworth's high opinion of it, as reported below by his nephew and chronicler, Christopher Wordsworth, has not been acknowledged: "A few days since, at Buxted, I was speaking to my father of Mr. Cary, who died lately: he said that my uncle, Wm. Wordsworth, with whom he had been spending some weeks this summer, expressed his opinion (I think on the occasion of Mr. Cary's death,) that Cary's translation of Dante was the best of all Translations (not of Dante only but of any foreign author whatever) in the English Language."[45] Since Wordsworth was himself an indefatigable translator, this is high praise indeed.[46] The words also suggest the poet's deep familiarity with both the English and Italian versions of the *Commedia*. The copies of Dante's work that Wordsworth owned support this last hypothesis, as they contain a number of marginal notes in the poet's own hand. Evidence also exists that, in the 1830s, Wordsworth became interested in Dante's life. In the edition of the *Commedia* that he purchased during his Italian tour of 1837, Wordsworth noted on the flyleaf of the first volume: "Query Boccaccio's Life of Dante."[47] In his notes on the text, Wordsworth did something unusual for his time: he highlighted a section of the *Purgatorio* (a theological disquisition on the Trinity, in 3.34–39), a canticle generally ignored outside of scholarly circles.

I believe Wordsworth changed his attitude toward Dante because, as he continued to edit and recast his *Prelude* and give up hope of ever completing the *Recluse,* he increasingly saw the links between his lifelong project of self-representation and Dante's own. Although one cannot speak of the *Prelude* as a poem influenced in its conception or procedures by the *Commedia,* the relationship between these two poems emerges as decidedly more complex than Wordsworth's public statements on Dante would lead one to believe. Both the *Prelude* and the *Commedia* have flourished as two of the most important autobiographical poems in the Western literary tradition. With the exception of, say, Walt Whitman, or to a lesser degree François Villon, the epic poem of the self remains largely a genre of two — the *Commedia* and *Prelude.* Both poems are over ten thousand lines in length; take as protagonist the author himself; and approach issues including moral philosophy, theology, the natural sciences, and political and literary history through the filter of personal experience. One can say that these are merely superficial common points, but in doing so, one has already said a great deal. In the beginning of the *Prelude* and the *Commedia,* each poet poses rhetorical questions that deal with the issue of self-representation and its transcendental analogue, election. Wordsworth adduces a list of possible models and their corresponding genres, including Miltonic epic and Spenserian romance, before settling on "some philosophic song / Of truth that cherishes our daily life" (*Prel.* 1.229–30). After learning from Virgil of his impending journey through the afterlife, Dante's Pilgrim asks, "Ma io, perché venirvi? . . . / Io non Enëa, io non Paulo sono" ("But I, why do I come there? . . . I am not Aeneas, I am not Paul") (*Inf.* 2.31–32). The invocation of literary epic (Virgil's *Aeneid*) and theological history (the apocryphal story, widely known in the Middle Ages, of Paul's journey to heaven and hell) serves the same function as Wordsworth's musings on genre in *Prelude* 1: establishing originality and necessity. Moreover, in the negative space of literary history, the paradigmatic models of the self recalled and rejected by the two poets will loom as the shadow selves of their narratives — points of reference against which to measure their personal development and literary skill.[48]

When considering the relationship between the *Commedia* and the *Prelude,* however, the differences are more instructive than any surface similarity. Wordsworth claimed to believe in God but seems to have done so as much out of sociopolitical as religious conviction. The steeple for him was an agent of community building, the vicar as much a humble mayor as a spiritual guardian. What Wordsworth most believed in, to the extent that he made it into a mystery and source of inscrutable force, was a generative rift within himself. A passage from the *Prelude* encapsulates how this unique experience of the self presented itself to him, and how he ultimately diverges from Dante in his understanding of the place of the self in the cosmos. "All shod with steel" and "hiss[ing] along the polished ice in games / Confederate" (*Prel.* 1.433–35), the poet and his friends are immersed in some of the glad, animal pleasure Wordsworth describes in "Tintern Abbey." One can almost hear the hiss of the blade against the surface of the frozen lake, and such is the feeling of solidarity that Wordsworth might just as well have written "we gave our body" and not "bodies" to the wind. But, even as a boy, he was not made for such scenes. He retires furtively from "the tumultuous throng" to silence, shadows, and stillness:

> Yet still the solitary cliffs
> Wheeled by me — even as if the earth had rolled
> With visible motion her diurnal round!
> Behind me did they stretch in solemn train,
> Feebler and feebler, and I stood and watched
> Till all was tranquil as a dreamless sleep. (*Prel.* 1.458–63)

"Till all was tranquil as a dreamless sleep" alliterates as delicately as the opening to one of the better-known "Lucy" poems, "A slumber did my spirit seal"; and "even as if the earth had rolled / With visible motion in her diurnal round!" nearly transliterates the final words of this same poem: "Rolled round in earth's diurnal course, / With rocks, and stones, and trees" (7–8).[49] In the *Prelude,* it is mountains that are being rolled, and in "A slumber did my spirit seal," it is the elusive Lucy. In each, however, the poet watches (or better, remembers watching) this rolling with utter passivity, without hopes, fears, or dreams. The passing scene before him elicits neither pathos nor wonder; it suffuses tranquility.

Ultimately, this eminently Wordsworthian stance of standing and watching — with none of the Christian resignation of the "standing and waiting" from Milton's sonnet on his blindness — suggests both the *Prelude*'s kinship with and distance from the *Commedia*.[50] The final canto of *Paradiso* challenges the reader to question the place of Dante's personal identity in the overall scheme of heaven and earth that unfolds before the Pilgrim, fittingly, in a textual metaphor:

> Nel suo profondo vidi che s'interna,
> legato con amore in un volume,
> ciò che l'universo si squaderna. (*Par.* 33.85–87)
>
> (In its depth I saw ingathered, bound by love in one single volume, that which is dispersed in leaves throughout the universe.)

Dante compares his role before the Trinity to that of a geometer who seeks to square the circle but lacks the knowledge to do so. Because the reader has followed the Pilgrim for a hundred cantos, his admission of insufficient skill in the face of the sublime comes across as genuine and admissible. The conjunction "but" then silences any anxiety he may have of representing the divine vision, while the closing image reveals that "già volgeva il mio disio e 'l *velle,* / sì come rota ch'igualmente è mossa, / l'amor che move il sole e l'altre stelle" ([the Pilgrim's] desire and will were [already] revolved, like a wheel that is evenly moved, by the Love which moves the sun and other stars) (143–45). Throughout the *Commedia,* aesthetic representation mediates between Dante's understanding of himself and his yearning for a higher, Christian register of experience. Only in the final lines, however, does one see personal identity and its attendant idiosyncrasies coalesce in a poetic image that renders indistinguishable the border between self and self-transcendence.

Wordsworth's *Prelude* also concludes with an apocalyptic vision; yet his "standing and watching" before the absolute differs from Dante's in kind even though it matches it in degree. Book 14 narrates the celebrated ascent of Mount Snowden, which affords Wordsworth a nocturnal vision that inspires a series of meditations on the poet's relations to society, the imagination, human and mineral nature, and the universal forces and feelings that make such relations possible. It is tempting to situate this vision in a tradition of apocalyptic literature, but Wordsworth anticipates this desire so adroitly as to thwart it.[51] In keeping with the principle of daily life and homely virtue that grounds his meditations on human nature and history, the preparation and execution for the ascent is carefully unspectacular. The evening of the climb is "breezeless," "wan," "dull," and "glaring" (*Prel.* 14.11, 12); the three climbers engage in "ordinary travellers' talk" (16); the narrator walks "with forehead bent / Earthward" (28–29). However, as in nearly all the scenes in which he amiably recreates with friends, Wordsworth separates himself the moment the physical experience begins to accrue affective or metaphysical meaning: "Each into commerce with his private thoughts: / Thus did we breast the ascent" (18–19).

Fittingly, the vision atop Mount Snowden finds Wordsworth "foremost of the band" (35) — once again alone:

> The Moon hung naked in a firmament
> Of azure without cloud, and at my feet
> Rested a silent sea of hoary mist.
> A hundred hills their dusky backs upheaved
> All over this still ocean; and beyond,
> Far, far beyond, the solid vapours stretched,
> In headlands, tongues, and promontory shapes,
> Into the main Atlantic, that appeared
> To dwindle, and give up his majesty,

> Usurped upon far as the sight could reach.
> Not so the ethereal vault; encroachment none
> Was there, nor loss; only the inferior stars
> Had disappeared, or shed a fainter light
> In the clear presence of the full-orbed Moon,
> Who, from her sovereign elevation, gazed
> Upon the billowy ocean, as it lay
> All meek and silent, save that through a rift —
> Not distant from the shore whereon we stood,
> A fixed, abysmal, gloomy, breathing-place —
> Mounted the roar of waters, torrents, streams
> Innumerable, roaring with one voice
> Heard over earth and sea, and, in that hour,
> For so it seems, felt by the starry heavens. (40–62)

Both Dante and Wordsworth experience their apocalyptic visions in full thrall of the stars. But as a "modern" artist who, in Coleridge's words, combined "poetry with sentiment," and who composed with "subjectivity," Wordsworth chooses to gloss, explicate, and elaborate upon the manifold meanings of this apocalypse. As a reflection of "majestic intellect," the vista afforded by Mount Snowden is the "emblem of a mind / That feeds upon infinity" (67, 70–71). Dante's choice of metaphor may differ—the *divino volume* of *Par.* 33.85–87—yet he also uses a poetic analogy to describe a universe at once infinite and harmonious. The difference lies in who or what is harmonizing this infinity for each poet. For Wordsworth, at one time (in the 1805 edition of *Prelude* 13.72–73), it was "the sense of God, or whatsoe'er is dim / Or vast in its [the mind's] own being." By the final edition of the poem, in 1850, these lines became

> a mind sustained
> By recognitions of transcendent power,
> In sense conducting to ideal form,
> In soul of more than mortal privilege. (74–77)

The editors Jonathan Wordsworth, M. H. Abrams, and Stephen Gill note that, in the transition from the 1805 to the 1850 versions of the text, few passages suffer as greatly as the ascent-of-Snowden episode (461n6). The distance between "sense of God" (1805) and "transcendent mind" (1850) is profound, and helps to explain why Wordsworth progressively sought to distance himself from a poem and a vision of the self, Dante's *Commedia* and its Pilgrim, that bear so many sympathies to his own. Each poet is concerned with election and exemplarity, for each poet senses that he has been called upon to bear witness for others about the plan and structure of the universe as well as about the place, both humbling and overwhelming, that a single individual occupies in this creation.⁵² But, whereas Dante's *Commedia* ends with the overcoming of the *principium individuationis* in the name of Christian community, the more naturalized Wordsworthian self is only further individuated by its apocalyptic encounter — more solitary than ever before in its new knowledge.

At the end of his history of a "poet's mind" in the *Prelude,* Wordsworth laments: "Yet much hath been omitted, as need was; / Of books how much!" (*Prel.* 14.312–13). Notwithstanding Wordsworth's assertions to the contrary, the *Commedia* of Dante was one such "omitted" book. The thematic sympathies between the *Commedia* and the *Prelude* suggest that, although the secular, heroic image of Dante in early nineteenth-century England was immensely popular, in many respects this very popularity hindered Dante's intended message from being heard. Wordsworth himself favored a "religionist" verse dissimilar to Dante's Christian poetic vision in kind but sympathetic to it in degree; and he was unique among English autobiographers in constructing, as Dante had done, a sustained narrative of the self that thematized the tension between self-representation and self-transcendence. Dante, however, came to be associated with sociopolitical causes and literary conventions that caused Wordsworth, in spite of his hidden sympathies for the *Commedia,* to label Dante "grotesque." In describing Dante this way, he was equating Dante's entire *Commedia* with his *Inferno.* The irony here is considerable: perhaps more than any other writer in Romantic England — indeed, in Romantic Europe — Wordsworth was best equipped to grasp the *Paradiso,* a text whose complexities have been understood by few, whose simplicity by even fewer.

PART III

Corpus Italicum

7

Italy as Woman and Wound, Dante to Leopardi

In one of the less popular corners of Santa Croce, the occasional tourist will pause in front of Foscolo's memorial tomb. Few will know that, because of Foscolo's poetry, this twelfth-century basilica played an invaluable role in forging Italian national identity during the Risorgimento; even fewer will realize that the success of "Dei sepolcri" helped the formerly neglected place of worship obtain necessary repairs and prestigious statuary.[1] Antonio Berti's statue of Foscolo from 1935 (fig. 5) recalls the autobiographical image created by the author of *Ultime lettere di Jacopo Ortis,* for the form radiates a martial vigor and emotional energy, the defining traits of the young lover, soldier, and suicide Ortis. But, as Foscolo himself emphasized throughout his career, Ortis represented only a single period of his literary life. The mature Foscolo repudiated the youthful extravagances of his earliest protagonist and promoted in their place the measured neoclassical restraint, tinged with cosmopolitan irony, of his second autobiographical alter ego, Didimo Chierico, a persona with whom Foscolo shared both an exile and an epitaph.[2]

The original statue of Foscolo chosen for the site, Zulimo Rossellini's funereal monument (1927), which depicts the poet on his deathbed surrounded by his muses, was decidedly less warlike (fig. 6). The literary iconography of this original monument reflects more accurately than its replacement the vast amounts of patriotic poetry and prose that Foscolo produced on behalf of Italy

Figure 5. Antonio Berti, *Monument to Ugo Foscolo*. Basilica of Santa Croce, Florence. Photo Credit: Scala / Art Resource, NY.

Figure 6. Zulimo Rossellini, *Monument to Ugo Foscolo*. Reprinted by permission of the Università degli Studi di Pavia, Area Servizi Generali, Patrimoniali e Logistici.

after his exile. Not surprisingly, the Fascist regime installed the replacement statue as part of its ongoing strategy of connecting Italy's military and cultural glories. The two decades of Mussolini's rule, the so-called *Ventennio* (1921–43), included many such acts, including conferences on the "Fascist" component of Machiavelli's political thought and Petrarch's militant *romanità* (Roman identity).[3] The replacement tomb of Foscolo in Santa Croce suggests the Fascist desire to promote a militarist and imperialist political agenda by underscoring the soldierly, virile qualities of its writers.[4] In representing authors like Foscolo in this way, the Fascists believed they were showing Italians that the literary avatars of their nation embodied Fascist ideals of war, glory, and statism — ideals that made these authors treasured heirs of an imperial Roman past.

The irony of the Fascist cultural policy is startling, because, in the minds of those same writers the Fascists used to promote a masculine national identity, Italy has always been a woman.[5] For example, in a celebrated funereal moment in Santa Croce by Antonio Canova (1810), Italia herself mourns the remains of the young Foscolo's idol, Alfieri, in typical allegorical and iconographic fashion (fig. 7). Draped in a classical toga and fitted with the proportions of an ancient

Figure 7. Antonio Canova, *Tomb of Vittorio Alfieri*. Basilica of Santa Croce, Florence. Photo Credit: Scala / Art Resource, NY.

Figure 8. Eugène Delacroix, *Liberty Guiding the People*. Louvre, Paris. Photo Credit: Erich Lessing / Art Resource, NY.

goddess, the elegant and graceful figure defers to standard neoclassical aesthetic strictures and visual devices. But she is weeping. In her emotional excess and bent, mournful posture, the figure establishes its allegiance to a literary metaphor of Italy that stretches back to Dante and continues to Canova and the Romantic age.[6] Canova's pitiful figure becomes all the more striking when one compares it to its national allegorical counterparts, especially France's Marianne. In Eugène Delacroix's acclaimed *La Liberté guidant le peuple* (Liberty guiding the people; 1830), a bare-breasted Marianne tramples over fallen bodies center stage and, with the audacity of an experienced soldier, leads into battle a wide social and demographic range of Frenchmen (fig. 8). One would be hard pressed to find such assertive iconography in Italian art of the Ottocento, where the most famous allegorical representation of Italia remained that of the baroque aesthetician Cesare Ripa (fig. 9). This figure owes its admirable qualities more to the glory of ancient Rome than to Ripa's own Italy,

Figure 9. From Cesare Ripa, *Iconologia*. New York: Garland, 1976. Reprint of edition published by P. P. Tozzi (Padua, 1611).

for he essentially reproduces the Virgilian trope of Roma and her castellated crown from *Aeneid* 6.781–87. In his widely disseminated collection *Iconologia* (Iconology; 1593; first illustrated ed., 1603), Ripa anticipates the type of power that Delacroix's Marianne later incarnated: strength (*fortezza*), he writes, should be a big-boned (*l'ossa grandi*), armed lady (*donna armata*) with a robust chest (*petto carnoso*).[7] Italian representations of these gender hybrids lacked altogether the French optimism and propagandistic resolve. Traditionally, the allegorical *corpus italicum* contained two dialectically related yet irreconcilable historical epochs: a corrupt and decadent modern Italy, represented in a beautiful but wounded body; and a martial and masculine ancient Roman Italia, with the bold heart and stalwart viscera of its imperial progenitor. The career of this hermaphroditic metaphor (that is, feminine Italian body mixed with a masculine ancient Roman soul) begins with Dante (*Purgatorio* 6; c. 1308–14); passes through Petrarch (canzone 128, "Italia mia"; 1344) and Machiavelli (*Il principe*; 1532); detours in Alfieri (sonnet to Dante; 1783); then culminates with Leopardi ("All'Italia"; 1818).[8] The transition from Dante's Italian "whore" to Leopardi's splendid, superficial "lady" never includes, however, the successful reconciliation by these authors of the historical tensions inherent in their divided body politics. Rather, the above writers actually emphasize the temporally heterogeneous nature of the *donna italica* in order to evoke more powerfully the sense of exile, nostalgia, and civil war (translated into images of *piaghe* [wounds]) that permeates their allegories. The more beautiful they made their Italy, the more they despaired of her.

I

The idea of Italy predates its actual foundation in 1861 by more than two thousand years. Indeed, though Italy is officially one of Europe's youngest states, as a cultural construct or "imagined community" (Anderson), it designates, alongside Greece, one of the two foundational nationalisms avant la lettre in the West.[9] In its bimillennial saga, "Italy" served, for example, as a slogan in the struggle for control of Rome after the death of Julius Caesar; a beacon for figures ranging from Boethius to Cassiodorus in emerging Christian Italy; and, in medieval times, the lamented "mother" of a *romanità* whose loss left Italians geopolitical orphans.[10] A major theoretician of *italianità* was Dante, whose *De vulgari eloquentia* describes Italy — the "bel paese là dove 'l sì suona" (fair land where *sì* is heard) (*Inf.* 33.80) — as a naturally circumscribed linguistic entity that should also enjoy political unity.[11] His *Commedia* promotes the image of Italy as the ancient "giardino" (garden) of Caesarean Rome as well as the future site of a renewed Holy Roman Empire (*Purg.* 6.105). Like Beatrice herself, Dante's Italy, rooted equally in the providential historicism of Virgil's Rome and the religious *terra sacra* that housed the Christian Church, emerges from the *Commedia* as a privileged site for the poem's sustained tension between the secular and spiritual. In Dante's hands, Rome is no less than the genius loci wherein the cities of God and Man coalesce.[12]

It has been a commonplace of Dante criticism to emphasize the importance of the ante-Purgatorial slopes in shaping Dante's vision of Italy, which culminates in his famous apostrophe to the "bordello" (brothel) Italia in *Purg.* 6.76–78. In these early cantos, the reader encounters political luminaries who, through their involvement in the intrigues of the Holy Roman Empire and their controversial means of salvation, embody the struggle between individual spiritual growth and collective political action that, with *Inferno* behind him, increasingly informs the Pilgrim's Purgatorial ascent. Freccero points out that, though wounded, the breast and brow of Manfred in Dante's *Purgatorio* 3 establish his valorous ties to Dante's beloved Holy Roman Empire as well as his transcendence of these same earthly links in the name of his figurative mothers, the Empress Constance and the Virgin Mary.[13] The political dimension of these wounds is clear enough. The spiritual purification and afterlife of Manfred, the scion of the former Holy Roman Emperor Frederick II, suggest the endurance of the historical and ideological principles of *imperium* that he biologically incarnated. To draw on an august medieval political metaphor, the wounded *petto* (breast) of Manfred represents the historical and temporally bound body of the king; but the eternal, symbolic aspect of this same king, his *caput* (head), manifested in Manfred's attractive blond locks, lives on after his mortal remains.[14] The body of Manfred thus encodes two competing metaphoric systems, spiritual and historical, which Dante masterfully blends in deference to the medieval practice of translating manly virtue into physical beauty.[15] The issue of gender is crucial to Freccero's reading, for instead of introducing himself as the son of the emperor, Frederick II, Manfredi announces his relation to the two Constances, his grandmother the empress and his pious daughter.[16] By omitting the name of Manfred's father in favor of his blessed grandmother and exemplary daughter, Dante replaces the standard patrilineal model of political succession (which he associates with historical violence) with a pacific, matrilineal, and Marian line that figuratively connects imperial and Christian discourses.

After Manfred, Dante's meditations on the body politic recommence in *Purgatorio* 5, whose penitents watch in awe as the rays of the Purgatorial sun do not pierce the Pilgrim's flesh. Virgil informs the group that " 'l corpo di costui è vera carne" (this man's [the Pilgrim's] body is true flesh) (33). Extending the solar trope, Dante writes that the sinners then dispersed as "sol calando, nuvole d'agosto" (August clouds at sunset) (39). In keeping with the corporeal violence that brought down most of the avatars in the early stages of *Purgatorio*, the first anonymous shade to introduce himself to Dante in *Purgatorio* 5 also succumbed, like Manfred, to "profondi fóri" (deep wounds) (73). Dante's subsequent encounter with Buonconte da Montefeltro shows the latter figure to be the biographical and rhetorical antithesis of his notorious father, Guido da Montefeltro, from *Inferno* 27. In contrast to his father, who exhibited his penitence bodily with his false friar's robe but experienced no interior contrition, Buonconte saves his soul at the end of his life by invoking the name of Mary. Buonconte emphasizes that he has broken the paternal link and is now his true self ("Io fui di Montefeltro, io son Bonconte" [I was of

Montefeltro, I am Buonconte]) (88). After rejecting his patronymic, Buonconte alludes to his shame with regard to his wife Giovanna, who now "non ha di me cura" (has no care for me) (89). The bodily site of repentance for Buonconte, as for Manfred, is the breast, which bears the actual and figurative *croce* (cross) that Buonconte tells the Pilgrim he made by devoutly folding his arms in a holy sign of pain and remorse as he lay dying (127).

Following his meeting with Buonconte, in *Purgatorio* 6 Dante encounters the body of the "alter[o] e disdegnos[o]" (lofty and disdainful) Sordello, a warrior, author of martial poetry, and son of Virgil's native Mantua. Dante's description of Sordello's animal presence suggests his grace, nobility, and power:

> e nel mover de li occhi onesta e tarda!
>   Ella non ci dicëa alcuna cosa,
> ma lasciavane gir, solo sguardando
> a guisa di leon quando si posa. (63–66)

> (And the movement of [Sordello's] eyes how grave and slow! He said nothing to us, but let us go on, watching only after the fashion of a couching lion.)

The corporeal imagery of early *Purgatorio,* masculine and martial to this point, then gives way to Dante's celebrated digression to his homeland, which begins:

> Ahi serva Italia, di dolore ostello
> nave sanza nocchiere in gran tempesta,
> non donna di provincie, ma bordello! (76–78)

> (Ah, servile Italy, hostel of grief, ship without a pilot in great tempest, no mistress of provinces, but brothel!)

The digression is extraordinary for its urgency and length (at seventy-six lines, it is the longest in the poem).[17] Drawing on the rhetoric of Jeremiah's Lamentations, Dante describes his female body politic as dominated, submissive ("serva"), and suffering ("di dolore ostello"). The wounds of Italia derive from her lack of self-governance and independence and, of equal importance, her poor choice of political allies and masters, especially Albert I of Austria and his father Rudolf I, who have allowed the "giardino" (garden) of the Holy Roman Empire (Italy) to be destroyed on account of their greed (97–105). The corruption of Italy is rhetorical as well as political: Dante's invective blends terminology and themes ranging from biblical apocalypse and the Latin epic of Lucan to crusade literature and the poetry of Dante's own much-maligned Guittone d'Arezzo.[18] In thematic analogy to the passage's formal confusion, the female Italian body politic is unable to govern itself, a "ship without a pilot," an image that recalls *Inferno* 26 and the fate of Ulysses' crew, who innocently perish because of their captain's egotistical pursuit and violation of their trust.

After chastising Italians for their inability to offer citizens hospitality in the manner of the noble-hearted Sordello, Dante notes of his countrymen that "l'un l'altro si rode" (one gnaws at the other) (83), which brings to mind the grotesque marriage of the jaws of Ugolino and the skull of Ruggieri in *Inferno* 32–33. The textual echo conflates the tropes of cannibalism and civil war and emphasizes the incontinence of the *donna italica,* who becomes increasingly bestial as the invective progresses.[19] Dante then asks Italians "guarda[rsi] in senno" (to look within [their] bosom), the bodily area established in the cantos of Manfred and Buonconte as the locus of contrition and penitence (86). This religious rhetoric is intensified by Dante's manipulation of a biblical source, "Cesare mio, perché non mi accompagne?" (My Caesar, why do you abandon me?) (114), an allusion to the abandonment of the Holy Roman Empire by the German Albert (a modern Caesar) that rewrites Christ's lament from the cross ("My God, my God, why hast thou forsaken me?") [Psalm 22:1]).[20] Similarly, Dante's description of modern Rome as "widowed" recalls both the city of Jerusalem widowed by the death of Christ in Jeremiah's Lamentations and, more pointedly, the Florence of the *Vita nuova* left bereft by the passing of Beatrice. By mixing ancient and biblical subtexts with his own medieval autobiography, Dante's metaphor of the Italian body politic blends three distinct temporal sites (antiquity, early Christianity, and contemporary Italy). In failing to achieve its imperial mission and reconnect to its Roman soul, the body politic of Italy becomes feminized, alternately promiscuous or merely feeble and old ("Vieni a veder la tua Roma che piagne / vedova e sola" [Come see your Rome that weeps, widowed and alone]) (*Purg.* 6.112–13). Florence is just as corrupt as Italy's ancient Roman *mater*: like Guido da Montefeltro, she is ready to strike a deal to save her skin and counterfeit her soul, offering empty words instead of genuine justice ("Il popolo tuo l'ha in sommo de la bocca" [Your (Dante's) people has it (justice) ever on its lips]) (132). Like Guido exchanging the robes of state for his friar's robe, Florence camouflages her deceitful acts with a suitable change of "legge, moneta, officio e costume" (laws, coinage, offices, and customs) (146). In sum, Florence is no better than the brothel Italy or the widow Rome. She is an "inferma" (sick woman) "che non può trovar posa in su le piume, / ma con dar volta suo dolor scherma" (who cannot find repose upon the down, but with her tossing seeks to ease her pain) (149–51). Through the images of the Italian *bordello* and the Florentine *inferma,* Dante returns to the sins of incontinence in upper hell—sloth, greed, lust, anger—and thereby forges, on a massive scale, a female political allegory of Italy's incapacity for self-governance.

Purgatorio 6 contains four apostrophes: to Italy (76–96), Albert (97–117), Jove (118–26), and Florence (127–51). The importance of the figures of apostrophe and address to Dante is well known: as Auerbach reminds us, although the address had been used in classical and medieval literature, Dante intensifies and personalizes the form to an unprecedented degree. The exhorting, prodding, and questioning in these addresses helps Dante create, according to Auerbach, a relationship with his reader similar to the one between a prophet and his audience.[21] By flanking his two invectives against promiscuous Italy and disabled Florence with overtures to the man (Albert) and the providential force (Jove) that have failed them, Dante establishes the pose of melancholic entreaty that will model later apostrophes by Italian poets to their nation. His manipulation of the female aspects of the allegorical body politic, especially its sexuality and need for the right husband or master, also anticipates the return by later writers to this paradigmatic metaphor. In formal terms, Dante creates of the *donna italica* a conversational ear that he, as poet, tries to bend to his call with the only arm at his disposal: language. But poetic utterance can be as much about self-articulation as communication, and in *Purgatorio* 6 Italia is not listening.

II

One can only marvel at the mixture of courage and audacity that compelled Petrarch to believe that, in essence, he ushered in a new cultural era that many consider to be the inauguration of Renaissance humanism.[22] The by now well-worn appositives of "crisis" and "belated" that often attend descriptions of the Petrarchan watershed can distract readers from Petrarch's own undeniable pleasure in pursuing his agenda and creating its metaphorical instantiations. It is ironic that, though few have been as actively psychologized as the supposedly and paradigmatically neurotic Petrarch, little attention has been given to the air of liberation that his lyric exudes in nearly reinventing poetics itself through the refashioning of traditional poetic forms.[23] Petrarch's predecessor Dante inhabited a poetic cosmos that refused to allow the aesthetic an autonomous sphere. Paolo and Francesca, in *Inferno* 5, fall into sin by reading only for pleasure ("per diletto") and failing to grasp the moral and ethical dimensions of the literary act (127). When the Pilgrim faints after hearing Francesca's tale, perhaps he does so because of his own overwhelming sense of guilt in having, early in life, composed that same supposedly idolatrous love lyric that enraptured and distracted Paolo and Francesca to the point of fatal transgression. Even when Dante does establish the legitimacy and even the priority of the aesthetic — see especially his conception in *Para-

diso 33 of the universe as a *divino volume,* and hence God as Supreme Poet—art must join hands with religion and theology if it is to express the inexpressible. A perception of ontological reciprocity between the aesthetic and the other intellectual disciplines and human faculties allowed Dante to infuse his imaginative construct *per eccellenza,* the 14,233-line *Commedia,* with a practical urgency that finds its purest distillation in the poem's many addresses to the reader.[24] The Dantesque *caveat lector* warns against the perils of aesthetic experience in the same breath that it reminds readers that God thinks more like a poet than anyone else, including theologians and philosophers. Yet poetry itself has little meaning for Dante outside of its dialectical tension with these other disciplines and faculties. Thus, the *Commedia* as a poem, if not read as a means to an overarching allegorical Christian meaning ("dottrina"), is so much dust in the wind ("versi strani" [strange verses]).[25]

To Petrarch, the scattering of this poetic dust could literally turn wind (*aura*) into golden (*aureo*) and physical splendor (*Laura*) if not poetry itself (*lauro*). His own apostrophes are not to Dante's anonymous reader or everyman but to a living or dead literary elite, separated from the poet in time and space but bound to him in a common pursuit of cultural reconstruction. In making Seneca, Cicero, Livy, and the rest into the poetic other or ear to his work, he proclaimed the independence of the aesthetic and the lyric moment from historical contingency, philosophical accuracy, ethical strictures, and theological precept. The refinements and technical innovations that his isolation of the aesthetic entailed compelled readers to replace their interest in the author as a human being seeking truth through literature—the case with Dante—with a more modern concern: the life of the man as creator of forms. Thus, the self-containment and self-reflexivity of the Petrarchan lyric, by hiding from us the authorial "I" as willfully as Dante exposes it, fuel autobiographical interest of a particularly formal nature. For few things are as existentially chastening, or hermeneutically challenging, as the thought that, in the final tally, the self might just be a self-fashioning entity. Hence the endless Freudian analysis of the supposedly fragile and fragmented Petrarch, especially in comparison with the "happier" Dante.[26]

My own sense is that, rather than the godless crisis that he and most later critics described his lyrical self-dramatization to be, Petrarch considered it a blissful slow-burn that carried its own rewards and justifications, notwithstanding his own highly stylized self-accusations. His poetic universe radiates the proportion, balance, and symmetry that, with its restricted lexicon, variation on a few select themes, and bold self-referentiality, never releases the dangerous energies, ranging from despair to ecstasy, that mark a Dante or such heirs as Alfieri and Foscolo. In the manner of his modern scion Leopardi, even when Petrarch writes of his persona in extremis, the existential pain is crafted with a formal perfection that neutralizes its darker elements and elicits melancholy or sadness in the reader but seldom dread or angst. Whereas Dante asks readers to look beneath the veil of his strange verses and find the doctrine hidden there, for Petrarch, the verses themselves are their own nondoctrinal recompense. As an end in itself that does not have "to mean," poetry, in Petrarch's hands, becomes, perhaps for the first time since Western antiquity, something that must be judged on its own terms, within a self-generated technical and thematic economy. No wonder, then, that he was among the first Western writers to be translated into an *-ism,* for by prioritizing aesthetic rhetoric and freeing it from the burdens of reference and meaning, he refined poetry to the point of, if not formula, at least reproducible code. Though, of course, Petrarch did not invent literary form, he may be said to have inaugurated its modern European history.

The figure of Italy, one of Petrarch's abiding poetic concerns, provides valuable insight into this epochal lyric transition. From beginning to end, the shadow of Dante enshrouds Petrarch's *Rerum vulgarium fragmenta* 128, the canzone "Italia mia" ("My Italy"; 1344). Though Petrarch claimed to have read Dante for the first time late in his life (about a decade after the composition of "Italia mia"), most critics now find this assertion rather unlikely.[27] In reality, Petrarch's engagement with Dante seems to have been a consistent and consistently anxious concern throughout the various genres in which he worked. In his poem to Italy, Petrarch's thematic debt to Dante includes the use of a feminized body politic to incarnate a political diatribe; a critique of contemporary Italy lacking in piety and humanity; and, above all, a privileging of the cult of ancient Rome. The technical borrowings from Dante are even more dramatic. Petrarch begins the poem with the phrase "Italia mia" (my Italy) (1), a genitive coupling that returns us to the very place where Dante concludes his digression of *Purgatorio* 6 ("Fiorenza mia" [my Florence]) (6.127).[28] He ends with an overture to his genetic connection to Italy (his "nido" [nest]) (82), just as Dante finishes his invective by localizing his *italianità* in his natal Florence. Petrarch follows Dante in emphasizing his Latin blood by unifying inhabitants of the Peninsula against the same common foreign enemy as Dante's: the Germans ("la tedesca rabbia" [the Teutonic rage]) (35). He also echoes Dante in excoriating Italian political *signori* for pursuing their selfish goals at the expense of the would-be nation's providential political history.[29] Last, and most important, each poet completes his digression with an appeal to the common Christian ground of the Italian nation.

Notwithstanding these similarities, the Petrarchan apostrophe to Italy profoundly differs from Dante's in nature if not in scope. In line with Thomas

Greene's notion of heuristic imitation (*Light in Troy* 40) — in which the later text formally approximates its source while also establishing a thematic distance — Petrarch rewrites Dante's heated conversational apostrophe by inscribing it within the impersonal rhetoric of the funereal dirge. Petrarch's elegiac apostrophe reveals his sense of the futility of the aesthetic mode vis-à-vis political affairs as well as his acknowledgment of fourteenth-century Italy's historical isolation from ancient Rome. Whereas Dante's tirade against the brothel Italy tries, albeit in vain, to reconcile the conflicting ancient and contemporary trajectories of the *corpus italicum*, Petrarch's melancholic overture accepts the ultimate impossibility of a renewed antiquity. Overall, the beauty of Petrarch's Italian maiden represents a stylized and idealized lamentation that seeks, as recompense for political failure, joy in the poetical image itself. Thus, the self-referential nature of Petrarch's Italia makes her, alongside Laura, a privileged example of the ambivalent dialogue between pleasure and pain that attends Petrarch's cult of the poetic image.[30]

After opening canzone 128 with an address to "Italia mia," Petrarch repeats the possessive and reflexive pronouns "mi" and "miei" (me and my) just a few verses later to express his intimate relationship to his allegorized nation. But his is the lonely passion of the necromancer, for the wounds of the body politic are mortal, and the poet's description of her draws on the figure of *eulogia* (eulogy), the formal blessing of the departed. The poet can only impotently admire the beautiful wounded *donna italica*, "ben che 'l parlar sia indarno / a le piaghe mortali / che nel bel corpo tuo sì spesse veggio" (although speech does not aid those mortal wounds of which in your lovely body I see so many) (1–3). This admission leads to two allusions to the *dolce stil novo*, the lyrical fusion of poetry and natural philosophy that nurtured, among others, the Dante of the *Vita nuova*. After beginning with a Cavalcantian trope of physical beauty mixed with mutilation, Petrarch adduces a *stilnovista* lexicon of "sospir" (sighs) and mourning ("doglioso et grave" [sorrowful and sad]) (4, 6). Why the suffering should be pleasing to Italy's major cities (which appear via the synecdoche of the rivers Tiber, Arno, and Po) escapes the reader in the first stanza, in which the poet admits there is little to be done on his country's behalf. Petrarch, however, remains one step ahead of us: his *impotentia* and pleasure-in-pain fuel two of his main concerns in constructing the female Italian body politic, nostalgia and exile, two themes he later exploits in his invocation of Italy as the bygone homestead of its now orphaned leaders.

In the second stanza, Petrarch asks God to return to his "diletto almo paese" (beloved, holy country) and soften "i cor' ch' endura et serra / Marte superbo et fero" (the hearts that proud fierce Mars makes hard and closed) (9, 12–13). The contrast between the aggressive, ill-intentioned bodies of Italy's rulers and the beautiful but broken Italian woman prepares the reader for the charged erotic rhetoric found in Dante. But whereas Dante's Italy is a brothel that lets in foreigners for the right price, Petrarch's Italia is a defenseless maiden overcome by rapacious Italian rulers and their foreign conspirators. To push the analogy a bit, in Dante, the Italic body sells itself, and so is a guilty perpetrator; in Petrarch, it is taken by force, the victim of a historical rape. The hardhearted exploiters of Italy no doubt possess physical strength, but they lack the corresponding *virtù* of Italy's Roman ancestors. Petrarch's only recourse in this situation is to invoke God directly ("ivi fa' che 'l tuo vero, / qual io mi sia, per la mia lingua s'oda" [cause Your truth (though I am unworthy) to be heard there through my tongue]) (14–15). Readers of Petrarch learn to be wary when he speaks of God, and by poem's end we learn that our possible suspicions in this regard are justified.

Petrarch uses the figure of antithesis to remind the reader of the woes besetting the Italian body politic. Though red and green are complementary colors, in canzone 128 they represent a grotesque pairing of "verde terreno" and "barbarico sangue" (green earth and barbarian blood) (21, 22), and the poet underscores this foreign contamination of Italy through the simile of an unnatural deluge that inundates Italy's sweet fields. In contrast to Dante, however, there is no rhetorical contamination in the Petrarchan construction, which blends in a coherent and refined linguistic-literary key its constituent parts.[31] Foreigners may have ruined this gorgeous lady, but the maiden herself bears part of the blame: "Se da le proprie mani / questo n'avene, or chi fia che ne scampi?" (If this [ruin] happens to us by our own hands, who can be there to rescue us?] (31–32). The language of civil war permeates the following stanzas: though nature, by providing the Alps, divided Italy from the German threat, Italy's political intrigue has permitted the invaders entry and "à procurato scabbia" in the "corpo sano" (contrived to make this healthy [Italian] body sick) (38). That this illness is caused by foreign troops is all the more lamentable because the Romans had once so harshly defeated this same "popol senza legge" (uncivilized people)—earlier described as "fiere selvaggia" (savage beasts)—that the rivers of Italy ran red with foreign blood (40, 43). This first allusion to the distance separating Petrarch's contemporary Italy from ancient Rome anticipates the ensuing apostrophe to "Latin sangue gentile" (noble Latin blood), which claims that the feminized state to which Italy has been reduced is "non natural cosa" (not a natural thing) (74, 80).[32] Rather, Petrarch writes, Germans from the north have conquered Italy, because its civil wars allowed barbarian blood to pollute the once noble *sangue* that coursed through Roman and Italian veins.

The lines following the apostrophe to Latinity contain a delicate appeal to the affective power of childhood memory. Petrarch asks the warring lords of Italy to recall their native land by posing themselves the following question:

> Non è questo 'l terren ch' i' toccai pria?
> non è questo il mio nido
> ove nudrito fui sì dolcemente?
> non è questa la patria in ch' io mi fido,
> madre benigna et pia,
> che copre l'un et l'altro mio parente? (81–86)
>
> (Is not this the ground that I touched first? Is not this my nest, where I was so sweetly nourished? Is not this my fatherland in which I trust, and my kind and merciful mother, which covers both of my parents?)

Here the shift from frail lovely Italy to martial male antiquity expresses itself in one of Warner's gender cocktails (*patria, madre,* and *l'un et l'altro parente*). The rhythmic repetition of the anaphora "non è questo" casts its spell as both the reader and the putative *Signore* are led back into the bosom of the initial ties that bind. We arrive at an Italy that is *nido* and *nutrice*, nest and nourishment, in a passage that implicitly invokes the etymological sense of the word *nation* as place of birth. The female functions that Petrarch emphasizes (Italy as mother, sustenance, and benign and pious lady) evoke the Dantesque counterimage of the Italian body politic as fallen and passive. Petrarch then exhorts her to become, so to speak, manly:

> Et pur che voi mostriate
> segno alcun di pietate,
> vertù contra furore
> prenderà l'arme, et fia 'l combatter corto;
> ché l'antico valore
> ne l'italici cor non è ancor morto. (91–96)
>
> (And, if you [God] merely show some sign of piety, manhood shall take up arms against rage, and the fighting shall be short: for ancient valor is not yet dead in Italic hearts.)

Italici signals the first time in the poem that Petrarch has used "Italian" as a qualifier; the Latinate *italico* implies the ancient Roman roots of the Italian national soil. Petrarch's message is clear: within the economy of his poem's organic metaphors, in order for the feminized, divided, and wounded Italian female body to become an integral, self-governing, and free male, she must acquire an ancient Italic (that is, Roman) heart, and thereby link modern Italy with Latin antiquity.

The final stanzas, however, suggest that this figurative transplant or *trans-*

latio imperii will never occur. The steady historical meditations of the poem cede to a prayer in the penultimate stanza, wherein the poet asks God to consider the fleeting nature of mortal time and the omnipotence of death in all matters human. The transcendental message contrasts with the civic and social agenda of the preceding lines, and the shift from an exhortation to action to a plea for quiet retirement paralyzes the poem's energies into that nostalgic and exilic state of unrequited longing typical of Petrarchan lyric. The poem ends with the traditional medieval *congedo* or farewell that sends the poem among its readers with instructions to speak courteously and seek out the few magnanimous and good readers or citizens, by asking: "Chi m'assicura? / I' vo gridando: Pace, pace, pace" (Who will protect me? I go crying: Peace, peace, peace!) (121–22). The present progressive form of "vo gridando" is a trademark Petrarchan grammatical construct that suggests the immanent physical coordinates of the narrator (see also Petrarch's earlier mention of an Italy in which he "now sit[s] sorrowful and sad") (6). This "situated" aspect of Petrarch's lyric voice in canzone 128 distinguishes it from Dante's tirade against Italy in *Purgatorio* 6 in two important ways. First, Dante's invective represents an abstract digression, outside of the narrative, unlike in Petrarch, whose narrative voice is embedded in the poem it articulates. Moreover, the phrase "vo gridando" heightens the subjective presence and present actions of the poet himself, thereby underscoring what Foscolo would often describe as Petrarch's tendency to reduce his field of experience to sentimental, autobiographical introspection.[33] The shift from elegy to lament in the final stanza of canzone 128 and its accompanying lexicon of exile and nostalgia convey Petrarch's despair over the future of his lovely national allegory. If, however, Italy and by extension Rome remained elegiac poetic figures for Petrarch, there was one Petrarchan locale that shared the promiscuous aspects of Dante's Italia: Avignon, the site during Petrarch's lifetime of the controversial "Babylonian captivity" (1309–77) of the papacy, during which seven popes (all French) resided in Avignon instead of Rome. Like Dante's *bordello* in *Purgatorio* 6, Petrarch's Avignon is alternately "Babylon," "den of thieves," and "scarlet woman," among other things.[34] But the elegiac-minded Petrarch stopped short of equating Italy with accursed Avignon. As familiar and fallen as the latter was to him, Italia was correspondingly upright and remote, asexual in her manner, passive in her mien, and prosopopoeial in her modality. In Petrarch, Dante's lively and angry apostrophe to his nation resurfaces with the melancholy resignation of epitaph.

III

The interpreter of the Italian body politic in Machiavelli faces a different species of challenge from that presented by Dante and Petrarch. Though the latter two incorporate a political element in their *donna italica,* they do so as poets, which is to say through metaphor and analogy. Machiavelli, by contrast, writes as a politician who adopts a poetical tone. Dante and Petrarch offer images and discourses whose political valence must be gauged through literary-critical sensitivity to the allusive and elusive qualities of a linguistic structure that is entirely figurative and, hence, as concerned with internal formal matters as it is with external historical reference. Machiavelli, instead, provides a doctrine that is principally political and only incidentally literary — but, by virtue of the author's rhetorical skill, prodigiously so.[35] This "ambidextrous" element of Machiavelli's writing tends to split his critics into two scholarly camps: the literary and the historico-political. The considerable challenges in establishing a dialogue between Machiavelli *poeticus* and *politicus* suggest the wily Machiavelli's success in dividing — or, to use his own terminology, outfoxing — his interpreters.[36]

One can only speculate as to why Machiavelli was so obsessed with the body. Perhaps because of his eschewal of disembodied abstractions in the name of concrete categories of analysis; perhaps because of his emphasis on appearance and spectacle over essence; perhaps even because of his own erotically charged, at times perverse, proclivities and concomitant knack for extrapolating the metaphysical from the sexual.[37] Whatever the reason, issues and themes of gender and corporeality limn the slim volume *Il principe* (*The Prince*), composed during the author's exile from Florence in 1512. Most famously, the prince must use his *virtù,* a polyvalent term drawn from the Latin *vir* (man), to combat that woman Fortuna, Machiavelli's female allegory for political vicissitude, historical contingency, the flux of time, and plain bad luck.[38] He even composed a poem, "Degli spiriti beati" (On the blessed spirits), which combines Dantesque and Petrarchan elements to urge Italians to rediscover their ancient *virtù* and rid Italy's "dolci campi" (sweet fields) of the "lungo strazio e 'nrimediabil danno" (long torment and irreparable harm) of foreign occupation. As a whole, Machiavelli's feminization of the Italian body politic in the *Principe* shares with Dante and Petrarch a preoccupation with Italy's lost Roman heritage and a religious appeal, however strategic, that Italians regain their providential historical destiny. Though the cloth or verbal skein covering Machiavelli's female national allegory is Petrarchan, her inner virtue or heart belongs to the more "Roman," vituperative Dante.[39]

Before turning to Machiavelli's treatment of the Italian body politic, it is crucial to note the human quality that sustains his corporeal metaphors if not worldview: desire. For Machiavelli, the wish or need to possess more than what one has, whether it be wealth, power, a sexual partner, even the assurance of the soul's afterlife, is rooted in the fundamental human tendency of unquenchable, ineluctable longing. In this regard, for all his supposed *dantismo*, Machiavelli seems to be the heir of the eternally unfulfilled Petrarch. Nearly all of Machiavelli's political systems and theories translate into figures of dominance, violence, and sexual pursuit. However unsettling his notion of desire, Machiavelli does not circumscribe this impulse with the Augustinian moralism or Petrarchan self-accusation that one finds, for example, in the *Secretum* (Secret; c. 1345). Early in the *Principe,* Machiavelli writes that it is natural and ordinary to seek personal gain, and that those who succeed in this regard will always be praised and never blamed. Desire, for Machiavelli, is simply the state of things, and thus a central concern in his treatises on governing human actions.[40] Machiavellian desire is less an ethical and moral dilemma than it is an ongoing hermeneutic or practical challenge — not dissimilar from something equally natural, like a fever, another problem best dealt with sooner than later. He writes:

> Prevedendosi discosto, facilmente vi si può rimediare, ma, aspettando che ti si appressino, la medicina non è a tempo, perché la malattia è divenuta incurabile. E interviene di questa come dicono e' fisici dello etico, che nel principio del suo male è facile a curare e difficile a conoscere, ma nel progresso del tempo, non l'avendo in principio conosciuta né medicata, diventa facile a conoscere e difficile a curare. Così interviene nelle cose di stato, perché, conoscendo discosto (il che non è dato se non a uno prudente) e mali che nascono in quello, si guariscono presto; ma quando per non li avere conosciuti si lasciono crescere in modo che ognuno li conosce, non vi è più rimedio. (*Principe* 10)
>
> (When you see trouble in advance, it is easily remedied, but when you wait till it is on top of you, the antidote is useless, the disease has become incurable. What doctors say about consumption applies here: in the early stages it is hard to recognize and easy to cure, but in the later stages, if you have done nothing about it, it becomes easy to recognize and difficult to cure. That is how it goes in affairs of state: when you recognize the evils in advance, as they take shape [which requires some prudence to do], you can quickly cure them; but when you have not seen them, and so let them grow till anyone can recognize them, there is no longer a remedy.) (*Prince* 8)

This medical simile naturalizes the polity as a coherent corporate, corporeal entity comprised of interrelated units, and pathologizes the challenges and disruptions that this body forces. What holds for the human body obtains for the body politic. Nature itself, Machiavelli argues, doctors the body politic, using famine, disease, flood, and other forms of *force majeure* to rid the polity of people it cannot feed, buildings it cannot maintain, and natural resources it cannot manage. Not surprisingly, for Machiavelli the preeminent doctors of the state were Italy's ancient Roman predecessors:

> Però e Romani vedendo discosto gli inconvenienti vi rimediorno sempre, e non li lasciorno mai seguire per fuggire una guerra, perché sapevono che la guerra non si leva ma si differisce a vantaggio di altri.... Né piacque mai loro quello che tutto dì è in bocca de' savii de' nostri tempi, di godere el benefizio del tempo, ma sì bene quello della virtù e prudenzia loro: perché el tempo si caccia innanzi ogni cosa, e può condurre seco bene come male e male come bene. (*Principe* 10)

> (Thus the Romans, who could see troubles at a distance, always found remedies for them. They never allowed a trouble spot to remain simply to avoid going to war over it, because they knew that wars don't just go away, they are only postponed to someone else's advantage.... They never went by that saying which you hear constantly from the wiseacres of our day, that time heals all things. They trusted rather their own character [*virtù*] and prudence —knowing perfectly well that time contains the seed of all things, good as well as bad, bad as well as good.) (*Prince* 8–9)

By combining force and action with foresight and calculation, the Romans displayed the talent or virtue necessary to trump the fickle mistress Fortuna, who, like temporality itself, brings all things in unpredictable manner and unequal measure. As adept as the ancients were in using *virtù* to control *fortuna*, modern Italy's own princes, with few notable exceptions like the infamous Cesare Borgia, were hapless. Whereas the Roman body politic was healthy and self-regulated, the modern Italian one is sick and contaminated by the use of mercenaries and auxiliary troops, who represent a disunited body and a major cause for Italy's ruin (*Principe* 13). But, unlike Dante and Petrarch, who berate the Italian *signori* without offering real political solutions, Machiavelli concludes the *Principe* by providing allegorical instruction as to how sick Italy can become healthy (and Roman) once again.

The infamous penultimate chapter 25 of *Il principe* compares Lady Fortuna to a flood: "uno di questi fiumi rovinosi, che, quando s'adirano, allagano e piani, ruinano li alberi e li edifizii, lievano da questa parte terreno, pongono da quell'altra" (one of those torrential streams, which, when they overflow, flood the plains, rip up trees and tear down buildings, wash the land away here and deposit it there) (*Principe* 80; *Prince* 67). Petrarch's image in canzone 128 of the barbarian tide overflowing his sweet Italy may have been on Machiavelli's mind here, as may have been the opening of Dante's *Inferno* 15, where flood metaphors anticipate the unbridled desire of the sodomites.[41] Independent of its possible antecedents, the scene represents the first instance in *Il principe* in which *fortuna* and Italy are set in binary opposition, with *fortuna* providing a flood that defenseless Italy cannot withstand. How is Italy to protect itself? By combining the foresight and audacity of the Romans alluded to earlier in *Principe,* chapter 3, and erecting dikes to channel the rising waters before they overflow. Then Machiavelli's sexual rhetoric hits full stride: "La fortuna è donna: ed è necessario, volendola tenere sotto, batterla et urtarla. E si vede che la si lascia più vincere da questi che da quelli che freddamente procedono" (*Principe* 82). (Fortune is a woman, and the man who wants to hold her down must beat and bully her. We see that she yields more often to men of this stripe than to those who come coldly toward her [*Prince* 69].)[42] Whereas Petrarch's Italy is defenseless and passive, Machiavelli's *fortuna* is a wild card, who "sempre, come donna, è amica de' giovani, perché sono meno respettivi, più feroci, e con più audacia la comandano" (like a woman ... is always a friend of the young, because they are less timid, more brutal, and take charge of her more recklessly (*Principe* 82; *Prince* 69). What began as a Petrarchan overture to the maiden Italy overrun by foreign hordes switches to a call for the right prince to come along to tame whorish Fortuna. Such an act would provide the vulnerable Italian body politic with the damming mechanisms — or security — she needs. By the end of chapter 25, though the corporeal imagery derives primarily from Petrarch's lament, the atmosphere, register, and tone are more akin to Dante's invective in *Purgatorio* 6.

The final chapter 26 of the *Principe* marks a switch in rhetorical mode, from analytical treatise to oratorical exhortation. Italy, Machiavelli claims, has descended to the necessary ground zero from which her political resurrection may now occur. She has been "sanza capo, sanza ordine, battuta, spogliata, lacera, corsa" (headless, orderless, beaten, stripped, scarred, overrun); and Fortune has rejected every prince who wished to heal "le sue ferite" (her wounds) (*Principe* 83; *Prince* 70). The reference to wounded Italy, which recalls Petrarch's *piaghe,* begins Machiavelli's figurative restructuring of Italy in feminine terms. Italy prays to a divinity for someone to rescue her, an allusion to Machiavelli's dedication of the text to Lorenzo de' Medici (grandson of Lorenzo the Magnificent), the man who will restore *antico valore* (ancient valor) by ridding Italy of the barbarians with Italian troops. Machiavelli describes Italy's current situation as an opportunity for Lorenzo to become Italy's redeemer by taming *fortuna* and serving as a suitable husband for fallen Italy. Lorenzo represents the homegrown version of the national helmsman that Dante wished could lead the Italian "nave sanza nocchiere" (ship without a pilot) (*Purg.* 6.77). Italians, Machiavelli writes, would repay her new prince with indescribable thirst for vengeance, deep devotion, dedication, and tears. His subsequent transcription of canzone 128.93–96 oscillates between a public endorsement of Petrarch's patriotic overture and a private channeling of the more politically resolute Dantesque voice:

> *Virtù contro a furore*
> *prenderà l'arme; e fia el combatter corto,*
> *ché l'antico valore*
> *nell'italici cor non è ancor morto.*
> (*Principe* 86; Machiavelli's italics for citation)

> (Then virtue boldly shall engage
> And swiftly vanquish barbarian rage,
> Proving that ancient and heroic pride
> In true Italian hearts has never died.) (*Prince* 72)

Petrarch, of course, concluded "Italia mia" with a prayerful appeal to solitude and peace; my sense is that Machiavelli avoided quoting the less politically engaged parts of canzone 128—and the inflammatory images in *Purgatory* 6—because they did not serve his propagandistic intents.[43] In the end, Machiavelli trumpets the more palatable and programmatic Petrarchan slogan while also infusing *Il principe* with Dante's polemical view that an ancient Roman *cuore* (heart) might beat inside a modern Italian organism, should the body politic find the right master or *caput* (head) to guide her. Like Dante's "ship without a pilot" looking for a Holy Roman Emperor to steer its course, Machiavelli's Italy is a woman looking for the right *virtù* to redeem her and protect her against that other less conscientious but eminently capable female rival, Fortuna. The notion might strike today's reader as old-fashioned, but Machiavelli's *donna italica* must, metaphorically speaking, marry well.

IV

The question of Italy in Machiavelli, with its synthesis of Dantesque and Petrarchan sources, takes a brief detour through an author who composed literary history's version of Machiavelli's *Principe*: the Alfieri of *Del principe e delle lettere*. The manner in which this text follows Machiavelli's lead is indicated by its penultimate chapter title: "Esortazione a liberar la Italia dai barbari" (Exhortation to free Italy from the barbarians). Echoing Machiavelli's description of Italia as overrun and beaten down by all manner of ruin, Alfieri in *Del principe* 3.11 invokes a "stanca, vecchia, battuta, avvilita, e . . . dispogliata" (weary, old, conquered, humiliated, despoiled) nation reminiscent of Dante's *inferma,* Florence, in *Purgatorio* 6 (*Del principe* 250; *Prince and Let-*

ters 154).⁴⁴ Like Machiavelli's national allegory, Alfieri's body politic in *Del principe* 3.11 has sunk to the necessary ground zero ("nell'apice della sua viltà e nullità" [at the peak of her baseness and nullity]) from which a total reconstruction, guided by a cadre of "caldi e ferocissimi spiriti" (fiery ferocious spirits), may occur (*Del principe* 250; *Prince and Letters* 155). The resurgence will be led by those who manage to retain the legacy of their ancient Roman *virtù*, for, Alfieri figuratively writes, a man born in the Rome of his day "si allegra ed innalza in sè stesso, nel rimare col tempo i Decj risorti ed i Regoli; stante che tutto ciò che ha potuto essere, può ritornare e sarà" (will rejoice and exult in foreseeing [the republican clans] the Decii and the Regoli resurrected. For all that has already been possible may return and exist once more) (3.11; *Del principe* 252; *Prince and Letters* 156).

The optimism of the masculine, martial rhetoric from *Del principe e delle lettere* undergoes a dramatic shift in one of the two sonnets Alfieri addressed to Dante in 1783:

> Dante, signor d'ogni uom che carmi scriva;
> E più di me, quant'ho mestier più forza
> Sopra gl'itali cori; la cui scorza,
> Debil quantunque, or fiamma niuna avviva:
>   Dante, non là di Flegetonte in riva,
> Dove pioggia di fuoco in sangue ammorza,
> Nè dove altro martíre a pianger sforza,
> Null'alma al par di me di pace è priva.
>   Strappato io son dal fianco di colei,
> Ch'a ogni nobile impresa impulso e norma,
> Mi ajutava a innalzare i pensier miei:
>   L'angiol del ciel, che sotto umana forma
> Meco venia, m'è tolto: invan vorrei
> Dietro a tue dotte piante or muover orma. (sonnet 54)⁴⁵

(Dante, master of all those who write verses — and especially me, if I do truly influence the hearts of Italians, whose skin, so weak, now no flame will revitalize. Dante, no soul is so bereft of peace as I am: not even by the bank of hell's Phlegethon River, where the rains of fire dissolve into blood; not even where the other intense suffering forces tears. I was torn from the side of her who helped me raise my thoughts to every noble impulse and principle. This angel of the sky, who came to me in a human form, is taken from me. Though in vain, I would like now to make tracks behind the learned soles of your feet.)

Using imagery reminiscent of Petrarch's canzone 128.95–96 ("l'antico valore / ne l'italici cor non è ancor morto" [ancient valor is not yet dead in Italic hearts]), Alfieri pessimistically notes that the Italian hearts of his own day are weak of skin (3–4). In a departure from Petrarch, however, in Alfieri the prevailing tone is martial, with a heavy dose of Dantesque rhetoric adduced to deepen the intensity of Alfieri's exegesis on the nature of political hope. In proposing himself as the *poeta vate* who might instill in Italian hearts the desire for virtue, Alfieri also adopts Dante's phenomenology of inspiration. Just as Dante defers to his Beatrice, whose beatific grace allowed him to transcend his own fallen state, so too does Alfieri submit to an angel of the sky who inspires only noble deeds.[46] Though a polemical tone reminiscent of Dante and Machiavelli fuels Alfieri's poem, he closes with Petrarchan resignation. The final sentiment is that the writer is in exile in this world, and that the evil inherent in human nature will inevitably strip the poet's life of meaning. But, unlike Dante, who writes in a world where spiritual transcendence is still possible, Alfieri can only wander without hope of redemption. The last lines of the sonnet evoke a feeling of belatedness and frustration to which even his irrepressible energy must defer. He links the negative qualifier "invan" (in vain) with the conditional "vorrei" (I would like) to emphasize that the master-pupil relationship between him and Dante will remain just that: an unequal pairing in which student will always lag far behind teacher (13). Like all comparatively lesser talents, he will imitate and idealize instead of challenge; his "angiol del ciel" (angel of the sky), Louisa of Stolberg, is no Beatrice; and the Italian *petto* and *cuore* he wishes to enflame with ancient virtue will remain weak and uninspired. Given the growing disillusionment with Italian culture and politics that eventually compelled Alfieri's complete withdrawal from public life, I consider the meditation on national identity in the above sonnet to be more representative of his overall views than the more hopeful, activist *Del principe e delle lettere*. Dante's and Petrarch's skepticism about Italia listening to its poets thus resurfaces in Alfieri's poem; but the nation's deaf ear reaches its apotheosis in Leopardi, whose *donna italica* combines the militant agenda of Dante and Machiavelli with the mournful nostalgia of Petrarch and Alfieri.

V

For all the mountains of scholarship on Leopardi, we have precious little on his use of his signature figure, apostrophe, those soliloquies masquerading as conversations that usually occur in the stillness of night and in an impenetrable yet strangely comforting solitude.[47] The addressees or ears to his apostrophes are figures with whom the poet most identifies: the female, dead, emotionally overwrought, and mentally or physically troubled—the moon, Sappho, Silvia, the wandering shepherd, even Leopardi himself and his *stanco cor* (tired heart) in "A se stesso" ("To Himself"). Unlike the effortlessly autobiographical Foscolo, the lyric self-articulation of the more reticent Leopardi depends, formally, on his invocation through apostrophe of an outside presence; thematically, on his overcoming of the seemingly insurmountable obstacles inherent in this communicative overture. An unlikely example of Leopardi's fragile apostrophe-as-autobiography appears in a poem to another figuratively "dead woman," the *donna italica* of "All'Italia" ("To Italy"), a work that says as much about Leopardi's construction of narrative lyric voice as it does about Italy. Leopardi's apostrophe to Italy recapitulates the previously mentioned female allegories yet also differs from them by seeking (albeit in vain) to reconcile a rift between ancient and modern Italy deemed inexorable by earlier allegorists. He achieves the militant synthesis by anchoring his imagery in a progressive *eloquenza* (eloquence) that infuses Petrarchan and Risorgimentalist rhetoric with the voices of contemporary authors, including Alfieri and Foscolo. The generally unacknowledged subtext of Foscolo's "Dei sepolcri" in "All'Italia" allows Leopardi to extend his female Italian national allegory past the historical impasses of the Dantesque and Petrarchan models and into a more engaged ritualistic, nationalist register.

Leopardi considered Petrarch's canzone 128 to be the epitome of lyric eloquence and, in his edition of Petrarch's poems, went to great lengths to praise this canzone's paradigmatic role in Italian literary history.[48] His own contribution to the six-hundred-year-old allegorical tradition of the *donna italica* was "All'Italia," written partly in response to the same bloody Napoleonic campaign of 1813 that inspired Foscolo's censure in *Lettere scritte dall'Inghilterra*. A series of civic and patriotic poems by Leopardi followed "All'Italia," including the aforementioned "Sopra il monumento di Dante" ("By Dante's Tomb") and "Ad Angelo Mai" ("To Angelo Mai"). Critics have tended to downplay the literary value of these more ideological poems, especially when compared to Leopardi's great contemporary idylls like "L'infinito" ("The Infinite"; 1819), "Alla luna" ("To the Moon"; 1819), "La sera del dì di festa" ("Sunday Evening"; 1820), and "Il sogno" ("The Dream"; 1821). Though the latter works are of a more sophisticated verbal texture and delicate emotional register than the didactic and discursive nationalist poems, common aesthetic and conceptual elements link the two subgenres. Many writers of the nineteenth century, including Manzoni, De Sanctis, and Carducci, praised "All'Italia" partly because of its overt Risorgimentalist rhetoric. Afterward, in a recurring scene of Italian critical history, Croce's endorsement of the refinement in Leopardi's idylls and his corresponding disdain for the poet's more historical lyric helped establish the terms of debate for a long-standing interpretive dichotomy. In a critique of Croce and echo of De Sanctis — who argued that though

"All'Italia" is not the most original work, it anticipates most of the later motifs and concerns of the artistically mature Leopardi — Binni argued on behalf of an active dialogue between the idyllic and heroic poetry by Leopardi. He proposed that the poet would never have achieved the elegiac, emotional, and stylistic brilliance of his introspective lyrics if he had not previously addressed the moral, historical, and "Romantic" problems of the civic poems.[49] Following Binni's cue, a comparison between the idyllic and political poems reveals how Leopardi employs the figure of apostrophe in each group:

> O donna mia,
> già tace ogni sentiero, e pei balconi
> rara traluce la notturna lampa:
> tu dormi, che t'accolse agevol sonno
> nelle tue chete stanze; e non ti morde
> cura nessuna; e già non sai né pensi
> quanta piaga m'apristi in mezzo al petto. ("La sera del dì di festa" 4–10)

> (Now, my dear,
> The narrow streets are still, only a few
> Last shutters are barred with lamplight:
> Taken easily by sleep, you lie
> Untroubled in your hushed rooms,
> Without a thought for the wound
> You've opened in my heart.) ("Sunday Evening" 5–11)[50]

> Piangi, che ben hai donde, Italia mia,
> le genti a vincer nata
> e nella fausta sorte e nella ria.
> Se fosser gli occhi tuoi due fonti vive,
> mai non potrebbe il pianto
> adeguarsi al tuo danno ed allo scorno;
> che fosti donna, or sei povera ancella. ("All'Italia" 18–24)

> (Weep on my Italy,
> for indeed you have reason to do so,
> for the Italian people were born to conquer,
> whether fortune be favorable or adverse!
> Even if your eyes were two living fountains
> never could your lament compare
> with your ills and scorn.
> For you were a great lady: now an impoverished servant.)[51]

In "La sera del dì di festa," Leopardi bends the ear of his lady ("donna mia") (3), the moon, with a finesse lacking in the stately, formal overture to Italy in the second poem. The silent, stolen moments of address in the idyll — for example, "tu dormi, che t'accolse agevol sonno / Nelle tue chete stanze" (Taken easily by sleep, you lie / Untroubled in your hushed rooms) — are a world away from the pathos and accusations of the patriotic work, with its talk of warfare, historical destiny, and a fallen national allegory. Yet Leopardi himself emphasized that politically engaged compositions like "All'Italia" ought to achieve an oratorical eloquence that he deemed crucial to establishing a native lyric Italian tradition. One of his prime examples of eloquent lyric — that is, verse that can hold an argument and move with persuasive conceptual force — was Petrarch's canzone 128, the acknowledged subtext of "All'Italia." Though highly politicized, the female national allegory in Leopardi shares much with the other dead women of his apostrophes, including the unfulfilled hopes and cruel *sorte* (destiny) of Sappho and Silvia ("Ultimo canto di Saffo" ["Sappho's Last Song"] 23; "A Silvia" ["To Sylvia"] 59). Glossing the rhetoric of mortality that subtends his poetic construction of Italy, Leopardi writes in his notebook, the *Zibaldone di pensieri* (Miscellany of thoughts), on November 10–11, 1823: "Nel 600, ed anche nel 700, l'Italia già uccisa, palpitava e fumava ancora. Così discorrasi della Spagna. Or l'una e l'altra sono immobili e gelate, e nel pieno dominio della morte" (2:2033).[52] (In the seventeenth and eighteenth centuries, having already been killed, Italy barely managed to breathe and smolder on. The same happened to Spain. And now both are immobile and frozen, in the full thrall of death.) His Italia exhibits the same lovely form of another of his beloved ladies, the "graziosa luna" (graceful moon) he serenades in the first line of "Alla luna." However much Leopardi's Italia differs in aspect and tone from his other apostrophized women, the common economy of images in "All'Italia" and the contemporary idylls (their intimacy of address, tears and wounds, paralyzing nostalgia) show that the boundaries separating Leopardi's historical and idyllic lyrics are more porous than traditionally thought.

Perhaps the most striking characteristic of "All'Italia" is philological: in typical Leopardian fashion, the poem is a soaring literary history-in-miniature. The archetypal Dantesque Italian national allegory resurfaces in Leopardi's "che fosti donna, or sei povera ancella" (For you were a great lady: now an impoverished servant) (24), an echo of Dante's transition from "donna di provincie" to "bordello" (*Purg.* 6.78). Leopardi's *ancella* (servant) is, of course, a less derogatory term than Dante's prostitute; but, like Dante, Leopardi in line 24 emphasizes a female fall from grace and corruption of morals, figured in his allegory's disheveled hair ("sparte le chiome") and uncovered flesh ("senza velo") ("All'Italia" 14). The preceding image of a once "formosissma donna" (gorgeous lady) (10), now lying tearful and battered ("Oimè quante ferite, / che lividor, che sangue!" [How many wounds, alas! / What blood and bruises!]) (8–

9), recalls the representations of the *donna italica* by Canova and Machiavelli. Canova's statue *Italia piangente,* completed less than a decade before Leopardi composed "All'Italia," anticipates the sorrow and shame of Leopardi's national allegory, for in each artist Italia turns her tear-stained face from view: "nascondendo la faccia / tra le ginocchia, e piange" (hiding her face between her knees / She weeps) ("All'Italia" 16–17). Similarly, Machiavelli writes in the final chapter of the *Principe* that Italy is a woman who is leaderless, beaten, bruised, and subjected to every kind of injury. The early section of "All'Italia" also contains an Alfierian overture to the poet's desire to enflame the weakened "Italic" national heart in sonnet 54 ("Dante, signor d'ogni uom che carmi scriva," discussed above): "Dammi, o ciel, che sia foco / agl'italici petti il sangue mio" (O Heaven, grant that my blood may inspire Italian breasts!) ("All'Italia" 39–40). Although Leopardi is unlikely to have had Alfieri's poem in mind here, I accept the critical view that a distinctly Alfierian lexicon suffuses the vocabulary of "All'Italia" with a patriotic fervor.[53]

However composite the subtext of "All'Italia," the verbal shadows cast by Petrarch's canzone 128 loom largest. Leopardi's Petrarchan debt is clear from the opening of "All'Italia," which begins "O patria mia" just as Petrarch's canzone 128 starts with the vocative "O Italia mia." Many other clues of poetic kinship appear immediately after: Leopardi alludes to twin Petrarchan symbols, "lauro" (laurel) in line 5 and "velo" (veil) in line 14; and Leopardi's Italy, like Petrarch's, is gorgeous, defenseless, uncovered, and riddled with wounds ("piaghe"). Leopardi dramatically invokes Petrarch's overture to the affective bonds of the childhood *nido* (nest) through his patriotic warrior's final lament: "Alma terra natia, / la vita che mi desti ecco ti rendo" (Sweet native land, the life you gave me, / behold, I offer up for you) (59–60).[54] Though the sprawling, hyperbolic, and uneven "All'Italia" lacks the tightly controlled, classical rhetorical structure of canzone 128, each aims to persuade its reader of a nationalist cause by combining historical argumentation with the music, imagery, and allusive force of lyric.[55] If the Roman-inspired Petrarch in "Italia mia" sought to combine the delicacy of Horace with the oratory of Cicero, the Hellenic-minded Leopardi aims in "All'Italia" to combine Pindar with Demosthenes.

For Leopardi, as for Petrarch and Italy's other national allegorists, the most distinctive aspect of Italia is temporal. A once great lady, she has fallen into decay and disgrace because of her corruption and foreign contamination. Like his predecessors, Leopardi imbues his "formosissima donna" with a beautiful if broken modern Italian body and an unattainable ancient Roman soul, then wistfully asks: "Dov'è la forza antica?" (Where is the ancient might?) (28). This unhappy corporeal dialectic appears as early as the opening lines, wherein Italy's physical appearance, however dazzling, serves as the mask to cover what she has lost:

> O patria mia, vedo le mura e gli archi
> e le colonne e i simulacri e l'erme
> torri degli avi nostri,
> ma la gloria non vedo. ("All'Italia" 1–4)
>
> (O my beloved land, the walls and the arches
> and the columns and the images do I behold
> and the solitary towers of our ancient ancestors.
> But the glory I do not behold.)

However bound to his precursors in establishing this ancient-modern dichotomy, Leopardi challenges the monolithic divisions he inherited by staking out a new aesthetic rhetoric permeated with the progressive political energies of his age. As Carolyn Springer notes,[56] the intended audience for Leopardi's apostrophe is not Petrarch's elite *signori*—or, for that matter, Alfieri's Dante or Machiavelli's Medici—but rather the *popolo* (people). The poet presents himself, to quote Wordsworth of the *Lyrical Ballads,* as a man speaking among other men.[57] The urgency of the Leopardian apostrophe to Italy also marks a distance from the Petrarchan source, because though the latter admitted its rhetorical impotence ("ben che 'l parlar sia indarno" [although speech does not aid]) (canzone 128.1), Leopardi fairly shouts at his Italia: "Attendi, Italia, attendi" (Listen closely, Italy, listen closely) ("All'Italia" 45). Within the fiction of the poem, moreover, Leopardi's narrator courts not the peaceful study and retirement of Petrarch but rather the glorious, Ortis-like gesture of self-sacrifice: "io solo / combatterò, procomberò sol io" (I, alone, shall do battle. / I, alone, advancing forward, shall die for you) (37–38). Leopardi's exhortation would have us believe that words do in fact matter, especially when the blood spilled for a nation consecrates this verbal message in a manner reminiscent of Foscolo's "Dei sepolcri."

Though we have some material on the relationship between Leopardi and Foscolo, the work on Leopardi's debt to Foscolo's poetry, especially "Dei sepolcri," is generally limited or dated.[58] Yet, I believe it is Foscolo who, above all, provides us the best clue as to why suddenly, midgallop as it were, Leopardi's narrative in "All'Italia" defers to Simonides. The second half of the poem, in which Leopardi rewrites Simonides' fragmentary hymn to the fallen heroes of Thermopylae, recalls Foscolo's ancient Greek invocations in "Dei sepolcri," first the Aegean travels of his friend Pindemonte and then the sustained meditation on the Italian political afterlife of the fallen Troy. Leopardi's "All'Italia," like Foscolo's "Dei sepolcri," sought to resolve the centuries-long crises of Italian fragmentation by anchoring its plea for national unity in the rhetoric of the sepulcher and the honor of dying for one's nation:

> Oh venturose e care e benedette
> l'antiche età, che a morte,
> per la patria correan le genti a squadre. ("All'Italia" 61–63)

> (O happy, loving, and blessed ancient days
> when men raced in droves to die for their country.)

Foscolo similarly writes "a' generosi / Giusta di gloria dispensiera è morte" (Death grants the great of soul their due) ("Sepolcri" 220–21; "Sepulchers" 223–24),[59] shortly after connecting Alfieri's stalwart patriotism with the glorious warriors' deaths in the Battle of Marathon ("Sepolcri" 190–212). Like "Dei sepolcri," "All'Italia" measures immortality less in terms of the soul's afterlife and more in the capacity of the departed to shape the memories of the living. For Leopardi, the spot where the dying soldier falls is soaked in a sanctifying blood that, as a metonymy, renders the site an actual physical locus for future nationalist reverence; as a metaphor, it suggests the sacrifices necessary for the establishment of an enduring transhistorical community:

> La vostra tomba è un'ara; e qua mostrando
> verran le madri ai parvoli le belle
> orme del vostro sangue. ("All'Italia" 125–27)

> (Your tomb is an altar and to it will come
> mothers pointing out the beautiful traces of
> your blood to their children.)

The lines recall the conclusion to "Dei sepolcri," where the blood-soaked tombs of the Trojan heroes serve as metonymic sites from which the Italian nation will spring via Aeneas's pilgrimage, as well as metaphorical analogies for the sepulchers of Santa Croce that elicit Foscolo's nationalist hymn:

> E tu onore di pianti, Ettore, avrai
> Ove fia santo e lagrimato il sangue
> Per la patria versato, e finchè il Sole
> Risplenderà su le sciagure umane. ("Sepolcri" 292–95)

> (And you, Hector, shall be honored by tears wherever men lament and hold
> sacred blood poured out for a fatherland, and as long as the sun shall shine on
> the calamities of man.) (Kroeber, 183)

Leopardi shrewdly noted that, though many early readers of "Dei sepolcri"—including the person to whom it is dedicated, Pindemonte—found distasteful Foscolo's introduction of Hector and the Trojan calamities, these same naysayers continue to read the passage with secret, passionate interest.⁶⁰ This hidden cult, Leopardi writes, derives from the fact that the Trojan episode, with all its graphic details, returns the Italian reader to his early childhood encounters with Homer's text. Like Foscolo's Pindemonte, Italian children roamed, Leopardi suggests, the imaginary vistas of Odysseus and Achilles. In underscoring this common affective literary experience, Leopardi anticipates Anderson's theories on imagined communities by diagnosing the crucial role that the death of Hector plays in the construction of Italian national identity and by grasping (like Foscolo) the profound effect of ancient myth on his people's collective psyche.

More than his prose defense of "Dei sepolcri," Leopardi's concluding stanzas in "All'Italia" vindicate Foscolo's distillation of Trojan blood into Italian spirit, for he follows Foscolo in projecting his poetic voice into an uncertain political future that he urges to heed the lessons of the ancients:

> Che se il fato è diverso, e non consente
> ch'io per la Grecia i moribondi lumi
> chiuda prostrato in guerra,
> così la vereconda
> fama del vostro vate appo i futuri
> possa, volendo i numi,
> tanto durar quanto la vostra duri. ("All'Italia" 134–40)

> (For if fate is adverse and does not allow me
> to shut my dying eyes in a war for Greece,
> still may the modest fame of your prophet-poet
> endure among future ages,
> if it pleases the gods,
> as long as your own fame endures.)

The proposed endurance of Leopardi's voice of Simonides, with its exaltation of soldierly blood, evokes the equally abiding concluding image of "sacred blood poured out for a fatherland, . . . as long as the sun shall shine on the calamities of man" in "Dei sepolcri." In the surpassing dignity, grace, and pathos of Foscolo's final verses, Leopardi discovered that gem of Petrarchan *eloquenza* whose nationalist aura he hoped would infuse his own youthful paean to Italy.

As with *Jacopo Ortis*, the reader of "All'Italia" often has the impression that the political discourse is more about the state of mind and spirit of the author himself rather than his country or his characters.⁶¹ In a sense, the truest Leopardian poetic heir to "Dei sepolcri" is his masterpiece "La ginestra, o il fiore del deserto" ("The Broom, or the Flower of the Desert"; 1836), which also draws imagery from Foscolo's poem and achieves a measured, humane emotional texture and seamless form akin to the Foscolian hymn.[62] Yet, for all their formal sympathies, an emotional and philosophical chasm divides the poets in these compositions. "Dei sepolcri," as we have seen, translates the razing of Troy and Italy's subsequent journey across the wilderness into a secular political discourse that culminates in the transhistorical community embodied in the tombs of Santa Croce. In "La ginestra," by contrast, the progressive musings on the national *ara* (altar) prophesied in "All'Italia" give way to reflections on a murderous flood of lava, burst forth from Vesuvius to destroy Pompeii and remind humankind of nature's indifference to its dreams of *"le magnifiche sorti e progressive"* (*splendid progress and destiny*) ("Ginestra" 51; Leopardi's ironic emphasis). The biblical epigraph to "La ginestra" may be the most indicative sign of Leopardi's vaunted philosophical pessimism and his distance from the solemn optimism of "Dei sepolcri": "E gli uomini vollero piuttosto le tenebre che la luce" (And men loved darkness rather than light) (John 3:19). Foscolo writes in "Dei sepolcri" that the eyes of one about to expire seek the light ("Perchè gli occhi dell'uom cercan morendo / Il Sole"), an image that epitomizes his desire to soften the brutal reality of mortality with stoic hope (122–23). In a chiasmus-like reversal, Leopardi claims instead that, though surrounded by the sweet light of life, we yearn for those shadows and tombs that Foscolo's Homer harrows out of their slumber. Though Leopardi never retracted his reflections on Italy as woman and wound in "All'Italia," by the time of his premature death in 1837, the martial, self-sacrificial voice of his early patriotism must have seemed as alien to him as the suicidal nationalism of Ortis seemed to the dying Foscolo.

8

The Body of Parini

To whom does the corpse belong? This is a question that Robert Harrison asks in his study of the debt binding us to our ancestors.[1] Critiquing Martin Heidegger, he argues that our sense of humanity derives from our living relationship with the dead and not from our consciousness of an abstract and inevitable state of death. We live in and through those specific predecessors who inspired, deluded, nourished, confounded, and loved us. When we lose them, we come to understand the notion of death as a real, concrete event instead of as a disembodied metaphysical certainty à la Heidegger. Moreover, the rituals we observe in disposing of their corpses serve as powerful cultural institutions that establish a sense of civic and social identity. Our lives in light of these deaths are ones of continued negotiation, silent conversation, and, to return to Heidegger, the discharging of *Schuld* (in both its meanings, debt and guilt) compelled by the deceased with whom we were intimate. Harrison writes that, in order to keep the dead alive, we need to possess their image; hence the signal value of the corpse. Only in confronting the corpse, identifying the body, verifying death, and performing the appropriate rites do we liberate the image of the deceased from its no longer animate organism. This is why parents and relations of the missing or kidnapped will so often speak of attaining closure when they finally receive or discover the remains of their loved ones. In order to gain access to the living image of the dead and give it an afterlife, we need first to occupy their death. The term *habeas corpus* (you must have the body) thus obtains as both a legal and an existential imperative.

In a poetic version of this line of thinking, Dylan Thomas concludes "A Refusal to Mourn the Death, by Fire, of a Child in London" (1936) with the cascading truism:

> Deep with the first dead lies London's daughter,
> Robed in the long friends,
> The grains beyond age, the dark veins of her mother,
> Secret by the unmourning water
> Of the riding Thames.
> After the first death, there is no other. (19–24)[2]

The vatic last sentence initially appeals to the reader for its clarity in the face of trauma. Yes, biology, insofar as we know, allows one life cycle, and so the body only dies once. Moreover, if we believe in the immortality of the soul, then yes again, this first death stands as but a minor prelude to an eternal life. But there is also a third way to interpret Thomas's seemingly naive conclusion, one in line with the notion of humanity implicit in Vico's discussion of burial as the returning of the body to the *humus* (earth). The poem ends with a solemn imagery of an interment and a subsequent life-affirming declaration that suggest that the first death of the girl belongs as much to her mourners as to her. The poem does not reveal whether the girl's burial was by human hands or nature itself during the fire; what matters is the invocation of a rite that betokens the symbolical separation of her spirit from her flesh. Her image can thereupon persist long after her charred remains; hence no further death is possible for her, as she continues to inhabit her ongoing relationships with her loved ones. These concluding lines thereby answer the question posed at the beginning of this chapter: if there is to be no second spiritual death after the first biological one, then the corpse must belong to the living.

Foscolo meditated long and hard on such matters. In his critique of Staël's *Corinne* in *Lettere scritte dall'Inghilterra,* he quarreled with the French author over her factual errors in discussing the graves in Santa Croce. He writes that Staël's confusion of the bones of Pietro Aretino and Leonardo Bruni reveal her "metaphysical" misreading of Italian history: that is, her misrepresentations of fact in light of her theoretical reflections on Italian cultural history. Because her musings on death bracket the actual details surrounding the dead she surveys, Staël is a Heidegerrian avant la lettre — and we have already witnessed the revulsion of Foscolo, like Wordsworth, for "Teutonic" metaphysics. For Foscolo, the principal question was not, to whom does the corpse belong?

Rather, it was, what do we owe the corpse? More specifically, what do we owe *a* corpse? In keeping with Harrison's distinction between an abstract notion of death and the concrete realities of the dead themselves, Foscolo carefully individuated the deceased according to the same categories that distinguished them while they lived. His thoughts on mortality also informed his views on the Italian body politic, with a major difference from those paradigmatic models discussed in the previous chapter: for Foscolo, Italy was both a man and a woman.

In a refreshing departure from more traditional Italian antecedents, recent American criticism has begun to address the issue of gender in Foscolo's work.[3] Though the philologist in Foscolo might have scorned a critical category of such recent coinage as "the body," his literary work reveals a long-standing fascination with corporeality, especially in its Lucretian declension. "Dei sepolcri" never speaks of a disembodied or immaterial soul; rather, it questions the afterlife of the individual in the minds, memories, and mythologies of humankind. It seems natural, then, that the metaphor of the Italian body politic should pique Foscolo's attention, since it conflates his perennial interests in nationalism and allegorical personification. Appropriately, the first sustained reflection on the Italian body politic by Foscolo appears in *Jacopo Ortis*, which, in the manner of *Corinne, ou l'Italie*, might have been retitled to carry the appositive: *Ortis, ovvero l'Italia*. Like Corinne, Ortis becomes, through his protracted self-sacrifice on behalf of his nation, an analogy for Italy; but before this occurs, the national allegory passes through both a matriarchal (Teresa) and a patriarchal (Parini) stage. The body of Parini fascinated Foscolo throughout his career, to such a degree that he transformed it into a privileged metaphor for the historical iniquities of the Risorgimento. Most important, Foscolo learns in and through Parini's body that, when we build our homes over the dead, we must make sure that the inhabitants of the necropolis share the same social order and legal rights that uphold the living city. For, as Foscolo writes in "Dei sepolcri," no plant can bloom in soil cursed by the dead.

In *Ultime lettere di Jacopo Ortis*, we first encounter the body of Teresa on December 3, 1797, when the protagonist writes to his friend and the text's narrator, Lorenzo:

> Era neglettamente vestita di bianco; il tesoro delle sue chiome biondissime diffuse su le spalle e sul petto, i suoi divini occhi nuotanti nel piacere, il suo viso sparso di un soave languore, il suo braccio di rose, il suo piede, le sue dita arpeggianti mollemente, tutto tutto era armonia: ed io sentiva una nuova delizia nel contemplarla. Bensí Teresa parea confusa, veggendosi d'improvviso un uomo che la mirava cosí discinta, ... essa tuttavia proseguiva. (*Ultime lettere* 26)

(She was casually dressed in white, the treasure of her blond hair overspread her shoulders and breast, her divine eyes were bathed in pleasure, her whole face evinced a gentle languor, her rosy arm, her foot, her fingers softly playing the harp—all was in complete harmony, and I felt an unwonted delight in contemplating her. Although Teresa seemed confused, suddenly finding a man gazing at her, carelessly dressed as she was, . . . she nevertheless went on playing.) (*Last Letters* 22)[4]

The virginal purity of Teresa's dress and the natural disposition of her clothes and manner suggest a lack both of coquetry and of sexual energy consistent with Foscolo's tendency to think of her as mother or friend rather than as lover. Her physical presence radiates a self-enclosure whose *armonia* (harmony), rather than drawing in the Dionysian Ortis, leaves him content to hold back and gaze upon her with Apollonian detachment. By reacting so delicately to her visible discomfort, Ortis reveals the purity of his own intentions toward Teresa and her unapproachable virtue. Yet she returns his objectifying look; in refusing to be objectified, she is an anti-Corinne who is able to meet defiantly the very stare that the male protagonist would wish to fix upon her. In glancing back at the man who beholds her, Teresa chafes at the allegorical chains, however lovely, with which Foscolo has shackled her.

The bodily musings assume a nationalist dimension in a subsequent, less ethereal encounter between Ortis and a Francophile woman just a week later on December 11, 1797. This patrician Italian wife is the antithesis of Teresa: her former beauty has lost its virginal innocence, she is gifted in feminine coquetry, and she happily reciprocates Ortis's gaze ("Ella sta con me volentieri" [She likes to be with me]) (*Ultime lettere* 27; *Last Letters* 22). As verdantly fresh as Teresa is, her opponent "Dea" (goddess), as Foscolo ironically refers to her, artificially perfumes the air of the boudoir to which she invites Ortis with a thousand scents. Ortis tries to defend himself from her charms by focusing on the Teresa-like allegorical and *vergine* Diana painted on the ceiling, but he makes the mistake of leafing through some *romanzi francesi* (French novels) strewn about the bedroom. These books distill the national essence of this alternately enchanting and disenchanting woman, and push Foscolo's representation of her into an allegorical key:

> E vedeva madama tutta molle e rugiadosa entrarsene presta presta e quasi intirizzita di freddo, e abbandonarsi sovra una sedia d'appoggio che la cameriera le preparò presso al fuoco. . . . Ella non era vestita che di una lunga e rada camicia la quale non essendo allacciata radeva quasi il tappeto, lasciando ignude le spalle e il petto ch'era per altro voluttuosamente difeso da una candida pelle in cui ella stavasi involta. (28)

(And I [Ortis] saw my fine lady, all soft and dewy, enter very quickly and almost numb with cold, and throw herself down on an easy chair which the maid had placed near the fire for her. . . . She was dressed only in a thin long gown which, being unlaced, almost grazed the carpet. It left her shoulders and her breast bare, but they were voluptuously protected by a white fur which she had wrapped around her.) (23–24)

The reader senses that Ortis would like to be more complacent in his subsequent rebuke of the dissolute woman, yet the pulse of his attraction is palpable, perhaps because she is so unlike the perfect, and hence perfectly remote, Teresa. The appealingly fragile woman must warm her numb bones by the fire, and she still wears the smoldering softness of recent sleep. Her feminine vulnerability attracts Ortis, who lingers over descriptions of her plush white arm and tiny foot "simile a quello che l'Albano dipingerebbe a una Grazia ch'esce dal bagno" (such as Albani would paint on a Grace issuing from her bath) (*Ultime lettere* 28; *Last Letters* 24). The passage is the most erotic in the entire novel, and the cadence of the prose, with its lush and unhurried invocations of female beauty, would seem to anticipate Ortis's sexual capitulation. But then a memory stays him: "Un genio benefico mi presentò la immagine di Teresa" (*Ultime lettere* 28). (A good angel brought Teresa's image to my mind [*Last Letters* 24].) He pictures Teresa, freshly arisen from bed and by the fireplace, and the recollection transforms his desire for the recumbent woman into reverence and awe for his *donna angelicata*. He apologizes immediately to the half-naked woman for his inopportune visit and excuses himself. Afterward, he tells Lorenzo that he composed the letter describing the woman and his misadventure with her in *lo bello stile* (the beautiful style), in order to mimic the extravagant rhetoric associated with his visit. Many of the effects of the seductive woman's room bear French traces: the novels, the perfumes, lap dog, and other feminine accoutrements that fill the pages of those same French novels that line her boudoir. The strident anti-Gallicism of Foscolo's early *maître à penser*, Vittorio Alfieri, seems to be hovering in the background of his negative descriptions of the idle chatter, coquetry, and opulent decadence that characterize the lady's domestic and social environment. By invoking the figure of the prototypical Italian maiden Teresa at the moment in which he is about to fall for the Gallic figure of the seductress, Foscolo lends to the sentimental education of his poet-protagonist Ortis a nationalist component permeated with patriotic ideology.

In a later entry, from March 17, 1798, Ortis responds to Lorenzo's fear "ch'io sia vinto oggimai dall'amore da *dimenticarmi di te e della patria*" (that I am, by now, so overwhelmed by love that I forget both you and my native land) (*Ultime lettere* 38; italics in original; *Last Letters* 34).[5] He reminds his friend that love for one's country can never be moderated let alone extinguished; then adds that, without Teresa, he would be in his grave. The subsequent allusions to Petrarch and Dante situate Ortis's discourse on *italianità* in the tradition of gender-inflected nationalist poetics. Quoting Petrarch (see italics), he tells Lorenzo that he weeps for his country, but his tears are lonely ones ("*Che le lagrime mie si spargan sole*" [(I desire) "*simply to shed some solitary tears*"]) (*Ultime lettere* 39; *Last Letters* 34). The allusion to *Rerum vulgarium fragmenta* 18.13–14 and Petrarch's unfulfilled longing for Laura locates Ortis's futile national tears in an elegiac mode similar to the dominant register of Petrarch's "Italia mia." Foscolo's long-standing interest in the Petrarchan national allegory extended into his British exile, where one of his last literary endeavors was to produce a collaborative English translation of Petrarch's canzone 128.[6] In a March 17, 1798, entry, he infuses the Petrarchan subtext with a Dantesque component, when Ortis claims that he cries for his country like Francesca da Rimini from *Inf.* 5.102: "*Che mi fu tolta*, e il modo ancor m'offende" (*Ultime lettere* 40; Foscolo's italics for citation). ([My homeland] was taken from me, "*in a way that still offends*" [*Last Letters* 35].) Foscolo continues in the Dantesque-Petrarchan line of nationalist gender reflection by immediately invoking a wounded Italian body politic ("le piaghe d'Italia" [the wounds of Italy]) with a rhetoric that also recalls Machiavelli. Just as the latter author spoke of a sick body politic incapable of regulating its parts, Ortis describes an Italy whose doctors, lawyers, merchants, nobles, priests, and professors fail to serve as proper guardians of the Italian organism. Echoing Alfieri's *Della tirannide,* Foscolo writes that the answer to this perennial crisis is an internal peace that will rid Italy of its contamination by foreigners (especially the French and Austrians) and restore Liberty to her throne.[7]

The conflation of love for Italy and love for Teresa comes shortly thereafter:

> Pur nondimeno io mi sento rinsanguinare piú sempre nell'anima questo furore di patria: e quando penso a Teresa — e se spero — rientro in un subito in me assai piú costernato di prima; e ridico: Quand'anche l'amica mia fosse madre de' miei figliuoli, i miei figliuoli non avrebbero patria; e la cara compagna della mia vita se n'accorgerebbe gemendo. — Pur troppo! alle altre passioni che fanno alle giovinette sentire sull'aurora del loro giorno fuggitivo, i dolori, e piú assai alle giovinette italiane, s'è aggiunto questo infelice amore di patria. (41)

> (Yet I feel that this passion of mine for a homeland is increasing all the time. And when I think of Teresa — and if I begin to hope — I suddenly come back to myself with greater consternation than before, and I say again, "Even if my friend were the mother of my children, my children would not have a homeland, and the dear companion of my life would to her sorrow realise it." It is

only too true! To the other passions which make girls, and especially Italian girls, sorrow at the dawning of their brief day, is added this unhappy love of their homeland.) (37)

Ortis will never have Teresa in the manner he wants her, as virginal wife, because the lack of a mother country elicits the tragic analogy of Teresa as a mother of children without a country. If Teresa cannot produce for him properly Italian offspring, Ortis is not sexually interested in her. His desire for Teresa thus assumes the form of an all-consuming but unconsummated living hell similar to the one experienced by the freshly invoked Paolo and Francesca. Ortis and Teresa are two passionate lovers lacking a bodily nexus and a body politic. Toward the end of the book, when Ortis realizes that he can longer have Teresa's body in its purity, he decides to commit suicide.[8] Because Teresa can never embody the Italy Foscolo seeks, she remains trapped for him in an immaterial and asexual allegorical form, akin to the beautiful but removed *donna italica* of Petrarch. For the Foscolo of *Ultime lettere di Jacopo Ortis,* the physical nature of love invariably gives way to its political dimensions.

These gender musings of *Ortis* assume a masculine turn through Foscolo's elaborate reconstruction of the body of Parini. It is to the pages of *Ultime lettere di Jacopo Ortis* that we owe the myth of Giuseppe Parini (1732–99) that would fuel the fire of much Risorgimento rhetoric. According to this legend, the fate of Parini, whose greatest work *Il giorno* (The day; 1763) satirizes the ignorance and decadence of a typical Lombard nobleman, reflects the fate of Italy's intellectuals and artists who sought to benefit their yet-to-be-born nation. Politically persecuted for his critique of the aristocracy, the aged Parini was forced to live in a state of poverty exacerbated by his own chronically degenerative physical health. In *Jacopo Ortis,* the reader encounters a Parini who is on his last legs: a broken and bruised figure who walks with difficulty yet who inspires the young Ortis to acts of patriotic resistance through his uncompromising virtue and unbendable will.[9] The early reception of Parini's work did not anticipate the elegiac and legendary turn it took in Foscolo and his contemporaries. Reactions to Parini by the major writers of his age ranged from outright hostility (Pietro Verri) to grudging respect (Alfieri) and admiration (Baretti); but nowhere in the Settecento does one find the heroic portrait created by Foscolo.[10] Whether positive or negative, the earliest readings of Parini tend to focus on his humble origins, personal dignity, physical ailments, and status as "cittadino integro e retto" (exemplary and upstanding citizen) (Caretti, *Parini* 17).

A contemporary of Foscolo's and the first major editor of Parini's work, Francesco Reina, laced his writings with a sustained meditation on Parini's body. An Italian patriot imprisoned during the Austrian occupation, Reina produced a biographical reading of Parini's poetry that conflated the author's poetic, thematic concerns with his physical, moral makeup—a move reminiscent of the use of Dante by Reina's hero, the Alfieri of *Del principe e delle lettere*. Reina writes in 1801:

> Una strana debolezza di muscoli lo aveva renduto dalla nascita gracile e cagionevole; ma la sua prima giovinezza piena di brio, e di alacrità non risentissi punto di quegl'incomodi, che tanto grave gli rendettero la virilità, e la vecchiaia. A ventun anno soffrí egli una violenta stiracchiatura di muscoli, ed una maggiore debolezza; perloché gambe, cosce, e braccia cominciarongli a mancar d'alimento, ad estenuarsi, e a perdere la snellezza, e la forza sí necessarie agli uffizi loro. Credevansi da principio, che il suo andare lento e grave fosse una filosofica caricatura, ma presto si conobbe proceder ciò da malattia, la quale crebbe in guisa di togliergli il libero uso delle sue membra. Egli è però da avvertire, che tanta era in lui la dignità e maestria del portamento, del porgere, e dello stampar orma, che ogni gentile persona era obbligata alla maraviglia, veggendo il suo difetto. Statura alta, fronte bella e spaziosa, vivacissimo grand'occhio nero, naso tendente all'aquilino, aperti lineamenti rilevati e grandeggianti, muscoli del volto mobilissimi e fortemente scolpiti, mano maestra di bei moti, labbra modificate ad ogni affetto speziale, voce gagliarda pieghevole e sonora, discorso energico e risoluto, ed austerità di aspetto raddolcita spesso da un grazioso sorriso indicavano in lui l'uomo di animo straordinariamente elevato, e conciliavangli una riverenza singolare.[11]

(A strange weakness of the muscles had rendered [Parini] from birth sickly and frail, but his early vivacious youth may have been completely free from those sufferings that rendered his adult life and old age so painful. At the age of twenty-one, he experienced a violent muscular affliction and a decline in health, so that his legs, thighs, and arms began to atrophy, attenuate, and lose that agility and force so necessary to their functioning. People believed at first that his slow and ponderous gait made him seem self-consciously philosophical, but soon they understood that it was the result of ill health, which spread in such a way as to deny him the free use of his limbs. It should be noted, however, that the dignity and majesty of his bearing, gestures, and movement were so impressive that any decent person was obliged to marvel when he saw Parini's handicaps. He was tall, with a broad and handsome brow, most lively and large black eyes, a nose tending toward the aquiline, and frank, impressive, and imposing features. His facial structure was quite strong and sculpted, his hand capable of graceful motion, and his lips of an unusual emotional expressiveness. He had a vigorous, supple, and sonorous voice, an energetic and resolute speech, and an austerity of aspect that would often be sweetened by a graceful smile. All these characteristics showed Parini to be a man of an extraordinarily elevated spirit and lent him an air of singular reverence.)

The endurance and dignity of the suffering figure implies the principled and stoic resistance of a *poeta vate* who will bear the slings and arrows of Italian political misfortune rather than enter into complicity with an insidious power structure. Limbs that do not bend to the ravages of illness suggest an individual who does not surrender to domestic corruption and foreign occupation. Parini's resistance in the face of physical misfortune reveals his capacity to transform this same misformed body into a thing of beauty and wonder. The physical and moral excellence of Parini, Reina writes, made this "Maestro di Libertà" (Master of Liberty) into a latter-day Socrates whose disciples included many of the leading writers of the age (for example, the now-forgotten Palamede Carpani, Antonio Conti, Giambattista Scotti, and Giovanni Torti). Foscolo added Ortis's name to this list and established him as Parini's most famous, if fictitious, disciple.

Ortis first meets Parini in his natal Milan, a city whose "body" surfaces elsewhere in Foscolo's work.[12] Their brief but crucial encounter represents a symbolic passing of the literary-historical baton. Parini is described repeatedly as "vecchio" (old), and he offers Ortis the compassionate advice that the fictional Alfieri denies the patriot. The intimacy of the meeting between Ortis and Parini, a master-apprentice tête-à-tête in the tradition of Dante-Virgil and Plato-Socrates, reveals their many shared characteristics. Each, unlike Alfieri, comes from humble origins, chooses democratic resistance over seclusion, and, most important, is ready to sacrifice himself in the name of his country. These "suicides" — actual in the case of Ortis, figurative for Parini — draw on the Foscolian myth of Cato. Just as Ortis sought to redeem Italy by shedding blood in the manner of Cato's self-sacrifice against the tyranny of Caesar in Lucan's *Pharsalia*, so too does Parini offer his body to the *corpus italicum*. He implores Ortis: "di'? spargerai tutto il sangue col quale conviene nutrire una nascente repubblica? arderai le tue case con le faci della guerra civile? unirai col terrori i partiti? spegnerai con la morte le opinioni? adeguerai con le stragi le fortune? ma se tu cadi tra via, vediti esecrato dagli uni come demagogo, dagli altri come tiranno (December 4, 1798; *Ultime lettere* 97). (Tell me, will you shed all the blood with which a nascent republic must be nourished? Will you burn your houses in the flames of civil war? Will you unite the parties with terror? Will you extinguish the opinions with death? Will you even out men's property with massacres? [But] if you fall by the wayside, you will find yourself cursed by some as a demagogue, by others as a tyrant [*Last Letters* 96].) Parini's speech to Ortis exudes despair, because he imagines that the lifetime of his literary and civic endeavors has been for naught: "E pensi tu, proruppe, che s'io discernessi un barlume di libertà, mi perderei ad onta della mia inferma vecchiaja in questi vani lamenti?" (*Ultime lettere* 96). ("And do you think,"

[Parini] burst out, "that if I could see one gleam of liberty, I would give myself over to these vain laments, despite my infirmity and old age?" [*Last Letters* 94–95].) Parini rejects the iconoclastic withdrawal of Alfieri and opts for the external display of one's sufferings, where the spectacle of a disgraced body becomes a morality play and public self-dramatization of the nation's woes. Ortis quickly grasps the historical resonance of his advice:

> Tacque—ed io dopo lunghissimo silenzio esclamai: O Cocceo Nerva! tu almeno sapevi morire incontaminato.—Il vecchio mi guardò:—Se tu nè speri, nè temi fuori di questo mondo—e mi stringeva la mano—ma io!—Alzò gli occhi al cielo, e quella severa sua fis[i]onomia si raddolciva di un soave conforto come s'ei lassú contemplasse tutte le sue speranze.—Intesi un calpestio che s'avanzava verso di noi; e poi travidi gente fra' tiglj; ci rizzammo; e l'accompagnai sino alle sue stanze. (97–98)

> ([Parini] fell silent. After a long silence I [Ortis] exclaimed: "O [Cocceius] Nerva![13] You at least knew how to die uncontaminated by the corruption you saw coming." The old man looked at me. "If you have no hope, and no fear of anything beyond this world"—and he clasped my hand—"but I. . . ." He raised his eyes to heaven, and his stern face became milder with some sweet comfort, as if he were contemplating all his hopes above. I heard a sound of trampling coming towards us, and then I caught a glimpse of people among the limes. We stood up, and I accompanied him to his apartments.) (96–97)

Foscolo's description of the body of Parini—which, like Lucan's Cato, bears the sign of its impending sacrifice—recalls Reina's bittersweet physical portrait, in which Parini's austerity of aspect would often be sweetened by a graceful smile. Also reminiscent of Reina's stance toward Parini, Foscolo's Ortis exhibits a profound reverence for what he refers to as an extraordinarily elevated spirit. The end of the above passage alerts the reader to the constant political persecution confronting the physically helpless Parini. The spectacle of Parini's body and the gist of his words move Ortis to angry expressions of violence and a call to arms; but the stoic and Cato-like Parini, in the passage's most explicit retrenchment of Foscolo's youthful adherence to Alfieri, questions the type of heroism that Ortis promotes. Heroism, according to Parini, is one-fourth daring, one-fourth crime, and one-half chance. The more noble action is to offer to the grave the same body that has recorded Italy's ignominious acts. Ortis, of course, will eventually heed his new teacher's defense of political martyrdom, thereby embracing the sepulcher of Parini and eschewing the solitude of Alfieri. After accompanying Parini to his apartment, Ortis writes to Lorenzo that the prosopopoeia of the poet is a more effective political voice than the oratory of the demagogue: "Io odo la mia patria che grida:—

SCRIVI CIÒ CHE VEDESTI. MANDERÒ LA MIA VOCE DALLE ROVINE, E TI DETTERÒ LA MIA STORIA. PIANGERANNO I SECOLI SU LA MIA SOLITUDINE; E LE GENTI S'AMMAESTRERANNO NELLE MIE DISAVVENTURE. IL TEMPO ABBATTE IL FORTE: E I DELITTI DI SANGUE SONO LAVATI NEL SANGUE" (December 4, 1798; 98; Foscolo's emphasis). (I hear my homeland crying out to me: "*Write what you have seen. I shall send my voice out from the ruins and tell you my story. The centuries will weep over my solitude, and the peoples will be taught by my misfortunes. Time strikes down the strong, and the crimes of blood are washed in blood*" [97].)

The passage anticipates both the Parinian transfiguration of Ortis's body at book's end ("If [God] had granted me a homeland, I would have spent all my intellect and my blood on its behalf" [March 25, 1799]) and the Homeric resurrection of the sacred blood poured out for the *patria* at the conclusion of "Dei sepolcri." The image of Parini in the December 4, 1798, entry thus forges a Risorgimentalist national allegory that offers an alternative to the centuries-old *donna italica* of Dante, Petrarch, and their successors in the form of a masculine, self-governing, self-sacrificial, and ancient Roman-like figure whose virtue no external polity nor internal corruption can compromise.

After *Jacopo Ortis,* the body of Parini resurfaces in the meditations on the link between death and democracy in "Dei sepolcri." The sepulcher's privileged access to questions of immortality, sacrifice, and transcendence—all crucial terms in the rhetoric of nationalism—inspired poets like Foscolo to connect the topos of graveyard poetry to the concerns and contingencies of nation building. "Dei sepolcri" critiques the inequality and corruption in the city of the dead in order to suggest that the necropolis must be governed by the same standards of law that regulate the living city. Failure to establish order in the realm of the sepulcher, Foscolo proposes, results in a comparable chaos in the same social and political units built upon the bedrock of the deceased. He approaches this matter by querying the muses about the treatment of Parini's corpse:

> Forse tu fra plebei tumuli guardi
> Vagolando, ove dorma il sacro capo
> Del tuo Parini? A lui non ombre pose
> Tra le sue mura la città, lasciava
> D'evirati cantori allettatrice,
> Non pietra, non parola; e forse l'ossa
> Col mozzo capo gl'insanguina il ladro
> Che lasciò sul patibolo i delitti.
> Senti raspar fra le macerie e i bronchi
> La derelitta cagna ramingando

> Su le fosse e famelica ululando;
> E uscir del teschio, ove fuggía la Luna,
> L'úpupa, e svolazzar su per le croci
> Sparse per la funerea campagna,
> E l'immonda accusar col luttúoso
> Singulto i rai di che son pie le stelle
> Alle obblïate sepolture. Indarno
> Sul tuo poeta, o Dea, preghi rugiade
> Dalla squallida notte. Ahi! sugli estinti
> Non sorge fiore ove non sia d'umane
> Lodi onorato e d'amoroso pianto. ("Sepolcri" 70–90)

> (Are you searching amidst common graves
> for the anointed head of your Parini?
> The city that gives herself only to singers
> who have sacrificed their manhood found no shade
> for him within its walls, not a stone,
> not a word. His bones might be bloodied
> by the severed head of some thief who paid
> the price on a scaffold. You can hear a stray
> bitch scratching at the graves among rubble
> and briars, howling with hunger. When the moon
> goes down, a hoopoe slips from the skull
> where it cowers and soars high above the crosses
> sown in death's furrows: it mocks
> the starlight that caresses long-forgotten
> burials. In vain, Goddess, you beg
> bleak night to sprinkle dew
> for your poet. No, flowers will not grow
> over the dead unless the living
> tend them with praise and loving tears.) ("Sepulchers" 74–92)[14]

The violence done to Parini's "sacro capo" (anointed head), like the symbolic head of Ernst Kantorowicz's proverbial king's two bodies, represents a desecration of what should be revered. The lack of care for this *caput* of Italian culture is emphasized by the fact that it may come into contact with the mutilated head of a common thief (76). The city itself, which should be the "tetto materno" (motherland) alluded to in line 65, is a perversion of the national female allegory of nourishing breast and womb that we encountered in Petrarch's canzone 128. The only poets protected by the city are "evirati cantori," the emasculated false rhetoricians whose empty words pervert Italy's historical destiny and encourage its foreign bondage (74). In his description of Parini, Foscolo may be recalling *Aeneid* 3, when Aeneas and his men are thwarted in their attempt to build a city over the remains of Polidorus, whose spirit surges forth to remind the Trojans of his ignominious death and the subsequent curse that afflicts his final place of rest. Independent of the possible Virgilian echo, Parini's abused corpse threatens the mineral realm as well as the human polity, for in lines 75 to 88, Foscolo offers an extended survey of a nature denatured, as it were, in a landscape of waste, vagrancy, and oblivion. The concluding image returns us to the beginning of the poem. It is not for mortals to ask if Parini's soul will outlive his body; rather, their task is to honor his corpse so that his metaphorical body — and by extension, his literary corpus — can regenerate in the mind of humankind. Moreover, it is the citizen's task to ensure that Parini's body receives suitable burial, so that his and other worthy corpses can render fecund the *humus* of the polis, whose figurative resurrection Foscolo translates into the image of a flower rising from the cemetery soil.

Foscolo believes that it is dangerous for the body of Parini to mingle with that of a common thief because, from the time that marriages, religious rites, and courts of law made humans feel compassion for themselves and others, people have protected the dead from the claims of nature.[15] The emphasis here, as throughout "Dei sepolcri," is on burial as a form of *domus* (house): a physical and ethical space that humans set up to shelter themselves from the unforgiving cycles of nature and its principle of survival of the fittest. In "Dei sepolcri," even nature, in the form of its "pie . . . stelle" (pitying stars), seems moved to incredulity by Italian transgressions in the city of the dead (85). One thinks of Lear's curse against nature, when his sanity begins to betray him, and he blasphemes the treachery of his daughters for poisoning the sanctity of family:

> Blow, winds, and crack your cheeks! rage! blow!
> You cataracts and hurricanoes, spout
> Till you have drench'd our steeples, drown'd the cocks!
> You sulphurous and thought-executing fires,
> Vaunt-couriers to oak-cleaving thunder-bolts,
> Singe my white head! And thou, all-shaking thunder,
> Strike flat the thick rotundity o' the world![16]

Parini's desecration invokes a comparable if less exclamatory rhetoric, for his corpse unlawfully mixes with outcasts and thieves; his tainted memory affronts those guardians of culture, the Muses; and the ground in which he lies is as barren as the dread landscape defiled by Lear's obscenities.

"Dei sepolcri" extends into an allegorical register the Risorgimentalist myth of Parini that Foscolo created in *Jacopo Ortis*. Parini sings to Italy from beneath his "povero tetto" (modest rooms), and then later stands as the venerable citizen ("vecchio" [old man]), symbol of stoic endurance ("Sepolcri" 55, 57; "Sepulchers" 68, 72–73). He died on August 15, 1799, not long after his fictive last meeting with Ortis, on December 4, 1798, and he was in fact buried with little fanfare in the common grave of Milan's Porta Comasina. His plight thus emerges from "Dei sepolcri" as a cautionary tale for the unenviable fate that awaits Italy's poet-prophets. It is not enough to say that Foscolo's paean to him in "Dei sepolcri" is an epitaph for an admired predecessor. Rather, Foscolo's literary struggle for the deceased Parini's rights continues that same campaign that marked Parini's endeavors as political crusader in a time of moral-ethical capitulation by many of Italy's public intellectuals. Parini's afterlife as a stain on the landscape, over whom no flower can grow, incarnates a violation of the pact between the living and the dead that Foscolo marks with the howling of beasts and the fluttering of an owl across a desert of unmarked and forgotten graves. Only by returning to Parini's writings and reading the historical iniquity grafted onto his body, "Dei sepolcri" implies, will Italians free themselves of a curse that has rendered infertile the "funerea campagna" (death's furrows) joining the polis to the necropolis ("Sepolcri" 83; "Sepulchers" 86). To return to the question posed at the beginning of this chapter (To whom does the corpse belong?), in order for Italians to hear Parini's message and liberate his image, they must first possess his corpse more humanely.

Foscolo's last major creative work, the *Lettere scritte dall'Inghilterra*, continues the construction of Parini as a Risorgimentalist allegory. In exile, Foscolo's mandate to promote Parinian cultural and political integrity intensified; and in *Lettere scritte dall'Inghilterra*, his principal enemy was not the France represented by Teresa's would-be rival in *Jacopo Ortis* but rather Germany, whose growing prestige in the new Romantic literature Staël tirelessly promoted, to Foscolo's chagrin. He writes that Italy's authors, "svogliati delle Muse, delle Grazie, e di tutte le Deità dell'Olimpo" (bored of the Muses, the Graces, and all the gods of Olympus), have begun to go "vagando fra gli avelli Teutonici" (wandering among the Teutonic graves) (457–58).[17] Foscolo proposes, instead, that these Italian authors should follow the example of Parini, who had "imparato da' latini e da' greci a raccogliere dalla natura sí ammirabile e insieme sí amabile nel nostro clima, le liete immagini che danno alla terra la luce eterna del cielo" (learned from the Latins and Greeks to gather, from a nature that is so admirable and lovable in our [Italian] climate, the happy images that the eternal light from heaven grants to earth) (458). The body of Parini, as a transcript of the Risorgimento, returns in a passage that begins in satire and ends in ironic censure—a rhetorical world away à la Didimo Chierico from the invective of Jacopo Ortis. Foscolo addresses his

"Saggio d'un gazzettino del bel mondo" (Essay from a high-society news circular) to a Milanese nobleman, Count C., whose city of origin makes him a compatriot of Parini in fact though not in spirit. The breezy, playful tone of the letter belies the sharp political observations that set the stage for Foscolo's impending Parinian anatomy. Foscolo writes that France is a more fashionable country than both Switzerland, which apes its more elegant Gallic neighbor, and England, where the love of liberty inspires its citizens to withstand that same "verga di nuovi signori" (oppression of new money) afflicting Italy (472). The Italians, Foscolo suggests, are quite capable of exhibiting the airs of fashion and *bon ton* (roughly, fashionable speech) because of their love of rhetoric, which Foscolo (citing Francis Bacon) connects to a capacity for telling lies.[18] Fashionable people, Foscolo claims, are generally great dissemblers: "Or il *Bon ton* non gira egli per tutti noi su l'unico cardine d'illuderci e piacerci scambievolmente?" (473). (For does not *bon ton* thrive because of its singular capacity to please us and, alternately, provide us with illusion?)

The discourse on fashion then takes a corporeal turn. Foscolo writes that, like the putative English gentleman who languidly receives visitors in pajamas until noon, he too has been reduced to a recumbent state because of an equestrian spill. Besides invoking Foscolo's early poetic composition "A Luigia Pallavicini caduta dal cavallo" (To Luigia Pallavicini fallen from her horse; 1799), the allusion also recalls the daring rider Alfieri from the autobiographical *Vita*, whom Foscolo mentions as a fellow horseman-gentleman like his interlocutor Count C. Before naming Alfieri, Foscolo cites a passage from Parini's *Il messaggio* (The message; 1793) to describe the foot injury that keeps him bedridden and drains his bodily strength. He then adds that, as opposed to the more comic, fashionable injuries of Count C., Alfieri, and himself, Parini was tragically and congenitally "infermo de' ginocchi fin dall'adolescenza" (afflicted with bad knees ever since adolescence) (475). This handicap did not mitigate, however, the fact that he "nacque anima ardente, educatasi per proprio vigore da sè: nè languí per età, nè per presentimento di morte" (was born an ardent soul and educated through his own native vigor; neither his age nor any fear of death caused him to languish) (475–76). The contrast between the unbreakable spirit of Parini and his broken body, framed by a larger discourse on the falseness of fashionable life and its deleterious national effects, culminates in a prolonged description of Parini's body as a mirror of Italian social injustice. The child of peasants, Parini suffered because he refused to prostitute his pen and sell politically palatable literary works, a virtue that echoes both Alfieri's unprotected *libero scrittore* from *Del principe e delle lettere* and, to push the genealogy further, Dante's incorruptible writer in *Convivio*:[19]

Leopoldo II, passando per la vostra città, vide un vecchio d'altero aspetto che strascinavasi sul bastone. Intese che era lo zoppo Parini; e volle che al suo stupendio di lettore di eloquenza il comune aggiungesse tanto che il vecchio s'ajutasse d'un calasetto. Ma i Luogotenenti de' Monarchi obbediscono per lo piú a ricchi della provincia; e gli avi e i padri vostri ottenero ch'ei continuasse a strascinarsi infermo e stramazzare nel fango e far ridere il volgo. Perchè ei deplorando i loro miseri obbrobrj, gli aveva redarguiti con severità giusta di cittadino, con dignità d'uomo, e con ingegno temuto ed odiato. Oggi lo celebrate come lume della vostra città. (*Lettere scritte dall'Inghilterra* 476)

([Holy Roman Emperor] Leopold II, upon passing through your city [Milan], saw a man of dignified aspect dragging himself along with a cane. He realized that this person was the lame Parini, and it was his wish that, in addition to Parini's stipend as a teacher of rhetoric, the community would give him enough money to provide him with a small coach. But the lieutenants of the king are more likely to obey the rich of their own provinces [than foreigners like Leopold]. And the elders and leaders of the city decreed that Parini was to continue to drag his lame body around, muck about in the mud, and make the rabble laugh. He suffered in this manner because he despised their petty hatreds and censured them with the just severity of a citizen, virile dignity, and respected and feared brilliance. Today, you revere him as a genius of your city.)

The haughty aspect of the slow-moving Parini recalls the equally *tardo,* deliberate Sordello in Dante; the description also recalls Reina's report: "People believed at first that [Parini's] slow and ponderous gait made him seem self-consciously philosophical." Foscolo combines these physical and moral virtues in his portrait of Parini: though "zoppo" (lame), his path continues unimpeded, through the actual and metaphorical "fango" (mud) of quotidian Milan, and he refuses to compromise his integrity to receive public funding. Parini wrote not for his peers but for posterity in a better, yet-to-be realized Italy. ("Today, you [Milanese] revere him as a genius of your city," Foscolo writes with fierce irony.) On a more optimistic note, Parini's posthumous appeal to his readers establishes the prophetic nature of his poetic voice and provides allegorical closure to the rhetoric of self-sacrifice offered by Foscolo's fictional Parini in *Jacopo Ortis* on December 4, 1798. That Milan now recognizes his value vindicates Parini's choice of political martyrdom and its public display of bodily suffering. Parini's *plebeo* and *infermo* qualities in *Lettere scritte dall'Inghilterra,* moreover, represent the antithesis of the trendy world of *bon ton* that, in Foscolo's eyes, makes the present Milan no different from that fallen version of the city in "Dei sepolcri" that nourishes only emasculated singers ("evirati cantori").

Foscolo's final words on the anglicized "Joseph Parini," in the *Essay on the*

Present Literature of Italy (1818), published the same year that Foscolo abandoned his composition of the *Lettere scritte dall'Inghilterra,* signal a shift from his more encomiastic previous words.[20] Though always respectful of Parini's character and patriotism, Foscolo notes that his erudition was "not remarkable" and that some of his odes were "absolutely bad" (*Essay* 2:1444, 1447). Above all, he criticizes Parini's overly descriptive and decorous poetry in the satirical *Giorno,* whose "sleepless irony somewhat fatigues the attention" (*Essay* 2:1439–40). Parini's physical symbiosis with Milan, rather than being a sign of patriotic authenticity, comes to embody for the exilic Foscolo a form of literary provincialism: "Another deficiency will be apparent to the foreign reader of Parini. The poet never saw any other city than Milan. His infirmities and his poverty confined him entirely at home. It was thus impossible that he should not give too much importance to objects which those accustomed to a wider sphere of action would consider unworthy of regard. It was natural, also, for the same reason, that his style, formed altogether on the classical writers, should occasionally degenerate into pedantry" (*Essay* 2:1440).[21]

I believe that Foscolo's views on Parini veered in a more negative direction toward the end of his life because of his shift from the Alfierian and Parinian Ortis model to the more critical and ironic autobiographical persona, Didimo Chierico.[22] In line with his depiction of Ortis, the younger Foscolo forged an elegiac Parini whose transcendent virtue recalls Italy's glorious ancient Roman past and martyrs like Cato. With maturity, however, and especially with his departure from Italy to his British exile, Foscolo came to question the self-sacrificial mandate of the Ortis-Parini stamp. Perhaps in England, Foscolo wondered if the fiery demise of an Italian political martyr would attract anyone to its flames. By the time of the *Essay* on Italian literature, Foscolo decided on a less dramatic form of literary engagement, the critical essay, a medium that left little space for both the self-glorification of Alfieri and the self-sacrifice of Parini. But Foscolo's spirit, like Parini's, was not broken. When the dream of poetry and poetic personae including Parini and Ortis faded in England, the sober Didimo was there to pick up the autobiographical pieces and serve as Foscolo's mouthpiece in his turn from creative writing to didactic criticism. The value of Foscolo's subsequent bilingual survey of Italian cultural history, vast in its scope and filled with vibrant poetic imagery and original theoretical speculations, cannot be overstated.[23]

In the British years, Foscolo finally came to terms with the shadow of Ortis and, by extension, Parini; in so doing, he cast aside the notion of suicide that each embodied. Self-slaughter, however ritualistic and deep with ancient Roman resonance, no longer seemed to Foscolo a viable political alternative after he left his Italian home and language for an England that, however much he admired it, never fully accepted him. Foscolo's British sojourn was a difficult one, marked by poverty, frustration, loneliness, and finally illness and a premature death. But "Italy" itself might never have come to be, at least as soon as it did, without those years of his in London. The essays on Italian history and culture that Foscolo produced during this time helped rally European support for the Risorgimento and eventual unification. To become Italy's international cultural spokesperson, Foscolo had to bid farewell first to Ortis, which he did in the "Notizia bibliografica" (Bibliographic note) of the edition of *Jacopo Ortis* from 1814, and next to the martyr Parini, which he did in the *Essay* on Italian literature from 1818. One can only speculate as to the poetry and prose that, without exile, might have followed his rejection of these self-sacrificial bodies in favor of the life-breathing pores of his diaphanous Graces, the subject of his last major poem, *Le Grazie* (The Graces), left unfinished in 1815.[24] His early death deprived us of many more masterpieces, as it cheated him of the elusive peace his self-described "spirto guerrier" (warrior's spirit) never allowed. But — and now I bring my speculation to that small grave in suburban London that received his body in 1827 — by rejecting the martyrdom of Parini-Ortis, Foscolo was able to possess the idea of his own death and free it from its nationalist and literary-historical associations. Perhaps this is a tall order for most of us: to accept our own mortality as a natural event and leave the work of figuring out the meaning of our lives to our loved ones. Perhaps this is what Foscolo was getting at when he writes in "Dei sepolcri," with breathtaking chiaroscuro, "gli occhi dell'uom cercan morendo / Il Sole" (the eyes of a dying man always seek the sun).

Epilogue: Italy's Broken Heart

In one of the more chilling scenes in Romantic literature, Goethe lies abed with his Roman mistress, enraptured by her body and overcome by pleasure, yet composed enough to discern the outline of metrical patterns along the contours of her back.[1] Some hundred years later, in an equally signatory Italian coming-of-age moment from E. M. Forster's *A Room with a View* (1909), Lucy Honeychurch and George Emerson stand together above the Arno, after witnessing a murder over a few liras. "Something tremendous has happened," George says to Lucy, something about the horror they observed, with its burst of primitive passion on an otherwise perfectly calm day, has brought them closer and, in a sense, sealed their love.[2] Into their staid world of English manners, an alien and unsettling "Italic" emotional economy has entered, and, George realizes, it will rend asunder the traditional, respectable bonds that their English identity was to have provided them. It will take several more months, a broken engagement with the hapless Cecil, and some two hundred pages of narrative for Lucy to arrive at a similar epiphany. But eventually the lessons she learns in Italy compel her to defy her family and return, with her new husband, George Emerson, to the very spot whose genius loci inspired the rupture: Florence and the Pensione Bertolini. One might label Lucy's journey from English decorum to Italian isolation a "Romanticism with a view" — a view into Italy's sublime city- and landscapes as well as into her own submerged passions, which before George only Beethoven could coax to the surface. Forster's novel appeared long enough after the Romantic age proper for him to look back on its more earnest aspects with gentle bemusement. But he was generous enough to suggest that Lucy's awakening, from the intellectual and moral to the emotional and sexual, could not have transpired without the Romantic dream of Italy that had inspired his English literary predecessors. When Lucy surrenders to this idea of Italy forged in Romantic Europe, and when Goethe capitulates to the body of a mistress who is as much a corpus of ancient cultural traditions as she is a living, breathing organism, a new way of living and conceiving art coalesce. For Goethe, Roman passion led to a desentimentalizing of art in the name of a puissant and indifferent natural world, whose forms by their very remoteness could bring a liberating objectivity to poetic composition. His memorable dictum—only by enjoying life's pleasures can we prepare for its inevitable tragedies—seems a fitting gloss to the nexus between *poesis* and lovemaking that transformed his erotic interludes into yet another discipline of study in his Roman *hohe Schule*.

A similar mix of affect, eros, and intellect in the star-crossed love of Oswald and Corinne reflects the main themes of Staël's novel and also reminds us of the dialogue between emotional and literary history in Goethe's *amore romano* and George and Lucy's Florentine romance. Staël's title suggests to the reader, in what Gérard Genette calls paratextual fashion, Corinne's dual identity, for the coordinating conjunction "ou" separating "Corinne" and "l'Italie" functions as a copulative that, in chiasmus-like fashion, nationalizes the heroine as it personifies the nation.³ Then the novel's epigraph anticipates Corinne's allegorical register: "Udrallo il bel paese, / Ch' Apennin parte, e 'l mar circonda e l'Alpe." ([Her name] will resound in the fair land parted by the Appenines and bounded by the sea and the Alps.) This citation of Petrarch's posthumous elegy of Laura highlights that the protagonist we are about to encounter carries the signs of her own imminent death.⁴ In a sense, the novel serves as a prosopopoeial call from beyond the grave and an epitaphic inscription. Like the Italian national allegories of Petrarchan and Leopardian stamp, in Staël's novel the physical space of Italy is beautiful ("bel paese"), divided (naturally by the Apennines, politically by its various factions and foreign spheres of influence), and unified only in nature. Yet Staël falls short in the epitaph-epigraph of proposing Corinne as a second Italy; instead, she is more a second Petrarchan Laura—which is to say, elegiac, forged in memory, and an elusive source of inspiration that inhabits the idealized history of the poet's imagination. Like Petrarch's allegorical Italia, Staël's protagonist Corinne suffers from a thwarted sexuality, externally imposed chastity, and limitations on her subjectivity imposed by an objectifying masculine gaze. Though Corinne strives for an independence that separates her from other allegorical constructions of Italy, the rhetoric of death shadows her initial and final appearances, especially in the image of her actual and figurative broken heart that signals Staël's pessimistic reading of Italian cultural history and its future prospects within the European polity.

When we first encounter Corinne, she emerges as if cast—as even her admirer, Oswald, is forced to admit—from the epic romance of Ariosto. Corinne's appearance in the novel coincides with her coronation as poet laureate on the Capitoline Hill in Rome, where Petrarch had been crowned nearly five centuries earlier. Though she is "la femme la plus célèbre" (the most famous woman) in Italy, a crowd of mystery hangs over Corinne, who goes only by her first name and leaves Oswald to wonder whether she is a goddess surrounded by clouds or a mere mortal (2.2; Œuvres 664; Corinne, Italy 25).[5] The extravagant furniture that accompanies Corinne's entrance further suggests the surreal, fictive quality attendant upon her identity:[6] "Enfin les quatres chevaux blancs qui traînaient le char de Corinne se firent place au milieu de la foule. Corinne était assise sur ce char costruit à l'antique, et des jeunes filles, vêtues de blanc, marchaient à côté d'elle. Partout où elle passait, l'on jetait en abondance des parfums dans les airs. . . . Tout le monde criait: *Vive Corinne! vive le genie, vive la beauté!*" (2.1; Œuvres 662). (At last the four horses drawing Corinne's chariot made their way into the midst of the crowd. Corinne was sitting on the chariot, built in the style of ancient Rome, and white-robed girls walked alongside her. Everywhere she went people lavishly threw perfumes into the air. . . . Everyone shouted, *Long live Corinne! Long live genius! Long live beauty!* [Corinne, Italy 22–23].) Corinne's embodiment of the abstract qualities of genius and beauty prepares the reader for the national allegorizing for which Staël, for better or worse, became famous. Oswald tells himself that, to judge Corinne fairly, he must set aside "la réserve de l'Angleterre" and "les plaisanteries françaises" (English reserve and French jesting), an act he has trouble performing, for, in Staël, you are where you are born (2.1; Œuvres 662; Corinne, Italy 23). The reader, in turn, senses that he or she is about to encounter not just a person but *a people*, and that Staël uses the name "Corinne," beautiful and brilliant though also bereft of all honor not related to the arts, as a code for "Italy."[7] For evidence of this, we need only heed the words of Castel-Forte: "C'est l'image de notre belle Italie; elle est ce que nous serions sans l'ignorance, l'envie, la discorde et l'indolence auxquelles notre sort nous a condamnés" (2.2; Œuvres 665). ([Corinne] is the image of our beautiful Italy; she is what we would be but for the ignorance, the envy, the discord, and the indolence to which our fate has condemned us [Corinne, Italy 27].)

Both Corinne's mind and body serve as sites for nationalist reflection. On his way to her recitation, Oswald learns that she is "poëte, écrivain, improvisatrice, et l'un des plus belle personnes de Rome" (poetess, writer, and improviser, and one of the most beautiful women in Rome) — as lovely to hear as she is to see (2.1; *Œuvres* 664; *Corinne, Italy* 21). Though she is about to receive the poetic laurel, Corinne is not a writer per se but a performer. Women poets in the Italy of her age were denied access to publication and had to establish their merits via the performance and recitation of verse. Her literary reception and physical apprehension are, in fact, one and the same (her appearance triggers the anaphora of synonymous chants, "*Long live Corinne! Long live genius! Long live beauty!*"). Even though she appears to the reader as an author, Corinne is always a spectacle, since her reputation is beholden exclusively to her artistic performance in space and time. When she dies bodily, her literary vocation dies with her, for she is denied the prosopopoeia that the written text, in its capacity to outlive the human voice, provides male poets.

For her performance, Corinne dresses like the Sibyl of the Renaissance painter Domenichino, in a white dress and with noble and modest demeanor: "Ses bras étaient d'une éclatante beauté; sa taille grande, mais un peu forte, à la manière des statues grecques, caractérisait énergiquement la jeunesse et le bonheur" (2.1; *Œuvres* 663). (Her arms were dazzlingly beautiful; her tall, slightly plump figure, in the style of a Greek statue, gave a keen impression of youth and happiness [*Corinne, Italy* 23].) She then ascends the stage at the Capitoline to receive the laurel and, lyre in hand, begins a lyrical improvisation on Italian cultural history that covers topics ranging from Rome's mythical founding by Aeneas to Dante's poetry of exile and the nature of the *genus italicum*. Italy, she tells the crowd, delights in its sunshine, arts, architecture; in Italy, "le génie se sent à l'aise" (the genius feels at home) (2.3; *Œuvres* 667; *Corinne, Italy* 31). The encomium, after its initial vital imagery and talk of eternity, then slips into elegy, with countless allusions to Italy's sorrow and, to invoke a corporeal allegory, a broken heart: "Ici l'on se console des peines mêmes du cœur, en admirant un Dieu de bonté, en pénétrant le secret de son amour; les revers passagers de notre vie éphémère se perdent dans le sein fécond et majestueux de l'immortel univers" (2.3; *Œuvres* 663). (Here [in Italy] one finds consolation even for the sorrow of the heart by admiring a bountiful God and fathoming the secret of his love. The transitory misfortunes of our ephemeral life are lost in the fertile, majestic bosom of the immortal universe [*Corinne, Italy* 31].) Until this point, Corinne's allegorical *donna italica* squares with the images of Italy conceived by Petrarch and Leopardi. In all of them, Italy is physically splendid and blessed with sun, clear blue skies, and fecund fields; in all, she is of a melancholic nature, consoled for her political woes by her talent for arts and letters, and exploited and overcome by her foreign suitors and assailants. However, in a departure from her Italian predecessors, Staël introduces a judgmental narrative eye onto the beautiful Italian woman: ascetic, austere, democratic, and disapproving England. She writes:

> Corinne fut interrompue pendant quelques moments par les applaudissemens les plus impétueux. Le seul Oswald ne se mêla point aux transports bruyans qui l'entouraient. Il avait penché sa tête sur sa main, lorsque Corinne avait dit: *Ici l'on se console des peines mêmes du cœur;* et depuis lors il ne l'avait point relevée. Corinne le remarqua, et bientôt, à ses traits, à la couleur de ses cheveux, à son costume, à sa taille élevée, à toutes ses manières enfin, elle le reconnut pour un Anglais. Le deuil qu'il portait, et sa physionomie pleine de tristesse la frappèrent. Son regard, alors attaché sur elle, semblait lui faire doucement des reproches. (2.3; 667)
>
> (For some moments Corinne was interrupted by the most enthusiastic applause. Oswald alone did not join in the rapturous clamour around him. He had bowed his head onto his hands when Corinne said, *Here one finds consolation even for the sorrows of the heart,* and after that he had not looked up. Corinne noticed him and soon, by his features, by the colour of his hair, by his dress, by his tall stature, in short by his whole demeanour, she realized that he was an Englishman. She was struck by his mourning dress and his sad expression. Then his gaze, fixing on her, seemed to reproach her gently.) (31)

This scene dramatically represents the translation of the *donna italica* from a national feminine concern to a foreign one, via Oswald's visual appropriation of Corinne and the Italy that she allegorizes. Though, technically, Oswald's reproach stems from his disapproval of Corinne's celebratory hymn because he is in mourning over his father's death, his judgmental gaze also reflects his inability to accept Corinne's independence, extroversion, and subjectivity. She is too much of *a* woman for him: her individuality scandalizes him, and he seeks a type or class of *the* woman, exemplified in the generic "British" virginal purity of the domestic Lucile. Following Oswald's ocular rebuke, Corinne shifts her discourse from elegy to eulogy; Italy henceforth becomes essentially a collection of illustrious graves:

> Le Colisée, les obélisques, toutes les merveilles qui, du fond de l'Égypte et de la Grèce, de l'extrémité des siècles, depuis Romulus jusqu'à Léon X, se sont réunies ici, comme si la grandeur attirait la grandeur, et qu'un même lieu dût renfermer tout ce que l'homme a pu mettre à l'abri du temps; toutes ces merveilles sont consacrées aux monuments funèbres. . . . Le froid et l'isolement du sépulcre sous ce beau ciel, à côté de tant d'urnes funéraires, poursuivent moins les esprits effrayés. On se croit attendu par la foule des ombres; et,

de notre ville solitaire à la ville souterraine, la transition semble assez douce. (2.3; 668)

(The Colosseum, the obelisks, all the wonders which are collected here from the depths of Egypt and Greece, from the most distant centuries, from Romulus right up to Leo X, as if greatness attracted greatness, and as if one place had to contain everything man could shield from the ravages of time, all these wonders are in honour of the dead.... Under this beautiful sky and beside so many funereal urns, timorous minds are less haunted by the chill and solitude of the grave. We imagine a host of shades awaits us, and from our lonely city to the city of the underworld the passage seems quite smooth.) (32)

Smooth indeed. Corinne and Oswald will have their first outing by these same Roman tombs that Corinne invokes in her improvisation; thus their ill-fated and unrequited love bears the shadow of death from its inception. Corinne's own womanly virtues will fade with the passing of this love, and the slumbering yet obvious sexual charm of her great beauty will never find expression, for the poetess will die of heartbreak at an early age, depriving herself and her city of an extraordinary artistic potential. The transition in Corinne's Capitoline improvisation from encomium and elegy to eulogy recalls the novel's mournful Petrarchan epigraph-epitaph ("[Her name] will resound in the fair land parted by the Appenines and bounded by the sea and the Alps"). More important, this rhetorical transition maps out the structure of the entire text. It takes the length of this long novel to arrive at Corinne's actual death, but when the event transpires, the reader senses that a narrative trajectory—whose movement toward Corinne's demise is hinted at in the Petrarchan epigraph-epitaph—has come full circle. As in the novel written just a few years earlier than *Corinne, Ultime lettere di Jacopo Ortis,* the allegorical nexus between the demise of the protagonist and the nation he or she embodies serves as the text's Archimedean point. The death of Corinne and her appositive national tag, *l'Italie,* testify to what Petrarch reminds us in his canzone 128, "Italia mia": neither woman nor nation can live on poetry alone.[8] And so our story of the foreign romance with Italy, and of Italy's response to this bittersweet love, concludes with a national allegory of heartbreak.

A century or so after Staël's novel, Italy ceased to be the world's university that it was for the fictional Corinne and the historical Goethe. By the time of Forster's *Room with a View,* and especially when it came to matters of the heart, Italy had become an anticlassroom. Whereas the "traveler" Goethe sought anonymity, independence, and acculturation in his Italian environs, the emphatically British "tourists" in Lucy Honeychurch's circle sought to domesticate their foreign environs by following the Baedeker guide and moving toward what Paul Fussell calls "the security of pure cliché."[9] Let us recall that George Emerson and Lucy Honeychurch learn their most valuable lesson neither in the Uffizi nor in Santa Croce but in the warm air of the Piazza Signoria with its unexpected waft of murder. Somewhere between today's hedonistic junior year abroad and the sober Grand Tour of the *Goethezeit*, the Italy of George and Lucy balances formal modes of learning and cultural pedagogy with those life lessons best studied under Keats's sunny "skies Italian." In contrast with the snobbish and impotent erudition of Forster's Reverend Cuthbert Eager, a sadly anachronistic vestige of the Grand Tour and its high-cultural aspirations, the love of George and Lucy combines naturalist, pantheistic elements with the acquisition of polish and refinement. Though at times George and Lucy's experiences present themselves as elemental and ahistorical, and hence unmediated by cultural precedent, they are the heirs of the Romantic Italy forged in scenes like Corinne's Capitoline improvisations and Goethe's erotic hexameters. As usual, Lucy's jilted paramour, Cecil, is off the mark when he suggests that the British should travel to Italy to acquire subtlety and savoir faire instead of book smarts. For it is precisely in books, and in those books written throughout Europe in the late eighteenth and early nineteenth centuries, that Cecil's notion of Italy is born.

The reception of Italian traditions continues to challenge us to rethink our collective debt to the Italian past and, more important, the ways in which the lessons of the cultural *corpus italicum* can redefine our experience of modern life. Whether through such figures as the fictitious broken heart of Staël's Corinne or the actual desecrated corpse of Foscolo's Parini, many writers turned to Italy's traditions in order to launch a critique against what they perceived to be the particular crises of modernity. I have described Italy's "premodern" exceptionalism primarily in terms of the Italian capacity to feel antiquity in the blood, exploit the popular and political valence of high-cultural expression, maintain a spiritual connection to culture in a secular age, and resist innovation that fails to reconcile itself with tradition. My list is limited and selective in the manner of essayistic historical generalizations. But I stand by this précis in hopes of providing a practical guide to the vast and complex question of Italy in nineteenth-century Europe and beyond.

In lieu of further gloss, I close by recalling the image that, to my mind, summarizes the argument of this book and extends it in new directions that I leave the reader to follow as he or she sees fit. We are back in the concluding section of "Dei sepolcri," and Foscolo has just relayed Cassandra's prophecy of Troy's destruction. We know that, from the ashes of Troy, first ancient Rome and then modern Italy will spring; hence, these concluding lines drive home the poem's most overt political allegory. But a purely thematic interpretation of these verses fails to account for their strange energy and atmosphere. The last ten lines or so pulse with a pleasure that seems at odds with the message of war and destruction they narrate. The lexical choices "splendidamente" (splendidly), "bello" (beautiful), "placando" (placating), and "risplenderà" (will shine) contradict Foscolo's concluding and crushing overture to "le sciagure umane" (humanity's disasters). One does well to ask: just what is this poem so happy about?

The answer, I believe, is in Dante. I argued earlier that Foscolo's prophecy of Cassandra draws on the rhetorical and moral energy of Cacciaguida's prediction of Dante's exile in *Paradiso* 17. The final words of "Dei sepolcri" cement this connection. The *Commedia* ends with an absolute overcoming of the self in the name of the ultimate unity of the individual, the universe, and God, figured in the image of a divine volume that binds with love all that is scattered throughout the universe. Similarly, Foscolo's "Dei sepolcri" finishes with a survey of the cosmic unity that binds this modern Italian poet with his ancient ancestors, departed countrymen, fellow artists, even humanity. The overarching bliss sustaining the final stanzas derives from a sacralization of culture that borrows from the discourse of Christianity in order to heal a modern poet's sense of alienation from the historical traditions that, he believes, have not only formed his nation's past but also plan for its future. Such promotion of foundation myths, reverence for tradition, and recourse to religious locution are, of course, not for everyone. Yet I find Foscolo's faith in enduring high cultural forms and the transhistorical community they generate to be both courageous and visionary. It is ultimately the serenity of his poem in the face of death that suggests to me the scandal of Italian Romanticism and the subsequent difficulties it has encountered in foreign reception. Italian Romantics took what most of their European contemporaries conceived of in lyric, fragmentary, or immanent terms—for example, the spectral energies of the landscape, inchoate registers of subjectivity, and internalization of historical solitude—and sought to lend them the scope of epic and the sanctity of a secular religion. But to revisit, as Foscolo does, Homer's underworld and Dante's Trinity circa 1800 is a peculiar act. His poetic harrowing, I believe, is haunted by the same fear that hovers over many other Italian Romantic attempts to create a new literature still responsive to classical and Christian traditions: will the modern world understand, in Leopardi's words, "il suono / di que' popoli antichi," Italy's ancient voices?

Notes

Works are cited in full in each of the individual chapters where they appear. I refer to some commonly cited works through an abbreviation, which I provide following the first full citation of the work, as in the following examples: Ugo Foscolo, *Edizione nazionale delle opere di Ugo Foscolo,* 23 vols. (Florence: Le Monnier, 1933–) (abbrev. "*EN*"); and Voltaire, *Œuvres complètes de Voltaire,* ed. Louis Moland, 52 vols. (Paris: Garnier Frères, 1877–85) (abbrev. "M"). In some cases, references are given both to the internal division of a work and to its page number (for example, the shortened citation "1.3; *Del principe* 121; *Prince and Letters* 14" refers to book 1, chapter 3, and page 121 of Vittorio Alfieri's *Del principe e delle lettere,* as well as page 14 of its translation (*The Prince and Letters*). In my references to the correspondence of Voltaire and William Wordsworth, I use the character "D" followed by the number of the documented letter in question. In all cases, I cite from sources without modernizing the spelling; unless otherwise indicated, translations are my own.

For translations of foreign titles, only published translations cited in this book are italicized and capitalized title-style (e.g., *The Betrothed,* for *I promessi sposi* by Alessandro Manzoni); other translated titles are left in regular script and capitalized sentence-style (e.g., Letters written from England, for *Lettere scritte dall'Inghilterra* by Ugo Foscolo). All translations of poem titles by Giacomo Leopardi are given inside quotation marks and capitalized title-style (e.g., "By Dante's Tomb" for "Sopra il monumento di Dante"), regardless of whether these poems are quoted in English translation.

Introduction

1. I follow the definition of *modernity* as "an intellectual tendency or social perspective characterized by departure from or repudiation of traditional ideas, doctrines, and cultural values in favour of contemporary or radical values and beliefs (chiefly those of scientific rationalism and liberalism)" (s.v. "modernity, n^{1b}," *OED Online*, September 2002, Oxford University Press; Feb. 18, 2007, http://dictionary.oed.com/cgi/entry/00313111). This book's central argument focuses on Italy's embattled relationship with the modern project in light of the nation's resistance to many of the tectonic shifts in European cultural, religious, and sociopolitical life set in motion by the Enlightenment. My assumption is that Italy's eccentric role in literary Romantic Europe corresponds to its equally anomalous position vis-à-vis burgeoning European democratic and nationalist institutions along with their correlatives (e.g., a rising and increasingly literate middle and bourgeois class, the development of a public sphere, and the continued codification of such binding social elements as language and law).

2. For heuristic purposes, I use the controversial and mutable designations *Romantic* and *Romanticism* to refer to the antineoclassical literature produced in Italy and throughout Europe in roughly the end of the eighteenth and first quarter of the nineteenth century. My argument makes clear, however, that the terminology associated with Romanticism had varied and ever-changing meanings for individual authors and their respective national literary traditions. For a detailed history of the term and its uses, see Hans Eichner, ed., introduction to *"Romantic" and Its Cognates: The European History of a Word* (Toronto: University of Toronto Press, 1972), 3: "Ever since the word *romantic* and its many cognates in European languages began to be used self-consciously as technical terms towards the end of the eighteenth century, the quest for a satisfactory definition of their meanings has continued unabated. It has been estimated that in the last sixty years some seven hundred articles and treatises have been devoted to this quest, and there is no indication that scholarly concern with the problem is lessening." For the history of the word and its cognates in Italy, see Carlo Calcaterra, ed., introduction to *I manifesti romantici del 1816 e gli scritti principali del "Conciliatore" sul Romanticismo* (Turin: UTET, 1951), 13–15; Olga Ragusa, "Italy/Romantico-Romanticismo," in Eichner, *"Romantic" and Its Cognates* 293–340; and Mario Scotti, "Gli aggettivi 'romantic,' 'romantique,' 'romantische,' 'romantico' e l'affermarsi del termine e del concetto di Romanticismo," *Il primo Ottocento*, in *Storia della letteratura italiana*, dir. Enrico Malato, 14 vols. (Rome: Salerno, 1995–2005), 7:499–504. Many Italian works between the French and European revolutions (1789–1848) did not fit traditional or typical definitions of *Romantic*, especially those elements adduced in René Wellek's classic article: an emphasis on imagination, nature, historical consciousness, and symbolic representation ("The Concept of Romanticism in Literary History," *Concepts of Criticism*, ed. Stephen G. Nichols, Jr. [New Haven: Yale University Press, 1963], 128–98). I use the term *question of Italian Romanticism* to denote the debates over Romantic literature stimulated by the publication of Anne Louise Germaine de Staël's "De l'esprit des traductions" in the influential Milanese literary journal *Biblioteca italiana* in 1816 (for Staël's original version of the essay, see *Mélanges*, in *Œuvres complètes de Mme la baronne de Staël*, ed. Auguste Louis Staël-Holstein, 17 vols. [Paris: Treuttel and Würtz, 1820–21], 17:387–99; for the Italian

edition, see "Sulla maniera e la utilità delle traduzioni," trans. Pietro Giordani, *Biblioteca italiana* 1 [1816]: 9–18); English translation in "The Spirit of Translation," trans. Joseph Luzzi, *Romanic Review* 97 (2006): 275–84. The essay, which exhorts Italian authors to free themselves from their pedantic cultural isolation by familiarizing themselves with modern northern European literature, drew responses from such leading writers as Giovanni Berchet, Pietro Borsieri, Ludovico di Breme, and the then adolescent Giacomo Leopardi. A valuable synthesis of the polemics over Italian Romanticism is in Alessandro Manzoni, "Sul romanticismo: Lettera al marchese Cesare D'Azeglio," *Opere*, ed. Guido Bezzola, 3 vols. (Milan: Rizzoli, 1961), 3:425–57; "Letter on Romanticism," trans. Joseph Luzzi, *PMLA* 119 (2004): 299–316. For a discussion of the problems in establishing historical frameworks for the different national Romantic movements, see Lilian R. Furst, *The Contours of European Romanticism* (Lincoln: University of Nebraska Press, 1979), 6–10. See also the cautionary words of Stuart Curran, *Poetic Form and British Romanticism* (New York: Oxford University Press, 1986), 209–10:

> Romanticism, conceived as a European phenomenon, lasted well over a century, yet at the same time occurred in national phases. Thus Goethe was already being enthusiastically celebrated as a genius before any of the Italian or French Romantics were born and stood as sage and septuagenarian when the great commotion of French Romanticism began with the *Méditations poétiques* of Lamartine in 1820. Just four years after that milestone, with the death of Byron, the flowering of British Romanticism had abruptly ceased; but the central figure of the French movement, Victor Hugo, would not die until 1885, leaving, true to his nature as a cultural monument, two epic poems to be published after his death. The anomalies interwoven within such dates could be multiplied considerably but would only underscore the extent to which, even when we identify Romanticism as pan-European, it is keyed to the discrete exigencies of national cultures.

3. For insights on the relations between the cities of the living and the dead, see Robert Pogue Harrison, *Dominion of the Dead* (Chicago: University of Chicago Press, 2003), passim.

4. See Foscolo's inaugural oration, "Dell'origine e dell'ufficio della letteratura" (ed. Gianfranca Lavezzi, *Opere*, ed. Franco Gavezzeni, 2 vols. [Turin: Einaudi-Gallimard, 1994–95], 2:505–37), a text that anticipates his Vichian poetic philology in later works including *Lettere scritte dall'Inghilterra:* "Ogni uomo sa che la parola è mezzo di rappresentare il pensiero; ma pochi si accorgono che la progressione, l'abbondanza e l'economia del pensiero sono effetti della parola." (Everyone knows that the word is the means for expressing thought; but few realize that the progress, richness, and economy of thought are effects of the word.)

5. Ugo Foscolo, *Ultime lettere di Jacopo Ortis*, ed. Maria Antonietta Terzoli, *Opere* 2:3–140; *Last Letters of Jacopo Ortis; and, Of Tombs*, trans. J. G. Nichols (London: Hesperus, 2002). See *Opere* 1:cxxx–cxxxiv, for an extensive critical bibliography on the text that includes studies, in chronological order, by Mario Fubini (1947); Mario Puppo (1948 and 1978); Ezio Raimondi (1953); Giovanni Gambarin (1956); Walter Binni (1959 and 1982); Pino Fasano (1966 and 1984); Guido Bezzola (1978); Giuseppe Nic-

oletti (1978); Giorgio Bàrberi Squarotti (1978); Maria Antonietta Terzoli (1987, 1988, and 1989); Massimo Riva (1988); and Olga Ragusa (1989).

6. Benedict Anderson, *Imagined Communities* (London: Verso, 1983), 9.

7. See Foscolo's essay on Lucretius, "Della poesia, dei tempi e della religione di Lucrezio," *Scritti letterari e politici, dal 1796 al 1808*, ed. Giovanni Gambarin (1972), 239–50; vol. 6 of *Edizione nazionale delle opere di Ugo Foscolo*, 23 vols. (Florence: Le Monnier, 1933–) (abbrev. "*EN*").

8. Ugo Foscolo, "Dei sepolcri," ed. Franco Longoni, *Opere* 1:21–38; "Ugo Foscolo: Sepulchers, " trans. Peter Burian, *Literary Imagination* 4 (2002): 17–30 (references are to this translation unless otherwise indicated). I also use the translation, with useful analysis (see 47–61), by Karl Kroeber, *The Artifice of Reality: Poetic Style in Wordsworth, Foscolo, Keats, and Leopardi* (Madison: University of Wisconsin Press, 1964), 179–83. For studies of the genesis and composition of "Dei sepolcri," see Giovanni Getto, *La composizione dei "Sepolcri" di Ugo Foscolo* (Florence: Olschki, 1977); and Aldo Vallone, *Genesi e formazione dei "Sepolcri,"* 2nd ed. (Asti: Arethusa, 1946). See the discussion of the poem and related issues in Glauco Cambon, *Ugo Foscolo, Poet of Exile* (Princeton, NJ: Princeton University Press, 1980), 155–81; Dino Cervigni, "Religione e cristianesimo nei 'Sepolcri,'" *Canadian Journal of Italian Studies* 1 (1978): 249–61; Benedetto Croce, *Poesia e non-poesia: Note sulla letteratura europea del secolo decimonono* (Bari: Laterza, 1923), 83–86; Francesco De Sanctis, *Storia della letteratura italiana*, ed. Gianfranco Contini (Milan: TEA, 1989), 809–11 (abbrev. "*Letteratura italiana*"); Vincenzo Di Benedetto, *Lo scrittoio di Ugo Foscolo* (Turin: Einaudi, 1990), 119–38; Eugenio Donadoni, *Ugo Foscolo pensatore, critico, poeta*, ed. Riccardo Scrivano, 3rd ed. (Florence: Sandron, 1964), 383–400; Oreste Macrí, *Semantica e metrica dei "Sepolcri" del Foscolo: Con uno studio sull'endecasillabo* (Rome: Bulzoni, 1978); Tom O'Neill, *Of Virgin Muses and of Love: A Study of Foscolo's "Dei sepolcri"* (Dublin: Irish Academic Press, 1981); Giorgio Petrocchi, *L'ultima dea* (Rome: Bonacci, 1977); Mario Scotti, *Foscolo fra erudizione e poesia* (Rome: Bonacci, 1973), 7–75; and Carolyn Springer, *The Marble Wilderness: Ruins and Representation in Italian Romanticism, 1775–1850* (New York: Cambridge University Press, 1987), 117–35. I am especially indebted to the reading of the poem and other interpretive insights in the classic study by Mario Fubini, *Ugo Foscolo: Saggi, studi, note*, rev. ed. (Florence: La Nuova Italia, 1978), 179–214; see 326–27n10 for useful bibliography. For further bibliography, see Foscolo, *Opere* 1:cxx–cxxii.

9. "Lo seppi: Teresa è maritata. . . . Cos' è la vita per me? il tempo mi divorò i momenti felici: io non la conosco se non nel sentimento del dolore: ed ora anche l'illusione mi abbondona. . . . La sola morte, a cui è commesso il sacro cangiamento delle cose, promette pace" (March 5, 1799; *Ultime lettere* 115–16). (I know. Teresa is married. . . . What is life for me? Time has devoured my moments of happiness. I only know I am alive when I feel grief. And now even that illusion abandons me. . . . Only death, to which is committed the sacred transformation of everything, promises peace [*Last Letters* 115].) See the discussion in Di Benedetto, 152–61.

10. For analysis of Rome's links to the papacy and Napoleon in the context of the Risorgimento, see Springer, *Marble Wilderness* 117.

11. Dante Alighieri, *The Divine Comedy*, trans. with commentary Charles S. Singleton, 6 vols. (Princeton, NJ: Princeton University Press, 1970–75). Italian text based on *La*

commedia secondo l'antica vulgata, ed. Giorgio Petrocchi, 4 vols. (Milan: Mondadori, 1966–67).

12. For the poem's controversial reception, see the anthology of excerpts reprinted in *EN* 6:519–83.

13. Rainer Maria Rilke, *Letters to a Young Poet,* ed. Stephen Mitchell (New York: Modern Library, 2001), 22–23. Fittingly, this passage is invoked in a recent novel, whose protagonist, Alex Massolini, escapes to Italy, from American politics in the 1960s and the Vietnam War, in order to discover his literary vocation (Jay Parini, *The Apprentice Lover: A Novel* [New York: Harper Collins, 2002], 18–19).

14. Exhibition, "French Nineteenth-Century Drawings in the Robert Lehman Collection," Metropolitan Museum of Art, New York, January 2003.

15. Geoffrey H. Hartman, *Scars of the Spirit: The Struggle against Inauthenticity* (New York: Palgrave Macmillan, 2002), 234.

16. In a recent, anti-Romantic treatment of Goethe's maxim, J. M. Coetzee uses this phrase as the epigraph to his memoir *Youth* (New York: Viking, 2002), whose sustained self-criticism and self-parody of the author's literary pilgrimage from South Africa to England undermines the stately cultural principles motivating Goethe's remark.

17. Nathaniel Hawthorne, *The Marble Faun, or The Romance of Monte Beni,* ed. Richard H. Brodhead (New York: Penguin, 1990).

18. Jonah Siegel explores the journey south by northern writers as part of their effort to locate their work in the web of travel literature associated with Italy's cult of genius (*Haunted Museum: Longing, Travel, and the Art-Romance Tradition* [Princeton, NJ: Princeton University Press, 2005]). See 122–34 for his discussion of Hawthorne's *Marble Faun.*

19. Lord Byron, *Childe Harold's Pilgrimage,* 4.707–9; vol. 2 of *The Complete Poetical Works,* ed. Jerome J. McGann, 3 vols. (Oxford: Clarendon, 1980–81). Springer contrasts the elegiac descriptions of loss—typical of Byron and foreign Romantics in their encounter with Italy's past—with counterdescriptions by Italians of their ruins in a politically progressive, encomiastic mode (*Marble Wilderness* 1–18). The centrality of the fragment to the Romantic imagination is the subject of Thomas McFarland, *Romanticism and the Forms of Ruin: Wordsworth, Coleridge, and Modalities of Fragmentation* (Princeton, NJ: Princeton University Press, 1981).

20. For anticipation of Goethe's shift from a Romantic to a neoclassical stylistic register, see his description of his reading of *Iphigenia at Tauris* to a group of German artists in Rome. "Diese jungen Männer, an jene früheren, heftigen, vordringenden Arbeiten gewöhnt, erwarteten etwas Berlichingisches und konnten sich in den ruhigen Gang nicht gleich finden; doch verfehlten die edlen und reinen Stellen nicht ihre Wirkung" (January 10, 1787; *Italienische Reise* 158–59). (These young men, being accustomed to my earlier vehement, vigorous works [i.e., *Werther*], had expected something in the [*Götz von*] *Berlichingen* [1773] style, and could not immediately become reconciled to the calm pace: but the pure and noble passages did not fail to make their effect [*Italian Journey* 129].) Johann Wolfgang von Goethe, *Italienische Reise,* ed. Erich Trunz and Herbert von Einem (1960), vol. 11 of *Werke,* ed. Erich Trunz, 14 vols. (Hamburg: Wegner, 1960–62); *Italian Journey,* ed. Thomas P. Saine and Jeffrey L. Sammons, trans. Robert R. Heitner, vol. 6 of *Goethe's Collected Works* (New York: Suhrkamp, 1989).

21. In twentieth-century modernism, a preferred site for the cycles of life and death for European artists was once again Paris rather than Italy. See, for example, the opening words of Rainer Maria Rilke, *The Notebooks of Malte Laurids Brigge*, trans. M. D. Herter Norton (New York: Norton, 1949), 13: "So, then people do come here [to Paris] in order to live; I would sooner have thought one died here. I have been out. I saw: hospitals."

22. For a study of the relationship between the terms *Corinne* and *Italie* in Staël's title, see Marie-Claire Vallois, *Fictions féminines: Mme de Staël et les voix de la Sibylle* (Saratoga, CA: Anma Libri, 1987), 112–13.

23. A witty discussion of the ongoing controversies surrounding the afterlife of Romanticism is in the introduction of Richard Thomas Eldridge, *The Persistence of Romanticism* (Cambridge: Cambridge University Press, 2001), 1–27.

24. Stuart Curran notes that, although the vigorously popular element of the British publishing industry in the early nineteenth century is often overlooked, the era did represent a "high-water mark for poetry" with its "astonishing effusion of verse" of both lasting and ephemeral quality ("The Print Culture of British Romanticism," *The People's Voice: Essays on European Romanticism*, ed. Andrea Ciccarelli, John Claiborne Isbell, and Brian Nelson [Melbourne: School of European Languages and Cultures, Monash University, 1999], 68–69).

25. See Raymond Williams, *Marxism and Literature* (Oxford: Oxford University Press, 1977), 45–54; David Bromwich, *A Choice of Inheritance: Self and Community from Edmund Burke to Robert Frost* (Cambridge, MA: Harvard University Press, 1989), 1–19; and Ezio Raimondi, *Romanticismo italiano e romanticismo europeo* (Milan: Mondadori, 1997), 29–30.

26. Foscolo went so far as to refer to the debates about Romanticism as an "idle question," though in truth both his critical writings and private letters elaborated upon many of the issues circulating in the polemics about Romanticism in Italy. I agree with Mario Fubini's assessment that Foscolo's disdain for the polemics of his younger contemporaries stemmed in part from his belief that he had already resolved, both in theory and literary practice, Romanticism's central debates — debates, moreover, that took place in an Italy from which the exiled Foscolo would forever be separated after 1815. Though Manzoni did explicitly address the *questione del romanticismo* in "Sul romanticismo" and "Lettre à Monsieur Chauvet" (1820) on the dramatic unities, he was not a principal contributor to the pivotal debates occasioned by the publication of Staël's essay on translation in *Biblioteca italiana* in 1816. The eighteen-year-old Leopardi did weigh in on the matter by defending the mythological-classical tradition attacked by Staël; but his contribution ("Discorso di un italiano intorno alla poesia romantica") was not selected for publication, nor did the later Leopardi return to the debates with a comparable level of engagement. For an overview of the relationship of the Romantic *tre corone* to the *questione del romanticismo* as well as analysis of the major contributions to this literary dispute, see Fubini's *Romanticismo italiano: Saggi di storia della critica e della letteratura*, 2nd ed., enl. (Bari: Laterza, 1960), 9–59, esp. 9–11.

27. For a discussion of the critical differences between American and Italian approaches to Dante, see Robert Pogue Harrison, *The Body of Beatrice* (Baltimore: Johns Hopkins University Press, 1988), 1–13. See also the wide range of methodological avenues explored in two recent issues of *Annali d'Italianistica,* "New Landscapes in Contemporary

Italian Cinema," ed. Gaetana Marrone-Puglia, *Annali d'Italianistica* 17 (1999); and, on travel literature, "Hodoeporics Revisited/Ritorno all'odeporica," ed. Luigi Monga, *Annali d'Italianistica* 21 (2003).

28. The term *world literature* (*Weltliteratur*) derives from Goethe, as reported by Johann Peter Eckermann in *Gespräche mit Goethe in den letzten Jahren seines Lebens* (1836). For a discussion of world literature as a "mode" and related issues, see David Damrosch, *What Is World Literature?* (Princeton, NJ: Princeton University Press, 2003), 1–36.

29. See above, note 2, for Furst; and John Claiborne Isbell, *The Birth of European Romanticism: Propaganda and Truth in Staël's "De l'Allemagne," 1810–1813* (New York: Cambridge University Press, 1994).

30. See Virgil Nemoianu, *The Taming of European Romanticism: European Literature and the Age of Biedermeier* (Cambridge, MA: Harvard University Press, 1984), especially his comparison of Manzoni and Walter Scott (205–16).

31. See above, note 23, for Eldridge; Michael Löwy and Robert Sayre, *Romanticism against the Tide of Modernity*, trans. Catherine Porter (Durham, NC: Duke University Press, 2001); Ian Balfour, *The Rhetoric of Romantic Prophecy* (Stanford, CA: Stanford University Press, 2002); and Paul Hamilton, *Metaromanticism: Aesthetics, Literature, Theory* (Chicago: Chicago University Press, 2003).

32. Roy Porter and Mikuláš Teich, eds., *Romanticism in National Context* (New York: Cambridge University Press, 1988).

33. Mario Puppo, *Romanticismo italiano e romanticismo europeo* (Milan: Istituto Propaganda Libraria, 1985); and Raimondi, *Romanticismo*.

34. The lone English study I have found on the subject is the primarily descriptive Grazia Avitabile, *The Controversy on Romanticism in Italy: First Phase, 1816–1823* (New York: Vanni, 1959). For citation of Staël's essay, see note 2, above.

35. For welcome exceptions, see Antonia Arslan and Gabriella Romani, eds., *Writing to Delight: Italian Short Stories by Nineteenth-Century Women Writers* (Toronto: University of Toronto Press, 2006); and Antonio Illiano, *Invito al romanzo d'autrice '800–'900: Da Luisa Saredo a Laudomia Bonanni* (Florence: Cadmo, 2001).

36. See Albert Russel Ascoli and Krystyna Clara Von Henneberg, eds., *Making and Remaking Italy: The Cultivation of National Identity around the Risorgimento* (Oxford: Berg, 2001); Zygmunt G. Barański and Rebecca J. West, eds., *The Cambridge Companion to Modern Italian Culture* (New York: Cambridge University Press, 2001); and Peter E. Bondanella and Andrea Ciccarelli, eds., *The Cambridge Companion to the Italian Novel* (New York: Cambridge University Press, 2003).

37. Though it appeared too recently to be considered in my discussion of the European myth of Italy, Roberto M. Dainotto's *Europe (in Theory)* (Durham, NC: Duke University Press, 2007) provides a genealogy of Eurocentrism that analyzes the Continent's marginalization of southern countries, including Italy, in light of northern Enlightenment ideals of progress and rationality.

38. For the substantial amount of criticism on Manzoni by Goethe—who wrote the preface for an early edition of Manzoni's poetry published at Jena in 1827—see his "Teilnahme Goethes an Manzoni," *Schriften zur Literatur,* vol. 14 of *Werke,* ed. Ernst Beutler (Zurich: Artemis, 1950), 812–44.

Chapter 1. Did Italian Romanticism Exist?

1. Friedrich Wilhelm Nietzsche, "Zweites Stück: Vom Nutzen und Nachteil der Historie für das Leben," *Unzeitgemässe Betrachtungen,* ed. Alfred Baeumler (Stuttgart: Kröner, 1964); *Untimely Meditations,* ed. Daniel Breazeale, trans. R. J. Hollingdale (New York: Cambridge University Press, 1997). See discussion in Harold Bloom, *The Anxiety of Influence: A Theory of Poetry* (New York: Oxford University Press, 1973), 49–51; Paul de Man, "Literary History," *Blindness and Insight: Essays in the Rhetoric of Contemporary Criticism,* 2nd ed., rev. (Minneapolis: University of Minnesota Press, 1983), 142–52; and David Perkins, *Is Literary History Possible?* (Baltimore: Johns Hopkins University Press, 1992), 175–86.

2. René Wellek and Austin Warren, *Theory of Literature,* 3rd ed. (New York: Harcourt, Brace, 1956), 241.

3. I. A. Richards, *Practical Criticism: A Study of Literary Judgement* (London: Routledge and Kegan Paul, 1964), 12.

4. See especially Hans-Robert Jauss, "Literary History as a Challenge to Literary Theory," trans. Elizabeth Benzinger, *New Directions in Literary History,* ed. Ralph Cohen (Baltimore: Johns Hopkins University Press, 1974), 11–41; and discussion in Geoffrey H. Hartman, "Toward Literary History," *Beyond Formalism: Literary Essays, 1958–1970* (New Haven: Yale University Press, 1970), 356–86, esp. 356.

5. See Jerome McGann, "Who's Carving Up the Nineteenth Century?" *PMLA* 116 (2001): 1415–21; Charles J. Rzepka, "The Feel of Not to Feel It," *PMLA* 116 (2001): 1422–31; and Susan J. Wolfson, "Our Puny Boundaries: Why the Craving for Carving Up the Nineteenth Century?" *PMLA* 116 (2001): 1432–41.

6. A notable example of these new approaches is Denis Hollier and R. Howard Bloch, eds., *A New History of French Literature* (Cambridge, MA: Harvard University Press, 1989), an episodic and multiauthorial edition of French literary history sensitive to historical discontinuity and marked by a plurality of theoretical approaches. For critical perspectives on literary history, including feminism, Marxism, postcolonialism, and the New Historicism, see Marshall Brown, ed., *The Uses of Literary History* (Durham, NC: Duke University Press, 1995). For a recent discussion of the concept of the period in literary history, see "Periodization: Cutting Up the Past," special issue of *Modern Language Quarterly* 62, no. 4 (2001).

7. See Gina Martegiani, *Il romanticismo italiano non esiste: Saggio di letteratura comparata* (Florence: Seeber, 1908), vii–xvi.

8. See Giovanni Carsaniga, s.v. "The Romantic Controversy," *The Cambridge History of Italian Literature,* ed. Peter Brand and Lino Pertile, rev. ed. (Cambridge, MA: Harvard University Press, 1999), 399–402. For further background on the *questione del romanticismo,* see Dirk Vanden Berghe, s.v. "Literary Journals," *Encyclopedia of Italian Literary Studies,* 2 vols., ed. Gaetana Marrone (New York: Routledge, 2007), 1:982–83; and Graziella Corsinovi, s.v. "Romanticism," in Marrone, 2:1596–97.

9. For consideration of the complicated political issues surrounding Foscolo's exile, see Giuseppe Nicoletti, *Il "metodo" dell' "Ortis" e altri studi foscoliani* (Florence: La Nuova Italia, 1978), 107–45; and Glauco Cambon, *Ugo Foscolo, Poet of Exile* (Princeton, NJ: Princeton University Press, 1980), 300–301n1, 310–11n14.

10. For Silvio Pellico's description of the persecutions faced by Italian intellectuals and his own subsequent imprisonment (1820–30), see his *Le mie prigioni* (1832).

11. Francesco De Sanctis, *La letteratura italiana del secolo XIX: Scuola liberale – scuola democratica; lezioni raccolte da Francesco Torraca,* ed. Benedetto Croce (Naples: Morano, 1898).

12. For discussion of De Sanctis's text and, more generally, the issue of Romanticism's reception in Italy, see Domenico Vittorini, "The Realistic Approach in the Evaluation of Romanticism in Modern Italian Criticism," *Italica* 25 (1948): 274–81.

13. Carducci's anti-Romantic statements are scattered throughout his collected works (*Opere di Giosuè Carducci,* 20 vols. [Bologna: Zanichelli, 1889–1909]); for analysis and survey of such remarks, see Julius Giuntoni, "The Reaction of Giosuè Carducci to Romanticism," *Italica* 8 (1931): 9–12. For a bibliographical overview of works that explore the underlying links between Carducci and Romanticism, see Mario Puppo, "La reazione al romanticismo nella poetica del Carducci" and "Postilla sul romanticismo del Carducci," *Poetica e critica del romanticismo* (Milan: Marzorati, 1973), 181–87. Giuseppe Antonio Borgese is among the critics attuned to the continuities between the aesthetic platforms of Carducci and the Romantics ("Literary Criticism in Italy during the Romantic Period," *Italica* 23 [1946]: 69–70).

14. Croce elaborated a confusing tripartite division between (1) moral Romanticism, which he negatively associated with sentimentalism and the *mal du siècle;* (2) artistic Romanticism, which expressed itself as an opposition to classical principles of balance and order; and (3) philosophical Romanticism, the drive for truth through intuition and imagination rather than reason ("Le definizioni del romanticismo," *Problemi di estetica e contributi alla storia dell'estetica italiana* [Bari: Laterza, 1949], 297–98; see the discussion in Joseph Rossi, "The Distinctive Character of Italian Romanticism," *Modern Language Journal* 39 [1955]: 59).

15. René Wellek devotes a chapter to the "Italian Critics" (see *The Romantic Age,* in *History of Modern Criticism: 1750–1950,* 8 vols. [New Haven: Yale University Press, 1955–92], 2:259–78), but he draws on Martegiani's study and stresses the derivative nature of nineteenth-century Italian poetics. Though not primarily a scholar of Romanticism, Erich Auerbach did produce "Entdeckung Dantes in der Romantik," *Gesammelte Aufsätze zur romanischen Philologie* (Bern: Francke, 1967), 176–83; nowhere, however, does he substantively address Italian Romanticism.

16. Roy Porter and Mikuláš Teich, eds., *Romanticism in National Context* (New York: Cambridge University Press, 1988).

17. For the principal texts in the question of Italian Romanticism, see Carlo Calcaterra, ed., *Manifesti romantici e altri scritti della polemica classico-romantica,* 2nd ed., enl., ed. Mario Scotti (Turin: UTET, 1979). See also the anthologies of Egidio Bellorini, ed., *Discussioni e polemiche sul romanticismo, 1816–1826,* 2 vols. (Bari: Laterza, 1943); and Giuseppe Petronio, ed., *Il romanticismo* (Palermo: Palumbo, 1960).

18. Important moments in Italian Romantic criticism include, in chronological order and with original dates of publication, Francesco De Sanctis, "La nuova letteratura," *Storia della letteratura italiana* (1871) and *La letteratura italiana nel secolo XIX* (1898); Giuseppe Antonio Borgese, *Storia della critica romantica in Italia* (1905); Benedetto Croce, "Le definizioni del romanticismo," *Problemi di estetica e contributi alla storia*

dell'estetica italiana (1910); Francesco Flora, *Dal romanticismo al futurismo* (1925); Mario Praz, *La carne, la morte e il diavolo nella letteratura romantica* (1930); Benedetto Croce, "Romanticismo," *Storia d'Europa nel secolo XIX* (1932); Walter Binni, *Preromanticismo italiano* (1947); Mario Fubini, *Romanticismo italiano* (1953); Ettore Bonora, *Il preromanticismo in Italia* (1958); Giuseppe Petronio, *Il romanticismo* (1960); Sebastiano Timpanaro, *Classicismo e illuminismo nell'Ottocento italiano* (1965); Mario Puppo, *Poetica e critica del romanticismo* (1973); Enzo Noè Girardi, *Manzoni, De Sanctis, Croce e altri studi di storia della critica italiana* (1986); and Ezio Raimondi, *Romanticismo italiano e romanticismo europeo* (1997).

19. Although women intellectuals organized influential literary salons and gave public recitations of poetry, social taboos and gender politics prevented them from entering the Italian Romantic canon.

20. Leopardi's aforementioned familiarity with contemporary Continental philosophy made him one of the more Europe-oriented of the Italian Romantics, and he remains the only Italian poet from the era to have achieved a considerable translatability and literary reputation abroad. His foreign admirers included William Ewart Gladstone, Charles Augustin Sainte-Beuve, and Ezra Pound, and most of his major works are now available in English translation. See G. Singh, *I canti di Giacomo Leopardi nelle traduzioni inglesi: Saggio bibliografico e antologia delle versioni nel mondo anglosassone* (Recanati: Centro Nazionale di Studi Leopardiani, 1990).

21. Vittorio Alfieri, *Opere*, 40 vols. (Asti: Casa d'Alfieri, 1951-) (abbrev. "*Opera omnia*"). See also Francesco De Sanctis, *Storia della letteratura italiana*, ed. Gianfranco Contini (Milan: TEA, 1989) (abbrev. "*Letteratura italiana*"); *History of Italian Literature,* trans. Joan Redfern, 2 vols. (New York: Basic, 1959) (abbrev. "*Italian Literature*"): "Gli effetti della tragedia alfieriana furono corrispondenti alle sue intenzioni. Essa infiammò il sentimento politico e patriottico, accelerò la formazione di una coscienza nazionale, ristabilì la serietà di un mondo interiore nella vita e nell'arte. I suoi epigrammi, le sue sentenze, i suoi motti, le sue tirate divennero proverbiali, fecero parte della pubblica educazione" (803). (His [Alfieri's] work had the effect he had intended. It awakened patriotic and political feeling and a national consciousness, and Italy regained the seriousness of an inner world in life and in art. His epigrams, sayings, mottoes, and tirades passed into the language, and were made part of public education [2:898].)

22. With typical political mystification, the dedication of this edition reads: "To the people of free and united Italy, this translation of the works of her greatest tragic poet, whose writings did so much to bring about that independence which she at length achieved sixty years after his death, is inscribed" (*The Tragedies of Vittorio Alfieri,* ed. Edgar Alfred Bowring, 2 vols. [London: Bell, 1876]).

23. For two works that critique foreign attacks on Italian neoclassicism, especially Staël's, see Giacomo Leopardi, "Discorso di un italiano intorno alla poesia romantica," in Calcaterra-Scotti, *Manifesti romantici* 482–574; and Ugo Foscolo, *Lettere scritte dall'Inghilterra,* ed. Elena Lombardi, *Opere,* ed. Franco Gavezzeni, 2 vols. (Turin: Einaudi-Gallimard, 1994–95), 2:460–61.

24. The most representative text on the nexus between Christianity and Romanticism in Italy is Manzoni, "Sul romanticismo: Lettera al marchese Cesare D'Azeglio," *Opere,* ed. Guido Bezzola, 3 vols. (Milan: Rizzoli, 1961), 3:425–57; "Letter on Romanticism,"

trans. Joseph Luzzi, *PMLA* 119 (2004): 299–316; for a satire of Italian Catholicism, see Johann Wolfgang von Goethe, *Italienische Reise*, ed. Erich Trunz and Herbert von Einem (1960), vol. 11 of *Werke*, ed. Erich Trunz, 14 vols. (Hamburg: Wegner, 1960–62), 159–60 (January 13, 1787); *Italian Journey*, ed. Thomas P. Saine and Jeffrey L. Sammons, trans. Robert R. Heitner, vol. 6 of *Goethe's Collected Works* (New York: Suhrkamp, 1989), 130.

25. Though he admired Manzoni's verse tragedy *Il conte di Carmagnola* (The Count of Carmagnola; 1820), Goethe criticized the author for fixating on the historically verifiable and separating his characters into two classes, the historical and the ideal; see his "Manzonis *Carmagnola*" 159–85, esp. 166: "Für den Dichter ist keine Person historisch" (For the poet, nobody is historical), vol. 37 of *Goethes sämtliche Werke*, ed. Eduard von der Hellen, 40 vols. (Stuttgart: Cotta, 1902–7). See also the discussion in Wellek, *Modern Criticism* 2:262; Mario Puppo, *Poesia e verità: Interpretazioni manzoniane* (Messina: D'Anna, 1979), 24, 34; and Sandra Bermann, ed. and trans., introduction to *On the Historical Novel*, by Alessandro Manzoni (Lincoln: University of Nebraska Press, 1996), 25.

26. See, for example, Jean-Jacques Rousseau, *La nouvelle Héloïse*, ed. Henri Coulet and Bernard Guyon (1961), in *Œuvres complètes*, ed. Bernard Gagnebin and Marcel Raymond, 5 vols. (Paris: Gallimard, 1959–95), 2:78:

> Ce fut là que je démêlai sensiblement dans la pureté de l'air où je me trouvais, la véritable cause de changement de mon humeur, et du retour de cette paix intérieure que j'avois perdue depuis si longtems. En effet, c'est une impression générale qu'éprouvent tous les hommes, quoiqu'ils ne l'observent pas tous, que sur les hautes montagnes où l'air est pur et subtil, on se sent plus de facilité dans la respiration, plus de légéreté dans le corps, plus de sérénité dans l'esprit."

> (It was there [in the Alps] that, in the purity of the air where I found myself, I came to an understanding of the genuine cause of my change of humor, and of the return of that inner peace I for so long had lost. Indeed, it is a general impression experienced by all men, although they do not all notice it, that high in the mountains where the air is subtle, one breathes more freely, one feels lighter in the body, more serene of mind. (*Julie, or The New Heloise*, ed. and trans. Philip Stewart and Jean Vaché [1977], in *The Collected Writings of Rousseau*, ed. Roger D. Masters and Christopher Kelly [Hanover, NH: University Press of New England, 1990–], 6:64.)

27. See *Prelude* (1850) 6.592–608:

> Imagination—here the Power so called
> Through sad incompetence of human speech,
> That awful Power rose from the mind's abyss
> Like an unfathered vapour that enwraps,
> At once, some lonely traveller. I was lost;
> Halted without an effort to break through;
> But to my conscious soul I now can say—
> "I recognise thy glory": in such strength
> Of usurpation, when the light of sense
> Goes out, but with a flash that has revealed

> The invisible world, doth greatness make abode,
> There harbours, whether we be young or old.
> Our destiny, our being's heart and home,
> Is with infinitude, and only there;
> With hope it is, hope that can never die,
> Effort, and expectation, and desire,
> And something evermore about to be.

Unless otherwise indicated, references are from the 1850 edition of *The Prelude, 1799, 1805, 1850: Authoritative Texts, Context and Reception, Recent Critical Essays,* ed. Jonathan Wordsworth, M. H. Abrams, and Stephen Charles Gill (New York: Norton, 1979).

28. Ugo Foscolo, *Ultime lettere di Jacopo Ortis,* ed. Maria Antonietta Terzoli, *Opere,* ed. Franco Gavezzeni, 2 vols. (Turin: Einaudi-Gallimard, 1994–95), 2:3–140; *Last Letters of Jacopo Ortis; and, Of Tombs,* trans. J. G. Nichols (London: Hesperus, 2002).

29. Alessandro Manzoni, *Adelchi,* in *Poesie e tragedie,* ed. Valter Boggione (Turin: UTET, 2002); *Alessandro Manzoni's "The Count of Carmagnola" and "Adelchis,"* trans. Federica Brunori Deigan (Baltimore: Johns Hopkins University Press, 2004).

30. For a comparison of Manzoni and Scott, see Georg Lukács, *The Historical Novel,* trans. Hannah and Stanley Mitchell (Lincoln: University of Nebraska Press, 1983), 69–71.

31. For Manzoni's view on the supposed impossibility of the historical novel as a genre, see *Del romanzo storico, Opere* 3:473; *On the Historical Novel* 72.

32. Marilyn Butler, *Romantics, Rebels, and Reactionaries: English Literature and Its Background, 1760–1830* (1981; New York: Oxford University Press, 1982), 113–37.

33. One of the few foreign critics to note this intimately personal aspect of the "classical" in Italian Romantic literature is Karl Kroeber, in *The Artifice of Reality: Poetic Style in Wordsworth, Foscolo, Keats, and Leopardi* (Madison: University of Wisconsin Press, 1964), 54–55, 61.

34. Fubini censures the critical tendency to emphasize the poem's historical and political dimensions at the expense of its aesthetic and universal values (Fubini, *Ugo Foscolo: Saggi, studi, note,* rev. ed. [Florence: La Nuova Italia, 1978], 193–95).

35. For discussion of De Sanctis's *Storia della letteratura italiana,* Benedetto Croce's *Storia d'Italia dal 1871 al 1915* (1928), and Antonio Gramsci's *Letteratura e vita nazionale* (1950), see Ezio Raimondi, *La letteratura italiana: Il moderno, la tradizione, e l'identità nazionale: Appunti dalle lezioni del corso monografico 1993/94* (Bologna: CUSL, 1994), 319–408.

36. See De Sanctis, *Letteratura italiana* 805; *Italian Literature* 2:903:

> La vecchia generazione se ne andava ai suoni lirici di Vincenzo Monti, professore, cavaliere, poeta di corti. I repubblicani a Napoli e a Milano venivano gallonati nelle anticamere regie. E non si sentì una voce fiera, che ricordasse i dolori e gli sdegni e le vergogne fra tanta pompa di feste e tanto strepito di armi. Comparve *Iacopo Ortis.* Era il primo grido del disinganno, uscito dal fondo della laguna veneta, come funebre preludio di più vasta tragedia.

> (The old generation was withdrawing, to the lyrical strains of Vincenzo Monti, professor, knight, and court poet. At Naples and Milan the republicans waited in

the royal antechambers, decked in the gold and braid of their court dress. In the midst of those splendid festivals and clashes of arms not a single proud voice was raised to remind Italians of the suffering and contempt and shameful usage of the past. The *Iacopo Ortis* appeared. It was the first cry of disillusionment, coming from the shoals of a Venetian lagoon like the funeral prelude of a vaster tragedy.)

See also *Letteratura italiana* 807; *Italian Literature* 2:906: "I *Sepolcri* stabilirono la sua riputazione e lo alzarono accanto a' sommi. . . . E in verità, questo carme è la prima voce lirica della nuova letteratura, l'affermazione della coscienza rifatta, dell'uomo nuovo" (The work that raised him [Foscolo] to the level of the great was the *Sepolcri*. . . . And certainly this ode was the first lyrical voice of the new literature, the affirmation of the new consciousness, the birth of the new man.)

37. See Peter Carravetta, s.v. "Italian Theory and Criticism: Twentieth Century," *The Johns Hopkins Guide to Literary Theory and Criticism,* ed. Michael Groden and Martin Kreiswirth (Baltimore: Johns Hopkins University Press, 1994), 411. Borgese astutely diagnoses the mix between close reading and national mythmaking that pervades De Sanctis's monumental work:

No plateau of liberated contemplation attracted him [De Sanctis] unless it included a landmark, open or implicit, positive or negative, in the liberation of Italy and of the human spirit. An undercurrent of political, philosophic, and moral preferences — nay, partisanships — vibrated beneath the surface of his most noncommittal pages; and his *History of Italian Literature,* often extolled as the finest of any literature, is in substance a history of liberal civilization, from the wane of the Middle Ages to the eradication of the Papal State, exemplified in the national history of Italy, which in turn is embodied in an organic interpretation of literary masters and masterpieces. ("Romantic Period" 68)

38. Benedict Anderson, *Imagined Communities* (London: Verso, 1983), 9. For discussion of the "cultural roots of nationalism with death," see ibid., 10–12; and Ted Underwood, "Romantic Historicism and the Afterlife," *PMLA* 117 (2002): 237–51.

39. Foscolo wrote to Goethe on January 16, 1802, that "forse" (perhaps) his novel was inspired by *Werther.* He added that his *Ortis* afforded him no right to call himself author ("ho sdegnato il titolo di autore" [I have disdained the title of author]), only to that of man ("Non ho nissun merito nell'invenzione avendo tratto tutto del *vero*" [Having taken everything from the *truth,* I can take no credit for invention]) ("Lettere varie," in *Opere di Ugo Foscolo,* ed. Mario Puppo, 7th ed. [Milan: Mursia, 1977], 1235–36; Foscolo's italics).

40. Ugo Foscolo, "Notizia bibliografica intorno alle *Ultime lettere di Jacopo Ortis*" (1814), ed. Maria Antonietta Terzoli, *Opere* 2:167.

41. Foscolo echoes an early section of Rousseau's *Confessions:* "Que la trompette du jugement dernier sonne quand elle voudra; je viendrai ce livre à la main me présenter devant le souverain juge. Je dirai hautement: voila ce que j'ai fait, ce que j'ai pensé, ce que ju fus" (*Œuvres* 1:6). (Let the trumpet of the Final Judgment sound when it will. I will

come with this book [the *Confessions*] in hand and present myself to the Sovereign Judge. I will say loudly: here is what I did, what I thought, and what I was.) The discrepancies in the symbols of confession that separate Foscolo (blood, pure hands and heart) from Rousseau (the text of his life) epitomize the difference between Foscolo's political narrative, with its martial themes and imagery, and Rousseau's tendency to explicate the self with metaphors of rhetoric and textuality.

42. Compare Foscolo's language of political self-sacrifice ("If you had granted me a homeland, I would have spent all my intellect and my blood on its behalf" [March 25, 1799]) with Lucan's representation of Cato:

> O utinam caelique deis Erebique liceret
> Hoc caput in cunctas damnatum exponere poenas!
> . . . .
> Hic redimat sanguis populos, haec caede luatur,
> Quidquid Romani meruerunt pendere mores.
> . . . .
> Hic dabit, hic pacem iugulus finemque malorum
> Gentibus Hesperiis: post me regnare volenti
> Non opus est bello. (*Pharsalia* 2.306–7, 312–13, 317–19)

> (But would it be possible for me [Cato], condemned by the powers of heaven and hell, to be the scapegoat for the nation! . . . Let my blood redeem the nations, and my death pay the whole penalty incurred by the corruption of Rome. . . . My blood, mine only, will bring peace to the people of Italy and end their sufferings; the would-be tyrant need wage no war, once I am gone.) (Lucan, *The Civil War (Pharsalia),* trans. J. D. Duff (1928; Cambridge, MA: Harvard University Press, 1988)

Foscolo's recourse to Lucan's Cato is most likely mediated by his reading of Dante, who draws directly from Lucan in transforming Cato into a revered symbol of justice, making him a gatekeeper to purgatory instead of condemning him in hell along with other suicides like Pier delle Vigne in *Inferno* 13.

43. Foscolo refers here to Edward Young, *Night Thoughts* (1742–45); James Hervey, *Meditations among the Tombs* (1746–47); and Thomas Gray, *Elegy Written in a Country Church-Yard* (1751).

44. Ugo Foscolo, "Lettera a Monsieur Guill[on]" (June 22, 1807), *Opere* 1:39–52.

45. Pietro Giordani, *Lettere inedite a Lazzaro Papi* (Lucca: Baccelli, 1851), 105.

46. For a discussion connecting Manzoni's view of providence to both Dante and Vico, see Ernesto G. Caserta, *Manzoni's Christian Realism* (Florence: Olschki, 1977), 91–92.

47. For a definition of the term, see Hugh J. McCann, s.v. "Divine Providence," *The Stanford Encyclopedia of Philosophy* (Fall 2006 edition), ed. Edward N. Zalta; Jan. 26, 2007, http://plato.stanford.edu/archives/fa112006/entries/providence-divine/.

48. See Rocco Montano, *Comprendere Manzoni* (Naples: Vico, 1975), 6.

49. See Attilio Momigliano, *Alessandro Manzoni,* 3rd ed., rev. (Messina: Principato, 1933), 275–76:

> La fede serena e incrollabile lo separa dalla rivoluzione e dal romanticismo. . . . La sua tristezza è molto distante da quella romantica, il suo pensiero è più simile alla

geometria che alla *rêverie*. . . . Nella sua opera c'è una più larga verità che in quella dei romantici, perchè questi non riflettono l'anima qual è nei grandi momenti della vita, quando le morbosità e le complicazioni dileguano.

(Serene and indestructible faith separates him [Manzoni] from the revolutionary and Romantic worlds. . . . His melancholy is quite distant from the Romantic one, his thought is closer to geometry than to reverie. . . . In his work there is a larger truth than in that of the Romantics, because the latter do not capture the soul as it is in the greatest moments of life, when the morbidity and complications subside.)

50. For analysis of Manzoni's changing understanding of providence, see Luciano Parisi, "Il tema della Provvidenza in Manzoni," *Modern Language Notes* 114 (1999): 83–105, which traces Manzoni's notion of the term from its early reliance on the religious thought of Jacques-Bénigne Bossuet to his more personal vision in *I promessi sposi*.

51. See, for example, Giovanni Getto's description of the novel's *lieto fine* (happy ending) in *Letture manzoniane* (Florence: Sansoni, 1964), 19. In his preface to the widely diffused edition of Manzoni's *I promessi sposi* (Turin: Paravia, 1946), Giuseppe Petronio writes that the novel "si chiude con un trionfo del bene addirittura sfacciato" (closes with a truly impudent triumph of good). In a scathing Marxist critique of Manzoni, Alberto Asor Rosa writes that "l'inevitabile soggezione allo schema provvidenziale mette necessariamente Manzoni fuori della strada maestra della grande arte borghese" (the inevitable deferral to providential design necessarily places Manzoni outside of the mainstream of great bourgeois art); ultimately, Asor Rosa continues, this leaves Manzoni's readers with "un bagaglio di origine gesuitica," "un'operazione istituzionale," and "sapienti accorgimenti di un'alta didattica" (a baggage of Jesuit provenance, an insider's operation, and highly learned clichés), instructing them to give themselves over to providence (*Sintesi di storia della letteratura italiana* [Florence: La Nuova Italia, 1972]). These views and a comprehensive summary of other such interpretations are translated and discussed in Franco Triolo, "Manzoni and Providence," *The Reasonable Romantic: Essays on Alessandro Manzoni,* ed. Sante Matteo and Larry H. Peer (New York: Lang, 1986), 245–57.

52. See Triolo, "Manzoni and Providence" 254, for discussion of the tragic elements in the conclusion of *I promessi sposi*. In a similar vein, Ezio Raimondi's seminal *Il romanzo senza idillio: Saggi sui "Promessi sposi"* (Turin: Einaudi, 1974) notes that, even when characters' fates seem to reflect the patterns of providential design, there are mitigating socioeconomic factors that make any Christian notion of closure untenable within the novel's broader pessimistic worldview; see 213–22 for his discussion of providence. Angelo Raffaele Pupino notes that the word *provvidenza* is often used in the novel not to mean divine justice but rather as an ironic synonym for fate or good fortune (*Manzoni, religione e romanzo* [Rome: Salerno, 2005], 216–22).

53. For a comprehensive discussion of Manzoni's relationship to European intellectual and cultural currents, see Giovanni Getto, *Manzoni europeo* (Milan: Mursia, 1971).

54. I discuss some of the ideas presented here on the link between Christianity and Romanticism in the introduction to my translation of Manzoni, "Sul romanticismo": "On Romanticism"; see esp. 300.

55. Ibid., 300.

56. It is worth noting Manzoni's disdain for another author also known for his Roman-

tic Christianity, Chateaubriand, whose Christian God in *Le génie du christianisme* (1802) allowed for a more direct and sublime contact between humankind and nature by chasing away the fauns, nymphs, satyrs, and other vestiges of neoclassical mythology. In keeping with his rationalist bent and high Enlightenment education among the *philosophes* of Milan and Paris, Manzoni preferred Bossuet, Corneille, Montesquieu, Pascal, Rousseau, and Voltaire to what he considered to be the excessive and overwrought French Romantic authors Chateaubriand, Hugo, and Lamartine (see Rossi, "Distinctive Character" 59–60).

57. See especially Foscolo's critique of Manzoni in his essay "Della nuova scuola drammatica in Italia" (1826), which states that an author should not be overly concerned with historical accuracy, because "non giova per nulla alla storia e nuoce alla poesia" (it does not help the history at all and damages the poetry). He continues: "La poesia tende a farci fortemente e pienamente sentire la nostra esistenza, e sollevarla di là dalle noie che l'accompagnano; la storia invece tende a dirigere la vita in guisa che sappiamo giovarci del mondo com'è." (Poetry tends to make us feel our existence strongly and fully, and to raise it up above the tedium that accompanies it; history instead tends to make us utilize existence for what it is.) Ugo Foscolo, *Poetiche romantiche*, ed. Giorgio Pullini (Padua: Liviana, 1955), 50, 56; original text cited and discussed in Franco Betti, "Key Aspects of Romantic Poetics in Italian Literature," *Italica* 74 (1997): 192–93. See also Douglas Radcliff-Umstead, "Foscolo and the Early Romantics," *Italica* 42 (1965): 240–43.

58. See Puppo, *Poesia e verità* (11–21), for a discussion of the relationship between poetry and truth in Manzoni's "Lettre à Chauvet" and *Del romanzo storico*.

59. Alessandro Manzoni, *I promessi sposi*, ed. Ezio Raimondi and Luciano Bottoni (Milan: Principato, 1987); *The Betrothed*, trans. Bruce Penman (Harmondsworth: Penguin, 1972).

60. A character in one of Manzoni's heirs in the historical novel, Giuseppe Tomasi di Lampedusa's *Il gattopardo* (*The Leopard*; 1958), voices the Manzonian concerns of many Italian Catholic intellectuals during the Risorgimento. In the midst of the unification, the Leopard's spiritual advisor Father Pirrone asks: "I nostri beni, quei beni che sono il patrimonio dei poveri, saranno arraffati e malamente divisi fra i caporioni più impudenti; e chi, dopo, sfamerà le moltitudini di infelici che ancora oggi la Chiesa sostenta e guida?" (*Il gattopardo*, 78th ed. [Milan: Feltrinelli, 1961], 54). (Our [the Church's] property, which is the patrimony of the poor, will be seized and carved up among the most brazen of their [the antimonarchists'] leaders; who will then feed all the destitute who are sustained and guided by the Church today? [*The Leopard*, trans. Archibald Colquhoun (New York: Pantheon, 1960), 52].)

61. For description of the biblical subtext to the Cardinal's words, see the gloss of Raimondi and Bottoni in Manzoni, *Promessi sposi* 430n.

62. For Manzoni's negative view of the relationship between providence and power, see his note to Germaine de Staël, *Considérations sur les principaux événemens de la revolution françoise* (1818): "Hélas! Si pour croire à la Providence vous avez besoin de trouver moralité dans l'exercice du pouvoir, vous n'avez pas lu l'histoire, ou vous ne croyez pas à la Providence." (Alas! If you need to find morality in the exercise of power in order to believe in divine providence, then you have not read history—or you do not believe in Providence.) For the quotation, see Giuseppe Lesca, "Postille inedite di A.

Manzoni a storici della rivoluzione francese," *Nuova antologia* 66 (1931): 172; and discussion in Parisi, 101n30.

63. André Bazin, "Défense de Rossellini," *Qu'est-ce que le cinema?* 12th ed. (Paris: Cerf, 2000), 354; "Defense of Rossellini," *What Is Cinema?* ed. and trans. Hugh Gray, 2 vols. (Berkeley and Los Angeles: University of California Press, 1967–71), 2:99.

64. For a disquisition on free indirect style in film, see Pier Paolo Pasolini, "The 'Cinema of Poetry,'" *Heretical Empiricism,* ed. Louise K. Barnett, trans. Ben Lawton and Louise K. Barnett (Bloomington: Indiana University Press, 1988), 175–82.

65. See Bazin, "Défense de Rossellini" 352.

66. References to Leopardi's poetry are from the *Canti,* in vol. 1 of *Opere,* ed. Sergio and Raffaella Solmi, 2 vols. (Milan: Ricciardi, 1956); unless otherwise indicated, translations are from *Leopardi: Selected Poems,* trans. Eamon Grennan (Princeton, NJ: Princeton University Press, 1997).

Chapter 2. Italy without Italians: Goethe, Staël, and Foscolo

1. See Edward W. Said, *Orientalism* (1978; New York: Vintage, 1979); Michael Herzfeld, *Anthropology through the Looking-Glass: Critical Ethnography in the Margins of Europe* (New York: Cambridge University Press, 1987); James G. Carrier, "Occidentalism: The World Turned Upside-Down," *American Ethnologist* 19 (1992): 195–212; John Agnew, "Timeless Space and State-Centrism: The Geographical Assumptions of International Relations Theory," *The Global Economy as Political Space,* ed. Stephen J. Rosow, Naeem Inayatullah, and Mark Rupert (Boulder, CO: Lynne Rienner, 1994), 87–106; Carl Levy, ed., *Italian Regionalism: History, Identity and Politics* (Oxford: Berg, 1996); Robert Lumley and Jonathan Morris, eds., *The New History of the Italian South: The Mezzogiorno Revisited* (Exeter: University of Exeter Press, 1997); and Jane Schneider, ed., *Italy's "Southern Question": Orientalism in One Country* (New York: Berg, 1998). For a historical perspective on Italian stereotypes abroad, see Andrew M. Canepa, "From Degenerate Scoundrel to Noble Savage: Italian Stereotypes in 18th-Century British Travel Literature," *English Miscellany* 22 (1971): 107–46.

2. Jane Schneider, "The Dynamics of Neo-Orientalism in Italy (1848–1995)," in Schneider, *Southern Question* 5. See 6–8 for a critique of two influential studies of southern Italian "backwardness": Edward C. Banfield, *The Moral Basis of a Backward Society* (Chicago: Free Press, 1958); and Robert D. Putnam, Robert Leonardi, and Raffaella Nanetti, *Making Democracy Work: Civic Traditions in Modern Italy* (Princeton, NJ: Princeton University Press, 1993).

3. For a comprehensive study of the matter, see Nelson Moe, *The View from Vesuvius: The Italian Culture and the Southern Question* (Berkeley and Los Angeles: University of California Press, 2002); esp. ch. 1, "Italy as Europe's South," which considers representations of the Italian south in Leopardi (17–18), in Staël's *Corinne* (31–35), and in others. See also Gabriella Gribaudi, "Images of the South: The *Mezzogiorno* as Seen by Insiders and Outsiders," in Schneider, *Southern Question* 83–113.

4. See Benedict Anderson, *Imagined Communities* (London: Verso, 1983); Ernst Gellner, *Nations and Nationalism* (Ithaca, NY: Cornell University Press, 1983); E. J. Hobsbawm, *Nations and Nationalism since 1780: Program, Myth, Reality* (New York: Cam-

bridge University Press, 1990); and Hans Kohn, *The Idea of Nationalism: A Study in Its Origin and Background* (New Brunswick, NJ: Transaction, 1944). For a more historical perspective, see Vincenzo Gioberti, *Del primato morale e civile degli italiani* (1843); John Stuart Mill, *Considerations on Representative Government* (1861); and Ernest Renan, *Qu'est-ce qu'une nation?* (1882).

5. The dichotomy of north versus south draws on a long-standing tradition of equating physical geography with national character; see James Fernandez, "The North-South Axis in European Popular Cosmologies and the Dynamic of the Categorical," *American Anthropologist* 99 (1998): 713–30; and Nelson Moe, "North, South, and the Identity of Europe," *Nineteenth-Century Contexts* 26 (2004): 314–20. The persistence of the myth of Italian backwardness with respect to European modernity has been explored by John Agnew, "Italia arretrata, Europa moderna," *Il mulino* 43 (1994): 11–28. Two influential studies of this supposedly recalcitrant Italian exceptionalism by native Italians are Carlo Tullio-Altan, *La nostra Italia: Arretratezza socioculturale, clientelismo, trasformismo e ribellismo dall'Unità ad oggi* (Milan: Feltrinelli, 1986); and Luciano Gallino, *Della ingovernabilità: La società italiana tra premoderno e neo-industriale* (Milan: Comunità, 1987). See also Tim Mason, "Italy and Modernization: A Montage," *History Workshop Journal* 25 (1988): 127–47.

6. Although the majority of Grand Tourists followed traditional itineraries that included the major cities Venice, Florence, and Rome, the ancient cultural heritage of this last city afforded it a privileged status among writers searching for a common European heritage that had a comparable source only in the more inaccessible and geographically remote sites of ancient Greece. Herzfeld provides an anthropological perspective on how Italy's fellow classical Mediterranean culture, ancient Greece, became "the idealized spiritual and intellectual ancestor of Europe" (1; see "Romanticism and Hellenism: Burdens of Otherness," in *Anthropology through the Looking-Glass* 1–27).

7. The issue of an "Italy without Italians" is considered from a different, domestic perspective by Giulio Bollati in his analysis of the Risorgimentalist patriot Francesco Melzi d'Eril (*L'Italiano: Il carattere nazionale come storia e come invenzione*, 2nd ed. [Turin: Einaudi, 1984], 14–34).

8. Percy Bysshe Shelley, *The Letters of Percy Bysshe Shelley*, ed. Roger Ingpen, 2 vols. (London: Pitman, 1912), 2:651, 653. For further details of Shelley's formative Italian experience, see *With Shelley in Italy: Being a Selection of the Poems and Letters of Percy Bysshe Shelley Which Have to Do with His Life in Italy from 1818 to 1822*, ed. Anna Benneson McMahan (Chicago: McClurg, 1905). See also the analysis in Richard Cronin, "Asleep in Italy: Byron and Shelley in 1819," *Keats-Shelley Review* 10 (1996): 151–80; and Alan M. Weinberg, *Shelley's Italian Experience* (New York: St. Martin's, 1991), and "Shelley's Italy: A Paradise of Exiles," *Unisa English Studies: Journal of the Department of English* 30 (1992): 14–23.

9. See Carl Ipsen, *Dictating Demography: The Problem of Population in Fascist Italy* (New York: Cambridge University Press, 1996), 25.

10. The rare foreign author to have mastered the Italian language, Shelley was a Dantist of note, an indefatigable translator of Italian, and the only English poet up to that time to employ terza rima successfully.

11. Works from this period include: Giovanni Berchet, contributions to *Il conciliatore*

(1818–19); Giacomo Leopardi, "L'infinito," "La sera del dì di festa," "Alla luna," "Il sogno," and "La vita solitaria" (1819–21); Alessandro Manzoni, "La pentecoste" (1817–22), *Il conte di Carmagnola* (1816–20), and *Osservazioni sulla morale cattolica* (1818–19); Vincenzo Monti, *L'invito a Pallade* (1819); and Ippolito Pindemonte, *Sermoni* (1819).

12. For a study of the functions, history, and structure of this cemetery, see Carl Nylander, Antonio Menniti Ippolito, and Paolo Vian, *The Protestant Cemetery in Rome: The "Parte Antica"* (Rome: Unione Internazionale degli Istituti di Archeologia, Storia e Storia dell'Arte in Roma, 1989).

13. Lord Byron, *Childe Harold's Pilgrimage*, in vol. 2 of *The Complete Poetical Works*, ed. Jerome J. McGann, 3 vols. (Oxford: Clarendon, 1980–81). For analysis of Byron's interest in early Italian Catholic poetry as a challenge to English Protestant authoritarianism, see Caroline Franklin, "Cosmopolitanism and Catholic Culture: Byron, Italian Poetry, and *The Liberal*," *British Romanticism and Italian Literature: Translating, Reviewing, Rewriting*, ed. Laura Bandiera and Diego Saglia (New York: Rodopi, 2005), 255–68. See also *With Byron in Italy: Being a Selection of the Poems and Letters of Lord Byron Which Have to Do with His Life in Italy from 1816 to 1823*, ed. Anna Benneson McMahan (Chicago: McClurg, 1906); and studies by Peter Quennell, *Byron in Italy* (London: Collins, 1941); and Peter Vassallo, *Byron: The Italian Literary Influence* (New York: St. Martin's, 1984).

14. A similar sentiment on those same tombs of Santa Croce that Byron celebrates permeates the most famous poem on the basilica: Foscolo's "Dei sepolcri." Foscolo's essay on Italian literature was included in the influential critical study on Byron by John Cam Hobhouse: *Historical Illustrations of the Fourth Canto of "Childe Harold": Containing Dissertations on the Ruins of Rome; and an Essay on Italian Literature* [by Ugo Foscolo] (New York: Gilley, 1818), 221–302; and is in Ugo Foscolo, *Opere*, ed. Franco Gavezzeni, 2 vols. (Milan: Ricciardi, 1974), 2:1395–1562.

15. Among the public figures and works of art represented in the painting are, to the middle left, Zoffany himself and poet William Cowper beside Raphael's *Madonna col bambino*; to the front right, the diplomat Sir Horace Mann discusses Titian's *Venere di Urbino* with author and artist Thomas Patch; to the middle far right, explorer of Africa James Bruce contemplates the *Venere de' Medici*. See Ilaria Bignamini and Andrew Wilton, eds., *Grand Tour: The Lure of Italy in the Eighteenth Century* (London: Tate Gallery, 1996), 135–36.

16. Oliver Millar, *Zoffany and His Tribuna* (London: Routledge and Kegan Paul, 1967), 34.

17. For a study of the Italian Grand Tour as a cultural institution and its practical elements—including cost, lodging, transport, and food and drink—see Jeremy Black, *Italy and the Grand Tour* (New Haven: Yale University Press, 2003). See James Buzard, *The Beaten Track: European Tourism, Literature, and the Ways to Culture, 1800–1918* (Oxford: Clarendon, 1993), for an examination of modern tourism in light of its democratization and commodification after the Grand Tour. See also Cesare De Seta, *L'Italia del Grand Tour: Da Montaigne a Goethe* (Naples: Electa, 1992); and Marie-Madeleine Martinet, *Le voyage d'Italie dans les littératures européennes* (Paris: Presses Universitaires de France, 1996).

18. For consideration of "images and metaphors of decline and decadence" (162) in travelers' depictions of contemporary Italian politics and society, see Black, *Italy and the Grand Tour* 142–63. See 118–34 for description of British attitudes and practices with regard to the opportunities for sex, gambling, and drinking offered by the Grand Tour.

19. For background, see Harry G. Haile, *Artist in Chrysalis: A Biographical Study of Goethe in Italy* (Urbana: University of Illinois Press, 1973); Gerhart Hoffmeister, ed., *Goethe in Italy, 1786–1986: A Bi-Centennial Symposium, November 14–16, 1986, University of California, Santa Barbara: Proceedings Volume* (Amsterdam: Rodopi, 1988); and Roger Paulin, "Goethe's and Stolberg's Italian Journeys and the Romantic Ideology of Art," *Travel Fact and Fiction: Studies on Fiction, Literary Tradition, Scholarly Discovery, and Observation in Travel Writing*, ed. Z. R. W. M. von Martels (New York: Brill, 1994), 207–29.

20. See Lilian R. Furst, "Goethe's *Italienische Reise* in Its European Context," in Hoffmeister, *Goethe in Italy* 115–32. Furst situates Goethe's text in an ad hoc genre of major travel writing that includes Tobias Smollet, *Travels through France and Italy* (1766); Stendhal, *Rome, Naples et Florence* (1817); William Hazlitt, *Notes of a Journey through France and Italy* (1826); and Chateaubriand, *Voyage en Italie* (1827). Significantly for Goethe, his father, Johann Caspar, composed an account in Italian of his journey to the Peninsula: *Viaggio per l'Italia* (1739–40). Goethe himself was an avid consumer of travel writing, which, according to one commentator, composed 13 percent of his library; see Arthur G. Schultz, "Goethe and the Literature of Travel," *Journal of English and Germanic Philology* 48 (1949): 445–68.

21. Johann Wolfgang von Goethe, *Italienische Reise*, ed. Erich Trunz and Herbert von Einem (1960), vol. 11 of *Werke*, ed. Erich Trunz, 14 vols. (Hamburg: Wegner, 1960–62); *Italian Journey*, ed. Thomas P. Saine and Jeffrey L. Sammons, trans. Robert R. Heitner, vol. 6 of *Goethe's Collected Works* (New York: Suhrkamp, 1989).

22. Chateaubriand writes on encountering Rome: "Le lieu est propre à la réflexion et à la rêverie: je remonte dans ma vie passée; je sens le poids du présent, et je cherche à pénétrer mon avenir." (The place is suited for reflection and dreaming: I return to my past life, I feel the weight of the present, and I seek to penetrate my future.) *Voyage en Italie*, in *Œuvres romanesques et voyages*, ed. Maurice Regard, 2 vols. (Paris: Gallimard, 1969), 2:1439. See discussion in Furst, "*Italienische Reise* in European Context" 126–27. For evaluation of the Romantic encounter between the poet and nature, see J. H. Van Den Berg, "The Subject and His Landscape," *Romanticism and Consciousness: Essays in Criticism*, ed. Harold Bloom (New York: Norton, 1970), 57–64.

23. Jane Brown explores the stylistic force of Goethe's objective rhetorical mode, in which "objects and abstractions become powerful actors . . . while people are excluded," and in which conversations "turn into dramatic dialogues [and] language takes on its own independent existence" ("The Renaissance of Goethe's Poetic Genius in Italy," in Hoffmeister, *Goethe in Italy* 79).

24. For studies of Goethe's knowledge of contemporary Italy, see Matthew Bell, *Goethe's Naturalistic Anthropology: Man and Other Plants* (Oxford: Clarendon, 1994), 176–88; and János Riesz, "Goethe's 'Canon' of Contemporary Italian Literature in His *Italienische Reise*," in Hoffmeister, *Goethe in Italy* 133–46. Works that take a more skeptical view include: H. Buriot-Darsiles, "Une renommée injustifiée: Le *Voyage en Italie* de Goethe," *Etudes italiennes* (1932): 104–17, 174–91; Dieter Borchmeyer, *Die*

Weimarer Klassik: Eine Einführung, 2 vols. (Königstein/Ts.: Athenäum, 1980), 1:97–98; and Ludwig Uhlig, "Goethes *Römischer Carneval* im Wandel seines Kontexts," *Euphorion* 72 (1978): 84–95. For a discussion of Goethe's relations with his contemporary Italian writers, see Gerhard Hoffmeister, "Goethe und die Italienische Romantik," *Goethe und die Europäische Romantik* (Munich: Francke, 1984), 107–15.

25. See Bell, *Goethe's Naturalistic Anthropology* 181.

26. Edward Gibbon internalized a similar temporal dialectical tension during his visit to Rome. The contrast between the present-day decadence of Rome and its monuments to the past inspired him to compose his famous *Decline and Fall of the Roman Empire* (1776–88): "It was at Rome on the fifteenth of October 1764, as I sat musing amidst the ruins of the Capitol, while the barefooted fryars were singing Vespers in the temple of Jupiter that the idea of writing the decline and fall of the City first started to my mind" (*Edward Gibbon: Memoirs of My Life,* ed. George Alfred Bonnard [New York: Funk and Wagnalls, 1969], 136). See discussion in J. G. A. Pocock, *The Enlightenments of Edward Gibbon, 1737–1764,* in *Barbarism and Religion,* 4 vols. (Cambridge: Cambridge University Press, 1999–), 1:283.

27. A similar sentiment permeates Hawthorne's description of St. Peter's as "the world's Cathedral" and "the palace of the world's Chief-Priest," in *The Marble Faun, or The Romance of Monte Beni,* ed. Richard H. Brodhead (New York: Penguin, 1990), 107.

28. For consideration of Goethe's relationship with Winckelmann in light of Goethe's transition in Italy toward a more classical aesthetic, see Stuart Atkins, "*Italienische Reise* and Goethean Classicism," *Aspekte der Goethezeit,* ed. Stanley A. Corngold, Michael Curschmann, and Theodore J. Ziolkowski (Göttingen: Vandenhoeck and Ruprecht, 1977), 81–96.

29. See *Italienische Reise,* January 13, 1787:

> Wieviel tat Winckelmann nicht, und wieviel ließ er uns zu wünschen übrig! Mit den Materialen, die er sich zueignete, hatte er so geschwind gebaut, um unter Dach zu kommen. Lebte er noch, und er könnte noch frisch und gesund sein, so wäre er der erste, der uns eine Umarbeitung seines Werks gäbe. Was hätte er nicht noch beobachtet, was berichtigt, was benutzt, das von andern nach seinen Grundsätzen getan und beobachtet, neuerdings ausgegraben und entdeckt worden. Und dann wäre der Kardinal Albani tot, dem zuliebe er manches geschrieben und vielleicht manches verschwiegen hat. (*Italienische Reise* 160)

> (How much Winckelmann left undone, and how much he left us to wish for! The reason he built so swiftly with the materials he had acquired was to get them under roof. Were he still living—and he could still be vigorous and healthy—he would be the first one to give us a revision of his work [*History of Art in Antiquity*]. How much more he would have observed and corrected, how much he would have used of what others, following his principles, have done, observed, newly excavated, and discovered. And then, too, Cardinal Albani, for whose sake he wrote, and perhaps withheld, so much, would be dead.) (*Italian Journey* 130–31)

30. Brown notes that Goethe's rhetoric in describing the Italians as mischievous, natural, and primitive recalls his description of the apes in the witch's dark kitchen in *Faust* ("Renaissance of Goethe's Poetic Genius" 86).

31. Friedrich Schiller, *Uber naive und sentimentalische Dichtung*, ed. Rolf-Peter Janz, Hans Richard Brittnacher, Gerd Kleiner, and Fabian Störmer, *Theoretische Schriften, Werke und Briefe*, 12 vols. (Frankfurt: Deutscher Klassiker, 1992), 8:708. Translations from Schiller's *"Naive and Sentimental Poetry," and "On the Sublime": Two Essays*, ed. and trans. Julius A. Elias (1966; New York: Ungar, 1975), 85.

32. The sentimental conservatism of Goethe and his contemporaries in their idealization of early humanity has been explored by Lienhard Bergel, "Vico and the Germany of Goethe," *Forum Italicum* 2 (1968): 566–88.

33. "Nun noch ein Geschichtchen, wie lose man im heiligen Rom das Heilige behandelt. Der verstorbene Kardinal Albani war in einer solchen Festversammlung.... Einer der Schüler fing in einer fremden Mundart an, gegen die Kardinäle gewendet: 'Gnaja! gnaja!' so daß es ungefähr klang wie 'Canaglia! canaglia!' Der Kardinal wendete sich zu seinen Mitbrüdern und sagte: 'Der kennte uns doch!' " (*Italienische Reise* 160). (One more little story about how frivolously holy things are treated in holy Rome. The late Cardinal Albani was in a festive assembly.... One of the schoolboys, turning to the cardinals, began to say, "Gnaja! gnaja!" [Worship! Worship!] in such a strange dialect that it sounded approximately like "Canaglia! canaglia!" [riff-raff]. Albani turned to his fellow cardinals and said, "That one obviously knows us!" [*Italian Journey* 130].)

34. See, for example, Goethe's description of the Christmas Day celebration in St. Peter's: "Es ist ein einziges Schauspiel in seiner Art, prächtig und würdig genug" (January 6, 1787; *Italienische Reise* 156). (The spectacle is unique in its way, splendid and quite dignified [*Italian Journey* 127–28].) This cautious approval, however, quickly cedes to intolerance for ritual devoid of meaning: "Ich bin aber im protestantischen Diogenismus so alt geworden, daß mir diese Herrlichkeit mehr nimmt als gibt; ich möchte auch wie mein frommer Vorfahre zu diesen geistlichen Weltüberwindern sagen: 'Verdeckt mir doch nicht die Sonne höherer Kunst und reiner Menschheit' " (*Italienische Reise* 156). (But I am such a long-time Protestant Diogenist that I find this magnificence more repellent than attractive. Like my pious predecessor I would wish to say to these ecclesiastical world conquerors: "Do not hide the sun of higher art and pure humanity from me" [*Italian Journey* 128].)

35. Goethe's sense of Europe and its relation to his concept of *Weltliteratur* has been explored by Hoffmeister, "Goethe und die Weltliteratur," *Goethe und die Europäische Romantik* 11–20.

36. For analysis of Goethe's influence upon Staël's view of Italy, see Martinet, *Voyage d'Italie* 125–31. For discussion of Goethe's projected study in 1795–96 of Italian "history, art, people, fauna, flora, geology, etc.," see Paulin, "Goethe's Italian Journeys" 212.

37. Thirty-two editions of the text appeared in France between the years 1830–70 alone; the work has been referenced in some form by artists as diverse as Gioachino Rossini, Felicia Hemans, Eugène Delacroix, Honoré de Balzac, Louisa May Alcott, and Bob Dylan. See John Claiborne Isbell, introduction to *Corinne, or Italy*, trans. Sylvia Raphael (New York: Oxford University Press, 1998), x–xi; all translations are from this edition.

38. Staël's interest in the relationship between national character and culture led to the publication of her influential study of German art, institutions, society, and thought: *De l'Allemagne* (1810).

39. Anne Louise Germaine de Staël, *Corinne, ou l'Italie*; vol. 1 of *Œuvres complètes de*

Madame la baronne de Staël-Holstein (Paris: Didot, 1871) (abbrev. "*Œuvres*"); *Corinne, or Italy*, trans. Sylvia Raphael. For background, see Simone Balayé, *Madame de Staël: Écrire, lutter, vivre* (Geneva: Droz, 1994); Avriel H. Goldberger, ed., *Woman as Mediatrix: Essays on Nineteenth-Century European Women Writers* (New York: Greenwood, 1987); Madelyn Gutwirth, Avriel H. Goldberger, and Karyna Szmurlo, eds., *Germaine de Staël: Crossing the Borders* (New Brunswick, NJ: Rutgers University Press, 1991); and Karyna Szmurlo, ed., *The Novel's Seductions: Staël's "Corinne" in Critical Inquiry* (Lewisburg, PA: Bucknell University Press, 1999).

40. See 5.1: "On dirait que l'orgueilleuse nature a repoussé tous les travaux de l'homme, depuis que les Cincinnatus ne conduisent plus la charrue qui sillonnait son sein; elle produit des plantes au hasard, sans permettre que les vivants se servent de sa richesse" (*Œuvres* 692). (It is as if nature, in her pride, has spurned all the works of man since the Cincinnati ceased to drive the plough which furrowed her bosom; she produces plants at random without allowing the living to make use of of her abundance [*Corinne, Italy* 78].)

41. Leopardi deftly perceives Oswald's tendency to repress the affective and fanciful aspects of his character: "La soprabbondanza della immaginazione è quella che tormenta i fanciulli . . . , e perciò in luogo di cercarla nello straordinario, cercano di spegnerla o addormentarla col metodo. Cosa che accade anche agli uomini. V. il carattere di Lord Nelvil nella Corinna" (August 16, 1820; Giacomo Leopardi, *Zibaldone di pensieri: Edizione critica e annotata*, ed. Giuseppe Pacella, 3 vols. [Milan: Garzanti, 1991], 1:199). (The superabundance of the imagination is something that torments the young . . . , and so instead of developing it to an unusual degree, they seek to eliminate or paralyze it by rational means. This also happens to adults, as we see in the case of Lord Nelvil in *Corinne*.)

42. In *Reflections on the Revolution in France* (1790; ed. J. C. D. Clark [Stanford, CA: Stanford University Press, 2001]), Edmund Burke uses similar rhetoric to contrast the English with the French. He champions the "manly, moral, regulated liberty" of England and compares the "solid wisdom" of English political philosophy to the "cold hearts and muddy understandings" of the French *philosophes* (150, 240). In a memorable quotation that anticipates Staël's representation of the steady and somewhat plodding English national character, Burke describes the English as "thousands of great cattle, reposed beneath the shadow of British oak," creatures that "chew the cud and are silent" (248).

43. For a discussion of Staël's *Corinne* as part of the "feminization" of Italy in the foreign imagination, see Buzard, *Beaten Track* 132–39.

44. On Lucile's silence as a reflection of Staël's critique of England's subjugation of women, see Frank Paul Bowman, "Communication and Power in Germaine de Staël: Transparency and Obstacle," in Gutwirth, Goldberger, and Szmurlo, *Crossing Borders* 61.

45. Goethe was among the many artists of the era who aspired to produce work that was performative in nature and that allowed for more personal contact with the audience; see Riesz, "Goethe's 'Canon'" 140.

46. The European aspect of Staël's Romanticism has been studied by Furst, *European Romanticism* 56–73; and Isbell, *Staël's "De l'Allemagne*," passim.

47. For a discussion of how regional and national cultural values affected the marriageable nature of women in Staël's era, see Ellen Moers, *Literary Women* (Garden City, NY: Doubleday, 1976), 314–15.

48. On the general status of women in nineteenth-century European letters, see Eve Sourian, "Germaine de Staël and the Possibilities of Women in France, England, and Germany," in Goldberger, *Woman as Mediatrix* 31–38. See also Madelyn Gutwirth, *Madame de Staël, Novelist: Emergence of the Artist as Woman* (Urbana: University of Illinois Press, 1978); and Ellen Peel and Nanora Sweet, "*Corinne* and the Woman as Poet in England: Hemans, Jewsbury, and Barrett Browning," in Szmurlo, *Novel's Seductions* 204–20. Peel and Sweet note that Corinne's "Italian birth and habits make her an exile in England, just as her sex metaphorically makes her an exile in patriarchy" ("*Corinne* and the Woman as Poet" 205). Staël does speak of Italy in exilic terms: Corinne describes Rome to Oswald as "l'asile des exilés du monde" (the refuge of the world's exiles) (4.3).

49. Oswald uses similar rhetoric in a previously discussed passage: "The year he had just spent in Italy had no connection with any other period of his life. It was like a brilliant apparition which had completely struck his imagination but had not been able to alter completely the opinions or tastes which had constituted his life till then" (16.4).

50. See 16.5: "Les images du bonheur domestique s'unissaient plus facilement à la retraite de Northumberland qu'au char triomphal de Corinne: enfin, Oswald ne pouvait se dissimuler que Lucile était la femme que son père aurait choisie pour lui.... Il s'endormit en pensant à l'Italie; et néanmoins, pendant son sommeil, il crut voir Lucile qui passait légèrement devant lui sous la forme d'un ange" (*Œuvres* 814). (The pictures of domestic happiness were more easily linked to [Lucile's] North Umberland retreat than to Corinne's triumphal chariot. In short, Oswald could not conceal from himself that Lucile was the wife his father would have chosen for him.... He fell asleep thinking of Italy but nevertheless he dreamt he saw Lucile passing lightly before him in the shape of an angel [*Corinne, Italy* 310].)

51. Simone Balayé remarks that, because Corinne is "placée au-dessus des Anglais et des Italiens" (situated above the English and the Italians), "elle voit la vérité qu'ils n'aperçoivent pas") (she is able to perceive truths that neither group is able to recognize) (201). In agreement with Peel and Sweet's description of Corinne as an exile in terms of both gender and nation (see note 48), Balayé emphasizes the privileged perspective that Corinne's marginal status affords her: "Élevée dans deux civilisations, ayant connu deux mentalités, elle les a dépassées l'une et l'autre, pour réunir en elle le meilleur de chacune. . . . N'appartenant à aucun groupe et participant de tous, elle est fondamentalement seule." (Raised in two civilizations [England and Italy], having known two different mentalities, Corinne overcame each one in order to internalize the best from each. . . . Belonging to no single group yet participating in all of them, she is fundamentally alone.) I agree with Balayé's claim that Corinne's outsider, cosmopolitan status makes her a double for Staël herself, who, like Corinne, refused to succumb to any one group or nationalistic mentality and its accompanying prejudices in pursuing her artistic aims (*Madame de Staël* 201).

52. English Showalter, Jr., sums up the challenges with which de Staël confronts the reader at the book's conclusion: "*Corinne* is a dialogic novel, in the Bakhtinian sense; Italy argues with England, female genius with patriarchal duty, and the author has not rigged the debate so that one side scores a clear victory" ("Corinne as an Autonomous Heroine," in Gutwirth, Goldberger, and Szmurlo, *Crossing Borders* 192).

53. Works on Italian literature and culture that Foscolo produced in England include: *Essay on the Present Literature of Italy* and a piece on Dante in the *Edinburgh Review* (1818); *Narrative and Romantic Poems of the Italians* (1819); "An Account of the Revolution of Naples during the Years 1798, 1799" (1821); essays on Pier delle Vigne, Michelangelo, and Tasso (1822); the celebrated essays on Petrarch (1823); a partial edition of Dante's *Commedia* and *Discorso storico sul testo del Decamerone* (1825); and "Women of Italy" (1826). For a study of Foscolo's English sojourn, see E. R. Vincent, *Ugo Foscolo: An Italian in Regency England* (Cambridge: Cambridge University Press, 1953).

54. References are to Ugo Foscolo, *Lettere scritte dall'Inghilterra,* ed. Elena Lombardi, *Opere* 2:447–502. For consideration of the text, see Lucia Conti Bertini, ed., *Gli appunti per le "Lettere scritte dall'Inghilterra": Livorno, Biblioteca Labronica, ms. XIV, cc. 98v–143v* [by Ugo Foscolo] (Florence: La Nuova Italia, 1975); Glauco Cambon, *Ugo Foscolo, Poet of Exile* (Princeton, NJ: Princeton University Press, 1980), 300–331; Mario Fubini, *Ugo Foscolo: Saggi, studi, note,* rev. ed. (Florence: La Nuova Italia, 1978), 535–60; Matteo Palumbo, "Jacopo Ortis, Didimo Chierico e gli avvertimenti di Foscolo 'Al lettore,'" *Modern Language Notes* 105 (1990): 70–72; and Gustavo Costa, "Ugo Foscolo's Europe: A Journey from the Sublime to Romantic Humor," *Symposium* 47 (1993): 98–111.

55. See, for example, the following articles in *Giambattista Vico: An International Symposium,* ed. Giorgio Tagliacozzo and Hayden V. White (Baltimore: Johns Hopkins University Press, 1969): Enrico De Mas, "Vico and Italian Thought," trans. Elio Gianturco, 159–64; Alain Pons, "Vico and French Thought," trans. Elio Gianturco, 171–85; Ramón Ceñal, S.J., "Vico and Nineteenth-Century Spanish Thought," trans. Himilce Novás, 187–201; and George Whalley, "Coleridge and Vico" 225–44. For Foscolo's relation to Vico, see Glauco Cambon, "Vico e Foscolo," *Forum Italicum* 12 (1978): 498–511. Cambon notes that Vichian philosophy appears in Foscolo more systematically than in any other author of the eighteenth century; see 498–99 for his exploration of how Foscolo's understanding of Vico was beholden to his teacher, the great pre-Romantic scholar Melchiorre Cesarotti.

56. Ugo Foscolo, *Discorso sul testo della Divina commedia,* in *Studi su Dante,* ed. Giovanni Da Pozzo, 2 pts. (1979–81); *Edizione nazionale delle opere di Ugo Foscolo,* 23 vols. (Florence: Le Monnier, 1933–), 9:1.183.

57. See Erich Auerbach, "Vico's Contribution to Literary Criticism," *Gesammelte Aufsätze zur romanischen Philologie* (Bern: Francke, 1967), 259–65.

58. See especially Vico's "Discoverta del vero Omero," bk. 3 of *Principj di scienza nuova d'intorno alla comune natura delle nazioni,* ed. Marco Veneziano (1744; Florence: Olschki, 1994). A quest for the "poetic" nature of early linguistic communication also motivates the work of Jean-Jacques Rousseau's *Essai sur l'origine des langues* (pub. posthumously, 1781) and Johann Gottlieb Herder's *Abhandlung über den Ursprung der Sprache* (1772). Vico underscores the epistemological as well as the moral and affective character of early languages to a greater degree than these two works.

59. Giambattista Vico, *Scritti vari e pagine sparse,* ed. Fausto Nicolini, vol. 5 of *Opere* (Bari: Laterza, 1940), 79.

60. In his resistance to the vogue of French thought, Foscolo remained true to his predecessor Alfieri; see especially the latter's virulent *Il misogallo.* Unlike Foscolo, Leo-

pardi read Staël closely, for his *Zibaldone* is filled with careful commentary on *Corinne* and other works of hers; see, for example, his gloss on Staël's disquisition in *Corinne* 15.9 on the nexus between French literary style and national character, to which Leopardi contrasts the ancient and Italian character and manner of composition (January 8, 1820; *Zibaldone* 1:107–9).

61. See Foscolo on Staël, regarding tendencies shared by her protagonist Corinne: "Legge sovra una lapide *Leonardo Bruni Aretino;* non fa caso il nome e il casato, bastale che sia d'Arezzo, e compatriota di *Pietro Tacci Aretino.* Guarda il globo terraqueo e i suoi abitatori a un occhiata nell'universo; guarda gli anni confusi coi secoli nell'eternità e la scienza de' tempi è per essa superflua a ottenere la scienza de' fatti: nè le importa che Leonardo nascesse innanzi al 1370 e Pietro dopo il 1490. Le importa di ragionare con filosofiche antitesi" (460–61). (She reads *Leonardo Bruni the Aretine* on a tombstone without heeding either the name or the entombed, and noticing only that he is from Arezzo and a compatriot of Pietro Aretino. She sees the oceans and lands of the globe along with its inhabitants in a single glance at the universe, and she sees the years confused with the eternal centuries. For her, the attainment of facts is superfluous to the knowledge of history. Nor does it matter to her that Leonardo Bruni was born in 1370, whereas Pietro Aretino was born in 1490. What matters to her is reason based on philosophical synthesis.)

62. For a discussion of Foscolo's relation to major currents of European culture, see Mario Puppo, *Romanticismo italiano e romanticismo europeo* (Milan: Istituto Propaganda Libraria, 1985), 35–46.

63. According to Mario Praz, in Foscolo the desire for Greek serenity was intimately personal and not — as Praz believed it was for northern poets like Keats and Hölderlin — the quest for an alien and remote world (*Motivi e figure* [Turin: Einaudi, 1945], 47).

64. In *Lettere scritte dall'Inghilterra,* Foscolo indicts German literature for the twin abuses of excessive abstraction and pedantic erudition.

Chapter 3. The Death of Italy and Birth of European Romanticism

1. Franco Moretti, *Atlas of the European Novel, 1800–1900* (New York: Verso, 1998), 10. See also Pino Fasano, "The Geography and History of 'Romantic': The Word and the Thing," trans. Viktor Berberi, in *The People's Voice: Essays on European Romanticism,* ed. Andrea Ciccarelli, John Claiborne Isbell, and Brian Nelson (Melbourne: School of European Languages and Cultures, Monash University, 1999), 26–45.

2. Percy Bysshe Shelley, *The Letters of Percy Bysshe Shelley,* ed. Roger Ingpen, 2 vols. (London: Pitman, 1912), 2:649.

3. Thomas Warton's *History of English Poetry* (1774–81) traces the growth of English poetry from its earliest stages and acknowledges relations between literary history and sociopolitical forces that many other neoclassical critics ignored. Girolamo Tiraboschi's *Storia della letteratura italiana* (1772–82) anticipates Romantic practices by organizing the history of Italian letters into an organic narrative and stressing its value as a source of cultural unity. Louis-René de Caradeuc de La Chalotais' *Essai d'éducation nationale* (1763) is also an important precursor in establishing the links between cultural activity and national identity that would prove central to Romantic literary historiography.

4. Schiller to Goethe, August 23, 1794; Johann Wolfgang von Goethe and Friedrich Schiller, *Der Briefwechsel zwischen Schiller und Goethe,* ed. Siegfried Seidel, 3 vols. (Munich: Beck, 1984); *Correspondence between Goethe and Schiller, 1794–1805;* trans. Liselotte Dieckmann (New York: Lang, 1994), 5.

5. Geoffrey H. Hartman, *Scars of the Spirit: The Struggle against Inauthenticity* (New York: Palgrave Macmillan, 2002), 164.

6. Johann Wolfgang von Goethe, *Italienische Reise,* ed. Erich Trunz and Herbert von Einem (1960), vol. 11 of *Werke,* ed. Erich Trunz, 14 vols. (Hamburg: Wegner, 1960–62); *Italian Journey,* ed. Thomas P. Saine and Jeffrey L. Sammons, trans. Robert R. Heitner, vol. 6 of *Goethe's Collected Works* (New York: Suhrkamp, 1989).

7. "Die Begierde, dieses Land zu sehen, war überreif: da sie befriedigt ist, werden mir Freunde und Vaterland erst wieder recht aus dem Grunde lieb, und die Rückkehr wünschenswert, ja um desto wünschenswerter, da ich mit Sicherheit empfinde, daß ich so viele Schätze nicht zu eignem Besitz und Privatgebrauch mitbringe, sondern daß sie mir und andern durchs ganze Leben zur Leitung und Fördernis dienen sollen" (November 1, 1786; *Italienische Reise* 125). (My longing to see this land [Rome] was more than ripe. Only now that it is satisfied have my friends and fatherland truly become dear to me again. Now I look forward to my return, indeed all the more so because I feel certain that I shall not be bringing all these treasures back just for my own possession and private use, but so that they may serve both me and others as guidance and encouragement for an entire lifetime [*Italian Journey* 103].)

8. "Bei der Abreise fällt einem doch immer jedes frühere Schneiden und auch das künftige letzte unwillkürlich in den Sinn, und mir drängt sich, diesmal stärker als sonst, dabei die Bemerkung auf, daß wir viel zu viel Voranstalten machen, um zu leben, denn so kehren auch wir, Tischbein und ich, so vielen Herrlichkeiten, sogar unserm wohlausgestatteten eignen Museum den Rücken. Da stehn nun drei Junonen zur Vergleichung nebeneinander, und wir verlassen sie, als wenn's keine wäre" (February 21, 1787; *Italienische Reise* 177). (Somehow, leaving for a trip always brings every past departure spontaneously to mind, as well as the future final one. And at the same time, more forcefully now than usual, the thought is welling up in me that we encumber our lives with too many things. For here we are, Tischbein and I, turning our backs not only on these many splendors, but even on our well-stocked private museum [of Rome]. Three Junos are standing there now in a row, for comparison with each other, and we are leaving them as if none was there at all [*Italian Journey* 144].)

9. For inquiry into the early history of this cultural and geographical phenomenon, see Edward Chaney, *The Evolution of the Grand Tour: Anglo-Italian Cultural Relations since the Renaissance* (Portland, OR: Cass, 1988); and Paul Franklin Kirby, *The Grand Tour in Italy, 1700–1800* (New York: Vanni, 1952). See also the meditations of Francis Bacon in "Of Travel" (1625), *Bacon's Essays,* ed. Richard Whately and Franklin Fiske Heard (Boston: Lee and Shepard, 1884), 194–96. Whateley notes that Bacon's brother Anthony traveled extensively to Italy to "verify the localities of celebrated battles and other transactions recorded by . . . historians"; but, once his research was completed, "he hurried away without having, or seeking, any intercourse with any of the *people* now inhabiting Italy, . . . having set out with the conviction that they were, and ever must be, quite unworthy of notice" (196n). A similar, less prejudiced dichotomy — of the type well

known to readers of Goethe's *Italienische Reise* (see especially the aforementioned entry from December 29, 1786) — permeates a landmark in pre-eighteenth-century foreign literature about Italy, Joachim du Bellay's *Les antiquitez de Rome* (1558); see, for example, sonnet 15.1–5, 11–14:

> Palles Esprits, & vous Umbres poudreuses,
> Qui jouissant de la clarté du jour
> Fistes sortir cest orgueilleux sejour,
> Dont nous voyons les reliques cendreuses,
>   Dictes, Esprits . . .
> . . . .
> Ne sentez vous augmenter vostre peine,
>   Quand quelquefois de ces costaux Romains
> Vous contemplez l'ouvrages de voz mains
> N'estre plus rien qu'une poudreuse plaine? (*Les antiquitez de Rome et Les regrets* [Geneva: Droz, 1947])

(Pale spirits, and you, o dusty shades, who when you enjoyed the light of day, created this proud sojourning place, whose fragmented remains we see, Say, o spirits . . . , do you not feel increase of sorrow when sometimes from these Roman slopes you contemplate your handiwork, and see that it is now a dusty plain and nothing more?) (trans. L. Clark Keating, *Joachim du Bellay* [New York: Twayne, 1971], 92)

10. See Joseph Addison, *Remarks on Several Parts of Italy, etc., in the Years 1701, 1702, 1703*, in *The Works of Joseph Addison*, 3 vols. (New York: Harper, 1837), 3:370.

11. Edward Gibbon, *Gibbon's Journey from Geneva to Rome: His Journal from 20 April to 2 October 1764*, ed. George Alfred Bonnard (New York: Nelson, 1961), 179.

12. *With Shelley in Italy, Being a Selection of the Poems and Letters of Percy Bysshe Shelley Which Have to Do with His Life in Italy from 1818 to 1822*, ed. Anna Benneson McMahan (Chicago: McClurg, 1905), 64.

13. John Keats, *The Poetical Works of John Keats*, ed. H. W. Garrod (Oxford: Clarendon, 1939).

14. Goethe also praised foreign versions of his work and even claimed that he preferred to read his *Faust* in translation rather than the original; see David Damrosch, *What Is World Literature?* (Princeton, NJ: Princeton University Press, 2003), 6–7.

15. See Staël, "Esprit des traductions" 389; "Spirit of Translation" 280: "On pourroit goûter encore, par une traduction bien faite dans sa propre langue, un plaisir plus familier et plus intime. Ces beautés naturalisées donnent au style national des tournures nouvelles, et des expressions plus originales." (One might still experience a more familiar and intimate pleasure thanks to a fine translation done in one's own language. These naturalized beauties imbue a national literary style with new turns of phrase and original expressions.) For Staël's original version of the essay, see *Mélanges*, in *Œuvres complètes de Mme la baronne de Staël*, ed. Auguste Louis Staël-Holstein, 17 vols. (Paris: Treuttel and Würtz, 1820–21), 17:387–99; English translation in "The Spirit of Translation," trans. Joseph Luzzi, *Romanic Review* 97 (2006): 275–84.

16. See A. O. Lovejoy, "On the Discriminations of Romanticism," *PMLA* 39 (1924): 229–53. Wellek's "The Concept of Romanticism" offers a sustained critique of Lovejoy's paradigmatic thesis that Romantic ideas were by and large heterogeneous, independent, and often antithetical to one another. René Wellek, "The Concept of Romanticism in Literary History," *Concepts of Criticism*, ed. Stephen G. Nichols, Jr. (New Haven: Yale University Press, 1963), 128–98. See also the argument on behalf of European Romantic unity in Morse Peckham, "Towards a Theory of Romanticism," *PMLA* 66 (1951): 5–23.

17. In line with Wellek, the following situate English Romanticism in a European context: M. H. Abrams, *Natural Supernaturalism: Tradition and Revolution in Romantic Literature* (New York: Norton, 1971); Harold Bloom, *The Visionary Company: A Reading of English Romantic Poetry*, rev. and enl. ed. (Ithaca, NY: Cornell University Press, 1971), and "The Internalization of Quest-Romance," *Yale Review* 58 (1969): 526–35; Paul de Man, "Wordsworth and Hölderlin," *Schweitzer Monatschefte* 45 (1966): 1141–55, and "Intentional Structure of the Romantic Image," *Romanticism and Consciousness* 65–77; Geoffrey H. Hartman, "Romanticism and Antiselfconsciousness," *Centennial Review* 6 (1962): 553–65; E. D. Hirsch, *Wordsworth and Schelling: A Typological Study of Romanticism* (New Haven: Yale University Press, 1960); and Karl Kroeber, *The Artifice of Reality: Poetic Style in Wordsworth, Foscolo, Keats, and Leopardi* (Madison: University of Wisconsin Press, 1964). Three recent studies of the international aspects of Romanticism are Lilian R. Furst, *The Contours of European Romanticism* (Lincoln: University of Nebraska Press, 1979); Virgil Nemoianu, *The Taming of European Romanticism: European Literature and the Age of Biedermeier* (Cambridge, MA: Harvard University Press, 1984); and Henry H. H. Remak, "New Harmony: The Quest for Synthesis in West European Romanticism," *European Romanticism: Literary Cross-Currents, Modes, and Models*, ed. Gerhart Hoffmeister (Detroit: Wayne State University Press, 1990), 331–51. Though attuned to the differences among the different national Romantic movements, Löwy and Sayre consider a range of issues from a European and international perspective, including the movement's twentieth- and twenty-first century afterlife (Michael Löwy and Robert Sayre, *Romanticism against the Tide of Modernity*, trans. Catherine Porter [Durham, NC: Duke University Press, 2001], 214–55).

18. See Nemoianu, *Taming of European Romanticism* 19: "In the thirty years that have passed since [Wellek's article "Concept of Romanticism" in 1949], comparative and general theories of romanticism have refined and enriched Wellek's views rather than disproved them. Henry Remak and Geoffrey Hartman, Northrop Frye and Harold Bloom all accepted Wellek's basic insight and strove mostly to add to the features, clarify the priorities, and describe the organization of the system." Nemoianu emphasizes the central role of Abrams's *Natural Supernaturalism* in promoting interiority and self-consciousness as a paradigmatically European Romantic category of critical analysis and literary expression (19–22).

19. Marilyn Butler, *Romantics, Rebels, and Reactionaries: English Literature and Its Background, 1760–1830* (1981; New York: Oxford University Press, 1982), 1–10.

20. See Curran, *Poetic Form* 210: "The effort to discuss [Romanticism] in a transnational setting inevitably encourages a discourse about what is shared in, rather than what separates, these national Romanticisms, with the result that vital distinctions easily become blurred." See also Andrea Ciccarelli: "In recent years it has become increasingly

clear that when confronting a multifaceted cultural event such as Romanticism, in order to respect the actual evolution of the movement within each European country it is preferable to speak of *Romanticisms* in the plural" (introduction to *The People's Voice,* ed. Ciccarelli, Isbell, and Nelson, 1).

21. Jerome McGann, *The Romantic Ideology: A Critical Investigation* (Chicago: University of Chicago Press, 1983).

22. Geoffrey H. Hartman, "On the Theory of Romanticism," *The Fate of Reading and Other Essays* (Chicago: University of Chicago Press, 1975), 277.

23. Alessandro Manzoni, "Sul romanticismo: Lettera al marchese Cesare D'Azeglio," *Opere,* ed. Guido Bezzola, 3 vols. (Milan: Rizzoli, 1961), 3:425–57; "Letter on Romanticism," trans. Joseph Luzzi, *PMLA* 119 (2004): 299–316.

24. *Encyclopédie ou dictionnaire raisonné des sciences, des arts et des métiers [Nouvelle impression en facsimilé de la première éd. de 1751–1780],* ed. Denis Diderot and Jean Le Rond d'Alembert, 35 vols. (Stuttgart-Bad Cannstatt: Frommann, 1966); *Encyclopedia: Selections [by] Diderot, D'Alembert, and a Society of Men of Letters,* trans. and ed. Nelly Schargo Hoyt and Thomas Cassirer (Indianapolis: Bobbs-Merrill, 1965). Unless otherwise indicated, references are to this edition and translation.

25. For analysis of the contemporary critical animus against the term *universalism* within the context of feminist theory, see Naomi Schor, "French Feminism Is a Universalism," *Bad Objects: Essays Popular and Unpopular* (Durham, NC: Duke University Press, 1995), 3–27.

26. Vittorio Alfieri, *Giornali;* vol. 1 of *Opere,* ed. Arnaldo Di Benedetto (Milan: Ricciardi, 1977), 414 (abbrev. "*Opere* Milan").

27. See Alfieri's *Giornali* February 19, 1775: "Je me suis battu longtems, si j'écrirois, ou si je n'écrirois pas une si digne journée, je m'y suis enfin résolu, moitié par l'envie de me corriger, et moitié pour flatter mon amour propre, qui est assez ingénieux pour rattraper sur la générosité de cet aveu tout ce qu'il a perdu dans ce que cet aveu peut avoir d'humiliant. C'est un ami, qui trouve toujours son conte à tout. Enfin, ceci est écrit, et si je n'en retire point de profit, cela pourra du moins servir un jour à me faire rire." (I debated for a long time over whether to write down or not the events of such a "worthy" day. I finally decided to write, partly out of a desire for self-improvement and partly to flatter my own *amour propre,* which is somehow ingenious enough to make anything potentially humiliating about such a decision seem noble. This *amour propre* is a kind of friend that manages to rationalize everything. In any case, I have written, and so be it. If what I have jotted down does not manage to provide me any kind of instruction, then it may at least make me laugh some day [414].)

28. For a discussion of this quotation, and, more generally, Alfieri's relationship with Voltaire, see Guido Santato, *Alfieri e Voltaire: Dall'imitazione alla contestazione* (Florence: Olschki, 1988), 43 and passim.

29. See, for example, Dante's confession to Beatrice in the Earthly Paradise (*Purg.* 31–33); Petrarch's prayer to the Virgin Mary at the conclusion of his *Rerum vulgarium fragmenta* (canzone 366); and the sequence on the conversion of the Unnamed (*l'Innominato*) in Manzoni's *I promessi sposi* (esp. ch. 21).

30. References are from the *Vita di Vittorio Alfieri da Asti scritta da esso,* in *Opere* Milan; translations are from the first English version of the text, published anonymously

in 1810 and then reissued in an updated and corrected form by E. R. Vincent, ed., *Memoirs: The Anonymous Translation of 1810* [by Alfieri] (New York: Oxford University Press, 1961). As is generally the case with Alfieri's works, the *Vita* has a distinguished set of Italian critics who have written about it but few interpreters outside of Italy: see, for example, Neuro Bonifazi, "L'operazione autobiografica e la *Vita* di Vittorio Alfieri," *L'approdo letterario* 75–76 (1976): 115–42; Benedetto Croce, *La letteratura italiana del Settecento; note critiche* (Bari: Laterza, 1949), 325–35, 375–95; Giacomo Debenedetti, "Nascita delle tragedia," *Saggi critici: Terza serie* (Milan: Il Saggiatore, 1959), 39–66; Francesco De Sanctis, *Storia della letteratura italiana,* ed. Gianfranco Contini (Milan: TEA, 1989), 792–805; Giampaolo Dossena, ed., introduction to Alfieri, *La vita* (Turin: Einaudi, 1967), vii–xlii; Luigi Fassò, "Introduzione all'edizione critica della *Vita*," *Opera omnia* 1:xi–lxiv (for full citation of Alfieri's *Opera omnia,* see 230n21); Mario Fubini, *Ritratto dell'Alfieri e altri studi alfieriani,* 2nd ed. (Florence: La Nuova Italia, 1963), 43–58; Luigi Russo, "La *Vita* dell'Alfieri," *Ritratti e disegni storici* (Bari: Laterza, 1946), 17–86; and Riccardo Scrivano, *Biografia e autobiografia: Il modello alfieriano* (Rome: Bulzoni, 1976), 105–31. For further bibliography, see Alfieri, *Opere* Milan cv.

31. "Eccomi ora dunque, sendo in età di quasi anni venzette, entrando nel duro impegno e col pubblico e con me stesso, di farmi autore tragico" (4.1; *Vita* 166). (Thus then at twenty-seven years of age did I enlist myself in the service of the Muses and appear before the public as an author of tragedies [*Memoirs* 153].)

32. See, for example, his encounter with the Renaissance treatise on manners, Giovanni della Casa's *Il galateo* (1558), a work supposedly of the purest Tuscan lacking any trace of French (*contrario d'ogni franceseria*):

> Onde, pieno di mal talento contro quel *Galateo,* lo apersi. Ed alla vista di quel primo *Conciossiacosache,* a cui poi si accoda quel lungo periodo cotanto pomposo e sì poco sugoso, mi prese un tal impeto di collera, che scagliato per la finestra il libro, gridai quasi maniaco: "Ella è pur dura e stucchevole necessità, che per iscrivere tragedie in età di venzett'anni mi convenga ingoiare di nuovo codeste baie fanciullesche, e prosciugarmi il cervello con sì fatte pedanterie." (4.1; *Vita* 177–78)

> (I opened it [*Il galateo*], however, though with the greatest repugnance; but no sooner had I read the very first *conciossiacosache* [such that] and the following sentence, which equally disgusted me by its pomposity and insignificance, than I flung the book in a rage out of the window, violently exclaiming: "What an insufferable hardship, if in order to write tragedies I must at the age of twenty-seven be condemned to read such stuff, and harass my brain with such pedantic absurdities.") (*Memoirs* 162)

33. See *Vita* 179: "Mi fece finalmente risolvere di andare in Toscana per avvezzarmi a parlare, udire, pensare, e sognare in toscano, e non altrimenti mai più" (4.2). (I took in consequence the resolution of travelling into Tuscany with a view to accustom myself to speak, hear, think, and dream Tuscan and only Tuscan for ever afterwards [*Memoirs* 164].)

34. For a study of the role of anti-Gallicism in the formation of British national identity, see Linda Colley, *Britons: Forging the Nation, 1707–1837* (New Haven: Yale University Press, 1992).

35. Anne Louise Germaine de Staël, *Corinne, ou l'Italie;* vol. 1 of *Œuvres complètes de Madame la baronne de Staël-Holstein* (Paris: Didot, 1871) (abbrev. "*Œuvres*"); *Corinne, or Italy,* trans. Sylvia Raphael (New York: Oxford University Press, 1998).

36. "Mais il n'est pas moins vrai qu'Alfieri n'a pas créé ce qu'on pourrait appeler un théâtre italien, c'est-à-dire des tragédies dans lesquelles on trouvât un mérite particulier à l'Italie" (7.2; *Œuvres* 714). (But it is not less true that Alfieri has not created what one could call an Italian theater, that is to say, tragedies where one can find a merit peculiar to Italy [*Corinne, Italy* 119].)

37. For Staël's critique of the French tendency to promote overzealously their national literary style, see "Esprit des traductions" 389: "Mais, pour tirer de ce travail un véritable avantage, il ne faut pas, comme les François, donner sa propre couleur à tout ce qu'on traduit." (In order to gain the most from this practice [of translation], however, we must not follow the French and impose our own national style upon all that we translate ["Spirit of Translation" 280].)

38. See Staël, "Esprit des traductions" 398–99:

> Les Italiens sont très-enthousiastes de leur langue; de grands hommes l'ont fait valoir, et les distinctions de l'esprit ont été les seules jouissances, et souvent aussi les seules consolations de la nation italienne. Afin que chaque homme capable de penser se sente un motif pour se développer lui-même, il faut que toutes les nations aient un principe actif d'intérêt: les unes sont militaires, les autres politiques. Les Italiens doivent se faire remarquer par littérature et les beaux-arts.

> (Italians are extremely enthusiastic about their language. Great men have brought distinction to it; and these intellectual distinctions have been the sole pleasure, and often the sole consolation, of the Italian nation. In order for each reflective individual to believe that he is capable of self-improvement, all nations must take an active interest. Some nations are military, others are political. The Italians need to assert their prominence through literature and fine arts.) ("Spirit of Translation" 284)

This sentiment is echoed in the aforementioned *Corinne* 6.3, where Staël notes that, though Europe owes its arts and sciences to Italy, it has now turned these gifts against the Italians and thereby robbed them of that "last glory that is allowed to nations without military power or political liberty."

39. Ugo Foscoli, "Dei sepolcri," ed. Franco Longoni, *Opere,* ed. Franco Gavezzeni, 2 vols. (Turin: Einaudi-Gallimard, 1994–95), 1:21–38; "Ugo Foscolo: *Sepulchers,*" trans. Peter Burian, *Literary Imagination* 4 (2002): 17–30.

40. See Staël, 20.5: "Il n'y a rien d'étroit, rien d'asservi, rien de limité dans la religion. Elle est immense, l'infini, l'éternel; et loin que génie puisse détourner d'elle, l'imagination, de son premier élan, dépasse les bornes de la vie, et le sublime en tout genre est un reflet de la Divinité" (*Œuvres* 861). (There is nothing narrow, nothing servile, nothing restricted, in religion. It is the immense, the infinite, the eternal. Genius is far from being likely to turn away from it. The imagination, right from its first light, outstrips life's limits, and the sublime in every genre is a reflection of the divine [*Corinne, Italy* 401].)

Prologue

1. See Edward Moore, *Dante and His Early Biographers* (London: Rivingtons, 1890), for consideration of *vite* on Dante by authors including Boccaccio, Filippo Villani, Leonardo Bruni, Giannozzo Manetti, and Giovanni Mario Filelfo.

2. See also Foscolo's unsigned review of *Pétrarque et Laure* by the Countess of Genlis in the *Quarterly Review* 24 (1821): 565: "Dante . . . was, like Milton, one of those rare individuals who are above the reach of ridicule, and whose natural dignity is exalted even by the blows of malignity."

3. Thomas Carlyle, *On Heroes, Hero-Worship, and the Heroic in History: Six Lectures; Reported, with Emendations and Additions* (New York: Appleton, 1841), 103–4.

4. Dante Alighieri, *The Divine Comedy*, trans. with commentary Charles S. Singleton, 6 vols. (Princeton, NJ: Princeton University Press, 1970–75). Italian text based on *La commedia secondo l'antica vulgata*, ed. Giorgio Petrocchi, 4 vols. (Milan: Mondadori, 1966–67).

5. See Giuseppe Mazzotta, "Why Did Dante Write the *Comedy*? Why and How Do We Read It? The Poet and the Critics," *Dante Now: Current Trends in Dante Studies*, ed. T. J. Cachey (Notre Dame, IN: Notre Dame University Press, 1995), 66.

6. The twenty addresses are: *Inf.* 8.94–96, 9.61–63, 16.137–42, 20.19–24, 22.118, 25.46–48, 34.22–27; *Purg.* 8.19–22, 9.70–72, 10.106–11, 17.1–19, 19.98–103, 31.124–26, 33.136–39; and *Par.* 2.1–18, 5.109–14, 9.10–12, 10.7–27, 13.1–12, 22.106–11. See the discussion in Erich Auerbach, "Dante's Addresses to the Reader," *Romance Philology* 7 (1954): 268–78; Leo Spitzer, "The Addresses to the Reader in the *Commedia*," *Romanische Literaturstudien, 1936–1956* (Tübingen: Niemeyer, 1959), 574–95; and William Franke, *Dante's Interpretive Journey* (Chicago: University of Chicago Press, 1996), 37–81.

7. See T. S. Eliot, "Tradition and the Individual Talent," *The Sacred Wood: Essays on Poetry and Criticism* (London: Methuen, 1964), 54–59.

8. For studies of the autobiographical component in Dante, see Gianfranco Contini, "Dante come personaggio-poeta della *Commedia*," *L'approdo letterario* 4 (1958): 19–46; John Freccero, ed., *Dante: A Collection of Critical Essays* (Englewood Cliffs, NJ: Prentice-Hall, 1965), 1–7, and *Dante: The Poetics of Conversion*, ed. Rachel Jacoff (Cambridge, MA: Harvard University Press, 1986); Marziano Guglielminetti, *Memoria e scrittura: L'autobiografia da Dante a Cellini* (Turin: Einaudi, 1977), 3–100; and Albert Russell Ascoli, "Palinode and History in the Œuvre of Dante," in Cachey, *Dante Now* 55–86. For discussion of literary self-representation in the Middle Ages, see Leo Spitzer, "Notes on the Poetic and Empirical 'I' in Medieval Authors," *Traditio* 4 (1946): 414–22; Peter Dronke, *Poetic Individuality in the Middle Ages: New Departures in Poetry, 1000–1150* (Oxford: Clarendon, 1970), 1–32; and Paul Zumthor, "Autobiographie au Moyen Age?" *Langue, texte, énigme* (Paris: Seuil, 1975), 165–80. On the general question of individuality in the Middle Ages, see, in chronological order, Walter Ullman, *The Individual and Society in the Middle Ages* (Baltimore: Johns Hopkins University Press, 1966); Colin Morris, *The Discovery of the Individual, 1050–1200* (New York: Harper and Row, 1972); Robert W. Hanning, *The Individual in Twelfth-Century Romance* (New Haven: Yale University Press, 1977); and Caroline Walker Bynum, "Did the Twelfth

Century Discover the Individual?" *Jesus as Mother: Studies in the Spirituality of the High Middle Ages* (Berkeley and Los Angeles: University of California Press, 1982), 82–109.

9. See De Sanctis, *Letteratura italiana* 208; *Italian Literature* 1:173: "Se l'allegoria gli ha dato abilità a ingrandire il suo quadro e a fondere nel mondo cristiano tutta la coltura antica, mitologia, scienza e storia, ha d'altra parte viziato nell'origine questo vasto mondo, togliendogli la libertà e spontaneità della vita, divenuto un pensiero e una figura, una costruzione *a priori*, intellettuale nella sostanza, allegorica nella forma." (Allegory enlarged his [Dante's] picture, giving him power to dissolve in the Christian world all the culture, mythology, science, and history of the ancients; but on the other hand, it weakened that vast world at its source, depriving it of the freedom and spontaneity of life, making it into a thought and a figuration, an a-priori construction—intellectual in its substance, allegorical in its form.) Francesco De Sanctis, *Storia della letteratura italiana*, ed. Gianfranco Contini (Milan: TEA, 1989); *History of Italian Literature*, trans. Joan Redfern, 2 vols. (New York: Basic, 1959).

10. A. W. Schlegel, *Geschichte der romantischen Literatur* (Stuttgart: Kohlhammer, 1965), 172; vol. 4 of *Kritische Schriften und Briefe*, ed. Edgar Lohner; "Lectures on Art and Literature" (1802–3). Translation in *Dante, the Critical Heritage, 1314(?)–1870*, ed. Michael Caesar (New York: Routledge, 1989), 422.

11. Unless otherwise indicated, references are from the 1850 edition in *The Prelude, 1799, 1805, 1850: Authoritative Texts, Context and Reception, Recent Critical Essays*, ed. Jonathan Wordsworth, M. H. Abrams, and Stephen Charles Gill (New York: Norton, 1979).

12. See Victor Hugo, *William Shakespeare* (1864), in *Œuvres complètes de Victor Hugo*, 45 vols. (Paris: Ollendorff, 1904–52).

13. See, respectively, Gabriele Rossetti, *Disquisitions on the Antipapal Spirit Which Produced the Reformation; Its Secret Influence on the Literature of Europe in General, and of Italy in Particular*, trans. Caroline Ward, 2 vols. (London: Smith, Elder, 1834), 1:157–71; Eugène Aroux, *Dante hérétique, révolutionnaire et socialiste: Révélations d'un catholique sur le moyen âge* (Paris: Renouard, 1854); T. S. Eliot, "Tradition and the Individual Talent" (1920), *The Sacred Wood: Essays on Poetry and Criticism* (London: Methuen, 1964); Erich Auerbach, *Dante als Dichter der irdischen Welt* (1929; Berlin: de Gruyter, 1969); English ed., *Dante, Poet of the Secular World*, trans. Ralph Manheim (Chicago: University of Chicago Press, 1961); Jeremy Tambling, *Dante and Difference: Writing in the "Commedia"* (Cambridge: Cambridge University Press, 1988); Rachel Jacoff, "Our Bodies, Our Selves: The Body in the *Commedia*," *Sparks and Seeds: Medieval Literature and Its Aftermath: Essays in Honor of John Freccero*, ed. Alison Cornish and Dana E. Stewart (Turnhout, Belg.: Brepols, 2000), 119–37; and Jeffrey Schnapp "Dante's Sexual Solecisms: Gender and Genre in the *Commedia*," *Romanic Review* 79 (1988): 143–63.

14. In addition to the *Commedia*, Dante's so-called *opere minori* also experienced a rebirth of critical interest in the Romantic period. Between 1800 and 1850, twelve editions of the *Vita Nuova* appeared in Europe, seven of the *Convivio*, three of the *Monarchia*, five of *De vulgari eloquentia*, and twenty-nine of the *Rime*.

15. Thomas Medwin, *Conversations of Lord Byron: Noted during a Residence with His Lordship at Pisa, in the Years 1821 and 1822* (London: Colburn, 1824), 195.

16. See, respectively, Giuseppe Macaluso, *Dante, Foscolo, Mazzini e la tradizione iniziatica* (Rome: Pensiero e Azione, Ufficio Culturale, 1965); Glauco Cambon, *Ugo Foscolo, Poet of Exile* (Princeton, NJ: Princeton University Press, 1980), 88–89, 91–93, 150–55; Diane Festa-McCormick, "Victor Hugo poète de l'exile et Dante," *Revue de Littérature Comparée* 48 (1974): 304–12; Michael Pitwood, *Dante and the French Romantics* (Geneva: Droz, 1985), 75–84, 175–208; Elizabeth Stopp, "Ludwig Tieck and Dante," *German Romantics in Context: Selected Essays, 1971–86* [by Elizabeth Stopp], ed. Peter Hutchinson, Roger Paulin, and Judith Purver (1971; London: Bristol Classical, 1992), 163–87; and Steve Ellis, *Dante and English Poetry: Shelley to T. S. Eliot* (New York: Cambridge University Press, 1983), 1–66.

17. Stendhal, *Racine et Shakspeare,* ed. Leon Delbos (Oxford: Clarendon, 1907), 25.

Chapter 4. Dante and Autobiography in the Age of Voltaire

1. In Voltaire's lifetime, critics of Dante included the Italian philosophers Giovanni Mario Crescimbeni, Giovanni Vincenzo Gravina, Ludovico Antonio Muratori, and Giambattista Vico; English and Irish writers Thomas Gray, Martin Sherlock, Horace Walpole, and Thomas Warton; French critics Jean-François de La Harpe and Louis Racine; and German intellectuals Gotthold Ephraim Lessing, J. N. Meinhard, and Moses Mendelssohn.

2. Werner P. Friederich's comprehensive *Dante's Fame Abroad, 1350–1850* (Chapel Hill, NC: University of North Carolina Studies in Comparative Literature, 1950) typifies an exhaustive philological approach that—in part because of the breadth of the material it covers—bases its assumptions regarding the critical reception of Dante exclusively on the direct statements of authors. Though Friederich does not discuss in depth cultural or sociopolitical factors that may have caused critical silences and rejections, his treatment of Dante in eighteenth-century Europe is generally sensitive to the influence of cultural politics on interpretations of the *Commedia.* See, for example, his discussion of Voltaire's aggressive stance on Dante because of attacks on French neoclassicism both at home and abroad (98–99).

3. Of the few works that address Voltaire's reading of Dante, the most informative is Eugène Bouvy, *Voltaire et l'Italie* (Paris: Hachette, 1898), 35–96.

4. See Lionel Gossman, *French Society and Culture: Background for 18th-Century Literature* (Englewood Cliffs, NJ: Prentice-Hall, 1972), 126.

5. See Voltaire, *Dictionnaire philosophique,* s.v. "Goût": "[Le goût] n'est-il le partage que du très-petit nombre, toute la populace en est exclue. Il est inconnu aux familles bourgeoises, où l'on est continuellement occupé du soin de sa fortune, des détails domestiques, et d'une grossière oisiveté, amusée par une partie de jeu. Toutes les places qui tiennent à la judicature, à la finance, au commerce, ferment la porte aux beaux-arts." (Taste is the province of only a few: most will never know it. It is unknown to bourgeois families, who must continually work hard at maintaining their fortunes and oversee untold domestic details. These bourgeois are startingly idle and easily amused by the slightest games. Any sector of society that focuses on justice, finance, or trade can never know the pleasures of the fine arts.) In *Œuvres complètes de Voltaire,* ed. Louis Moland, 52 vols. (Paris: Garnier Frères, 1877–85), 19:282 (abbrev. "M").

6. See, for example, Voltaire's description of the diplomatic debacle that culminated in the Seven Years War, 1756–63. After cataloging the deceptions that sparked the war, he describes how Frederick II, with great hypocrisy, politely received the French ambassador-poet, the Duke of Nivernais, on the same day that he signed a treaty with England against France and wrote "une épigramme contre le poëte" (an epigram against the poet [the duke]). Voltaire's reaction to this unhappy union of belletrism and diplomacy is to comment mockingly: "C'était alors le privilège de la poésie de gouverner les États." (It was then the privilege of poetry to rule the governments.) In *Mémoires pour servir à la vie de M. de Voltaire écrits par lui-même;* M 1:46.

7. See Voltaire to Nicolas Claude Thieriot, August 9, 1756: "Je me trouve trop bien de ma retraitte des Délices. Heureux qui vit chez soy avec ses nièces, ses livres, ses jardins, ses vignes, ses chevaux, ses vaches, son aigle, son renard, et ses lapins qui se passent la patte sur le nez. J'ai tout cela, et les Alpes par dessus, qui font un effet admirable. J'aime mieux gronder mes jardiniers que de faire ma cours aux rois." (I am so content here in my retreat at Les Délices. Happy is he who lives at home with his nieces, books, gardens, vineyards, horses, cows, falcon, fox, and rabbits who rub their noses with their paw. I have all this, and above me the Alps, which create an admirable effect. I would rather berate my gardeners than court the favor of kings.) In *Correspondence and Related Documents,* ed. Theodore Besterman, in *The Complete Works of Voltaire,* vols. 85–135 (Geneva: Voltaire Foundation, 1968–77), D6965 (abbrev. "OC").

8. In the *Essai,* Voltaire mentions only that Dante wrote "dans un temps, où l'on n'avait pas encore un ouvrage de prose supportable" (in an age where there was not yet a single work of acceptable prose). In *The English Essays of 1727,* ed. D. Williams; OC, vol. 3b (1996), 439, ll. 16–17.

9. See *Purg.* 20.49–52 (for full citation of Dante's *Commedia,* see 224–25n11):

> Chiamato fui di là Ugo Ciappetta;
> di me son nati i Filippi e i Luigi
> per cui novellamente è Francia retta.
>   Figliulo fu' io d'un beccaio di Parigi.
>
> (I was called Hugh Capet in that other place; and from me were born the Philips and the Louises, who lately have come to rule France. I was the son of a Parisian butcher.)

After ridiculing Dante's genealogy of the French monarchy, Bayle remarks: "Ce seroit abuser de son loisir et de la patience des lecteurs que de réfuter cet homme." (It would be waste of one's free time and the patience of the reader to deign to refute this man [Dante].) In *Dictionnaire historique et critique,* 11th ed., 16 vols. (Paris: Desoer, 1820), 4:398.

10. By 1746, Voltaire was proficient enough in Italian to submit an essay entitled *Saggio intorno ai cambiamenti convenuti sul globo* to the Bologna Academy of Sciences, of which he was a member. He corresponded with many Italians throughout his lifetime, belonged to several Italian academies (including the prestigious Accademia della Crusca), and at one point even retained an Italian secretary. In 1769, he composed some Italian verses as part of the chorus to *Baron d'Otrante,* an *opera buffa.* For an overview of Voltaire's time in Italy, see Bouvy, *Voltaire et l'Italie,* passim.

11. Giuseppe Baretti, *Prefazioni e polemiche*, ed. Luigi Piccioni, 2nd ed. (Bari: Laterza, 1933), 89.

12. For Akenside's text, see *Dodsley's Museum* 19 (December 6, 1746): 165–69, in *Dante, the Critical Heritage, 1314(?)–1870*, ed. Michael Caesar (New York: Routledge, 1989), 359–60. Akenside's literary tastes were patriotic and traditional: Homer and Shakespeare top his list with a final rating of eighteen out of a perfect twenty, and Milton is next with seventeen. Dante languishes well below with a tally of thirteen.

13. See Winckelmann's "Thoughts on the Imitation of the Painting and Sculpture of the Greeks" (1755), *German Aesthetic and Literary Criticism: Winckelmann, Lessing, Hamann, Herder, Schiller, Goethe*, ed. and trans. H. B. Nesbit (New York: Cambridge University Press, 1985), 32–35.

14. See René Wellek, *History of Modern Criticism, 1750–1950*, 8 vols. (New Haven: Yale University Press, 1955–92), 1:41.

15. In *Inferno* 4 and 5, Dante debunks any aesthetic autonomy that ignores spiritual considerations (in Limbo) and moral responsibilities (in the case of Paolo and Francesca). In Limbo, the encyclopedic catalogue of literary antiquity demonstrates that even the highest achievements by the pagan poets does not mitigate the fact that they lived through, and now suffer in, the haze of desire without hope ("sanza speme vivemo in disio") (*Inf.* 4.42). The *Inferno* 5 scene where Paolo and Francesca succumb to adultery through a reading of the story of Lancelot and Guinevere reveals that aesthetic pleasure (the reading process marking the transition from the narrative of Guinevere and Lancelot's kiss to the actual one by Paolo and Francesca) cannot escape a Christian moral economy that views this adulterous rapture as sin.

16. Dante Alighieri, *The Divine Comedy*, trans. with commentary Charles S. Singleton, 6 vols. (Princeton, NJ: Princeton University Press, 1970–75). Italian text based on *La commedia secondo l'antica vulgata*, ed. Giorgio Petrocchi, 4 vols. (Milan: Mondadori, 1966–67).

17. For all his similarity to Voltaire, Baretti takes pains to distance himself and Dante from Voltairean neoclassicism: "That spirit of method and geometry that hath taken possession, for more than an age, of the poetry of the principal European nations, hath been the consequence of rigid observation and exact criticism, and could not be found in the time of Dante, as he was the first great poet and great writer" (*Prefazioni* 110). Although Voltaire disavowed a science of aesthetics, Baretti was correct in indicating that in the criticism of the age a "spirit of method and geometry" was in full force. The following works represent neoclassical attempts to infuse aesthetic evaluation with a rationalist bias: Boileau, *L'art poétique* (1674); René Le Bossu, *Traité du poème épique* (1675); Nicolas Malebranche, *Recherche de la vérité* (1694); Charles Batteux, *Les beaux arts reduits à un même principe* (1746); and Étienne Bonnot de Condillac, *Essai sur l'origine des connaissances humaines* (1746).

18. In *Dante Studies in the Age of Vico* (Ottawa, Ont.: Dovehouse, 1988), Domenico Pietropaolo analyzes Dante's fate in eighteenth-century Italy; see 11–21 for a bibliographical review of scholarship on eighteenth-century Italian criticism of Dante. See also Aldo Vallone, *La critica dantesca nel Settecento ed altri saggi danteschi* (Florence: Olschki, 1961), 3–64.

19. This rebirth was partly due to the publication of three important editions of the

Commedia. Gaetano Volpi's *La divina commedia, già ridotta a miglior lezione dagli Accademici della Crusca ed ora accresciuta di un doppio rimario e di tre indici* (1727) provided Italian readers with a well-indexed and accessible text that explained the poem's rhyme scheme. In 1728, Carlo d'Aquino produced the first Latin translation of the *Commedia* in over three hundred years. And in 1732, d'Aquino's Jesuit associate Pompeo Venturi published a much-needed annotated version of the text that markedly differed from the predominantly Neoplatonic glosses of the Renaissance commentaries.

20. References to Bettinelli's text are from *Opere di Francesco Algarotti e di Saverio Bettinelli,* ed. Ettore Bonora (1969), in *Illuministi italiani,* 7 vols. (Milan: Ricciardi, 1958–71), 2:629–83.

21. The allusion is to the briefly fashionable Mantuan poet, Signor Pascali, a military official in the Austrian army.

22. "Pur de' bellissimi versi, che a quando incontravansi, mi facean tal piacere che quasi gli perdonava" (Bettinelli, *Opere* 2:638). (Such was the beauty of some [of Dante's] verses, that when I encountered them, they gave me so much pleasure that I almost forgave him.)

23. Voltaire's definition of the epic hero is consistent with Bettinelli's understanding of the term. According to Voltaire, the epic protagonist defines the identity of both himself and his poem through his actions. He is a public creature whose private life and inner thoughts are of minor concern in the genre: "Quelle sera donc l'idée que nous devons former de la poésie épique? Le mot *épique* vient du grec επος, qui signifie *discours:* l'usage a attaché ce nom particulièrement à des récits en vers d'aventures héroïques.... Le poème épique, regardé en lui-même, est donc un récit en vers d'aventures héroïques." (So what should we think about epic poetry? The word *epic* comes from the Greek επος signifying *discourse.* Colloquial use has, in particular, employed this word to define verse narratives of heroic adventures.... The epic poem in itself is therefore a poetic narrative of heroic events.) In *Essai sur la poésie épique;* OC 3b:401, ll. 109–12, 117–18.

24. This letter indicates the extent to which Voltaire imagined himself to be a public enemy of the *Commedia.* He chides Algarotti for having abandoned the cause of the *Lettere virgilianae:* "Algarotti a donc abandonné le Triumvirat comme Lepidus?" (Algarotti has thus abandoned the triumvirate like Lepidus?). Voltaire then adds that Algarotti's unwillingness to join in the anti-Dante attacks resulted from his fear of public censure in Italy, and that deep down he shared Bettinelli's antipathy toward Dante.

25. Voltaire bases his representation of Dante and his world almost entirely upon Bayle's impressionistic and inaccurate discussion in the *Dictionnaire historique et critique* from 1702.

26. For a discussion of Voltaire's religious thought, see René Pomeau, *La religion de Voltaire,* rev. ed. (Paris: Nizet, 1956).

27. In *A History of the Italian Tongue,* Baretti similarly observes that some elements of Dante's poetry have withstood the passage of time, while others have become obsolete and unintelligible (*Prefazioni* 124).

28. See Lionel Gossman, *Medievalism and the Ideologies of the Enlightenment: The World and Work of La Curne de Sainte-Palaye* (Baltimore: Johns Hopkins University Press, 1968), 352 ff. Eighteenth-century intellectuals did show an interest in the supposedly primitive aspects of the Middle Ages, but not in the way that their Romantic

successors would idealize the medieval period. Enlightenment representations of the Middle Ages from the period 1750–60 listed by Gossman include Rousseau, the *Discourses;* Salomon Gessner, *Idyll* (French translation); Paul Henri Mallet, *Histoire de Dannemarc;* Robert Wood, *Essay on Homer;* and James MacPherson's influential *Ossian* fragments.

29. In the same *Essai sur les mœurs* in which he critiques Dante, Voltaire writes:

> Il résulte de ce tableau que tout ce qui tient intimement à la nature humaine se ressemble d'un bout de l'univers à l'autre: que tout ce qui peut dépendre de la coutume est différent, et que c'est un hasard s'il se ressemble. L'empire de la coutume est bien plus vaste que celui de la nature; il s'étend sur les mœurs, sur tous les usages; il répand la variété sur la scène de l'univers: la nature y répand l'unité; elle établit partout un petit nombre de principes invariables: ainsi le fonds est partout le même, et la culture produit des fruits divers. (ch. 197; M 13:182)

> (The result of this vast tableau [of mores] is that everything that is truly inherent in human nature will be the same from one end of the universe to the other, everything in the realm of custom will be different, and only chance can make things similar. The world of customs is much more vast than that of human nature: customs affect morals and everyday forms of behavior and are responsible for the world's variety. Human nature is responsible for the world's unity and for establishing everywhere a limited number of invariable principles. Thus, the basis for human activity is everywhere the same, and culture produces different manifestations.)

30. Consistent with the attitudes of *philosophes* on human nature, the *Encyclopédie* defines *Humaine (espèce)* in the following manner: "Il n'y a donc eu originairement qu'une seule race d'hommes qui, s'étant multipliée & répandue sur la surface de la terre, a donné à la longue toutes les variétés dont nous venons de faire mention" (8:348). (In the beginning, there was only a single race of humankind that, having expanded and multiplied throughout the surface of the globe, has given us by and large all the different peoples and cultures that we have been discussing.) *Encyclopédie ou dictionnaire raisonné des sciences, des arts et des métiers [Nouvelle impression en facsimilé de la première éd. de 1751–1780],* ed. Denis Diderot and Jean Le Rond d'Alembert, 35 vols. (Stuttgart-Bad Cannstatt: Frommann, 1966).

31. For Enlightenment notions of progress, see Abbé de Saint-Pierre, *Projet de paix perpétuelle* (1713); Anne-Robert-Jacques Turgot, *Tableau philosophique des progrès de l'esprit humain* (1750); and Marquis de Condorcet, *Esquisse d'un tableau historique des progrès de l'esprit humain* (1774). The notion of the *philosophes* that individuals could and should divest themselves of habits and prejudices that separated them from progress had its opponents, most notably Edmund Burke (see David Bromwich, *A Choice of Inheritance: Self and Community from Edmund Burke to Robert Frost* [Cambridge, MA: Harvard University Press, 1989], 43–78).

32. See *Encyclopédie* 15:27: "Par le *sens commun* on entend la disposition que la nature a mise dans tous les hommes, ou manifestement dans la plûpart d'entr'eux, pour leur faire porter, quand ils ont atteint l'usage de la raison, un jugement commun & uniforme, sur des objets différens du sentiment intime de leur propre perception." (By

common sense, we mean the capacity for common and uniform judgment that nature has placed in all men and women — or at least in the majority of them — in order to enable them, once they have reached maturity, to translate the intimate and individual sensations of their perceptions into common, shared judgments.)

33. In M 1:5–65. Because of the controversial nature of the work, Voltaire insisted that it remain unpublished during his and Frederick II's lifetime. After a dramatic career as a manuscript — which included its theft by Jean-François de La Harpe during his sojourn at Ferney in 1768 — the text was published for the first time in 1784 (see discussion in M 1:5–6).

34. See especially Voltaire, *Lettres philosophiques* 13: "Sur M. Locke," and 14: "Sur Descartes et Newton" (M 22:121–32). Analysis of Locke's influence on the *philosophes* is in Jørn Schløser, *John Locke et les philosophes français: La critique des idées innées en France au dix-huitième siècle* (*Studies on Voltaire and the Eighteenth Century* 353 [1997]).

35. Voltaire, *Lettres philosophiques* 13, "Sur M. Locke" (M 22:122).

36. Etienne Bonnot de Condillac, *Traité des sensations; Traité des animaux* (1798; Paris: Fayard, 1984), 11.

37. Ernst Cassirer, *The Philosophy of the Enlightenment,* trans. Fritz C. A. Koelln and James P. Pettegrove (Princeton, NJ: Princeton University Press, 1951), 24.

38. Voltaire admired Condillac for his systematic thinking and promotion of Newton and Locke. In 1756, he invited Condillac to come and write a philosophical magnum opus at Les Délices; see *Correspondence* D6998. See also discussion in Isabel F. Knight, *The Geometric Spirit: The Abbé de Condillac and the French Enlightenment* (New Haven: Yale University Press, 1968), 1.

39. See *Gargantua* 1.21 ("Comment Gargantua fut insitiué par Ponocrates en telle discipline qu'il ne perdait heure du jour") (How Gargantua was taught by Ponocrates in such a way that he did not waste a moment of the day), and 1.22 ("Comment Gargantua employait le temps quand l'air était pluvieux") (How Gargantua spent his time in rainy weather); in François Rabelais, *Les cinq livres: Gargantua, Pantagruel, Le tiers livre, Le quart livre, Le cinquième livre,* ed. Jean Céard, Gérard Defaux, and Michel Simonin (Paris: Librairie Générale Française, 1994).

40. Voltaire later refers to the king with the hermaphroditic tag "Alcine-Frédéric." The episode is a masterful rewriting of a section of canto 6 in Ludovico Ariosto's *Orlando furioso,* in which Alcina the sorceress lures the knight Astolfo into her magic palace, floods him with pleasure, and after she tires of him imprisons him in a myrtle. Voltaire, like Astolfo, is the center of a sort of love triangle (Voltaire, Frederick, and Mme. du Châtelet: Astolfo, Alcina, and Ruggiero). For both Voltaire and Astolfo, loss of self-awareness also includes a loss of country and community: "Je déplus fort au roi de France" (I heartily displeased the king of France) (M 1:37); "Né di Francia né d'altro mi rimembra" (I remembered neither France nor anything else) (*Orlando furioso* 6.47.5). Voltaire's reworking of the Ariostean source text shows how desire and irony work in tandem to unmask any pretense to coherence by the self. Yet neither Astolfo nor Voltaire expresses any regret over his plight, as if each knew even before the episodes took place that some external factor would eventually crumble the individual codes he had spent his life establishing. After his capitulation to Frederick, Voltaire ironically describes the

comforts purchased with his loss of freedom: "Me voilà donc avec une clef d'argent doré pendue à mon habit, une crois aux cou, et vingt mille francs de pension" (M 1:37). (There I was with a key of gilded silver on my suit, a cross around my neck, and a twenty-thousand franc pension.) Similarly, Astolfo recounts his pleasures with the sorceress to a fellow knight, only to emphasize—in the manner of Francesca da Rimini in *Inferno* 5— the difficulty of remembering former happiness in times of woe:

> Deh! perché vo le mie piaghe toccando,
> senza speranza poi di medicina?
> Perché l'avuto ben vo rimembrando
> quando io patisco estrema disciplina? (6.49.1–4)

(Oh! Why do I touch these old wounds, when there is no hope of remedy? Why do I keep on recalling the pleasure I experienced, when I suffer such grave punishment?)

References to Ariosto's text are to *Orlando furioso*, ed. Lanfranco Caretti (Milan: Ricciardi, 1954).

41. The only character to emerge from the *Mémoires* with her identity intact is Mme. du Châtelet. Voltaire never provides, however, a direct description of her; he lists instead her general characteristics and attributes: her style embodies the universal principles of *la clarté, la précision,* and *l'élégance* to which Voltaire aspires. In sum, he represents her as an undifferentiated pastiche of virtue and talent—and as a woman who stands in the way of Frederick's desire to keep Voltaire in Germany: "Le roi de Prusse, à qui j'avais souvent signifié que je ne quitterais jamais Mme du Châtelet pour lui, voulut à toute force m'attraper quand il fut défait de sa rivale" (M 1:35). (The King of Prussia, whom I often told that I would never leave Mme. du Châtelet for him, wished at any cost to capture me when he learned of his rival's passing away.)

42. See Hume, *My Own Life,* in *An Inquiry Concerning Human Understanding, and Selections from a Treatise of Human Nature* (Chicago: Open Court, 1938), v–xvi.

43. In Hume's *A Treatise of Human Nature,* "On Personal Identity" begins with an attack on those philosophers who "imagine we are every moment intimately conscious of what we call SELF, that we feel its existence and its continuance in existence; and are certain, beyond the evidence of a demonstration, both of its perfect identity and simplicity." Foreshadowing his self-representation in *My Own Life,* Hume writes:

> I may venture to affirm of the rest of mankind, that they are nothing but a bundle or collection of different perceptions, which succeed each other with an inconceivable rapidity, and are in a perpetual flux and movement. . . . The mind is a kind of theatre, where several perceptions successively make their appearance; pass, repass, glide away, and mingle in an infinite variety of postures and situations. There is properly no *simplicity* in it at one time, nor *identity* in different; whatever natural propension we may have to imagine that simplicity and identity. (*A Treatise of Human Nature,* ed. L. A. Selby-Bigge, 2nd ed. [Oxford: Clarendon, 1978], 1.4.6)

Chapter 5. Alfieri's Prince, Dante, and the Romantic Self

1. See Vittorio Alfieri, *Del principe e delle lettere*, ed. Pietro Cazzani (1951), 1.8; vol. 1 of *Scritti politici e morali*, vols. 3–5 of *Opere*, 40 vols. (Asti: Casa d'Alfieri, 1951–) (abbrev. "*Opera omnia*"); *The Prince and Letters*, ed. Beatrice Corrigan, trans. Beatrice Corrigan and Julius A. Molinaro (Toronto: University of Toronto Press, 1972).

2. These five editions appeared in England (London, 1778); France (Paris, 1787); and Germany (Nuremberg, 1781; Berlin and Strasbourg, 1788; Berlin, 1799).

3. Important translations include William Hayley's English version of *Inferno* 1–3 (1782), Antoine de Rivarol's *L'enfer, traduction nouvelle en prose* (1783), and A. W. Schlegel's German translation of fragments of the *Commedia* (1790). See Paul Colomb de Batines, *Bibliografia dantesca; ossia, Catalogo delle edizioni, traduzioni, codici manoscritti e comenti della Divina commedia e delle opere minori di Dante, seguito dalla serie de' biografi di lui*, trans. Giovanni Costantini and Zanobi Bicchierai, 2 vols. (Prato: Aldina, 1845–46), 1:252–53, 264–66, 271; and Werner P. Friederich, *Dante's Fame Abroad, 1350–1850* (Chapel Hill: University of North Carolina Studies in Comparative Literature, 1950), 114–16, 226–29, 375–84.

4. An early sign of interest in Dante from the Jena Romantics was an essay on the *Commedia* by A. W. Schlegel in 1791; then followed Friedrich Schelling's lecture "Uber Dante in philosophischer Beziehung," delivered as part of a series of talks in Jena in 1802 and 1803. In these same two years, A. W. Schlegel discussed the poet in his lectures on literature and art in Berlin. A leader of the Jena group, Friedrich Schlegel, drew on Dante's tripartite division of *Inferno, Purgatorio,* and *Paradiso* in elaborating his three-stage theory of tragedy in *Geschichte der alten und neuen Literatur* (1812). See René Wellek, *History of Modern Criticism: 1750–1950*, 8 vols. (New Haven: Yale University Press, 1955–92), 2:21–22; Erich Auerbach, "Entdeckung Dantes in der Romantik," *Gesammelte Aufsätze zur romanischen Philologie* (Bern: Francke, 1967); and Ralph Pite, *The Circle of Our Vision: Dante's Presence in English Romantic Poetry* (New York: Oxford University Press, 1994), 22.

5. Vincenzo Martinelli's edition of the *Commedia* (London and Livorno: Masi, 1778) includes a laudatory *vita* of Dante and two letters defending the poet from Voltaire's attacks. Also noteworthy was the *Commedia* edited by Gian Jacopo Dionisi (Parma: Bodoni, 1795), whose philological accuracy and thoroughness were such that Foscolo labeled him the "ristoratore del testo dantesco" (restorer of Dante's text; in Giuliano Mambelli, *Annali delle edizioni dantesche* [Bologna: Zanichelli, 1931], 77). Unless otherwise indicated, references to the textual history of the *Commedia* are to Mambeli.

6. Alfieri had an opportunity to meet Rousseau in Paris in 1771 but declined to do so. He stated that the Swiss writer's already legendary abrasiveness would probably have caused him to begin despising a man he wished to continue admiring. Although it is tempting to view this evasion as a manifestation of literary anxiety vis-à-vis a formidable predecessor, by 1771 Alfieri had neither read much of Rousseau nor expressed any desire to pursue a literary career (see *Vita* 3.12).

7. See especially Foscolo's description of the failed attempt by Ortis to meet Alfieri (August 27, 1798; Ugo Foscolo, *Ultime lettere di Jacopo Ortis*, ed. Maria Antonietta Terzoli, *Opere*, ed. Franco Gavezzeni, 2 vols. [Turin: Einaudi-Gallimard, 1994–95], 2:3–

140; *Last Letters of Jacopo Ortis; and, Of Tombs,* trans. J. G. Nichols [London: Hesperus, 2002]). Alfieri, typically, wanted nothing to do with the adulation of admirers and went so far as to affix to his door a public notice warning away literary pilgrims (see *Opera omnia* 2:294).

8. See Aurelia Accame Bobbio's summary and bibliography in *Enciclopedia dantesca,* dir. Umberto Bosco, 6 vols. (Rome: Istituto della Enciclopedia Italiana, 1970–78), 1:120–21; and Assunta Borselli, "Dante nella ricerca stilistica di Alfieri," *L'Alighieri* 37 (1996): 89–101.

9. The definitive catalog of Alfieri's library books lists thirteen copies of the *Commedia,* including those with commentaries by Cristoforo Landino (1481), Alessandro Vellutello (1544), and Bernardino Daniello (1568), as well as the landmark edition of the Accademia della Crusca (1595). The catalogue also contains influential critical studies on Dante by Pietro Francesco Giambullari (1544), Belisario Bulgarini (1573), and Jacopo Mazzoni (1573). See Guido Santato, *Alfieri e Voltaire: Dall'imitazione alla contestazione* (Florence: Olschki, 1988), 74–76.

10. Alfieri borrowed verses from *Paradiso* 16 to serve as epigraph to the satire *La plebe* and cited Dante's sonnet "Gente più vana assai" in his satirical attack on his political enemies in sonnet 5 of *Il misogallo* (ed. Clemente Mazzotta [1984], in *Opera omnia* 5:242). In 1790, Alfieri remarked that the entire *Inferno* warranted recopying, for he believed that one learned more from the errors of Dante than from the successes of other poets; see Batines, *Bibliografia dantesca* 1:206. In contrast, Bettinelli claimed that only a hundred verses in the entire *Commedia* merited preservation.

11. Vittorio Alfieri, *Esquisse du jugement universel,* ed. Clemente Mazzotta (1984), 1.279–92, vol. 3 of *Scritti politici e morali,* and vol. 5 of *Opera omnia.*

12. For traditional memoirs written between 1750 and 1800, see Voltaire, *Mémoires pour servir à la vie de M. de Voltaire écrits par lui-même;* Carlo Goldoni, *Mémoires;* and Giovanni Giacomo Casanova, *Histoire de ma vie.* Examples of *cursus studiorum* in the first half of the eighteenth century are Muratori, *Intorno al metodo seguito ne' suoi studi;* and Giambattista Vico, *Vita scritta da sè medesimo.* For fictionalized autobiographical accounts in the period between 1770 and 1800, see Goethe, *Die Leiden des jungen Werther;* Restif de la Bretonne, *Monsieur Nicolas;* and Foscolo, *Ultime lettere di Jacopo Ortis.* A representative diary is Alfieri's *Giornali* (1774–77); and a major life history from the period is Gibbon's *Memoirs of My Life and Writings* (pub. posthumously, 1796). I outline the above categories of self-representation in s.v. "Autobiography," *Encyclopedia of Italian Literary Studies,* 2 vols., ed. Gaetana Marrone (New York: Routledge, 2007), 1:107–8. For a survey of the different types of autobiography during this period, see Franco Fido, "At the Origins of Autobiography in the 18th and 19th Centuries: The *Topoi* of the Self," *Annali d'Italianistica* 4 (1986): 168–80. See also Marziano Guglielminetti, "Per un'antologia degli autobiografi del Settecento," *Annali d'Italianistica* 4 (1986): 140–51; and Andrea Battistini, *Lo specchio di Dedalo: Autobiografia e biografia* (Bologna: Il Mulino, 1990).

13. For critical discussions of the distinction between autobiography and memoir, see Philippe Lejeune, *L'autobiographie en France* (Paris: Colin, 1971), 42–71; and Karl J. Weintraub, "Autobiography and Historical Consciousness," *Critical Inquiry* 1 (1975): 821–48. See also, in chronological order, Georges Gusdorf, "Conditions et limites de

l'autobiographie," *Formen der Selbstdarstellung: Analekten zu einer Geschichte des literarischen Selbstportraits,* ed. Günter Reichenkron and Erich Haase (Berlin: Duncker and Humblot, 1956); Jean Starobinski, "The Style of Autobiography," trans. S. Chatman (1971), repr. in *Autobiography, Essays Theoretical and Critical,* ed. James Olney (Princeton, NJ: Princeton University Press, 1980), 73–83; Karl J. Weintraub, *The Value of the Individual: Self and Circumstance in Autobiography* (Chicago: University of Chicago Press, 1978); Paul de Man, "Autobiography as De-Facement," *Modern Language Notes* 74 (1979): 919–30; John Sturrock, *The Language of Autobiography: Studies in the First Person Singular* (New York: Cambridge University Press, 1993); and Philippe Lejeune, *Le pacte autobiographique,* 2 vols. (Paris: Seuil, 1975–2005).

14. See the description on Alfieri's situation in Corrigan and Molinaro, *Prince and Letters* ix–xii.

15. Voltaire fled persecution in France as early as 1726, Diderot was imprisoned in 1749, Claude Adrien Helvétius's *De l'esprit* from 1758 was burned, and Rousseau went into exile in 1762. See Corrigan and Molinaro, introduction to *Prince and Letters* xiii–xvii.

16. One region that had a fairly liberal policy regarding freedom of expression was Tuscany, home of the literary language Alfieri wished to emulate and the region to which he eventually immigrated (see ibid., xv).

17. The following works from the period between 1740 and 1780 contain either cautious disapproval or outright rejection of the principles of *la clarté, l'élégance,* and *le dessein* that Voltaire and others defined as characteristic of the tasteful literary work: Johann Jacob Bodmer, *Kritische Betrachtungen über die poetischen Gemählde der Dichter;* Diderot, *Discours sur la poésie dramatique;* Alessandro Verri, *Degli errori utili;* Baretti, *Discours sur Shakespeare et Monsieur de Voltaire;* and Horace Walpole, *History of the Modern Taste in Gardening.*

18. See Voltaire's letter to Frederick II of Prussia from May 26, 1742: "J'aime peu les héros, ils font trop de fracas, / Je hais les conquérants, fiers ennemis d'eux mêmes, / Qui dans les horreurs des combats / Ont placé le bonheur supreme. / . . . Plus leur gloire a d'éclat, plus ils sont haïssables." (I hardly like heroes, for they make too much noise. I hate conquerors, those fierce enemies of themselves who have placed their greatest happiness in the horrors of combat. . . . The more their glory resounds, the more hateful they are.) (OC D2611).

19. *Encyclopédie ou dictionnaire raisonné des sciences, des arts et des métiers [Nouvelle impression en facsimilé de la première éd. de 1751–1780],* ed. Denis Diderot and Jean Le Rond d'Alembert, 35 vols. (Stuttgart-Bad Cannstatt: Frommann, 1966); *Encyclopedia: Selections [by] Diderot, D'Alembert, and a Society of Men of Letters,* trans. and ed., Nelly Schargo Hoyt and Thomas Cassirer (Indianapolis: Bobbs-Merrill, 1965). For an example of the balance between study and sociability in *philosophe* thought, see David Hume, *An Enquiry Concerning Human Understanding* (Buffalo: Prometheus, 1988), 11–12: "The most perfect character is supposed to lie between . . . extremes; retaining an equal ability and taste for books, company, and business; preserving in conversation that discernment and delicacy which arise from polite letters; and in business, that probity and accuracy which are the natural result of a just philosophy. . . . Man is a sociable, no less than a reasonable being."

20. See Voltaire, *Mémoires* (note 12 above); and Hume, *Story of My Own Life* (1776).

21. Vittorio Alfieri, *Rime,* ed. Francesco Maggini (1954), *Opera omnia* 9:50.

22. "Di Bologna mi deviai per visitare in Ravenna il sepolcro del Poeta, e un giorno intero vi passai fantasticando, pregando, e piangendo" (4.10; *Vita* 227). (After Bologna, I left the direct road with the view of visiting the tomb of Dante at Ravenna, where I passed a whole day in melancholy meditation [*Memoirs* 216].) References are from the *Vita di Vittorio Alfieri da Asti scritta da esso,* vol. 1 of *Opere,* ed. Arnaldo Di Benedetto (Milan: Ricciardi, 1977); translations are from the first English version of the text, published anonymously in 1810 and then reissued in an updated and corrected form by E. R. Vincent, ed., *Memoirs: The Anonymous Translation of 1810* [by Alfieri] (New York: Oxford University Press, 1961).

23. An author who influenced Alfieri, Vico (see *Del principe e delle lettere* 2.2), provides a similar formulation of the untimely and marginal heroism of the self-styled visionary writer in his *Vita scritta da sè medesimo.*

24. See an unsigned essay by Foscolo in the *Edinburgh Review* 30 (1818): 334: "The haughtiness of demeanour, attributed to him [Dante] by all the writers from Giovanni Villani [c. 1275–1348] to the present day, probably is not exaggerated."

25. See Ettore Bonora, *Il preromanticismo in Italia; compendio delle lezioni di letteratura italiana dell'anno accademico, 1958–59* (Milan: La Goliardica, 1959), 34.

26. Alfieri initially welcomed the storming of the Bastille with an ode: "Parigi sbastigliato," ed. Pietro Cazzani (1966); in *Scritti politici e morali, Opera omnia* 4:101–11.

27. See, for example, *Vita* 3.10; 109–17.

28. A journal entry from early in Alfieri's career sums up his desire to be unlike any other person of his time:

> Non perdo mai occasione d'imparare a morire: il più gran timore ch'io abbia della morte, è di temerla: non passa giorno in cui non vi pensi; pure non so davvero se la sopporterò da eroe, o da buon Cattolico, cioè da vile: bisogna esservi per saperlo. . . . In mio pensiero, che non ad altro è volto ch'alla gloria, rifaccio spesso il sistema di mia vita, e penso ch'a quarantacinque anni, non voglio più scrivere; godere bensì della fama che sarommi procacciata in realtà, o in idea, ed attendere soltanto a morire. Temo una sola cosa; che avanzando verso la meta giudiziosamente prefissami, non la allontani sempre più, e ch'agli anni quarantacinque non pensi se non a vivere; e forse a sciccherar carta. Per quanto mi sforzi a credere, e far credere ch'io sia diverso dal comune degli uomini, tremo d'essere simigliantissimo.
>
> (I never miss any opportunity to learn how to die. The greatest fear I have of death is that I will fear it. Not a day passes where I do not think of this. I have no idea of whether I will face death as a hero or as a good Catholic—that is, coward. One needs to be there to know this. . . . In my thoughts, which are only ever about glory, I often rethink the plan of my life, and imagine that when I am forty-five years old I will no longer wish to write. I would rather enjoy the fame that has been allotted to me in reality or my fantasy, and wait only to die. I fear only that when the end of that time judiciously granted me comes, I will not push it away, think only of living longer, and perhaps of wasting more paper. As much as I force myself to believe and make others believe that I am different from the common run of men, I shudder about being most similar to it.) (April 26, 1777; Vittorio Alfieri, *Giornali;* vol. 1 of *Opere,* ed. Arnaldo Di Benedetto [abbrev. "*Opere* Milan"], 421–22)

29. See Voltaire, *Lettres philosophiques* 13: "Sur M. Locke," and 14: "Sur Descartes et Newton" (M 22:121–32); *Œuvres complètes de Voltaire,* ed. Louis Moland, 52 vols. (Paris: Garnier Frères, 1877–85), 19:282 (abbrev. "M").

30. "E questi quattro grandissimi, dopo sedici anni oramai ch'io li ho giornalmente alle mani, mi riescono sempre nuovi, sempre migliori nel loro ottimo, e direi anche utilissimi nel loro pessimo; chè io non asserirò con cieco fanatismo, che tutti e quattro a luoghi non abbiano e il mediocre ed il pessimo; dirò bensì che assai, ma assai, vi si può imparare anche dal loro cattivo; ma di chi ben si addentra nei loro motivi e intenzioni: cioè da chi, oltre l'intenderli pienamente e gustarli, li sente" (4.10; *Vita* 228). (For the sixteen years that I have read these works [by Dante, Petrarch, Ariosto, Tasso] they have always appeared new to me: on each perusal I have discovered fresh beauties in those parts of them which are truly excellent; and even the faults of such authors are not destitute of utility. I dare not here affirm with blind fanaticism that they have never written indifferent and even bad verses, I only contend that valuable lessons may be learned even from their defects. In forming a judgment of their merits it is necessary, however, to enter into their intentions and be well acquainted with their motives: it is necessary also not only to comprehend and taste their beauties but to feel them [*Memoirs* 217].)

31. See Bettinelli, "Lettera diretta al signor canonico De Giovanni del Collegio delle Arti Liberali di Torino sulla nuova edizione delle tragedie di Vittorio Alfieri," *Illuministi italiani,* 7 vols. (Milan: Ricciardi, 1958–71), 2:1181: "Ha studiato Petrarca, Ariosto, e Dante; ma l'ultimo solo campeggia nel suo stile, perch'è il più robusto, e però il vidi ognor preferito dai pensatori in prosa." ([Alfieri] studied Petrarch, Ariosto, and Dante; but only the latter dominates his style, because he is the most robust, and unfortunately the one I increasingly see preferred by prose authors.)

Chapter 6. Wordsworth, Dante, and British Romantic Identity

1. Edward Quillinan, diary entry, July 9, 1847. Trans.: "I say that her most noble soul departed in the first hour of the ninth day of the month." Quillinan adds the following gloss: "Dante's Beatrice (la Beatrice Portinari) died in her 26th year on the ninth of June 1290, at Florence where she was born.—see Vita Nuova." The diary belongs to the Wordsworth Library in Grasmere, England; I am indebted to the library's former director, the late Robert Woof, for pointing out this item to me and for his many other valuable suggestions.

2. Selected adaptations of the Paolo and Francesca episode in Britain alone between 1800 and 1850 attest to the interdisciplinary breadth of Dante's popularity: oil paintings by John Raphael Smith (1803) and Archer James Oliver (1810); Hunt's poem *Story of Rimini* (1816); an oil painting by Henry Fuseli (1818); Byron's poem *Francesca da Rimini* (1820); an anonymous translation in the *Edinburgh Review* (1821); Henry Perronet Briggs's oil painting (1827); illustrations by William Blake (1827); the second edition of Hunt's *Story of Rimini* (1832); John Rogers Herbert's oil painting (1832); a translation by J. H. Merivale (1838); Richard Westamacott's sculpture (1838); an oil painting by Henry Nelson O'Neil (1842); Lord John Russell's translation (1842); Hunt's translation of *Inferno* 5 (1846); a drawing from Lord Leighton (1850); Dante Gabriel Rossetti's

painting (1850); and an unidentified translation in *Tait's Edinburgh Magazine* (1850). See Paget Jackson Toynbee, *Britain's Tribute to Dante in Literature and Art: A Chronological Record of 540 Years (c. 1380–1920)* (London: Oxford University Press, 1921), 39–104.

3. See Georg Wilhelm Friedrich Hegel, *Aesthetics: Lectures on Fine Art*, trans. T. M. Knox, 2 vols. (Oxford: Clarendon, 1975), 2:1104: "While the Homeric heroes have been made permanent in *our* memories by the muse, [Dante's] characters have produced their situation for *themselves*, as individuals, and are eternal in themselves, not in our ideas."

4. Thomas Love Peacock, *Nightmare Abbey* (New York: Norton, 1964), 30. For a detailed account of the presence of Dante in nineteenth- and twentieth-century England, see Steve Ellis, *Dante and English Poetry: Shelley to T. S. Eliot* (New York: Cambridge University Press, 1983). For a bibliography and history of Dante studies in England, see Steven Botterill, "Dante Studies in the British Isles since 1980," *Dante Studies* 111 (1993): 245–61. For the role of Italian poetry in British literature of the mid-eighteenth to mid-nineteenth century, see Beatrice Corrigan, ed., *Italian Poets and English Critics, 1755–1859: A Collection of Critical Essays* (Chicago: University of Chicago Press, 1969).

5. William Wordsworth to Walter Savage Landor, January 21, 1824, D123; *The Later Years: Part 1, 1821–1828*, rev., ed., and arr. Alan G. Hill; vol. 4 of *The Letters of William and Dorothy Wordsworth*, ed. Ernest de Sélincourt, Chester L. Shaver, and Alan G. Hill, 2nd ed., 8 vols. (Oxford: Clarendon, 1967–93).

6. The relevant bibliography is essentially a corpus of annotations regarding the occasions Wordsworth read Dante or incorporated him into his work: see Werner P. Friederich, *Dante's Fame Abroad, 1350–1850* (Chapel Hill: University of North Carolina Studies in Comparative Literature, 1950), 243–44; Paget Jackson Toynbee, *Dante in English Literature from Chaucer to Cary, c. 1380–1844*, 2 vols. (London: Methuen, 1909), 2:1–5; Duncan Wu, *Wordsworth's Reading, 1770–1799* (New York: Cambridge University Press, 1993), 43–44, and *Wordsworth's Reading, 1800–1815* (New York: Cambridge University Press, 1995), 69–70. The general misunderstanding of the subject is distilled in Friederich's dismissal: "Though references to Dante in William Wordsworth are relatively numerous, there existed between the two men no deep spiritual relationship" (243). Two studies attempt to move beyond a strictly philological approach, but their formalist readings do little to engage the cultural and historical contexts that shaped Wordsworth's view of Dante: Myungbok Kim, "The Poetics of *Praeludere*: Dante and Wordsworth" (Ph.D. diss., University of Illinois at Urbana-Champaign, 1989); and Marion Montgomery, *The Reflective Journey toward Other: Essays on Dante, Wordsworth, Eliot, and Others* (Athens: University of Georgia Press, 1973), 97–112.

7. "Autobiographical Memoranda Dictated by William Wordsworth, P[oet] L[aureate], at Rydal Mount, November 1847," *The Prose Works of William Wordsworth*, ed. Alexander Balloch Grosart, 3 vols. (London: Moxon, 1876), 3:222 (abbrev. "*Prose*").

8. Unless otherwise indicated, references are from the 1850 edition in *The Prelude, 1799, 1805, 1850: Authoritative Texts, Context and Reception, Recent Critical Essays*, ed. Jonathan Wordsworth, M. H. Abrams, and Stephen Charles Gill (New York: Norton, 1979).

9. For discussion of Wordsworth's Italian studies, see Ben Ross Schneider, Jr., *Wordsworth's Cambridge Education* (Cambridge: Cambridge University Press, 1957), 99–103.

10. See April 7, 1846, "Reminiscences of Wordsworth," by Lady Richardson and Mrs. Davy, in "Conversations and Personal Reminiscences," *Prose* 3:456: "I never engaged in the proper studies of the university, so that in these I had no temptation to envy any one; but I remember with pain that I *had* envious feelings when my fellow-student in Italian got before me. I was his superior in many departments of mind, but he was the better Italian scholar, and I envied him." See also June Sturrock, "Wordsworth's Italian Teacher," *Bulletin of the John Rylands University Library of Manchester* 67 (1985): 797–812.

11. Later in life, Wordsworth recalled a passage cited in translation by Thomas Gray during his tour of the Lake District: "Even Gray himself, describing, in his Journal, the steeps at the entrance of Borrowdale, expresses his terror in the language of Dante: — 'Let us not speak of them, but look and pass on'" ("Kendal and Windermere Railway: Two Letters Reprinted from the *Morning Post* [1844]," *Prose* 2:327). Dante's original reads: "Non ragionam di lor, ma guarda e passa" (*Inf.* 3.51). Dante Alighieri, *The Divine Comedy*, trans. with commentary Charles S. Singleton, 6 vols. (Princeton, NJ: Princeton University Press, 1970–75). Italian text based on *La commedia secondo l'antica vulgata*, ed. Giorgio Petrocchi, 4 vols. (Milan: Mondadori, 1966–67).

12. See E. R. Vincent, lecture notes to *Pieces Selected from the Italian Poets [and Translated into English Verse by Some Gentlemen of the University]*, ed. Agostino Isola, 2nd ed. (Cambridge: Archdeacon, 1784); microfilm of Fitzwilliam Museum, Cambridge. This edition belonged to Wordsworth and in all likelihood served as his textbook at Cambridge. The editorial choices by his teacher Isola reflect the neoclassical predilections of late eighteenth-century English academe: one selection from Giovanni Battista Guarini and Giambattista Marino, two from Tasso and Alessandro Tassoni, three from Petrarch, five from Ariosto, and a full twenty-six from the Enlightenment court poet-playwright Pietro Metastasio; none from Dante. See discussion in Toynbee, *Dante in English Literature* 1:358–59.

13. William Wordsworth to Sir George Beaumont, October 17 and 24, 1805, D281; *The Early Years, 1787–1805*, rev. Chester L. Shaver, vol. 1 of *Letters*.

14. See *Inf.* 3.1–3: "Per me si va ne la città dolente, / per me si va ne l'etterno dolore, / per me si va tra la perduta gente" (Through me you enter the woeful city, through me you enter eternal grief, through me you enter among the lost). Wordsworth provides the citation (a slight textual variant of the above) with no mention of its source, which implies that he was either quoting from memory or copying verses he sensed were so well known as to need no bibliographical explication; see *Prose* 1:160.

15. June Sturrock claims in "Wordsworth: An Early Borrowing from Dante" (*Notes and Queries* 27 [1980]: 204–5) that the following lines from "Salisbury Plain" (begun 1793, pub. 1798) were influenced by Dante's verses in *Inf.* 5: "The thoughts which bow the kindly spirits down / And break the springs of joy, their deadly weight / Derive from memory of pleasures flown / Which haunts us in some sad reverse of fate" (19–22). Compare Dante: "Nessun maggior dolore / che ricordarsi del tempo felice / ne la miseria" (There is no greater sorrow than to recall, in wretchedness, the happy time) (121–23). I agree with the counterarguments of both Wu, *Wordsworth's Reading, 1770–1799* 43–44, and W. J. B. Owen, "Literary Echoes in *The Prelude*," *Wordsworth Circle* 3 (1972): 3–16. The nostalgic regret that accompanies the recollection of happier times is a commonplace notion almost synonymous with the Wordsworthian tendency to look back

wistfully and thematize the accompanying emotional tug. Moreover, nothing in the rest of "Salisbury Plain" would lead one to conclude that this general existential observation by Wordsworth carries with it any specifically Dantesque connotations. Wu also mentions that a recent edition of Wordsworth published by Longman argues that the "little boat" in "Peter Bell" (begun 1798, pub. 1819) refers to "la navicella del mio ingegno" from the opening lines of *Purgatorio*. There is no conclusive evidence, however, that Wordsworth had read *Purgatorio* by 1798–1819, a period when criticism of Dante was mostly limited to the *Inferno*. Also, the boat image often recurs in Wordsworth's poetry, usually with personal and purposefully non-literary-historical associations (see, for instance, the poet's nocturnal row along the Bay of Ullswater as well as his boat journey with friends to a deserted island in, respectively, *Prel.* 1.357–400 and 2.138–97).

16. Robert Morehead, "Observations on the Poetical Character of Dante," in Robert Woof, ed., vol. 1 of *William Wordsworth: The Critical Heritage* (New York: Routledge, 2001), 1020. Morehead's remarks may have been influenced by his cousin, Francis Jeffrey, editor of the *Edinburgh Review* and one of Wordsworth's most influential detractors.

17. See, for example, Dante's description of the role of memory in the composition of "Donne ch'avete intelletto d'amore" (Women who have understanding of love) in *Vita nuova* ch. 19, and Wordsworth's well-known claim in "Preface to *Lyrical Ballads*" that his poetry begins from a "spontaneous overflow of feeling," which is then tempered by reflection: "The emotion is contemplated till, by a species of reaction, the tranquillity gradually disappears, and an emotion, kindred to that which was before the subject of contemplation, is gradually produced" (*Prose* 2:96).

18. William Wordsworth, *"Lyrical Ballads," and Other Poems, 1797–1800*, ed. James Butler and Karen Green (Ithaca, NY: Cornell University Press, 1992), 116–20 (abbrev. "*LB*").

19. From the vast bibliography on "Tintern Abbey," I limit myself to a list of some recent influential interpretations. For a reading of the poem in terms of Wordsworth's aesthetic evasion of industrial spread in the Wye Valley, see Marjorie Levinson, *Wordsworth's Great Period Poems: Four Essays* (New York: Cambridge University Press, 1986), 14–57. A similar perspective informs Jerome McGann, *The Romantic Ideology: A Critical Investigation* (Chicago: University of Chicago Press, 1983). Geoffrey H. Hartman writes on the dialectic between self- and nature-consciousness in *Wordsworth's Poetry, 1787–1814*, 2nd ed. (New Haven: Yale University Press, 1971), esp. 31–69. A reading of "Tintern Abbey" that highlights the anxieties that accompany introspection is Harold Bloom, *The Visionary Company: A Reading of English Romantic Poetry*, rev. and enl. ed. (Ithaca, NY: Cornell University Press, 1971), 131–40. David Bromwich argues that as seemingly ethereal a poem as "Tintern Abbey" carries with it Wordsworth's personal and political guilt over his experiences in revolutionary France (*Disowned by Memory: Wordsworth's Poetry of the 1790s* [Chicago: University of Chicago Press, 1998], 69–91).

20. My understanding of pleasure in Wordsworth is indebted to Bromwich, *Disowned by Memory* 127–33; and Lionel Trilling, "The Fate of Pleasure: Wordsworth to Dostoevsky," *Romanticism Reconsidered: Selected Papers from the English Institute*, ed. Northrop Frye (New York: Columbia University Press, 1963), 73–106.

21. Wordsworth writes in his notes to "Tintern Abbey": "No poem of mine was

composed under circumstances more pleasant for me to remember than this" (*Prose* 3:45).

22. William Hazlitt, *The Complete Works of William Hazlitt*, ed. P. P. Howe, 21 vols. (Toronto: Dent, 1930–34) (abbrev. "*CW*").

23. Morehead provides a similar view: "One of Wordsworth's finest peculiarities is perfectly possessed by Dante, and much better applied; . . . we mean that close observation of nature. . . . The error with Wordsworth is, that he makes observations of this kind the staple of his poetry. . . . Dante lived among political intrigues, and the turmoil of factions, yet it is astonishing, that he had as fine an eye for these glimpses of nature . . . as the poet who has passed all his days musing on the banks of Grassmere [sic], or Rydalwater. But the Chief Magistrate of Florence, as our poet [Dante] was in one year . . . knew very well that the mind of a being like man . . . cannot be permanently occupied with, though it may, with deep feeling, take a sidelong glance at, dancing daffodils, or the reflection of a lamb in a lake" ("Poetical Character of Dante" 1020–21).

24. See Samuel Taylor Coleridge, "Lecture on Dante," in *Dante, the Critical Heritage, 1314(?)–1870*, ed. Michael Caesar (New York: Routledge, 1989), 439–47.

25. Compare Friedrich Schelling: "It would be of subordinate interest to represent by itself the Philosophy, Physics, and Astronomy of Dante, since his true particularity lies only in his manner of fusing them with his poetry. . . . If . . . his philosophy is to be characterized in general as Aristotelian, we must not understand by this the pure Peripatetic philosophy, but a peculiar union of the same with the ideas of the Platonic then entertained, as may be proved by many passages of the poem." See "The *Divina Commedia* from the German of Schelling," trans. Henry Wadsworth Longfellow, *"Divine Comedy" of Dante Alighieri* (Boston: Houghton, Mifflin, 1913), 485 (abbrev. "Schelling").

26. Compare ibid.: "In order to make his poem universal [Dante] was obliged to make it historical. An invention entirely uncontrolled, and proceeding from his own individuality, was necessary to unite [the astronomy, the theology, and the philosophy of the time], and form them into an organic whole."

27. For an account of Shelley's relationship to Dante, see Stuart Curran, "Figuration in Shelley," *Dante's Modern Afterlife: Reception and Response from Blake to Heaney*, ed. N. R. Havely (New York: St. Martin's, 1998), 49–59; and Ellis, *Dante and English Poetry* 3–35.

28. See Marilyn Butler, *Romantics, Rebels, and Reactionaries: English Literature and Its Background, 1760–1830* (1981; New York: Oxford University Press, 1982), 138–54.

29. Percy Bysshe Shelley, *The Complete Poetical Works of Percy Bysshe Shelley*, ed. Neville Rogers, 4 vols. (Oxford: Clarendon, 1972–), 2:10.

30. Shelley, *A Defence of Poetry*, in *Shelley's Poetry and Prose: Authoritative Texts, Criticism*, ed. Donald H. Reiman and Sharon B. Powers (New York: Norton, 1977), 496.

31. Shelley's reading of Dante as "bridge" between antiquity and modern times has antecedents in the Jena critics and also appears three years earlier (1818) in Hazlitt's "Lectures on the English Poets"; see *CW* 5:17. One of the more evocative Dantesque images from the *Defence* (Dante as "Lucifer of the starry flock," who brought light to "benighted" medieval Italy) echoes Giuseppe Baretti, *Dissertation upon the Italian Poetry* (1753): "The Muses began to free themselves from their rusty shackles in the schools [of Brunetto Latini and other early humanist scholars]. Florentines, putting their helping hand

to the work, brightened a little the face of reason; but Dante appeared and like a morning-sun, almost dispersed the mists that hovered for so many ages over the Parnassean mountain" (*Prefazioni e polemiche,* ed. Luigi Piccioni, 2nd ed. [Bari: Laterza, 1933], 98).

32. In Peacock's *Nightmare Abbey,* Shelley (in the character of Scythrop) sits brooding over a copy of *Purgatorio* after an unsuccessful attempt to seduce Marionetta. Unfortunately for Dante, Scythrop "pretend[s] to be deeply interested" but "kn[ows] not a word he was reading." The object of Scythrop's affections, Marionetta, realizes full well that her suitor is bluffing. The following dialogue ensues: " 'I see you are in the middle of Purgatory.' [Marionetta said] — 'I am in the middle of hell,' said Scythrop, furiously" (29–30).

33. See Butler, *Romantics, Rebels* 113–37.

34. A signal difference between the English and Italian cases was the imbalance in power between Italy and France that England never experienced. Long before the Napoleonic invasion (1796), the French presence in Italy stretched back to the Norman rule of southern Italy in the Middle Ages and Charles VIII's military expedition in 1494–95.

35. For a similar point, see the review of Leigh Hunt's *The Story of Rimini: A Poem* (an adaptation of Dante's *Inferno* 5) in *Edinburgh Review* 26 (1816): 476: "[Hunt's poetry] reminds us . . . of that pure and glorious style that prevailed among us before French models and French rules of criticism were known in this country [England], and to which we are delighted to see there is now so general a disposition to recur. Yet its more immediate prototypes, perhaps, are to be looked for rather in Italy than in England."

36. Before the crisis of Campoformio, many Italians falsely believed Napoleon would be the nation's great emancipator; in reality, his policies in Italy were dictated by his overall strategy vis-à-vis Austria. For analysis of Napoleon's complex relationship to Italian liberty in the 1790s, see Stuart Woolf, *A History of Italy, 1700–1860: The Social Constraints of Political Change* (London: Methuen, 1979), 162–67.

37. See, for example, Staël, *Corinne* 2.3: "L'Italie, au temps de sa puissance, revit tout entière dans le Dante. Animé par l'esprit des républiques, guerrier aussi-bien que poëte, il souffle la flamme des actions parmi les morts, et ses ombres ont une vie plus forte que les vivants d'aujourd'hui" (*Œuvres* 666). (Italy, at the height of its power, lives again to the full in Dante's work. Animated by the spirit of the Republic, a warrior as well as a poet, he fans the flames of action amongst the dead, and his shades are more vibrantly alive than those living today [*Corinne, Italy* 29].) Anne Louise Germaine de Staël, *Corinne, ou l'Italie;* vol. 1 of *Œuvres complètes de Madame la baronne de Staël-Holstein* (Paris: Didot, 1871) (abbrev. "*Œuvres*"); *Corinne, or Italy,* trans. Sylvia Raphael (New York: Oxford University Press, 1998) (abbrev. "*Corinne, Italy*").

38. For a survey of the landmark aesthetic responses to these political events, see James K. Chandler, *England in 1819: The Politics of Literary Culture and the Case of Romantic Historicism* (Chicago: University of Chicago Press, 1998), passim.

39. See Coleridge, "Lecture on Dante" 447; and Dante, *The Vision, or Hell, Purgatory, and Paradise,* trans. Henry Francis Cary, 2nd ed. corr., 3 vols. (London: Taylor and Hessey: 1819), xliii.

40. For Landor's praise of Wordsworth, see his Latin work *Idyllia heroica decem* (Pisa: Nistri, 1820), 215.

41. See Morehead on this connection: "There is another singular resemblance between Dante and Wordsworth. . . . In the Paradiso, especially, he indulges to an excess in certain

long bewildered metaphysical and theological discussions, which are extremely in the wandering unsatisfactory style of our good friend the Pedlar in [Wordsworth's] the Excursion.... The mystical style of writing, however, is very excusable ... in the oldest poet of Christian Europe; ... the only wonder is, that, in the nineteenth century Mr Wordsworth should have carried it so much further, and interwoven it so much more closely with the tissue of his poem" ("Poetical Character of Dante" 1021).

42. Wordsworth writes in this same letter to Landor: "As to the low-bred and headstrong Radicals, they are not worth a thought" (D123).

43. Caroline Fox, *Memories of Old Friends. Being Extracts from the Journals and Letters of Caroline Fox . . . from 1835 to 1871*, ed. Horace N. Pym, rev. ed. (London: Smith, Elder, 1883), 244.

44. Wordsworth alludes to Dante in the following poems: "White Doe of Rylstone," "Poems of the Imagination Composed during a Tour in the Summer of 1833," "Sonnet on the Sonnet" (1827), and "Florence" (1837). See Toynbee, *Dante in English Literature* 2:1–5.

45. Note, September 23, 1844, on flyleaf of vol. 1 of Dante, *Vision, or Hell, Purgatory, and Paradise*, trans. Cary; from Wordsworth Library. Even as astute a Wordsworthian as Alan G. Hill, an editor of the poet's correspondence, inaccurately remarks: "Wordsworth does not seem to have returned to the [*Commedia*] with much pleasure in later life" ("Wordsworth and Italy," *Journal of Anglo-Italian Studies* 1 [1991]: 116).

46. Two projects that intermittently occupied Wordsworth were his modernization of selected poems by Geoffrey Chaucer and his partial translation of Virgil's *Aeneid*. A discussion of the above as well as a consideration of Wordsworth's methods and achievements as translator is in Bruce E. Garver, ed., introduction to William Wordsworth, *Translations of Chaucer and Virgil* (Ithaca, NY: Cornell University Press, 1998), 3–29.

47. Dante, *La divina commedia*, ed. Paolo Costa, 3 vols. (Florence: Magheri, 1835–36); from Wordsworth Library.

48. For Dante's synthesis of Viriglian and Pauline (via St. Augustine) elements, see Giuseppe Mazzotta, *Dante, Poet of the Desert: History and Allegory in the "Divine Comedy"* (Princeton, NJ: Princeton University Press, 1979), 147–91.

49. *The Poetical Works of William Wordsworth*, ed. Ernest de Selincourt, vol. 2 (Oxford: Clarendon, 1940), 216.

50. See John Milton, "When I consider how my light is spent," l. 14; sonnet 19 of *Poems* (1673).

51. For a discussion of apocalypse in Wordsworth, see Hartman, *Wordsworth's Poetry* 45–60.

52. Compare Wordsworth: "Prophets of Nature, we to them will speak / A lasting inspiration, sanctified / By reason, blest by faith: what we have loved, / Others will love, and we will teach them how" (*Prel.* 14.446–49); and Dante:

> O somma luce che tanto ti levi
> da' concetti mortali, a la mia mente
> ripresta un poco di quel che parevi,
>   e fa la lingua mia tanto possente,
> ch'una favilla sol de la tua gloria possa
> lasciare a la futura gente. (*Par.* 33.67–72)

(O Light Supreme that art so far uplifted above mortal conceiving, relend to my mind a little of what Thou didst appear, and give my tongue such power that it may leave only a single spark of Thy glory for the folk to come.)

Chapter 7. Italy as Woman and Wound, Dante to Leopardi

1. See Guido Mazzoni, "Ugo Foscolo e Santa Croce," in Guido Mazzoni et al., *Ugo Foscolo e Firenze* (Florence: Le Monnier, 1928), 8–10, 25–26.

2. For retrospective analysis of Jacopo Ortis, in comparison to Goethe's Werther, see Foscolo, "Notizia bibliografica intorno alle *Ultime lettere di Jacopo Ortis*" (1814), ed. Maria Antonietta Terzoli, *Opere*, ed. Franco Gavezzeni, 2 vols. (Turin: Einaudi-Gallimard, 1994–95), 2:174–201. See also "Notizia intorno a Didimo Chierico," Foscolo's biographical note about the fictitious translator of *Viaggio sentimentale di Yorick lungo la Francia e l'Italia* (Foscolo's translation in 1813 of Laurence Sterne, *A Sentimental Journey through France and Italy*; 1766), *Opere* 2:345–53. At the conclusion of this fictitious biographical note, Foscolo's Chierico composes the following Latin epitaph for himself: "Didymi Clerici / vitia, virtus, ossa / hic post annos +++ / conquiescere coepere" (The vices, virtues, and bones of Didimo Chierico, after . . . years of life, here began to repose) (353). In a letter from August 22, 1812, to Isabella Teotochi Albrizzi, Foscolo composed a similar autobiographical epitaph: "Hugonis Phoscoli / vitia virtus ossa / hic post an . . . / quiescere coeperunt" (*Epistolario* 4:108; in *Opere* 2:911n6). References to the *Epistolario* (Correspondence), ed. Plinio Carli, Giovanni Gambarin, Francesco Tropeano, and Mario Scotti (1949–) are from vols. 14–23 of *Edizione nazionale delle opere di Ugo Foscolo*, 23 vols. (Florence: Le Monnier, 1933–).

3. For analysis of the debates about Machiavelli's relation to Fascist political thought and his reception during the *Ventennio*, see Michele Ciliberto, "Appunti per una storia della fortuna di Machiavelli in Italia: F. Ercole e L. Russo," *Studi storici* 10 (1969): 799–832. For interpretation of Petrarch's cult of ancient Rome—especially in his allegiance to Cola di Rienzo, a fourteenth-century politician who sought to restore ancient virtues but whose policies ultimately dissolved into murderous tyranny—see Foscolo, "On the Character of Petrarch"; *Opere* 2:618–19.

4. For consideration of Italy's masculine constructions in Fascist cinema, see Angela Dalle Vacche, *The Body in the Mirror: Shapes of History in Italian Cinema* (Princeton, NJ: Princeton University Press, 1992), 18–56.

5. Many lines of inquiry in this chapter are indebted to Millicent Marcus's "The Italian Body Politic Is a Woman: Feminized National Identity in Postwar Italian Film," in *Sparks and Seeds: Medieval Literature and Its Aftermath: Essays in Honor of John Freccero*, ed. Alison Cornish and Dana E. Stewart (Turnhout, Belg.: Brepols, 2000), 329–47. For a historical perspective on the matter, see Joan M. Ferrante, *Woman as Image in Medieval Literature: From the Twelfth Century to Dante* (New York: Columbia University Press, 1975).

6. Springer notes that Canova's figure of Italia mourning Alfieri's death was the first representation of the Italian nation in the monumental sculpture of the nineteenth century; and that, in recognition of his exemplary *italianità*, Alfieri was the first non-Tuscan to be allowed burial in Santa Croce (Carolyn Springer, *The Marble Wilderness: Ruins and Representation in Italian Romanticism, 1775–1850* [New York: Cambridge University Press, 1987], 187n36).

7. Cesare Ripa, *Iconologia* (Padua, 1611; New York: Garland, 1976), 179; see discussion in Marina Warner, *Monuments and Maidens: The Allegory of the Female Form* (New York: Atheneum, 1985), 65.

8. Representations of the Italian body politic as a woman are also found in the poetry of Gabriello Chiabrera, Vincenzo da Filicaia, and Vincenzo Monti.

9. Benedict Anderson, *Imagined Communities* (London: Verso, 1983).

10. For discussion of the notion of "Italy" inherited by Dante, see Giulio Vallese, "Dante e la canzone 'Italia mia' del Petrarca," *Le parole e le idee* 10 (1968): 3. See Ronald Syme, *The Roman Revolution* (1939; London: Oxford University Press, 1966), for discussion of the future Emperor Augustus's use of Italian identity to unite the Peninsula's landed gentry against Marc Antony—who, Augustus claimed, represented the interests of corrupt, "urban" Rome (276–93).

11. Dante Alighieri, *The Divine Comedy,* trans. with commentary Charles S. Singleton, 6 vols. (Princeton, NJ: Princeton University Press, 1970–75). Italian text based on *La commedia secondo l'antica vulgata,* ed. Giorgio Petrocchi, 4 vols. (Milan: Mondadori, 1966–67). Dante returns to the question of Italy's need for linguistic coherence in his philosophical summa, *Convivio* (c. 1304–7): see 1.10.5, 1.10.12, 1.11.1–2, 1.12.5, and 1.13.12. See also Filippo Brancucci, s.v. "Italia," *Enciclopedia dantesca,* dir. Umberto Bosco, 6 vols. (Rome: Istituto della Enciclopedia Italiana, 1970–78), 2:529–33. For a critique of the supposed coherence of the term *Italy,* see John Dickie, "The Notion of Italy," *The Cambridge Companion to Modern Italian Culture,* ed. Zygmunt G. Barański and Rebecca J. West (New York: Cambridge University Press, 2001), 17–33.

12. See Charles Till Davis, *Dante and the Idea of Rome* (Oxford: Clarendon, 1957), passim.

13. John Freccero, "Manfred's Wounds and the Poetics of *Purgatorio,*" *Dante,* ed. Harold Bloom (New York: Chelsea House, 1986), 139–49.

14. See Ernst Hartwig Kantorowicz, *The King's Two Bodies: A Study in Mediaeval Political Theology* (1957; Princeton, NJ: Princeton University Press, 1997); and Jacques Le Goff, "Head or Heart? The Political Use of Body Metaphors in the Middle Ages," trans. Patricia Ranum, *Fragments for a History of the Human Body,* ed. Michel Feher, Ramona Naddaff, and Nadia Tazi, 3 vols. (New York: Zone, 1989), 3:13–26, esp. 17.

15. For discussion of this topos, see Ernst Robert Curtius, *European Literature and the Latin Middle Ages,* trans. Willard R. Trask (Princeton, NJ: Princeton University Press, 1953), 180–82.

16. See Manfred's description of his grandmother in *Purg.* 3.112–13: "poi sorridendo disse: 'I son Manfredi, / nepote di Costanza imperadrice' " ("then [he] said smiling, 'I am Manfred, grandson of the Empress Constance' "). Manfred also mentions his daughter in 3.143 ("la mia buona Costanza").

17. For examination of Dante's use of ancient, especially Ciceronian, rhetoric in the passage, see Maurizio Perugi, "Canto VI," in *Purgatorio* (2001), *Lectura dantis turicensis,* ed. Georges Güntert and Michelangelo Picone, 3 vols. (Florence: Cesati, 2000–2002), 2:85–91.

18. For analysis of *Purg.* 6.76 ff. and its rhetorical complexities, see Zygmunt Barański, "*Purgatorio* VI," *Lectura dantis* 12 supp. (1993): 81–97; Teodolinda Barolini, *Dante's Poets: Textuality and Truth in the "Comedy"* (Princeton, NJ: Princeton University Press,

1984), 153–73; and Maurizio Perugi, "Il Sordello di Dante e la tradizione mediolatina dell'invettiva," *Studi danteschi* 55 (1983): 23–135. For bibliography on the canto, see Barański, "*Purgatorio* VI" 95n1; and Perugi, "Sordello di Dante" 23–28.

19. For a link between cannibalism and civil war in Dante, see John A. Scott, *Dante's Political Purgatory* (Philadelphia: University of Pennsylvania Press, 1996), 100–101. For evidence of the increasingly animalistic nature of Dante's allegorical *Italia*, see *Purg.* 6.91–96:

> Ahi genti che dovresti esser devota,
> e lasciar seder Caesar in la sella,
> se bene intendi ciò che Dio ti nota,
>   guarda come esta fiera è fatta fella
> per non esser corretta da li sproni,
> poi che ponesti mano a la predella.

(Ah, people that ought to be obedient and let Caesar sit in the saddle, if you rightly understand what God notes to you! See how this beast has grown vicious, through not being corrected by the spurs, since you did put your hand to the bridle!)

20. *The New Oxford Annotated Bible with the Apocrypha*, rev. standard ed., ed. Herbert Gordon May and Bruce Manning Metzger (New York: Oxford University Press, 1977).

21. Erich Auerbach, "Dante's Addresses to the Reader," *Romance Philology* 7 (1954): 275.

22. Two landmark studies of the Petrarchan historiographical moment are Theodore E. Mommsen, "Petrarch's Conception of the 'Dark Ages,'" *Speculum* 17 (1942): 226–42; and Franco Simone, "La coscienza della Rinascita negli Umanisiti," *La rinascita* 2 (1939): 838–71, and 3 (1940): 163–86. See also Giuseppe Mazzotta, *The Worlds of Petrarch* (Durham, NC: Duke University Press, 1993), 14–33: "For Petrarch [the term *Middle Ages*] designates the limits of vision—the limit of a culture that ignores the values of the classical world and that spans the time between the birth of Christ and his own age.... The decline of Rome and the concomitant eclipse of classical antiquity ... cast a thick shadow on man's earthly life" (17). For a reading of Petrarch's confrontation between medieval and classical worlds, see Thomas M. Greene, *The Light in Troy: Imitation and Discovery in Renaissance Poetry* (New Haven: Yale University Press, 1982), 28–53, esp. 36. For analysis of gender and the body in Petrarch, see Margaret Brose, "Petrarch's Beloved Body: 'Italia mia,'" *Feminist Approaches to the Body in Medieval Literature*, ed. Linda Lomperis and Sarah Stanbury (Philadelphia: University of Pennsylvania Press, 1993), 1–20; see especially her discussion of the male-female binary gender system in "All'Italia" (2) and Petrarch's attempt to revive "Roman virile laws and virtues" with his poem (9).

23. Freccero notes that Petrarch's poetry was fairly conservative vis-à-vis the techniques he inherited from the Middle Ages, and that he refined rather than recast such existing forms as the sonnet, sestina, Dantesque canzone, and lexicon and themes of the *dolce stil novo* ("The Fig Tree and the Laurel: Petrarch's Poetics," *Diacritics* 5 [1975]: 34–40). I discuss the Petrarchan watershed in the Italian tradition of literary self-representation in s.v. "Autobiography," *Encyclopedia of Italian Literary Studies*, 2 vols., ed. Gaetana Marrone (New York: Routledge, 2007), 1:107.

24. For the relationship between poetry and the medieval organization of knowledge, see Giuseppe Mazzotta, *Dante's Vision and the Circle of Knowledge* (Princeton, NJ: Princeton University Press, 1993), passim. See also Warren Ginsberg, *Dante's Aesthetics of Being* (Ann Arbor: University of Michigan Press, 1999).

25. See, for example, Dante's apostrophe in *Inf.* 9.61–63: "O voi ch'avete li 'ntelletti sani / mirate la dottrina che s'asconde / sotto 'l velame de li versi strani" (O you who have sound understanding, mark the doctrine that is hidden under the veil of the strange verses).

26. For a pioneering example of this critical subgenre of comparing Dante and Petrarch, see Ugo Foscolo, "A Parallel between Dante and Petrarch," *Opere* 2:633–60.

27. References are to Petrarch, *Petrarch's Lyric Poems: The "Rime sparse" and Other Lyrics,* trans. and ed. Robert Durling (Cambridge, MA: Harvard University Press, 1976). For analysis of Petrarch's relation to Dante, see Aldo Bernardo, "Petrarch's Attitude toward Dante," *PMLA* 70 (1955): 488–517; and Umberto Bosco, *Petrarca* (Turin: UTET, 1946), 259–62.

28. I am indebted to Ronald Martinez for bringing this to my attention.

29. See Vallese, "Dante e la canzone" 11.

30. Petrarch's alternately celebratory and guilty relationship with his poetic creations is the subject of his imaginary conversation with the ghost of St. Augustine in the *Secretum* (c. 1342–53). For a reading of Petrarch's potentially sacrilegious cult of Laura, see Robert M. Durling, "Petrarch's 'Giovene donna sotto un verde lauro,'" *Modern Language Notes* 86 (1971): 1–20.

31. For a rhetorical analysis of Petrarch's canzone alongside Leopardi's "All'Italia," see Carolyn Springer, "Petrarch and Leopardi: The Two Canzoni all'Italia," *Canadian Journal of Italian Studies* 10 (1987): 15–22. Springer notes: "Petrarch's verse form is fashioned to contain his argument: enjambments are rare; close end-of-line rhymes are used to reinforce syntactic relationships and aid transitions; . . . the stanzas even resemble paragraphs in that each seems to develop a discrete argument" (17).

32. "Latin sangue gentile: / sgombra da te queste dannose some, / non far idolo un nome, / vano, senza oggetto; / ché 'l furor de lassù, gente ritrosa, / vincerne d'intelletto / peccato è nostro, et non natural cosa" (Noble Latin blood: throw off these harmful burdens, do not make an idol of an empty name; it is on account of our own sins, and not a natural thing, that the slow northerners should conquer us in intellect) (74–80).

33. See Foscolo, "Parallel" 2:645–46: "Petrarch makes us see every thing through the medium of one predominant passion, habituates us to indulge in those propensities which by keeping the heart in perpetual disquietude, paralize intellectual exertion—entice us into a morbid indulgence of our feelings, and withdraw us from active life."

34. See *Babylon on the Rhone: A Translation of Letters by Dante, Petrarch, and Catherine of Siena on the Avignon Papacy,* ed. and trans. Robert Coogan (Madrid: Turanzas, 1983).

35. For a discussion of the dialectic between politics and literature in an early composition by Machiavelli, see Stefano Ugo Baldassarri,"Costanti del pensiero machiavelliano nel *Decennale* 1 e nel 'Capitolo di Fortuna,'" *Italian Quarterly* 33 (1996): 17–28. For a recent anthology that combines political and literary analysis, see Albert Russell Ascoli and Victoria Ann Kahn, eds., *Machiavelli and the Discourse of Literature* (Ithaca, NY: Cornell University Press, 1993).

36. On Machiavelli's political caginess, see Susan Behuniak-Long, "The Elusive Machiavelli," *Review of Politics* 52 (1990): 318–19.

37. For a general study of Machiavelli's body politic, see Hanna Fenichel Pitkin, *Fortune Is a Woman: Gender and Politics in the Thought of Niccolò Machiavelli* (Berkeley and Los Angeles: University of California Press, 1984). For Machiavelli's preoccupation with spectacle, see *Principe* 21: "Debbe . . . tenere occupati e populi con le feste e spettaculi. E perché ogni città è divisa in arte o in tribù, debbe tenere conto di quelle università, raunarsi con loro qualche volta" (*Principe* 74). ([The prince] should . . . entertain his people with festivals and spectacles. And because every city is divided into professional guilds and family groupings, he should be inward with these people, and attend their gatherings from time to time [*Prince* 63].) References to the text are from Niccolò Macchiavelli, *Opere*, ed. Mario Bonfantini (Milan: Ricciardi, 1954); *The Prince*, ed. and trans. Robert M. Adams, 2nd ed. (New York: Norton, 1992). For discussion of Machiavelli's acceptance—compared with Dante's rejection—of ambition, desire, and fraud, see Joseph Anthony Mazzeo, *Renaissance and Seventeenth-Century Studies* (New York: Columbia University Press, 1964), 90–91.

38. For discussion of the ancient political dichotomy *fortuna-virtù*, see J. G. A. Pocock's magisterial *Machiavellian Moment: Florentine Political Thought and the Atlantic Republican Tradition* (Princeton, NJ: Princeton University Press, 1975), 31–48. See especially Pocock's notion that the *fortuna-virtù* opposition was often expressed "in the image of a sexual relation: a masculine active intelligence was seeking to dominate a feminine passive unpredictability which would submissively reward him for his strength or vindictively betray him for his weakness" (37). See also Felix Gilbert, "On Machiavelli's Idea of Virtù," *Renaissance News* 4 (1951): 53–55; and Thomas M. Greene, "The End of Discourse in Machiavelli's *Prince*," *Yale French Studies* 67 (1984): 57–71. Cary J. Nederman points out that the complex classical and medieval sources for *fortuna* available to Machiavelli included Dante's Christian image of Fortune as a "quasi-autonomous force working in concert with the divine plan yet not simply reducible to God's will" ("Amazing Grace: Fortune, God, and Free Will in Machiavelli's Thought," *Journal of the History of Ideas* 60 [1999]: 626).

39. For discussion of Machiavelli's critique of Petrarch's politics, see Emanuela Scarpa, "Machiavelli e la 'neutralità' di Francesco Petrarca," *Lettere italiane* 27 (1975): 263–85. For further analysis of the anti-Petrarchan line in Machiavelli, see A. E. Quaglio, "Dante e Machiavelli," *Cultura e scuola* 9 (1970): 160–73, esp. 173.

40. See Machiavelli's *Discorsi sopra la prima deca di Tito Livio* 1.37 (1531): "La natura ha creato gli uomini in modo che possono desiderare ogni cosa e non possono conseguire ogni cosa: talché essendo sempre maggiore il desiderio che la potenza dello acquistare, ne risulta la mala contentezza di quello che si possiede, e la poca sodisfazione d'esso" (*Discorsi* 170). (Nature has created men so that they desire everything, but are unable to attain it; desire being thus always greater than the faculty of acquiring, discontent with what they have and dissatisfaction with themselves result from it [*Discourses* 208].) References to the text are in *Opere*; and the translation of Christian E. Detmold in *The Prince and the Discourses* (1940; New York: Modern Library, 1950).

41. See Petrarch, canzone 128.28–30: "O diluvio raccolto / di che deserti strani / per inondar i nostri dolci campi!" (Oh deluge gathered in what strange wilderness to overflow our sweet fields!); and Dante, *Inf.* 15.4–6, 10: "Quali Fiamminghi tra Guizzante e

Bruggia, / temendo 'l fiotto che 'nevr' lor s'avventa, / fanno lo schermo perché 'l mar si fuggia; / . . . a tale imagine eran fatti quelli" (As the Flemings between Wissant and Bruges, fearing the tide that rushes in on them, make the bulwark to drive back the sea; . . . in like fashion were these banks [in hell] made). For Machiavelli's naturalizing of political metaphors, see Charles D. Tarlton, "Fortuna and the Landscape of Action in Machiavelli's *Prince*," *New Literary History* 30 (1999): 737–55.

42. Ezio Raimondi describes the relationship *fortuna-virtù* in terms of a sexual conflict permeated with sadistic and masochistic rhetoric (introduction to Niccolò Machiavelli, *Opere*, 2nd ed. [Milan: Mursia, 1966], xix).

43. Brose notes that Machiavelli was "aware of Petrarch's ambivalent political stance," and that the ironies of his citation would not have been lost on his readers ("Beloved Body" 7).

44. Vittorio Alfieri, *Del principe e delle lettere*, ed. Pietro Cazzani (1951); vol. 1 of *Scritti politici e morali*, vols. 3–5 of *Opere*, 40 vols. (Asti: Casa d'Alfieri, 1951–) (abbrev. "*Opera omnia*"); *The Prince and Letters*, ed. Beatrice Corrigan, trans. Beatrice Corrigan and Julius A. Molinaro (Toronto: University of Toronto Press, 1972).

45. Vittorio Alfieri, *Rime*, ed. Francesco Maggini (1954), *Opera omnia* 9:52.

46. The poem, in biographical terms, refers to a hiatus in Alfieri's love affair with Louisa of Stolberg during her divorce proceedings with Stuart.

47. The sole study I have found on the subject is David Castronuovo, "The Apostrophic Prayer: A Guiding Figure in Leopardi's Earliest Poetry," *Romance Languages Annual* 10 (1998): 216–24. Two general treatments of apostrophe are Jonathan Culler, "Apostrophe," *Diacritics* 7 (1977): 59–69; and, for a conflicting view, J. Douglas Kneale, "Romantic Aversions: Apostrophe Reconsidered," *ELH* 58 (1991): 141–65.

48. See the gloss to canzone 128 in Petrarch, *Le rime*, ed. Giacomo Leopardi, 3rd ed. (Firenze: Le Monnier, 1851):

> Ma non è meraviglia che l'Italia non abbia lirica, non avendo l'eloquenza, la quale è necessaria alla lirica a segno che se alcuno m'interrogasse qual composizione mi paia la più eloquente fra le italiane, risponderei senza indugiare, le sole composizioni liriche italiane che si meritino questo nome, cioè le tre Canzoni del Petrarca, "O aspettata," "Spirto gentil," "Italia mia."

> (But it is no wonder that Italy lacks a lyric tradition, for it lacks eloquence, which is so necessary for lyric that if someone were to ask me what I thought were the most eloquent works in Italian literature, I would answer without hesitation that there are only three Italian works that merit this designation: Petrarch's three canzoni, "O aspettata," "Spirto gentil," and [canzone 128] "Italia mia.")

49. Walter Binni, preface to *La nuova poetica leopardiana*, 3rd ed. (Florence: Sansoni, 1979), xiv–xvi.

50. References to Leopardi's poetry are from the *Canti*, in vol. 1 of *Opere*, ed. Sergio and Raffaella Solmi, 2 vols. (Milan: Ricciardi, 1956); unless otherwise indicated, translations are from *Leopardi: Selected Poems*, trans. Eamon Grennan (Princeton, NJ: Princeton University Press, 1997).

51. Translations of the poem are from Ray Fleming, "Leopardi's 'All'Italia' and 'Sopra

il monumento di Dante': A Translation," *Canadian Journal of Italian Studies* 2 (1979): 149–52.

52. Giacomo Leopardi, *Zibaldone di pensieri: Edizione critica e annotata*, ed. Giuseppe Pacella, 3 vols. (Milan: Garzanti, 1991).

53. For a discussion of Leopardi's Alfierian lexical choices *vile* and *feroce* in "All'Italia" 45, see Luigi Russo, *Ritratti e disegni storici: Serie terza, dall'Alfieri al Leopardi*, 3rd ed. (Florence: Sansoni, 1963), 227.

54. Compare Petrarch, "All'Italia": "Is not this the ground that I touched first? Is not this my nest, where I was so sweetly nourished? Is not this my fatherland in which I trust, and my kind and merciful mother, which covers both of my parents?" (81–86).

55. See Springer for an examination of the differences in intended audience, rhetorical register, and ancient sources in "Italia mia" and "All'Italia" ("Petrarch and Leopardi" 15–20).

56. Ibid.

57. See *Zibaldone* August 26, 1821: "La virtù, l'eroismo, la grandezza d'animo non può trovarsi in grado eminente, splendido e capace di giovare al pubblico, se non che in uno stato popolare, o dove la nazione è partecipe del potere" (*Zibaldone* 1:924). (Virtue, heroism, and greatness of spirit can only express itself with eminence, splendor, and public appeal if it does so either in a popular forum or in a nation whose people are empowered.)

58. In a letter from February 25, 1828, Leopardi asks Viesseux to send him a recent edition of Foscolo's poetry and prose; a later correspondence (January 21, 1832) expresses Leopardi's interest in consulting a new biography on Foscolo. More important, Leopardi included lines 1–90 and 213–95 from Foscolo's "Dei sepolcri," as well as his odes "A Luigia Pallavicini caduta da cavallo" and "All'amica risanata," in his anthology of selected works of Italian literary masterpieces, *Crestomazia italiana poetica* (Milan: Stella, 1828). See *Leopardi nel carteggio Viesseux: Opinioni e giudizi dei contemporanei, 1823–1837*, ed. Elisabetta Benucci, Laura Melosi, and Daniela Pulci (Florence: Olschki, 2001), lx, 101, 267n, 483n, 532n, 596n, 600, 620. For the presence of Foscolo's poetry in Leopardi, see Lucia Pagano, "Di alcuni influssi foscoliani nelle tre canzoni patriottiche di Giacomo Leopardi," *Rassegna nazionale* 5 (September 16, 1917): 126–35; Binni, *Poetica leopardiana* xvii; Giovanni Getto, *Saggi leopardiani*, 2nd ed. (Messina: D'Anna, 1977), 59; and Gian-Paolo Biasin, *Italian Literary Icons* (Princeton, NJ: Princeton University Press, 1985), 38–42. Among more recent critics, Vittoriano Esposito ("Rilettura delle canzoni patriottiche: 'All'Italia' e 'Sopra il monumento di Dante,'" *Rivista di sudi italiani* 16 [1998]: 234–42) comes close to suggesting the presence of "Dei sepolcri" in "All'Italia," but he limits himself to grouping Foscolo along with Alfieri and Monti as a generic influence on Leopardi's civic voice.

59. Ugo Foscolo, "Dei sepolcri," ed. Franco Longoni, in *Opere*, 2 vols., ed. Franco Gavezzeni (Turin: Einaudi-Gallimard, 1994–95), 1:21–38; "Ugo Foscolo: *Sepulchers*," trans. Peter Burian, *Literary Imagination* 4 (2002): 17–30 (references are to this translation unless otherwise indicated). I also use the translation, with useful analysis (see 47–61), by Karl Kroeber, *The Artifice of Reality: Poetic Style in Wordsworth, Foscolo, Keats, and Leopardi* (Madison: University of Wisconsin Press, 1964), 179–83.

60. See *Zibaldone*, February 1, 1829: "Tutti, cominciando dal Pindemonte, . . . hanno

biasimato l'introduzione di Ettore e delle cose troiane nel Carme dei Sepolcri; e tutti leggono quell'episodio con grande interesse, e segretamente vi provano un vero piacere. Certo, quell'argomento è rancido; ma appunto perch'egli è rancido, perchè la nostra *acquaintance* con quei personaggi dáta dalla nostra fanciullezza, essi c'interessano sommamente, c'interessano in modo, che non sarebbe possibile, sostituendone degli altri, produrre altrettanto effetto" (2:2527). (Everyone, beginning with Pindemonte, ... has complained of the introduction of Hector and the Trojan references in the poem "Dei sepolcri." Yet everyone reads that episode with great interest and secretly takes true pleasure in it. The argument is certainly raw, but it is so precisely because our acquaintance with those characters dates from our childhood—and so it interests us profoundly and in a way that it would have been impossible to achieve by substituting some other effect.)

61. See Getto, *Saggi leopardiani* 39: "Ma il sentimento politico, sia nel discorso sia nella canzone, rimane piuttosto generico e privo di quella concretezza storica propria della poesia patriottica manzoniana." (But the political sentiment, whether in argument or in the poetry [of "All'Italia"], remains rather generic and devoid of that historical concreteness typical of the patriotic poetry of Manzoni.)

62. See Binni, *Poetica leopardiana* 180n.

Chapter 8. The Body of Parini

1. Robert Pogue Harrison, *The Body of Beatrice* (Baltimore: Johns Hopkins University Press, 1988), 142.

2. Dylan Thomas, *Collected Poems, 1934–1952* (1952; London: Dent, 1953), 101.

3. A recent gender-inflected reading of Foscolo is Margaret Brose, "Back to the Body of the Mother: Foscolo's 'A Zacinto,'" *Italica* 74 (1997): 164–84.

4. Ugo Foscolo, *Ultime lettere di Jacopo Ortis*, ed. Maria Antonietta Terzoli, *Opere*, ed, Franco Gavezzeni, 2 vols. (Turin: Einaudi-Gallimard, 1994–95), 2:3–140; *Last Letters of Jacopo Ortis; and, Of Tombs*, trans. J. G. Nichols (London: Hesperus: 2002).

5. For a description of the Christological associations of Teresa, see Maria Antonietta Terzoli, *Il libro di Jacopo: Scrittura sacra nell' "Ortis"* (Rome: Salerno, 1988), 237–48.

6. See Frederick May, "The Hughes-Foscolo Translation from Petrarch," *Amor di libro* 11 (1963): 25–30, 97–101, 139–43.

7. See Tom O'Neill, "The Figure of Alfieri in 'Dei sepolcri,'" *Italica* 55 (1978): 321–37.

8. See Ortis to Lorenzo, March 5, 1799, 11 P.M.: "Lo seppi: Teresa è maritata. Tu taci per non darmi la vera ferita—ma l'infermo geme quando la morte il combatte, non quando lo ha vinto." (I know. Teresa is married. You stay silent, not wishing to inflict on me the final wound, but the man who is ill groans while death is attacking him, not when death has conquered him.) Lorenzo glosses his friend's letter by remarking: "apparisce che Jacopo decretò in quel dí di morire" (it appears that on that day Jacopo decided to die) (*Ultime lettere* 115; *Last Letters* 114).

9. For Foscolo's relation to Parini, see Dante Isella, "Foscolo e l'eredità pariniana," *Lezioni sul Foscolo*, ed. Marino Berengo (Florence: La Nuova Italia, 1981), 21–41.

10. Baretti praises Parini's poetry in *An Account of the Manners and Customs of Italy* (1768); in his correspondence with his brother Pietro, Alessandro Verri tags Parini an "animale" and "canaglia" (animal and riff-raff) (in Lanfranco Caretti, ed., *Parini e la critica: Storia e antologia della critica*, 2nd ed., rev. and enl. [Florence: La Nuova Italia, 1970], 8–9). Alfieri's view of Parini contains a similar aristocratic bias; later in his life, Pietro Verri's opinion on Parini changed to a positive appraisal of his virtue. In Ottocento criticism, Pietro Giordani compares Parini to Dante; other authors who focused on Parini's *italianità* include Giovanni Berchet, Vincenzo Gioberti, and Giuseppe Giusti. Leopardi had little patience for Parini's verse, but found his character admirable enough to inspire one of the more autobiographical of the *Operette morali*, "Il Parini, ovvero della gloria," a meditation on the writer's uneasy position in society and the fragility of literary glory (*Operette morali: Essays and Dialogues*, ed. and trans. Giovanni Cecchetti [Berkeley and Los Angeles: University of California Press, 1982], 200–269). The apotheosis of the biographical reading of Parini was De Sanctis's representative view that Parini the man was worthier than Parini the artist: "La sua forza è più morale che intellettuale" (*Letteratura italiana* 789). (His strength lay more in morality than in intellect [*Italian Literature* 2:882].) Francesco De Sanctis, *Storia della letteratura italiana*, ed. Gianfranco Contini (Milan: TEA, 1989) (abbrev. "*Letteratura italiana*"); *History of Italian Literature*, trans. Joan Redfern, 2 vols. (New York: Basic, 1959) (abbrev. "*Italian Literature*"). A similar sentiment appears in Croce: "È stato talvolta segnato l'inizio della nuova letteratura italiana nel Parini; ma il Parini è di mente e d'animo uomo del Settecento, del periodo razionalistico e delle riforme; e settecentesca sebbene elegantissima è l'arte didascalica e ironica nei suoi toni maggiori, erotica e gallante nei minori." (It has been occasionally argued that the new Italian literature began with Parini. But Parini is in mind and spirit a man of the eighteenth century, of the period of rationality and reform; and eighteenth-century art, however elegant, is didactic and ironic in its major expressions and erotic and gallant in its minor ones.) Benedetto Croce, *Poesia e non-poesia; note sulla letteratura europea del secolo decimonono* (Bari: Laterza, 1923), 7. For a revision of such biographical readings and promotion of Parini's formal innovations—a view shared by an early admirer of Parini's poetry, Manzoni—see Ettore Bonora, *Parini e altro Settecento: Fra classicismo e illuminismo* (Milan: Feltrinelli, 1982).

11. In Caretti, *Parini* 98; for Reina's detailed portrait of Parini, see his "Vita di Giuseppe Parini," in Giuseppe Parini, *Dalle opere di Giuseppe Parini*, ed. Francesco Reina, 6 vols. (Milan: 1801–4), 1:v–lxvi. Subscribers to Reina's edition included Alfieri, Napoleon Bonaparte, Foscolo, Manzoni, and Monti (see Caretti, *Parini* 18n2). For a dramatic example of Parini's transfiguration, see Giuseppe De Marini, *Lo spirito dell'abate Parini accolto all'altro mondo dall'ombra dell'abate Pietro Metastasio* . . . (1799), in which Metastasio receives the spirit of Parini in the Elysian fields and presents him to such illustrious shades as Ariosto, Dante, Petrarch, Tasso, and Tassoni.

12. For Foscolo's long-standing antipathy for Milan, see his letter of February 5, 1817, to the Countess of Albany (Louisa of Stolberg): "Questo paese col suo clima, con le sue fisionomie, col suo gergo mi dà noja micidiale, mi adira, mi attrista in tutti i pensieri, mi snerva tutte le fibbre" (Ugo Foscolo, *Epistolario* [Correspondence], ed. Plinio Carli, Giovanni Gambarin, Francesco Tropeano, and Mario Scotti [1949–]; vols. 14–23 of *Edizione nazionale delle opere di Ugo Foscolo*, 23 vols. [Florence: Le Monnier, 1933–],

5:38). (This city [Milan] with its climate, its physiognomies, and dialect gives me a mortal ennui, angers me, saddens all of my thoughts, and enervates me to the very fiber.)

13. Cocceius Nerva was a Roman patrician and close associate of the Emperor Tiberius who, in the manner of Ortis's role model Cato, took his life in protest against the corruption of the Roman state (see Tacitus, *Annals* 6.26).

14. Ugo Foscolo, "Dei sepolcri," ed. Franco Longoni, *Opere* 1:21–38; "Ugo Foscolo: Sepulchers," trans. Peter Burian, *Literary Imagination* 4 (2002): 17–30 (references are to this translation unless otherwise indicated). I also use the translation, with useful analysis (see 47–61), by Karl Kroeber, *The Artifice of Reality: Poetic Style in Wordsworth, Foscolo, Keats, and Leopardi* (Madison: University of Wisconsin, 1964), 179–83.

15. "Dal dí che nozze e tribunali ed are / Dier alle umane belve esser pietose / Di sè stesse e d'altrui, toglieano i vivi / All'etere maligno ed alle fere / I miserandi avanzi che Natura / Con veci eterne a sensi altri destina" ("Sepolcri" 91–96). (Ever since marriage, and courts of law, / and the altar taught us human beasts / to be kind to ourselves and to one another, / the living have snatched from predator's jaws / and the ravages of weather / the poor remains that Nature assigns to her cycle of change ["Sepulchers" 93–98]).

16. William Shakespeare, *King Lear*, in *The Works of William Shakespeare*, ed. William George Clark and William Aldis Wright (London: Macmillan, 1938), 3.2.1–7.

17. Ugo Foscolo, *Lettere scritte dall'Inghilterra*, ed. Elena Lombardi, *Opere* 2:447–502.

18. See Bacon's "Of Truth," and his statement that "A mixture of a lie doth ever add pleasure" (Francis Bacon, *Bacon's Essays*, ed. Richard Whately and Franklin Fiske Heard [Boston: Lee and Shepard, 1884], 2).

19. In *Conv.* 1.9.5, Dante uses the word *litteratura* to designate those Latin works of high aesthetic quality whose exploitation for profit or honors ("denari o dignitate") by avaricious writers resulted in the prostitution of classical letters (1.9.3). Dante, *Il convivio ridotto a miglior lezione e commentato,* ed. Giovanni Busnelli and Giuseppe Vandelli, 2nd ed., 2 vols. (Florence: Le Monnier, 1954).

20. The *Essay*—which first appeared in the London edition of Hobhouse's *Historical Illustrations of the Fourth Canto of "Childe Harold": Containing Dissertations on the Ruins of Rome; and an Essay on Italian Literature* (New York: Gilley, 1818)—is in Foscolo, *Opere* 2:1395–562.

21. The *Essay* also contains a passage (2:1451–52) similar to the aforementioned description of Leopold II's sighting of the handicapped, persecuted Parini in *Lettere scritte dall'Inghilterra* (476).

22. For Foscolo's many writings incorporating the Didimo Chierico persona—including his playful portrait "Notizia intorno a Didimo Chierico," the fictitious translator of *Viaggio sentimentale* (see chapter 7, note 2, above); and *Didymi clerici prophetae mimini hypercalypseos liber singularis* (1816), a satire of the Milanese elite written in biblical Latin—see the anthology Foscolo, *Didimo Chierico, profeta minimo,* ed. Sebastiano Aglianò (Milan: Bompiano, 1945).

23. Patriotic reactions to Foscolo's death in England were immediate. See, for example, John Watson Dalby's connection of Foscolo's life to the cause of Italian freedom in "To the Memory of Ugo Foscolo," *Robin's New and Improved Series of Arliss's Magazine* 11

(1827): 285–87. See also the obituary on Foscolo in the *Liverpool Commerical Chronicle*, September 22, 1827.

24. See Ugo Foscolo, *Dalle "Grazie,"* ed. Franco Longoni, *Opere* 1:113–68.

Epilogue

1. "Oftmals hab ich auch schon in ihren Armen gedichtet / Und des Hexameters Maß leise mit fingernder Hand / Ihr auf den Rücken gezählt." (Often I even compose my poetry in her embraces, / Counting hexameter beats, tapping them out on her back / Softly, with one hand's fingers.) Johann Wolfgang von Goethe, *Roman Elegies, and the Diary*, trans. David Luke (London: Libris, 1988), 7.149–51.

2. E. M. Forster, *A Room with a View*, ed. Malcolm Bradbury (New York: Penguin, 2000), 39–42.

3. See Gérard Genette, *Palimpsests: Literature in the Second Degree*, trans. Channa Newman and Claude Doubinsky (Lincoln: University of Nebraska Press, 1997), 3.

4. Naomi Schor describes this epitaphic quality of Corinne as an allegory for feminist criticism, in "Depression in the Nineties," *Bad Objects: Essays Popular and Unpopular* (Durham, NC: Duke University Press, 1995), 161–63. See also Jean Starobinski, "Suicide et mélancolie chez Mme de Staël," *Madame de Staël et l'Europe: Colloque de Coppet* (Paris: Klincksieck, 1970), 246.

5. Anne Louise Germaine de Staël, *Corinne, ou l'Italie;* vol. 1 of *Œuvres complètes de Madame la baronne de Staël-Holstein* (Paris: Didot, 1871) (abbrev. "*Œuvres*"); *Corinne, or Italy*, trans. Sylvia Raphael (New York: Oxford University Press, 1998) (abbrev. "*Corinne, Italy*").

6. Maddalena Pennachia Punzi notes that de Staël draws on the biographies of many other illustrious women, including Sappho and Cleopatra, in her allegorical representation of Corinne (*Il mito di Corinne: Viaggio in Italia e genio femminile in Anna Jameson, Margaret Fuller e George Eliot* [Rome: Carocci, 2001], 33). See also Joan E. Dejean, "De Staël's *Corinne*: The Novel's Other Dilemma," *Stanford French Review* 11 (1987): 77–87, and *Fictions of Sappho, 1546–1937* (Chicago: University of Chicago Press, 1989), 167 ff.

7. See 2.1: "Dans l'état actuel des Italiens, la gloire des beaux-arts est l'unique qui leur soit permise; et ils sentent le génie en ce genre avec une vivacité qui devrait faire naître beaucoup de grands hommes, s'il suffisait de l'applaudissement pour les produire, s'il ne fallait pas une vie forte, de grands intérêts et une existence indépendante, pour alimenter la pensée" ("In their present state, the only glory permitted to the Italians is that of the arts. They appreciate this kind of genius with a keenness which would give birth to many great men if acclaim would produce them, if strength of purpose, great interests, and an independent existence were essential food for thought") (*Œuvres* 662; *Corinne, Italy* 20).

8. See the aforementioned lines from Petrarch, canzone 128.1–2, 4–5: "Italia mia, ben che 'l parlar sia indarno / a le piaghe mortali / . . . piacemi almen che' miei sospir sian quali / spera 'l Tevero et l'Arno." (My Italy, although speech does not aid those mortal wounds, . . . I wish at least my sighs to be such as Tiber and Arno hope for.) Petrarch, *Petrarch's Lyric Poems: The "Rime Sparse" and Other Lyrics*, trans. and ed. Robert

Durling (Cambridge, MA: Harvard University Press, 1976). Compare Castel-Forte's admission that Italians could follow Corinne's footsteps and "se créer un monde" (make a world for themselves), "si notre génie . . . pouvait s'allumer toute entier au seul flambeau de la poésie" (if the fire of our [Italian] genius . . . could be fully set alight by the torch of poetry alone) (2.2; *Œuvres* 665; *Corinne, Italy* 27).

9. Paul Fussell, *Abroad: British Literary Traveling between the Wars* (New York: Oxford University Press, 1980), 39. The basis of my distinction between the itineraries of Goethe and Lucy Honeychurch derives from Buzard, who explores the cultural implications of the modern opposition between "travel" (with its associations of authentic, individual experience) and the more commodified, generic qualities linked to tourism (*Beaten Track* 18).

Index

The index does not include the names of historical figures and events as they appear in fictionalized literary accounts (e.g., Virgil as character in Dante's *Commedia* and Saverio Bettinelli's *Lettere virgilianae* is not indexed, whereas Virgil as author of the *Aeneid* is). I omit references to complete works, collected correspondence, and other larger texts when indexing their self-contained individual units (e.g., Dante's *Commedia* does not appear in the index, whereas its individual *cantiche*, *Inferno*, *Purgatorio*, and *Paradiso*, do). The index does not include the names of authors, texts, or historical figures and events cited in the notes, but it does indicate thematic references to the notes (e.g., "Alfieri, Vittorio: autobiography in, 250n27").

Abelard, Peter, 100
Abrams, M. H., 19, 82, 158
Addison, Joseph, 80–81, 142
Akenside, Marc, 108
Alfieri, Vittorio: on Ariosto, 138, 266n30; autobiography in, 103, 127–28, 137–40, 250n27, 265n28; on Boccaccio, 87; Canova's statue of, 165–66; on Dante, 87, 125–26, 128, 130–32, 134–40, 174, 185–86, 191, 202, 262n10, 265n22, 266nn30–31; Dante, in library, 136, 263n9; Dante, sonnets to, 134, 169, 185–86; Enlightenment, critique of, 125–26, 129–32, 134–35, 137; exile of, 15, 129; in Florence, 88; Foscolo, influence on, 140, 199–200, 204, 211; Foscolo's representation of, 8, 192, 262–63n7; on French culture, 85–86, 89–90, 126, 137, 199; de-Frenchification and Italianization of, 87–89, 93; Goethe, compared to, 90; heroism, defense of, 131; Italian body politic in, 184–86; and Leopardi, 187, 190; *libero scrittore*, notion of, 84, 88,

Alfieri, Vittorio (*continued*)
93, 132–35, 147, 209; Machiavelli's influence on, 184; patriotic reputation of, 30, 230n22; on Milton, 130; on Petrarch, 87, 138, 266n30; and Rousseau, 262n6; solitary nature of, 262–63n7; Staël's representation of, 89–90; on Tasso, 138, 266n30; *tramelogedia* in, 126, 139; Tuscanization of, 88, 251nn32–33; Voltaire's influence on, 86, 88–89, 124–25, 129

Alfieri, Vittorio, works of: *Del principe e delle lettere*, 124–26, 128–32, 137–39, 184–86, 202, 209; *Della tirannide*, 129, 200; *Esquisse du jugement universel*, 126–28; *Estratto di Dante*, 126; *Etruria vendicata*, 129; *Giornali*, 86; *Il misogallo*, 126; *Ugolino*, 126, 139; *Vita*, 86–90, 126, 128, 136–140

Algarotti, Francesco, 109
Alitalia, 1
Anderson, Benedict, 5, 37, 169, 193
Antologia, 28
Archimedes, 144
Aretino, Pietro, 74, 196
Arezzo, Guittone d', 171
Ariosto, Ludovico: Alfieri's view of, 138; in Isola's edition, 143; as model, 109; in Staël, 215; in Voltaire, 119, 122
Aroux, Eugène, 102
Auerbach, Erich, 19, 29, 102, 173
Augustine, Saint, 100
Austria, 28, 150, 200
Avignon, 179

Bacon, Francis, 209
Balfour, Ian, 19
Baretti, Giuseppe: censorship of, 129; on Dante and Voltaire, 107–9, 257n17, 258n27, 270–71n31; on Parini, 201, 281n10
Bayle, Pierre, 106–7
Bazin, André, 49–50, 52
Beccaria, Cesare, 28
Belli, Giuseppe Gioachino, 19

Berchet, Giovanni, 28, 55
Berti, Antonio, 163–64
Bettinelli, Saverio: on Alfieri, 137, 266n31; Dante, critique of, 109–12, 263n10; enthusiasm in the arts, notion of, 136–37; and Voltaire, 109, 112, 136, 258n24
Biblioteca italiana, 28
Binni, Walter, 18, 188
Bloom, Harold, 19, 82
Boccaccio, Giovanni: in Alfieri, 87; in Byron, 56; as Dante's biographer, 98, 110, 136; in Staël, 74; in Wordsworth, 154
Boethius, 100, 169
Boileau-Despréaux, Nicolas, 106–7
Borgese, Giuseppe Antonio, 18, 29, 37
Borgia, Cesare, 182
Borsieri, Pietro, 28
Breme, Ludovico di, 28
Britain: in comparative literary studies, 19; cult of sensibility in, 109; Dante's popularity in, 150, 266–67n2; and France, 150, 256n6; freedom of the press in, 128; Italy, contrast to, 66–71, 76, 244nn49–51; in Keats's poetry, 82; national identity of, 150; public law and order in, 66, 69–70, 243n42
Brose, Margaret, 18
Browning, Elizabeth Barrett, 76
Browning, Robert, 76
Bruni, Leonardo, 24, 196
Buffon, 85
Burckhardt, Jacob, 100
Burke, Edmund, 137
Butler, Marilyn, 35, 83
Byron: *Childe Harold's Pilgrimage*, 13, 56, 59; on Dante, 102, 142; in Hawthorne, 13; on Italian Catholic poetry, 239n13; on Italy, 16, 57, 225n19; popularity of, 65; on Wordsworth, 146

Caesar, Julius, 169, 203
Il caffè, 28, 85

Index   287

Cambon, Glauco, 6, 18
Canova, Antonio, 165–67, 190
Capponi, Gino, 28
Carducci, Giosuè, 29, 187
Carlyle, Thomas, 98–99
Carpani, Palamede, 203
Cary, Henry Francis, 98, 148, 152, 154
Cassiodorus, 169
Cato: Foscolo's myth of, 203–4, 211, 234n42, 282n13; in Lucan, 38
Charlotte, Queen, 57
Chateaubriand, François-René de: Dante in, 102; in Italy, 13; Manzoni's critique of, 235–36n56; religion of, 35; on Rome, 250n22
Châtelet, Émilie du: death of, 117, 119, 261n41; and Voltaire, 106, 115, 260n40
Ciccarelli, Andrea, 18, 83
Cicero, 30, 174, 190
Colbert, Jean-Baptiste, 108
Coleridge, Samuel Taylor: on Dante, 142, 147–48, 152, 154, 158; religion of, 35; and Wordsworth, 148, 153–54
comparative literature, 18–19
Il conciliatore, 28, 55
Condillac, Étienne Bonnet de, 116–17, 120
Conti, Antonio, 203
Corneille, Pierre, 88, 106, 150
Crane, Hart, 12
Croce, Benedetto: on Dante, 99–100; and De Sanctis, 3, 29, 37; on Italian Romanticism, 29, 229n14; on Leopardi, 187; metaphysics in, 42; on Parini, 281n10
Curran, Stuart, 83

Dante: aesthetics, notion of, 173–74, 257n15; apostrophe in, 169, 173, 276n25; autobiography in, 99–100; in Bettinelli, 110–12; biographies or *vite* of, 98, 125, 135–36; Britain, reception in, 141, 266–67n2, 268n12; in Byron, 56; in Coleridge, 148; Europe, reception in, 125, 255n1; exile from Florence, 98; Foscolo, influence on, 7, 9–11, 102, 174, 200, 219–20; in Foscolo's "Dei sepolcri," 8; Germany, reception in, 125, 262n4; in Hazlitt, 146–8, 270n31; Italian body politic in, 16, 171–73, 176–77, 180, 186, 203, 275n19; Italy, reception in, 109, 125; literature, definition of, 282n19; and Milton, 98, 263n2; providential imagination of, 41; publication history of, 103, 125, 254n14, 257–58n19, 262nn2–3, 262n5; rating of, 257n12; Rome, notion of, 169; in Schelling, 148; in Shelley, 149; in Staël, 216, 271n37; and Tuscan vernacular, 87; Wordsworth, compared to, 143–44, 270n23, 271–72n41; in Vico, 73
Dante, works of: *Convivio*, 2; *De vulgari eloquentia*, 99, 143, 169; *Inferno*, 108, 126, 159, 170, 262n4; *Inf.* 1: 47, 108; *Inf.* 2: 155; *Inf.* 4: 110–11; *Inf.* 5: 173, 200; *Inf.* 15: 98–99, 182–83; *Inf.* 26: 13, 110, 172; *Inf.* 27: 170; *Inf.* 32: 126, 139, 172; *Inf.* 33: 109, 126, 139, 169, 173; *Monarchia*, 99; *Paradiso*, 98, 102; *Par.* 17: 3, 9–11, 220; *Par.* 33: 101, 156–58, 174; *Purgatorio*, 98, 102; *Purg.* 1: 9; *Purg.* 3: 154, 170; *Purg.* 5: 170–71; *Purg.* 6: 169, 171–73, 175, 179, 183–84, 189; *Vita nuova*, 141, 144, 149, 172, 176
Delacroix, Eugène, 167–68
Della Casa, Giovanni, 88
de Man, Paul, 19, 29, 82
Demosthenes, 190
Denina, Carlo, 129
De Sanctis, Francesco: on Alfieri, 30, 230n21; on Dante, 99–100, 254n9; on Foscolo, 232–33n36; and Italian Romanticism, 29; on Leopardi, 187–88; on Manzoni, 42; nationalist criticism of, 36–37, 233n37; on Parini, 281n10
Descartes, René, 115–16, 132, 136

Diderot, Denis, 15, 136
dolce stil novo, 176
Dombroski, Robert, 18

Eldridge, Richard, 19
Eliot, T. S., 100, 102
Emerson, Ralph Waldo, 17
England. *See* Britain
Enlightenment: Alfieri's critique of, 125–26, 129–32, 134–35, 137; anthropology, 114; categorical imperative, 41; common sense, 259–60n42; Dante's reception in, 97, 102, 104; human nature, 113–14, 259n30; in Italy, 28, 85; literary historiography, 78; literature, notions of, 15, 77, 85, 87, 89–90, 93, 125, 131; in Manzoni, 236n56; memoir, 103, 114, 127–28; and modernity, 222n1; neoclassicism, 150; noble savage, 41; Romantic critique of, 83; separation of church and state, 2, 38, 41; sociability, 15, 264n19; tabula rasa, 41; taste, 106, 113, 264n17; travel in, 57
Ercilla y Zuniga, Alonso de, 106

Fasano, Pino, 18
Fascist cultural policy (Italy), 165
Fichte, Johann Gottlieb, 154
Flora, Francesco, 18
Florence: Alfieri in, 88; capital of Italy, 11; corruption of, 182; Dante's exile from, 98; in Dante's *Purg.* 6, 172–73, 175, 184; in Dante's *Vita nuova*, 172; in Foscolo's "Dei sepolcri," 8–9, 93; genius loci of, 213; Machiavelli's exile from, 180
Forster, E. M., 17, 213–14, 218–19
Foscolo, Ugo: Alfieri's influence on, 140, 199–200, 204, 211; antiquity in, 75, 246n63; autobiography in, 5, 163, 187, 211; body of Parini in, 16–17, 197, 201, 203–12, 219; Dante's influence on, 7, 9–11, 102, 174, 200, 219–20; Didimo Chierico, alter ego, 4, 163, 208, 211, 273n2; editor of Dante, 102; exile of, 4, 28, 71–72, 76, 211–12; French style, critique of, 74; German thought, critique of, 85, 196, 208; Goethe, letter to, 233n39; Italian body politic in, 197–201; and Leopardi, 187, 191–94, 279n58, 279–80n60; living and dead, view of, 3, 6, 51, 282n15; life of, 4; Lucretius's influence on, 7, 197; on Manzoni, 43, 236n57; Manzoni, contrast to, 48; Manzoni and Wordsworth, compared to, 31–34; on Milan, 281–82n12; mythology in, 2, 34; nationalist readings of, 36–37; nationalist rhetoric in, 38–41; on Petrarch, 179, 276n33; Petrarch's influence on, 200; poetics of, 44, 48; *questione della lingua* in, 8; reception of, 17, 36–37, 232–33n36; religion in, 6; on Romanticism, 4, 226n26; Staël, critique of, 74–76, 196, 208, 246n61; statues of, 163–65; translation of, 19; Troy, myth of, 6, 8–11, 20, 35, 40, 52, 191–94, 219–20; Vico's influence on, 72–73, 223n4
Foscolo, Ugo, works of: "A Luigia Pallavicino," 209; "Dei sepolcri," 3–11, 18, 36–37, 39–41, 52, 93, 163, 187, 191–94, 197, 205–8, 210, 219–20; *Essay on the Present Literature of Italy*, 210–12; *Le Grazie*, 212; "Lettera a Monsieur Guill[on]," 39; *Lettere scritte dall'Inghilterra*, 55, 71–76, 187, 196, 208–11; "Notizia bibliografica intorno alle *Ultime lettere di Jacopo Ortis*," 212; *Ultime lettere di Jacopo Ortis*, 4–6, 11, 13, 30–32, 34, 36–38, 163, 193–94, 197–201, 203–5, 208, 210, 212, 218
Foucault, Michel, 20
France: Alfieri's aversion to, 137; and Britain, 150, 256n6; censorship in, 129; in comparative literary studies, 19; cultural preeminence of, 12; in Foscolo, 208–9; and Italy, 271n34; Mari-

anne, symbol of, 167–68; modernism in, 226n21; national identity of, 150
Freccero, John, 100, 170
Frederick II of Prussia, 117–20
Frugoni, Carlo, 109
Fubini, Mario, 19
Furst, Lilian, 19
Fussell, Paul, 219

Galileo, 4, 8
Garibaldi, Giuseppe, 30
Genette, Gerard, 214
Germany: antiquity in, 35; censorship in, 129; in comparative literary studies, 19; Foscolo's critique of, 208; and Goethe, 13, 80; Hellenism in, 2; metaphysical traditions of, 42; nationhood in, 79–80; Sturm und Drang in, 27, 109, 121
Gibbon, Edward, 81
Gill, Stephen Charles, 158
Gilson, Etienne, 100
Giordani, Pietro, 28
Givone, Sergio, 18
Goethe, Johann Wolfgang von: Alfieri, compared to, 90; autobiography in, 121; classicism and neoclassicism of, 35, 61, 82, 225n20; erotic poetry of, 219; on Italian religion, 63–64, 242nn33–34; and Italian Romanticism, 29; on Italy and Rome, 12, 16–17, 21, 49, 54, 59–65, 67, 75, 79–80, 98, 218, 247nn7–8; life of, 12–13; and literary history, 90; on Manzoni, 17, 21, 43, 48, 227n38, 231n25; maxim of, 12; popularity of, 65; portrait by Tischbein, 59; as pre-Romantic figure, 126; and Roman mistress, 213–14; and Romanticism, 223n2; in Schiller, 78–79, 89; on translation, 81–82, 248n14; *Weltliteratur* in, 77, 227n28; and Winckelmann, 61, 63-64, 241nn28–29
Goethe, Johann Wolfgang van, works of: *Italienische Reise*, 12, 54, 59–65, 71, 76, 79–80; *Die Leiden des jungen Werthers*, 23, 38; *Römische Elegien*, 17, 213–14, 219
Goldsmith, Oliver, 143
Gramsci, Antonio, 3, 42
Grand Tour: and Italian language, 142; and Italy, 17, 49–50, 54, 57–58, 80–81, 97–98, 219, 239n15; itinerary, 60, 238n6; length of, 61; modern tourism, compared to, 12
Gray, Thomas, 39, 79, 142–43
Greene, Thomas M., 175–76

Hamilton, Paul, 19
Harrison, Robert Pogue, 195, 197
Hartman, Geoffrey H., 19, 29, 79, 82–83
Hawthorne, Nathaniel, 12–13
Hazlitt, William, 142, 146–48, 150, 152–54
Hegel, Georg Wilhelm Friedrich, 47, 141
Heidegger, Martin, 195
Héloïse, 100
Helvétius, Claude Adrien, 127
Herder, Johann Gottfried, 64
Hervey, James, 39
Hobbes, Thomas, 71, 73
Hölderlin, Friedrich, 35
Holland, 128
Homer: in Alfieri, 130, 139; in Dante, 110; in Foscolo, 50, 194, 205, 220; in Hazlitt, 148; in Hegel, 267n3; in Keats, 81–82; in Leopardi, 193; rating of, 257n12; in Vico, 73, 109
Hugo, Victor: 20, 102
Hume, David: in Alfieri, 130; autobiography of, 120–22, 133, 136; personal identity, definition of, 261n43; Voltaire's letter to, 121
Hunt, Leigh, 77, 142

Isbell, John, 19
Isola, Agostino, 142–43
Italy: antiquity of, 2, 11, 54; and artistic traditions, 66–68, 92, 283–84nn7–8; Canova's statue of, 165–67;

Italy (*continued*)
  censorship in (Tuscany), 128, 264n16; effeminacy of, 54, 67–68, 76; foreign occupation of, 28, 72–73; as haven for women, 69; high culture and national identity in, 3, 11; as idea, 169, 274n10; law and order, lack of, 67–68; modernity and premodernity of, 1–11, 52, 54, 68, 71, 76, 219, 222n1; mores, lack of, 70; myth of, 2, 17, 48–52, 54–55, 76; primitiveness or violence of, 54, 62–65; religious imagination in, 3; Ripa's allegory of, 167–68; society, lack of, 58, 68

James, Henry, 76
Jeremiah, Book of, 171–72
John, Book of, 194
Johnson, Samuel, 103, 143
Joyce, James, 15, 76

Kant, Immanuel, 41, 154
Kantorowicz, Ernst, 206
Keats, John: beauty and truth in, 14, 17; on Dante, 142; "Happy is England!" 82, 219; lyric style of, 6; mythology in, 35, 246n63; "On First Looking into Chapman's Homer," 81–82; on translation, 81–82; on Wordsworth, 146
Kierkegaard, Søren, 35

Lamartine, Alphonse de, 35
Landino, Cristoforo, 98, 136
Landor, Walter Savage, 152–54
Latini, Brunetto, 99
Lawrence, D. H., 76
Leopardi, Giacomo: and Alfieri, 187, 190; apostrophe in, 186–87, 191; and Canova, 190; and Continental philosophy, 17, 230n20; Dante's influence on, 189; and Foscolo, 187, 191–94, 279n58, 279–80n60; Italian body politic in, 16, 186–194, 214, 216; and Machiavelli, 190; and Manzoni, 187, 280n61; mythology, 2; and national identity, 279n57; on Petrarch, 278n48; Petrarch, difference from, 191, 276n31; Petrarch's influence on, 174, 189–90, 193; poetics of, 44; reception of, 17; and Romanticism, 4, 223n2, 226n26; and Staël, 223n2, 243n41, 245–46n60; translation of, 19; writings of (1818–22), 55, 239n11
Leopardi, Giacomo, works of: "Ad Angelo Mai," 30, 187; "All'Italia," 169, 187–94; "A se stesso," 187; "A Silvia," 189; "La ginestra," 193–94; "L'infinito," 20, 187; "La luna," 187, 189; "La sera del dì di festa," 52, 187–89; "Il sogno," 187; "Sopra il monumento di Dante," 30, 187; "Ultimo canto di Saffo," 189; Zibaldone, 189
Lessing, Gotthold Ephraim, 103
Livy, 174
Locke, John, 41, 115–16, 137
Louis XIII, 107
Louis XIV, 106, 108
Louisa of Stolberg, 128–29, 137, 186
Lovejoy, A. O., 82–83
Lowy, Michael, 19
Lucan, 38, 171, 203–4
Lucian, 127

Machiavelli, Niccolò: in Byron, 56; Dante's and Petrarch's influence on, 180–82, 184; "Degli spiriti beati," 180; desire in, 191, 277n40; exile of, 180; in Fascist Italy, use of, 165; *fortuna* and *virtù* in, 190, 192–94, 277n38, 278n42; in Foscolo, 8; Italian body politic in, 169, 180–84, 186; and Leopardi, 190; and the Medici, 183, 191; on Petrarch, 278n43; *Il principe*, 180–84, 190; in Santa Croce, 4; sexual rhetoric in, 180–81, 183–84, 277n38, 278n42; spectacle in, 277n37
Manzoni, Alessandro: antimodernism of, 36; Catholicism of, 35, 41–48; and Enlightenment, 236n56; family of, 28; Florentine sojourn of, 88; Foscolo and

Goethe, contrast to, 48; Foscolo and Wordsworth, compared to, 31–34; and French culture, 235–36n56; and Leopardi, 187, 280n61; in Martegiani, 27; obscurity of, 97; providence in, 42, 48, 235nn50–52; *questione della lingua* in, 8, 17; reception of, 17, 37; and Romanticism, 4, 14, 43–45, 48, 84, 226n26; self-translation in, 3; and Staël, 236n62; transcendental imagination of, 98; translation of, 19, 81–82; writings of (1818–22), 55, 239n11

Manzoni, Alessandro, works of: *Adelchi*, 31–34; *Del romanzo storico*, 34; *I promessi sposi*, 3, 18, 20, 34, 36, 41–48; "Sul romanticismo," 14, 20, 31, 43–45, 84

Martegiani, Gina, 27–29
Mazzini, Giuseppe, 29–30, 36, 41, 102
Mazzotta, Giuseppe, 99
McGann, Jerome, 83
Metastasio, Pietro, 88
Metternich, Prince von, 6
Michelangelo, 4, 8, 143, 152
Millar, Oliver, 57
Milton, John: in Alfieri, 130; and Dante, 98, 263n2; rating of, 257n12; sonnet on his blindness, 156; and Wordsworth, 143, 155
Molière, 88, 150
Montano, Rocco, 42
Montesquieu, 103
Monti, Vincenzo, 19, 28, 55
Morehead, Robert, 143–44
Moretti, Franco, 77

Napoleon: defeat of, 28, 149–50; and Foscolo, 3, 4, 31, 73; and Italian liberty, 271n36; and Leopardi, 187; and papacy, 8; and Treaty of Campoformio, 150
nationalism: in Alfieri, 93; and allegory, 3; and death, 5, 37–38, 205; in Foscolo, 11, 38–41, 204–5; and Italian literature, 3, 36–37, 52; and Italian Romanticism, 18, 27; in Italy, 169; religious rhetoric in, 37–38; and Romanticism, 14, 78
Nemoianu, Virgil, 19
Newton, Isaac, 115
New York City, 12
Nietzsche, Friedrich, 25–27, 35, 108
Nigro, Salvatore, 18
Novalis, 35, 52

Parini, Giuseppe: 103; body as national symbol, 17, 197, 201–12; reception of, 281nn10–11
Pascal, Blaise, 106
Pasolini, Pier Paolo, 50
Paul, Saint, 155
Peacock, Thomas Love, 55, 59, 78, 102, 141, 150
Pellico, Silvio, 28
Perkins, David, 26
Petrarch: in Alfieri, 138, 266nn30–31; ancient and medieval worlds in, 275n22; in Byron, 56; Dante, compared to, 173–75; Dante's influence on, 175; Fascist image of, 165; in Foscolo's criticism, 276n33; in Foscolo's "Dei sepolcri," 8; in Foscolo's *Ultime lettere di Jacopo Ortis*, 5, 200; Italian body politic in, 169, 175–80, 182–86, 200–201, 205–6, 214, 216; Leopardi, difference from, 191, 276n31; in Leopardi's criticism, 278n48; in Machiavelli, 181, 278n43; as model, 109; poetics of, 173–75, 275n23, 276n30; as poet laureate, 215; rhetoric of, 276n31; in Shelley, 149; and Tuscan vernacular, 87; in Wordsworth, 150
Petrarch, works of: "Italia mia," 169, 175–79, 182, 184–85, 187, 189–91, 200, 206, 218; *Secretum*, 181
Petronio, Giuseppe, 18
Pindar, 190
Pindemonte, Ippolito, 19, 55, 191–93
Pope, Alexander, 79
Pound, Ezra, 76

Praz, Mario, 18
Puppo, Mario, 18–19, 42–43

Quillinan, Edward, 141

Rabelais, François, 117
Racine, Jean, 88, 106, 150
Raimondi, Ezio, 18–19
Raphael, 81
Reina, Francesco, 201–4, 210
Richards, I. A., 26
Richelieu, Cardinal, 108
Rilke, Rainer Maria, 11–12
Ripa, Cesare, 167–68
Risorgimento: Britain and France, compared to, 150; and Catholic Church, 236n60; and Dante, 99; and Foscolo, 39, 163, 205, 207–8; and Italian history, 6; and Italian Romanticism, 20, 30; and Leopardi, 187; and myth of Parini, 197, 201, 205, 207–8; and national allegory, 3; and Rome, 8
Romanticism: autobiography in, 102–3; in Britain, 27, 35, 43, 146, 159, 223n2, 226n24; in cultural and national context, 83, 223n2, 249n20; definition of, 222–23n2; in Europe, 14, 16, 82–84, 90–91, 93–94, 159, 222–23n2; in France, 27, 35, 43, 223n2; in Germany, 2, 35, 43, 92, 146, 148; in Greece, 29; and Hugo, 224n2; in Hungary, 29; irony, 27–28; literary history, 77–78, 246n3; literature, definitions of, 2, 15, 77–78; and Manzoni, 14, 43–45, 48, 84, 226n26; sublime, 31; in Switzerland, 29
Romanticism, Italian: and antiquity, 30, 34–35; Catholicism of, 30, 34–35, 41–48; in Croce, 29, 229n14; defining characteristics of, 2–4, 11, 222–23n2; derivative nature of, 27; in De Sanctis, 29; exceptional nature of, 20, 30, 34, 52, 220, 222n1; and Foscolo, 4, 226n26; and Goethe, 29; historical focus of, 30, 34–36; and Leopardi, 223n2, 226n26; reception of, 17–21, 27–29, 50; and Risorgimento, 30; and Staël, 29; and Stendhal, 29; women authors in, 20, 230n19
Rome: ancient, Italian body politic and, 16, 165, 167–69, 175, 177–80, 182–85, 190–91; contrast between past and present in, 241n26; and foreign writers, 54; and Goethe, 22, 59–65, 70, 79, 80, 82; and Risorgimento, 8; ruins of, 248n9; and Shelley, 55–56, 59, 64, 77; as site for reverie, 240n22; and Staël, 65–66, 101–3, 253n40
Rossellini, Roberto, 36, 41, 49–52
Rossellini, Zulimo, 163, 165
Rossetti, Gabriele, 102
Rousseau, Jean-Jacques: and Alfieri, 262n6; autobiography in, 103, 105, 114, 231n26, 233–34n41; exile of, 15, 264n15; in Foscolo, 71, 73, 75; noble savage in, 41; as pre-Romantic figure, 126, 128; and Voltaire, 121–22

Sablet, Jacques, 58–60, 65
Said, Edward, 53
Santa Croce: Alfieri's monument in, 166, 273n6; in Byron, 56–57; and Foscolo, 4–5, 9, 11, 36, 40, 74, 163–65, 192, 194, 196
Sayre, Robert, 19
Schelling, Friedrich: 101; and Coleridge, 148; on Dante, 101, 270n25–26; in Wordsworth, 154
Schiller, Friedrich, 63–64, 78–79, 89, 113, 147
Schlegel, August Wilhelm, 2, 35, 101, 142, 147, 153
Schlegel, Friedrich, 2, 14, 27, 35, 101, 103, 147, 153
Schliemann, Heinrich, 11
Scott, Walter, 17, 20, 43, 65
Scotti, Giambattista, 203
Seneca, 174
Shakespeare, William, 207
Shelley, Percy Bysshe: classicism of, 35;

on Dante, 102, 142, 149–50, 270n31; exile in Italy, 13, 98; and Italy, 16, 49, 78, 80, 238n10; poetics of, 14; on Protestant Cemetery (Rome), 55–56, 59–60, 65; on Raphael's *St. Cecilia*, 81; on Rome, 55–56, 59, 64, 77; satirized by Peacock, 150, 271n32; and Wordsworth, 146, 149
Shelley, Percy Bysshe, works of: *Defence of Poetry*, 149–50; "To Wordsworth," 149
Simonides, 191, 193
Sismondi, Jean Charles Léonard de, 147, 150
Spain, 43, 150, 189
Springer, Carolyn, 191
Staël, Anne-Louise Germaine de: Alfieri in, 89–90; and allegory, 2, 214–18, 283n3, 283n6; on Dante, 216, 271n37; Foscolo's critique of, 74–76, 196, 208, 246n61; French style, critique of, 252n37; in Hawthorne's *Marble Faun*, 13–14; Italian body politic in, 215–18; and Italian Romanticism, 29, 75, 222–23n2; and Italy, 49, 64–71, 76, 98, 244nn49–50, 252n38, 283–84nn7–8; and Leopardi, 223n2, 243n41, 245–46n60; national character in, 50, 242n38; Petrarch's influence on, 214, 218; popularity of, 65; publication history, 242n37; on religion, 252n40; on Rome, 65–66, 101–3, 253n40; on translation, 75, 81–82, 92, 222–23n2, 248n15, 252n37; on Virgil, 216
Staël, Anne-Louise Germaine de, works of: *Corinne, ou l'Italie*, 13–14, 27, 50, 55, 59, 61, 65–71, 74, 76, 89–94, 196–98, 214–19; *De l'Allemagne*, 92; "De l'esprit des traductions," 19, 75, 92; *De la littérature considerée dans ses rapports avec les institutions sociales*, 128
Stein, Gertrude, 12
Stendhal, 29, 49, 55, 102, 141

Stevens, Wallace, 15
Stuart, Charles Edward, 128, 137
Switzerland, 29, 128, 209

Tasso, Torquato: in Alfieri, 138, 266n30; Boileau, attacked by, 106; in Isola's edition, 143, 268n12; as model, 109; in Voltaire, 119, 122
Thomas, Dylan, 196
Tieck, Ludwig, 102
Timpanaro, Sebastiano, 18
Tischbein, Johann Heinrich Wilhelm, 59, 60, 80
Torraca, Francesco, 29
Torti, Giovanni, 203
travel, versus tourism, 284n9
Trissino, Giangiorgio, 106

Vellutello, Alessandro, 136
Verdi, Giuseppe, 41
Verri, Alessandro, 28
Verri, Pietro, 28, 201
Vico, Giambattista: 2; Alfieri's similarity to, 137; burial, notion of, 196; on Dante, 73, 109; in Foscolo, 72–73; providential imagination of, 41
Vieusseux, Giovan Pietro, 28
Villon, François, 155
Virgil: *Aeneid*, 6, 40, 111, 155, 168, 206–7; in Alfieri, 130; legend of, 119; Rome, notion of, 169; Wordsworth, translated by, 272n46
Visconti, Ermes, 19, 28, 55
Vittorio Amadeo III, 128–29
Voltaire: Alfieri, influence on, 86, 88–89, 124–25, 129; Ariosto in, 260–61n40; autobiography in, 115–21, 136; and Bettinelli, 109, 113, 136, 258n24; and Châtelet, 106, 115, 117, 119, 261n41; and Condillac, 260n38; on Dante, 16, 102–7, 109, 111–14, 116, 118–19, 122–23, 141; Descartes, critique of, 115–16; epic, notion of, 119, 122, 258n23; and exile, 106, 264n15; and Frederick II, 117–20, 260–61nn40–

Voltaire (*continued*)
41; *gens de lettres,* definition of, 84–86, 89, 94, 128; heroism, critique of, 131, 264n18; on human nature, 132, 259n29; Hume, letter to, 121; and Italian authors, 109, 258n24; Italian studies of, 256n10; literature, notion of, 15, 105–6, 108, 137; Locke, promotion of, 115–16; poetry and politics in, 105, 256n6; and Rousseau, 121–22; society and writer in, 133; taste in, 255n5

Voltaire, works of: "Article de Voltaire sur Voltaire," 115; *Candide,* 105; *Commentaire historique sur les œuvres de l'auteur de la "Henriade,"* 119–22; *Dictionnaire philosophique,* 112–13, 129; *Eléments de la philosophie de Newton,* 115; *Essai sur les mœurs,* 107; *Essai sur la poésie épique,* 106; *L'Henriade,* 115, 119; "Lettre à Monsieur de ***, professeur en histoire," 106–7; *Lettres chinoises, indiennes et tartares,* 118–19, 122; *Lettres philosophiques,* 104, 107; *Memoires pour servir à la vie de Voltaire,* 115, 117–20; *Temple du goût,* 108

Warner, Marina, 178
Warren, Austin, 26
Wellek, René, 19, 26, 29, 82–83
Whitman, Walt, 12, 155
Winckelmann, Johann Joachim, 35, 54, 61, 63–64, 108
Wordsworth, Christopher, 154
Wordsworth, Jonathan, 158

Wordsworth, William: autobiography in 144–46, 155, 159; and Byron, 146; at Cambridge, 142–43, 148, 268n10, 268n12; and Coleridge, 148, 152–54; and contemporary writers, 146, 149, 153–54, 272n42; on Dante, 102, 142–43, 150, 152–55; Dante, allusions to, 154, 268n11, 268n14, 272n44; Dante, compared to, 143–44, 155–59, 268–69n15, 269n17, 270n23, 271–72n41; Foscolo and Manzoni, compared to, 31–34; on German philosophy, 153–54, 196; and Gray, 142–43, 268n11; and Italian politics, 150; and Keats, 146; literature, idea of, 15; Milton in, 143, 155; and Morehead, 143–44, 270n23, 271–72n41; Petrarch in, 150; pleasure, concept of, 145–46, 269–70nn20–21; politics of, 150–52, 272n42; religion in, 35, 153, 155, 159; and Shelley, 146, 149; as translator, 272n46

Wordsworth, William, works of: *Convention of Cintra,* 143, 150; "Michael," 151–52; "Preface to *Lyrical Ballads,*" 3, 89, 143, 145, 191; *Prelude,* 6, 31–32, 34, 101, 103, 142, 148, 155–59; "A slumber did my spirit seal," 156; "Tintern Abbey," 20, 144–46, 156

world literature, 18–19

Young, Edward, 39

Zoffany, Johann, 57–59
Zola, Emile, 49